Software Engineering Guides

Software Engineering Guides

Edited by
Jon Fairclough

PRENTICE HALL
London New York Toronto Sydney Tokyo Singapore
Madrid Mexico City Munich

First published 1996 by
Prentice Hall Europe
Campus 400, Maylands Avenue
Hemel Hempstead
Hertfordshire, HP2 7EZ
A division of
Simon & Schuster International Group

Printed and bound in Great Britain by
Redwood Books, Trowbridge, Wiltshire.

Library of Congress Cataloging-in-Publication Data

Available from the publisher

British Library Cataloguing in Publication data

A catalogue record for this book is available
from the British Library

ISBN 0-13-449281-1

 3 4 5   00 99 98 97

TABLE OF CONTENTS

CONTRIBUTORS

C. Mazza

J. Fairclough

B. Melton

D. de Pablo

A. Scheffer

R. Stevens

M. Jones

G. Alvisi

PREFACE

This book contains the guides to software engineering produced by the European Space Agency (ESA). The guides contain advisory material for software developers applying ESA's Software Engineering Standards (PSS-05-0), which have been published in the book *Software Engineering Standards*[1]. The production of this book version of the guides has been sponsored by ESA's Technology Transfer programme.

The guides have been produced between 1991 and 1995, and have proved to be invaluable for software engineers applying ESA's standards. They have been compiled from experiences of people using the standards, discussions with software engineers, and research of the software engineering literature.

The *Software Engineering Guides* explain how to apply the *Software Engineering Standards* effectively. This is done by describing a process to be followed, and identifying the methods and tools that can be used to perform each step of the process. Information about the contents of the documents required by the *Software Engineering Standards*, mostly obtained from relevant ANSI/IEEE standards, is also provided.

The ESA Software Engineering Standards and Guides are controlled by the ESA Board for Software Standardisation and Control (BSSC). The board, one of whose roles is to define and promote the use of the Standards and Guides, welcome comments and suggestions from users.

The following past and present BSSC members have contributed to the production of the guides: Carlo Mazza, Bryan Melton, Daniel de Pablo, Adriaan Scheffer, Richard Stevens, Michael Jones and Gianfranco Alvisi. The BSSC wishes to thank Jon Fairclough for his work in researching, drafting and editing the guides, Bill Burke for his proof-reading, Ian Alexander for his contributions on detailed design and production, and all those software engineers in ESA and Industry who have made useful suggestions about how to implement the *Software Engineering Standards*.

M.Jones, BSSC co-chairman
European Space Operations Centre
Robert Bosch Str 5
D-64293 Darmstadt
Germany

U.Mortensen, BSSC co-chairman
European Space Technology Centre
P.O.Box 299
2200 AG Noordwijk
The Netherlands

May 1995

---

[1]   Software Engineering Standards, C.Mazza, J.Fairclough, B.Melton, D. de Pablo, A.Scheffer, R.Stevens, Prentice Hall, ISBN 0-13-106568-8, 1994

INTRODUCTION

1 PURPOSE OF THE GUIDES

This book contains guidance for users of the *Software Engineering Standards,* also published by Prentice-Hall. The *Software Engineering Standards* define the mandatory and recommended practices for specifying, developing and maintaining software. The *Software Engineering Guides* collected in this book discuss the practices in more detail, and describe the methods and tools for performing them. The guides also contain instructions for writing the documents required by the *Software Engineering Standards.*

2 STRUCTURE OF THE STANDARDS AND GUIDES

The *Software Engineering Standards* and *Software Engineering Guides* form the two level document tree shown in Figure 1.

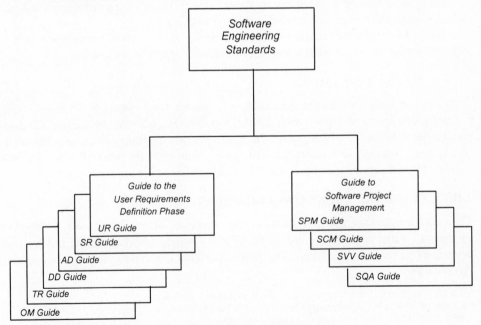

Figure 1: The Document Tree

The top level is the book '*Software Engineering Standards'.* The lower level comprises the *Software Engineering Guides,* which are collected in this book.

Software Engineering Standards divides the software engineering activity into two parts: the products themselves and the procedures used to make them.

The process of production is partitioned into six phases, and there is a guide for each:

- Guide to the User Requirements Definition Phase (UR guide)
- Guide to the Software Requirements Definition Phase (SR guide)
- Guide to the Architectural Design Phase (AD guide)
- Guide to the Detailed Design and Production Phase (DD guide)
- Guide to the Transfer Phase (TR guide)
- Guide to the Operations and Maintenance Phase (OM guide)

Each of the above guides contains an overview of the phase, guidelines on methods and tools that can be used in the phase, and instructions for documentation.

The procedures to be followed in the life cycle are divided amongst four management activities, and there is a guide for each:

- Guide to Software Project Management (SPM guide)
- Guide to Software Configuration Management (SCM guide)
- Guide to Software Verification and Validation (SVV guide)
- Guide to Software Quality Assurance (SQA guide).

Each of the above guides contains an overview of the activity, guidelines on methods and tools that can be used, and instructions for planning.

This book contains the ten guides described above. Each guide is a standalone entity, with its own introduction, table of contents, main text, appendices and index.

3 HOW TO USE THIS BOOK

Although this book can be read from start to finish, we have assumed that readers will primarily use it as a reference book for the *Software Engineering Standards*. Readers should therefore decide which part of the Standards they require help on (e.g. phase or management activity), and locate the start of the guide from the main table of contents in this introduction, and then turn to the table of contents of the appropriate guide.

4 IEEE STANDARDS ACKNOWLEDGEMENT

The software engineering standards of the Institute of Electrical and Electronic Engineers (IEEE) have been used as the primary source of terminology and for the definitions of products and plans. The IEEE standards that have been used to prepare this book are:

IEEE Std 610. 12-1990, IEEE Glossary of Software Engineering Terminology
IEEE Std 830-1993, IEEE Recommended Practice for Software Requirements Specifications
IEEE Std 1016-1987, IEEE Recommended Practice for Software Design Descriptions (Reaffirmed 1993)
IEEE Std 1063-1987, IEEE Standard for Software User Documentation (Reaffirmed 1993)
IEEE Std 1058.1-1987, IEEE Standard for Software Project Management Plans (Reaffirmed 1993)
IEEE Std 828-1990. IEEE Standard for Software Configuration Management Plans
IEEE Std 1012-1986, IEEE Standard for Verification and Validation Plans (Reaffirmed 1992)
IEEE Std 1028-1988, IEEE Standard for Software Reviews and Audits
IEEE Std 829-1983, IEEE Standard for Software Test Documentation (Reaffirmed 1991)
IEEE Std 730-1989, IEEE Standard for Software Quality Assurance Plans

Guide to the user requirements definition phase

TABLE OF CONTENTS

CHAPTER 1
INTRODUCTION

1.1 PURPOSE

Software Engineering Standards [Ref 1] defines the first phase of the software life cycle to be the 'User Requirements Definition Phase' (UR phase). Activities and products are examined in the 'UR review' (UR/R) at the end of the phase.

The UR phase can be called the 'problem definition phase' of the life cycle. The phase refines an idea about a task to be performed using computing equipment, into a definition of what is expected from the computer system.

This document provides a definition of what user requirements are, suggests how they can be captured and gives guidelines on how they should be stated in a URD. This guide should be read by all active participants in the user requirements phase, i.e. initiators, user representatives, software project managers and authors and reviewers of the URD.

1.2 OVERVIEW

Chapter 2 discusses the UR phase. Chapters 3 and 4 discuss methods and tools for user requirements definition. Chapter 5 describes how to write the URD, in particular how to fill out the document template. Chapter 6 summarises the life cycle management activities, which are discussed at greater length in other guides.

All the mandatory practices in *Software Engineering Standards* relevant to the UR phase are repeated in this document. The identifier of the practice is added in parentheses to mark a repetition. This document contains no new mandatory practices.

CHAPTER 2
THE USER REQUIREMENTS DEFINITION PHASE

2.1 INTRODUCTION

The UR phase can be called the 'concept' or 'problem definition' phase of the *Software Engineering Standards* life cycle. User requirements often follow directly from a spontaneous idea or thought. Even so, wide agreement and understanding of the user requirements is more likely if these guidelines are applied. The definition of user requirements is an iterative process.

User requirements are documented in the User Requirements Document (URD). The URD gives the user's view of the problem, not the developer's. A URD may have to go through several revisions before it is acceptable to everyone.

The main outputs of the UR phase are the:
- User Requirements Document (URD);
- Software Project Management Plan for the SR phase (SPMP/SR);
- Software Configuration Management Plan for the SR phase (SCMP/SR);
- Software Verification and Validation Plan for the SR Phase (SVVP/SR);
- Software Quality Assurance Plan for the AD phase (SQAP/SR);
- Acceptance Test Plan (SVVP/AT).

2.2 CAPTURE OF USER REQUIREMENTS

The capture of user requirements is the process of gathering information about user needs. *Software Engineering Standards* recommends that:
- user requirements should be clarified through criticism and experience of existing software and prototypes;
- wide agreement should be established through interviews and surveys;
- knowledge and experience of the potential development organisations should be used to help decide on implementation feasibility, and, perhaps to build prototypes.

Above all, user requirements should be realistic [Ref 5]. Realistic user requirements are:
- clear;
- verifiable;
- complete;
- accurate;
- feasible.

Clarity and verifiability help ensure that delivered systems will meet user requirements. Completeness and accuracy imply that the URD states the user's real needs. A URD is inaccurate if it requests something that users do not need, for example a superfluous capability or an unnecessary design constraint (see Section 2.4).

Realistic user requirements must be feasible. If the resources and timescales available for its implementation are insufficient, it may be unrealistic to put them in a URD.

When a system is to replace an existing one, the best way to make the user requirements realistic is to describe the current way of doing things and then define the user requirements in terms of the changes needed. The description of the current system should use the concrete, physical terms familiar to the user [Ref 7, 8, 9].

Methods for capturing user requirements are discussed in Chapter 3.

2.3 DETERMINATION OF OPERATIONAL ENVIRONMENT

A clear description of the real world that the software will operate in should be built up, as the user requirements are captured. Chapter 3 describes several user requirements definition methods that can be used. This description of the operational environment must clearly establish the problem context.

In a system development, each subsystem will have interfaces to other, external, systems. The nature of these exchanges with external systems should be specified and controlled from the start of the project. The information may reside in an Interface Control Document (ICD), or in the design documentation of the external system.

The roles and responsibilities of the users and operators of software should be established by defining the:

- characteristics of each group (e.g. experience, qualifications);
- operations they perform (e.g. the user of the data may not operate the software).

2.4 SPECIFICATION OF USER REQUIREMENTS

The specification of user requirements is the process of organising information about user needs and expressing them in a document.

A requirement is a 'condition or capability needed by a user to solve a problem or achieve an objective' [Ref 2]. This definition leads to two principal categories of requirements: 'capability requirements' and 'constraint requirements'. These categories and their subcategories are described in detail in this chapter. Unless otherwise indicated, all types of requirements can be stated in the User Requirements Document.

2.4.1 Capability requirements

Capability requirements describe the process to be supported by software. Simply stated, they describe 'what' the users want to do.

A capability requirement should define an operation, or sequence of related operations, that the software will be able to perform. If the sequence contains more than approximately five related operations, the capability requirement should be split.

The operations should be organised to describe the overall process from start to finish. Where there are many operations to describe, it is recommended that they are grouped hierarchically to help manage the complexity.

Operations may be routine, (e.g. normal tasks) or non-routine (e.g. error handling, interruptions). Non-routine operations may be grouped separately from those related to the normal processing.

In the Software Requirements Definition Phase, capability requirements will be analysed to produce a set of functional requirements. If duplication of capability requirements occurs, the analyst may be able to replace them with a single functional requirement. A single function may support a process at many different times, therefore a function can map to many capability requirements.

Quantitative statements that specify performance and accuracy attributes should form part of the specification of capability. This means that a capability requirement should be qualified with values of:

- capacity;
- speed;
- accuracy.

The performance attribute is the combination of the capacity and speed attributes.

2.4.1.1 Capacity

The capacity attribute states 'how much' of a capability is needed at any moment in time. Each capability requirement should be attached with a quantitative measure of the capacity required. For example the:

- number of users to be supported;
- number of terminals to be supported;
- number of satellites that can be controlled simultaneously;
- amount of data to be stored.

2.4.1.2 Speed

The speed attribute states how fast the complete operation, or sequence of operations, is to be performed. Each capability requirement should be attached with a quantitative measure of the speed required. There are various ways to do this, for example the:

- number of operations done per unit time interval;
- time taken to perform an operation.

For example: '95% of the transactions shall be processed in less than 1 second', is acceptable whilst, '95% of the transactions will be done as soon as possible' is not.

Note that a system may react quickly to a command but take quite a long time to complete the operations requested. Such 'response' requirements should be stated as HCI requirements.

2.4.1.3 Accuracy

The accuracy of an operation is measured by the difference between what is intended and what happens when it is carried out.

Examples are:

- 'the accuracy of accounting reports shall be one accounting unit';
- 'the program shall predict the satellite's altitude to within 10 metres, seven days in advance'.

Accuracy attributes should take account of both systematic errors and random errors.

2.4.2 Constraint requirements

Constraint requirements place restrictions on how the user requirements are to be met. The user may place constraints on the software related to interfaces, quality, resources and timescales.

Users may constrain how communication is done with other systems, what hardware is to be used, what software it has to be compatible with, and how it must interact with human operators. These are all interface constraints.

An interface is a shared boundary between two systems; it may be defined in terms of what is exchanged across the boundary.

Interfaces are important kinds of constraints. The user may define external interfaces (i.e. state how interactions with other systems must be done) but should leave the developers to define the internal interfaces (i.e. to state how software components will interact with each other).

Users may constrain the quality required of the final product. Typical quality characteristics are: adaptability, availability, portability, security and safety.

2.4.2.1 Communications interfaces

A communications interface requirement may specify the networks and network protocols to be used. Performance attributes of the interface may be specified (e.g. data rate).

The ISO reference model for Open Systems Interconnection, with its seven layers of abstraction, can be used for describing communications interfaces. This means that a communications interface requirement should use terminology consistent with the model. Communications interface requirements should avoid mixing the layers of abstraction.

2.4.2.2 Hardware interfaces

A hardware interface requirement specifies all or part of the computer hardware the software is to execute on. This may be done by stating the make and model of the device, physical limitations (e.g. size, weight), performance (e.g. speed, memory), qualifications (e.g. project approved, space qualified) and also perhaps whether any hardware selected has to be derated (e.g. for operation at altitude). Environmental considerations that affect the selection of hardware may be stated (e.g humidity, temperature and pressure).

2.4.2.3 Software interfaces

A software interface requirement specifies whether the software is to be compatible with other software (e.g other applications, compilers, operating systems, programming languages and database management systems).

2.4.2.4 Human-Computer Interaction

A Human-Computer Interaction (HCI) requirement may specify any aspect of the user interface. This may include a statement about style (e.g. command language, menu system, icons), format (e.g. report content and layout), messages (e.g. brief, exhaustive) and responsiveness (e.g. time taken to respond to command). The hardware at the user interface (e.g. colour display and mouse) may be included either as an HCI requirement or as a hardware interface requirement.

2.4.2.5 Adaptability

Adaptability measures how easily a system copes with requirements changes. Adaptable (or flexible) systems are likely to live longer, although the extra design work needed may be extensive, especially for optimising modularity. An example of an adaptability requirement is: 'it shall be possible to add new commands without retesting existing commands'.

In the operations and maintenance phase the software may undergo continuous adaptation as the user requirements are modified by experience.

When considering the adaptability, note that any change involves some risk, and to change reliable parts of the system may not be acceptable.

2.4.2.6 Availability

Availability measures the ability of a system to be used during its intended periods of its operation. Availability requirements may specify:
- mean and minimum capacity available (e.g. all terminals);
- start and end times of availability (e.g. from 0900 to 1730 daily);
- time period for averaging availability (e.g. 1 year).

Examples of availability requirements are:
- 'the user shall be provided with 98% average availability over 1 year during working hours and never less than 50% of working hours in any one week';
- 'all essential capabilities shall be at least 98% available in any 48 hour period and at least 75% available in every 3 hour period'.

When a system is unavailable, some, or even all, of its capabilities cannot be used. A loss of capability is called a 'failure' and is caused by one or more 'faults'. The average time between the occurrence of faults internal to the software (i.e. 'bugs') measures the 'reliability' of the software. The average time taken to fix such faults measures its 'maintainability'. A system may also become unavailable due to external factors (e.g. loss of input service).

Users only need to state their availability requirements. The availability requirements are decomposed into specific reliability and maintainability requirements in the SR phase.

2.4.2.7 Portability

Software portability is measured by the ease that it can be moved from one environment to another. Portable software tends to be long lived, but more code may have to be written and performance requirements may be more difficult to meet. An example of a portability requirement is: 'the software shall be portable between environments X and Y'.

Portability can be measured in terms of the number of lines of code and/or the number of modules that do not have to be changed to port the software from one computer to another. Either absolute or relative measurements can be used.

If migration to another hardware base or operating system is intended, then any requirements to run with different hardware and software interfaces should be stated as portability requirements. New interfaces should be described (e.g. name the new operating system or computer hardware).

2.4.2.8 Security

A system may need to be secured against threats to its confidentiality, integrity and availability. For example, a user may request that unauthorised users be unable to use the system, or that no single event such as a fire should cause the loss of more than 1 week's information. The user should describe threats that the system needs to be protected against, e.g. virus intrusions, hackers, fires, computer breakdowns.

The security of a system can be described in terms of the ownership of, and rights of access to, the capabilities of the system.

A secure system protects users from their own errors as well as the malicious interference, or illegal activities, of unauthorised users.

2.4.2.9 Safety

The consequences of software failure should be made clear to developers. Safety requirements define the needs of users to be protected against potential problems such as hardware or software faults. They may define scenarios that the system should handle safely (e.g. 'the system should ensure that no data is lost when a power failure occurs')

2.4.2.10 Standards

Standards requirements normally reference the applicable documents that define the standard.

Two kinds of standards can be specified: process standards and product standards. Examples of product standards are export file formats and legal report formats. Examples of the process standards are product assurance standards and accounting procedures to be followed. Adherence to process standards should be specified in the Software Project Management Plan.

A standards requirement may specify the methods that are to be employed by the developers in subsequent phases. Such methods must be compatible with the life cycle defined in *Software Engineering Standards*.

2.4.2.11 Resources

The resources available for producing and operating the software are a constraint on the design. If this information is available then it should be stated in the Software Project Management Plan in terms of one or more of financial, manpower and material limits.

As with any other product, the quality and sophistication of a software product are limited by the resources that are put into building it.

Resource requirements may include specifications of the computer resources available (e.g. main memory). They may define the minimum hardware that the system must run on. Care should be taken to include only the necessary resource constraints.

2.4.2.12 Timescales

A constraint on the design of the software may be the acceptable timescales for its development and production. Requirements for the achievement of specific life cycle milestones may be stated in the Software Project Management Plan.

2.5 ACCEPTANCE TEST PLANNING

Validation confirms whether the user requirements are satisfied when the software is delivered. This is done by performing acceptance tests in the Transfer Phase.

Acceptance Test Plans must be generated in the UR phase and documented in the Acceptance Test section of the Software Verification and Validation Plan (SVVP/AT). The Acceptance Test Plan should describe the scope, approach and resources required for the acceptance tests, and take account of the user requirements. See Chapter 6.

2.6 PLANNING THE SOFTWARE REQUIREMENTS DEFINITION PHASE

Plans of SR phase activities must be drawn up in the UR phase by the developer. Planning of the SR phase is discussed in Chapter 6. Planning should cover project management, configuration management, verification, validation and quality assurance. Outputs are the:
* Software Project Management Plan for the SR phase (SPMP/SR);
* Software Configuration Management Plan for the SR phase (SCMP/SR);
* Software Verification and Validation Plan for the SR phase (SVVP/SR);
* Software Quality Assurance Plan for SR phase (SQAP/SR).

2.7 THE USER REQUIREMENTS REVIEW

Producing the URD and the SVVP/AT is an iterative process. The initiator should organise internal reviews of a document before its formal review.

The outputs of the UR phase must be formally reviewed during the User Requirements Review (UR08). This should be a technical review. The recommended procedure is described in the Guide to Software Verification and Validation, and is derived from the IEEE standard for Technical Reviews [Ref 4].

Normally, only the URD and the Acceptance Test Plan undergo the full technical review procedure involving users, developers, management and quality assurance staff. The Software Project Management Plan (SPMP/SR), Software Configuration Management Plan (SCMP/SR), Software Verification and Validation Plan (SVVP/SR), and Software Quality Assurance Plan (SQAP/SR) are usually reviewed by management and quality assurance staff only.

The objective of the UR/R review is to verify that:
- the URD states user requirements clearly and completely and that a general description of the process the user expects to be supported is present;
- the SVVP/AT is an adequate plan for validating the software in the TR phase.

The UR/R should conclude with a statement about the project's readiness to proceed.

CHAPTER 3
METHODS FOR USER REQUIREMENTS DEFINITION

3.1 INTRODUCTION

This chapter discusses methods for user requirements capture and specification in current use. Methods can be combined to suit the needs of a particular project.

3.2 METHODS FOR USER REQUIREMENTS CAPTURE

While user requirements ultimately come from an original idea, one or more of the methods described below can be used to stimulate the creative process and record its output.

3.2.1 Interviews and surveys

Interviews should be structured to ensure that all issues are covered. When it is not practical to interview all the potential users, a representative sample should be selected and interviewed; this process is called a survey. Interviews and surveys can be useful for ensuring that:
- the user requirements are complete;
- there is wide agreement about the user requirements.

3.2.2 Studies of existing software

New software is often written to replace existing software. An investigation of the good and bad features of what exists can identify requirements for what is to be built. Examination of user manuals, requirements documentation and change proposals can be especially helpful.

3.2.3 Study of system requirements

If software is part of a larger system, many of the user requirements can be derived from the System Requirements Document.

3.2.4 Feasibility studies

A feasibility study is the analysis and design of the principal features of a system. The amount of detail in the design will not normally allow its implementation, but may show whether implementation is possible.

3.2.5 Prototyping

A prototype is an 'executable model of selected aspects of a proposed system' [Ref 6]. If requirements are unclear or incomplete, it can be useful to develop a prototype based on tentative requirements to explore what the user requirements really are. This is called 'exploratory prototyping'. Hands-on experience can be an excellent way of deciding what is really wanted.

3.3 METHODS FOR REQUIREMENTS SPECIFICATION

3.3.1 Natural language

The obvious way to express a requirement is to use natural language (e.g. English). Natural language is rich and accessible but inconsistency and ambiguity are more likely. For example, the statement:
　　'The database will contain an address'
might be read as any of:
　　'There will be one and only one address'
　　'Some part of the database will be designated as an address'
　　'There will be at least one address in the database'.

3.3.2 Mathematical formalism

Mathematical formulae should be described or referenced in the URD where they clarify the statement of requirement. All symbols used in an expression should be defined or referenced.

3.3.3 Structured English

Structured English is a specification language that makes use of a limited vocabulary and a limited syntax [Ref 7]. The vocabulary of Structured English consists only of:
- imperative English language verbs;
- terms defined in a glossary;
- certain reserved words for logic formulation.

The syntax of a Structured English statement is limited to these possibilities:
- simple declarative sentence;
- closed end decision construct;
- closed end repetition construct.

Structured English is normally used to describe the basic processes of a system and is suitable for expressing capability requirements. Examples are:

Sequence:

```
GET RAW DATA
REMOVE INSTRUMENT EFFECTS
CALIBRATE CORRECTED DATA
```

Condition:

      IF SAMPLE IS OF NOMINAL QUALITY THEN
          CALIBRATE SAMPLE
     ELSE
          STORE BAD SAMPLE

Repetition:

     FOR EACH SAMPLE
          GET POINTING DIRECTION AT TIME OF SAMPLE
          STORE POINTING DIRECTION WITH SAMPLE

Formalising the English structure may allow automated processing of requirements (e.g. automated checking, analysis, transformation and display) and makes it easier to define acceptance tests.

3.3.4 Tables

Tables are an effective method for describing requirements completely and concisely. Used extensively in later phases, they can summarise relationships more effectively than a plain text description.

3.3.5 System block diagrams

Block diagrams are the traditional way of depicting the processing required. They can also demonstrate the context the software operates in when it is part of a larger system.

3.3.6 Timelines

Timelines can describe sequences of operations that software must perform, especially if there is a real-time aspect or processing schedule. They convey a sense of interval more powerfully than a text description.

3.3.7 Context diagrams

A context diagram contains one bubble, representing the system, and dataflow arrows, showing the inputs and outputs. Context diagrams show external interfaces.

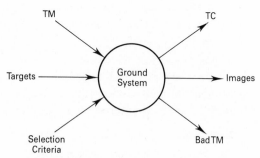

CHAPTER 4
TOOLS FOR USER REQUIREMENTS DEFINITION

4.1 INTRODUCTION

This chapter discusses tools for user requirements capture and specification. Tools can be combined to suit the needs of a particular project.

4.2 TOOLS FOR USER REQUIREMENTS CAPTURE

The questionnaire is the primary tool of a survey. To get useful data, careful consideration should be given to its contents and presentation.

A feasibility study may be performed using CASE tools for analysis and design. Similarly, prototyping of code may employ tools used for detailed design and production.

Capturing user requirements from studies of existing software may require building models that describe what the existing software does [Ref 7, 8, 9]. CASE tools are available for the construction of such models.

When the software is being developed as part of a system development, any tools used for system requirements analysis may also prove useful in identifying the user requirements.

4.3 TOOLS FOR USER REQUIREMENTS SPECIFICATION

4.3.1 User requirements management

Tools for managing user requirements information should support one or more of the following functions:
- insertion of new requirements;
- modification of existing requirements;
- deletion of requirements;
- storage of attributes (e.g. identifier) with the text;
- searching for requirements attributes and text strings;
- cross-referencing;
- change history recording;
- access control;
- display;
- printing, in a variety of formats.

Database Management Systems (DBMS), available on a variety of hardware platforms (e.g. PC, minicomputer, mainframe), provide many of these functions. For large systems, a requirements DBMS becomes essential.

The ability to export requirements data to the word processor used for URD production is essential for preserving consistency.

4.3.2 Document production

A word processor or text processor should be used for producing a document. Tools for the creation of paragraphs, sections, headers, footers, tables of contents and indexes all facilitate the production of a document. A spell checker is desirable. An outliner may be found useful for creation of sub-headings, for viewing the document at different levels of detail and for rearranging the document. The ability to handle diagrams is very important.

Documents invariably go through many drafts as they are created, reviewed and modified. Revised drafts should include change bars. Document comparison programs, which can mark changed text automatically, are invaluable for easing the review process.

Tools for communal preparation of documents are beginning to be available, allowing many authors to comment and add to a single document in a controlled manner.

CHAPTER 5
THE USER REQUIREMENTS DOCUMENT

5.1 INTRODUCTION

The URD is a mandatory output of the UR phase (UR10) and must always be produced before the software project is started (UR11). The URD must:
- provide a general description of what the user wants to perform with the software system (UR12);
- contain all the known user requirements (UR13);
- describe the operations the user wants to perform with the software system (UR14);
- define all the constraints that the user wishes to impose on any solution (UR15);
- describe the external interfaces to the software system or reference them in ICDs that exist or are to be written (UR16).

The size and content of the URD should reflect the complexity of the problem and the degree of expertise and understanding shared by the initiator, users, URD author and software developer.

The URD needs to state the problem as completely and accurately as possible. The cost of changing the user requirements increases rapidly as the project proceeds through the life cycle.

When software is transferred to users after development, acceptance tests are held to determine whether it meets the user requirements. The URD should be detailed enough to allow the definition of acceptance tests.

The URD should be a balanced statement of the problem and should avoid over-constraining the solution. If the software described in the URD is a part of a larger system (i.e. it is a subsystem), then the URD may replace the descriptive information with references to higher level documents. The purpose of the software, however, should always be clear from the URD.

Software Engineering Standards defines the minimum required documents for a software project and the URD has a definite role to play in this documentation scheme. URD authors should not go beyond the bounds of that role.

The URD should not:
- contain an exhaustive analysis of the requirements on the software (this is done in the SR phase);
- define any design aspects (this is done in the AD and DD phases);
- cover project management aspects (which form part of the SPMP/SR).

If definition of design aspects is unavoidable, then such definitions should be categorised as constraint requirements.

The URD should define needs accurately and leave the maximum scope for the software engineer to choose the most efficient solution.

5.2 STYLE

The style of a URD should be plain and concise, and be written using language, vocabulary and style which is easily understandable to the user community. The URD should be clear, consistent and modifiable. Wherever possible, requirements should be stated in quantitative terms to increase their verifiability.

5.2.1 Clarity

A URD is 'clear' if each requirement is unambiguous and understandable to project participants. A requirement is unambiguous if it has only one interpretation. To be understandable, the language used in a URD should be shared by all project participants and should be as simple as possible.

Each requirement should be stated in a single sentence. Justifications and explanations of a requirement should be clearly separated from the requirement itself.

Clarity is enhanced by grouping related requirements together. The capability requirements in a group should be structured to reflect any temporal or causal relationships between them. Groups containing more than about ten requirements should be broken down into sub-groups. Subgroups should be organised hierarchically. Structuring the user requirements is one of the most important ways of making them understandable.

5.2.2 Consistency

A URD is consistent if no requirements conflict. Using different terms for what is really the same thing, or specifying two incompatible qualities, are examples of lack of consistency.

Where a term used in a particular context could have multiple meanings, a single meaning should be defined in a glossary, and only that meaning should be used throughout.

5.2.3 Modifiability

A URD is modifiable if any necessary requirements changes can be documented easily, completely, and consistently.

A URD contains redundancy if there are duplicating or overlapping requirements. Redundancy itself is not an error, and redundancy can help to make a URD more readable, but a problem arises when the URD is updated. If a requirement is stated in two places, and a change is made in only one place, the URD will be inconsistent. When redundancy or overlapping is necessary, the URD should include cross-references to make it modifiable.

The removal of redundancy can lead to errors. Consider the situation of two similar requirements from separate users being combined. A change of mind on the part of one user may result in the removal of the combined requirement. The requirement of the other user has been lost, and this is an error. Source attributes should be retained when merging requirements to show who needs to be consulted before an update is made.

5.3 EVOLUTION

Changes to the URD are the user's responsibility. The URD should be put under change control by the initiator at soon as it is first issued. The document change control procedure described in *Software Engineering Standards* Part 2, Section 3.2.3.2.1 is recommended. This requires that a change history be kept.

New user requirements may be added and existing user requirements may be modified or deleted. If anyone wants to change the user requirements after the UR phase, the users should update the URD and resubmit it to the UR/R board for approval. Note that in the OM phase, the Software Review Board (SRB) replaces the UR/R board.

The initiator of the project should monitor the trend in the occurrence of new user requirements. An upward trend signals that the software is unlikely to be successful.

5.4 RESPONSIBILITY

The definition of the user requirements must be the responsibility of the user (UR01). This means that the URD must be written by the users, or someone appointed by them. The expertise of software engineers, hardware engineers and operations personnel should be used to help define and review the user requirements.

Typically the capability requirements are generated by the people who will use the system, while the constraint requirements may come from either hardware, software, communications or quality assurance experts. Human-computer interfaces are normally best defined by a joint effort of users and developers, ideally through prototypes.

In a system development, some of the user requirements for the software come from the System Requirements Document. The preferred approach is to refer to system requirements in the URD. Alternatively, relevant requirements can be extracted from the System Requirements Document, perhaps reformulated, and then inserted in the URD. This approach may pose problems from a change control point of view, but may also be the only possible alternative when the system requirements are not clearly identifiable or when the requirements applicable to the software components are embedded in other requirements.

It should never be assumed that all the user requirements can be derived from system requirements. Other techniques for capturing user requirements should always be considered (see Chapter 2). In other cases there could be multiple user groups, each having their own set of requirements. A single URD, with sections compiled by the different groups, or multiple URDs, one for each group, are both possible ways of documenting the user requirements.

In summary, there is no single scheme for producing a URD. Nevertheless:
- responsibilities should be clearly defined before URD production is started;
- the real users of the system are responsible for determining the capability requirements (UR01);

- the software engineers to be in charge of the development should take part in the URD creation process so that they can advise the users on the real practicalities of requirements, point out the potential of existing software and technology, and possibly develop prototypes.

The roles and responsibilities of the various people must be clarified and accepted by everybody involved before the process starts. Whatever the organisation, users should avoid dictating solutions while developers should avoid dictating capabilities.

5.5 MEDIUM

It is usually assumed that the URD is a paper document. There is no reason why the URD should not be distributed electronically to participants with the necessary equipment.

5.6 CONTENT

The URD should be compiled according to the table of contents provided in Appendix C of *Software Engineering Standards*. This table of contents is derived from ANSI/IEEE Std 830-1993 'Recommended Practice for Software Requirements Specifications' [Ref 3].

Section 1 should briefly describe the purpose and scope of the software and provide an overview of the rest of the document. Section 2 should provide a general description of the world the software operates in. While rigour is not necessary, a clear physical picture should emerge. Section 3 should provide the formal requirements, upon which the acceptability of the software will be judged. Large URDs (forty pages or more) should contain an index.

References should be given where appropriate. A URD should not refer to documents that follow it in the *Software Engineering Standards* life cycle. A URD should contain no TBDs by the time of the User Requirements Review.

Software Engineering Standards recommends the following table of contents for a URD:

Service Information:
a - Abstract
b - Table of Contents
c - Document Status Sheet
d - Document Change records made since last issue

1 INTRODUCTION[1]
    1.1 Purpose
    1.2 Scope
    1.3 Definitions, acronyms and abbreviations
    1.4 References

---

[1] The User Requirements Document contents lists is based upon extracts from IEEE Std 830-1993, IEEE Recommended Practice for Software Requirements Specifications, copyright © 1993 by the Institute for Electrical and Electronic Engineers Inc. The IEEE disclaims any responsibility or liability resulting from the placement and use in this publication. Information is reprinted with the permission of the IEEE.

1.5 Overview

2 GENERAL DESCRIPTION
2.1 Product perspective
2.2 General capabilities
2.3 General constraints
2.4 User characteristics
2.5 Operational environment
2.6 Assumptions and dependencies

3 SPECIFIC REQUIREMENTS
3.1 Capability requirements
3.2 Constraint requirements

Material unsuitable for the above contents list should be inserted in additional appendices. If there is no material for a section then the phrase 'Not Applicable' should be inserted and the section numbering preserved.

5.6.1 URD/1 INTRODUCTION

This section should provide an overview of the entire document and a description of the scope of the software.

5.6.1.1 URD/1.1 Purpose (of the document)

This section should:
(1) define the purpose of the particular URD;
(2) specify the intended readership of the URD.

5.6.1.2 URD/1.2 Scope (of the software)

This section should:
(1) identify the software product(s) to be produced by name;
(2) explain what the proposed software will do (and will not do, if necessary);
(3) describe relevant benefits, objectives, and goals as precisely as possible;
(4) be consistent with similar statements in higher-level specifications, if they exist.

5.6.1.3 URD/1.3 Definitions, acronyms and abbreviations

This section should provide the definitions of all terms, acronyms, and abbreviations, or refer to other documents where the definitions can be found.

5.6.1.4 URD/1.4 References

This section should provide a complete list of all the applicable and reference documents, identified by title, author and date. Each document should be marked as applicable or reference. If appropriate, report number, journal name and publishing organisation should be included.

5.6.1.5 URD/1.5 Overview

This section should:
   (1) describe what the rest of the URD contains;
   (2) explain how the URD is organised.

5.6.2 URD/2 GENERAL DESCRIPTION

This chapter should describe the general factors that affect the product and its requirements. This chapter does not state specific requirements but makes those requirements easier to understand.

5.6.2.1 URD/2.1 Product perspective

This section puts the product into perspective with other related systems. If the product is to replace an existing system, the system should be described and referenced. Ancestors of the product that are no longer in use might be mentioned. If the product is 'standalone', it should be stated here.

5.6.2.2 URD/2.2 General capabilities

This section should describe the main capabilities and why they are needed. This section should describe the process to be supported by the software, indicating those parts of the process where it is used.

5.6.2.3 URD/2.3 General constraints

This section should describe any items that will limit the developer's options for building the software.
   This section should not be used to impose specific requirements or specific design constraints, but should state the reasons why certain requirements or constraints exist.

5.6.2.4 URD/2.4 User characteristics

This section should describe those general characteristics of the users affecting the specific requirements.
   Many people may interact with the software during the operations and maintenance phase. Some of these people are users, operators and maintenance personnel. Certain characteristics of these people, such as educational level, language, experience and technical expertise impose important constraints on the software.
   Software may be frequently used, but individuals may use it only occasionally. Frequent users will become experts whereas infrequent users may remain relative novices. It is important to classify the users and estimate the likely numbers in each category. If absolute numbers cannot be stated, relative numbers can still be useful.

5.6.2.5 URD/2.5 Operational environment

This section should describe the real world in which the software is to operate in. This narrative description may be supported by context diagrams, to summarise external interfaces, and system block diagrams, to show how the activity fits within the larger system. The nature of the exchanges with external systems should be specified.

If a URD defines a product that is a component of a parent system or project then this section should:

- outline the activities that will be supported by external systems;
- reference the Interface Control Documents that define the external interfaces with the other systems;
- describe the computer infrastructure to be used.

5.6.2.4 URD/2.4 Assumptions and dependencies

This section should list the assumptions that the specific requirements are based on. Risk analysis should be used to identify assumptions that may not prove to be valid.

A constraint requirement, for example, might specify an interface with a system that does not exist. If the production of the system does not occur when expected, the URD may have to change.

5.6.3 URD/3 SPECIFIC REQUIREMENTS

Specific requirements should be described in this section, which is the core of the URD. The acceptability of the software will be assessed with respect to the specific requirements.

Each requirement must be uniquely identified (UR02). Forward traceability to subsequent phases in the life cycle depends upon each requirement having a unique identifier.

Essential requirements have to be met for the software to be acceptable. If a requirement is essential, it must be clearly flagged (UR03). Non-essential requirements should be marked with a measure of desirability (e.g. scale of 1, 2, 3).

Some user requirements may be 'suspended' pending resources becoming available. Such non-applicable user requirements must be clearly flagged (UR09).

The priority of a requirement measures the order, or the timing, of the related software becoming available. If the transfer is to be phased, so that some parts of the software come into operation before others, then each requirement must be marked with a measure of priority (UR04).

Unstable requirements should be flagged. These requirements may be dependent on feedback from the UR, SR and AD phases. The usual method for flagging unstable requirements is to attach the marker 'TBC'.

The source of each user requirement must be stated (UR05). The source may be defined using the identifier of a system requirement, a document cross-reference or even the name of a person or group. Backwards traceability depends upon each requirement explicitly referencing its source.

Each user requirement must be verifiable (UR06). Clarity increases verifiability. Each statement of user requirement should contain one and only one requirement. A user requirement is verifiable if some method can be devised for objectively demonstrating that the software implements it. For example statements such as:

- 'the software will work well';

- 'the product shall be user friendly';
- 'the output of the program shall usually be given within 10 seconds';

are not verifiable because the terms 'well', 'user friendly' and 'usually' have no objective interpretation.

A statement such as: 'the output of the program shall be given within 20 s of event X, 60% of the time; and shall be given within 30 s of event X, 99% of the time', is verifiable because it uses concrete terms and measurable quantities. If a method cannot be devised to verify a requirement, the requirement is invalid.

The user must describe the consequences of losses of availability and breaches of security, so that the developers can fully appreciate the criticality of each function (UR07).

5.6.3.1 URD/3.1 Capability requirements

The organisation of the capability requirements should reflect the problem, and no single structure will be suitable for all cases.

The capability requirements can be structured around a processing sequence, for example:
   a) RECEPTION OF IMAGE
   b) PROCESSING OF IMAGE
   c) DISPLAY OF IMAGE
perhaps followed by deviations from the baseline operation:
   d) HANDLING LOW QUALITY IMAGES
Each capability requirement should be checked to see whether the inclusion of capacity, speed and accuracy attributes is appropriate.

5.6.3.2 URD/3.2 Constraint requirements

Constraint requirements may cover any topic that does not directly relate to the specific capabilities the users require.

Constraint requirements that relate to interfaces should be grouped around the headings:
- communications interfaces;
- hardware interfaces;
- software interfaces;
- human-computer interactions (user interfaces).

If the software is part of a larger system then any documents (e.g. ICDs) that describe the interfaces should be identified.

Requirements that ensure the software will be fit for its purpose should be stated, for example:
- adaptability;
- availability;
- portability;
- security;
- safety;
- standards.

CHAPTER 6
LIFE CYCLE MANAGEMENT ACTIVITIES

6.1 INTRODUCTION

Plans of SR phase activities must be drawn up in the UR phase. These plans cover project management, configuration management, verification and validation, quality assurance and acceptance tests.

6.2 PROJECT MANAGEMENT PLAN FOR THE SR PHASE

By the end of the UR review, the SR phase section of the SPMP (SPMP/SR) must be produced (SPM02). The SPMP/SR describes, in detail, the project activities for the SR phase. As part of its introduction, the SPMP/SR must outline a plan for the whole project (SPM03).

A rough estimate of the total cost of the software project should be included in the SPMP/SR. Technical knowledge and experience gained on similar projects help make this estimate.

A precise estimate of the effort involved in the SR phase must be included in the SPMP/SR (SPM04). Specific factors affecting estimates for the work required in the SR phase are the:

- number of user requirements;
- level of user requirements;
- stability of user requirements;
- level of definition of external interfaces;
- quality of the URD.

An estimate based simply on the number of user requirements might be very misleading - a large number of detailed low-level user requirements might be more useful, and save more time in the SR phase, than a few high-level user requirements. A poor quality URD might imply that a lot of requirements analysis is required in the SR phase.

6.3 CONFIGURATION MANAGEMENT PLAN FOR THE SR PHASE

By the end of the UR review, the SR phase section of the SCMP (SCMP/SR) must be produced (SCM42). The SCMP/SR must cover the configuration management procedures for all documentation, CASE tool outputs and prototype code, to be produced in the SR phase (SCM43).

6.4 VERIFICATION AND VALIDATION PLAN FOR THE SR PHASE

By the end of the UR review, the SR phase section of the SVVP (SVVP/SR) must be produced (SVV09). The SVVP/SR must define how to trace user requirements to software requirements, so that each software requirement can be justified (SVV10). It should describe how the SRD is to be evaluated by defining the review procedures. It may include specifications of the tests to be performed with prototypes.

6.5 QUALITY ASSURANCE PLAN FOR THE SR PHASE

By the end of the UR review, the SR phase section of the SQAP (SQAP/SR) must be produced (SQA03). The SQAP/SR must describe, in detail, the quality assurance activities to be carried out in the SR phase (SQA04). The SQAP/SR must outline the quality assurance plan for the rest of the project (SQA05).

SQA activities include monitoring the following activities:

- management;
- documentation;
- standards, practices, conventions, and metrics;
- reviews and audits;
- testing activities;
- problem reporting and corrective action;
- tools, techniques and methods;
- code and media control;
- supplier control;
- records collection maintenance and retention;
- training;
- risk management.

6.6 ACCEPTANCE TEST PLANS

The initiator(s) of the user requirements should lay down the acceptance test principles. The developer must construct an acceptance test plan in the UR phase and document it in the SVVP (SVV11). This plan should define the scope, approach, resources and schedule of acceptance testing activities.

Specific tests for each user requirement are not formulated until the DD phase. The Acceptance Test Plan should deal with the general issues, for example:

- where will the acceptance tests be done?
- who will attend?
- who will carry them out?
- are tests needed for all user requirements?
- what kinds of tests are sufficient for provisional acceptance?
- what kinds of tests are sufficient for final acceptance?
- must any special test software be used?
- if the acceptance tests are to be done by users, what special documentation is required?
- how long is the acceptance testing programme expected to last?

APPENDIX A
GLOSSARY

A.1 LIST OF TERMS

Except for the definitions listed below, the definitions of all terms used in this document conform to the definitions provided in or referenced by *Software Engineering Standards*.

capability requirement
A capability requirement describes an operation, or sequence of related operations, that the software must be able to perform.

constraint requirement
A constraint requirement restricts the way the software is implemented, without altering or describing the capabilities of the software.

end user
A person who utilises the products or services of a system.

initiator
The person, or group of people, who originates a project and is responsible for accepting its products.

language
A symbolic method of expressing information. Symbols convey meaning and are used according to convention.

operator
A person who controls and monitors the hardware and software of a system.

outliner
A word processing program that allows the viewing of the section headings in isolation from the rest of the text.

risk
The amount of uncertainty in being able to satisfy a requirement.

user[2]
A person who utilises the products or services of a system, or a person who controls and monitors the hardware and software of a system (i.e. an end user, an operator, or both).

---

[2] In *Software Engineering Standards*, a user is the same as an 'end user', and an operator is not a user. The meaning of user has been generalised in these guides to include the operator, to follow normal usage.

A.2 LIST OF ACRONYMS

AD	Architectural Design
ANSI	American National Standards Institute
AT	Acceptance Tests
BSSC	Board for Software Standardisation and Control
DD	Detailed Design and production
ESA	European Space Agency
OM	Operations and Maintenance
PSS	Procedures, Specifications and Standards
SCM	Software Configuration Management
SCMP	Software Configuration Management Plan
SPM	Software Project Management
SPMP	Software Project Management Plan
SQA	Software Quality Assurance
SQAP	Software Quality Assurance Plan
SR	Software Requirements
SRB	Software Review Board
SVV	Software Verification and Validation
SVVP	Software Verification and Validation Plan
TBC	To Be Confirmed
TBD	To Be Defined
TR	Transfer
UR	User Requirements
UR/R	User Requirements Review

APPENDIX B
REFERENCES

1. Software Engineering Standards, C.Mazza, J.Fairclough, B.Melton, D.DePablo, A.Scheffer, R.Stevens, Prentice Hall, 1994
2. IEEE Standard Glossary for Software Engineering Terminology, ANSI/IEEE Std 610.12-1990.
3. IEEE Guide to Software Requirements Specifications, ANSI/IEEE Std 830-1984.
4. IEEE Standard for Software Reviews and Audits, IEEE Std 1028-1988.
5. Realistic User Requirements, G.Longworth, NCC Publications, 1987.
6. Software Evolution Through Rapid Prototyping, Luqi, in COMPUTER, May 1989.
7. Structured Analysis and System Specification, T.DeMarco, Yourdon Press, 1978.
8. SSADM Version 4, NCC Blackwell publications, 1991.
9. Structured Systems Analysis and Design Methodology, G.Cutts, Paradigm, 1987.

APPENDIX C
UR PHASE MANDATORY PRACTICES

This appendix is repeated from *Software Engineering Standards*, Appendix D.2.

UR01   The definition of the user requirements shall be the responsibility of the user.

UR02   Each user requirement shall include an identifier.

UR03   Essential user requirements shall be marked as such.

UR04   For incremental delivery, each user requirement shall include a measure of priority so that the developer can decide the production schedule.

UR05   The source of each user requirement shall be stated.

UR06   Each user requirement shall be verifiable.

UR07   The user shall describe the consequences of losses of availability, or breaches of security, so that developers can fully appreciate the criticality of each function.

UR08   The outputs of the UR phase shall be formally reviewed during the User Requirements Review.

UR09   Non-applicable user requirements shall be clearly flagged in the URD.

UR10   An output of the UR phase shall be the User Requirements Document (URD).

UR11   The URD shall always be produced before a software project is started.

UR12   The URD shall provide a general description of what the user expects the software to do.

UR13   All known user requirements shall be included in the URD.

UR14   The URD shall describe the operations the user wants to perform with the software system.

UR15   The URD shall define all the constraints that the user wishes to impose upon any solution.

UR16   The URD shall describe the external interfaces to the software system or reference them in ICDs that exist or are to be written.

APPENDIX D
INDEX

Guide
to the
software requirements
definition
phase

TABLE OF CONTENTS

CHAPTER 1
INTRODUCTION

1.1 PURPOSE

Software Engineering Standards [Ref. 1] defines the second phase of the software life cycle to be the 'Software Requirements Definition Phase' (SR phase). Activities and products are examined in the 'SR review' (SR/R) at the end of the phase.

The SR phase can be called the 'problem analysis phase' of the life cycle. The user requirements are analysed and software requirements are produced that must be as complete, consistent and correct as possible.

This document provides guidance on how to produce the software requirements. This document should be read by all active participants in the SR phase, e.g. initiators, user representatives, analysts, designers, project managers and product assurance personnel.

1.2 OVERVIEW

Chapter 2 discusses the SR phase. Chapters 3 and 4 discuss methods and tools for software requirements definition. Chapter 5 describes how to write the SRD, starting from the template. Chapter 6 summarises the life cycle management activities, which are discussed at greater length in other guides.

All the SR phase mandatory practices in *Software Engineering Standards* are repeated in this document. The identifier of the practice is added in parentheses to mark a repetition. No new mandatory practices are defined.

CHAPTER 2
THE SOFTWARE REQUIREMENTS DEFINITION PHASE

2.1 INTRODUCTION

In the SR phase, a set of software requirements is constructed. This is done by examining the URD and building a 'logical model', using recognised methods and specialist knowledge of the problem domain. The logical model should be an abstract description of what the system must do and should not contain implementation terminology. The model structures the problem and makes it manageable.

A logical model is used to produce a structured set of software requirements that is consistent, coherent and complete. The software requirements specify the functionality, performance, interfaces, quality, reliability, maintainability, safety etc., (see Section 2.4). The software requirements and the logical model are documented in the Software Requirements Document (SRD). The SRD gives the developer's view of the problem rather than the user's. The SRD must cover all the requirements stated in the URD (SR12). The correspondence between requirements in the URD and SRD is not necessarily one-to-one. The SRD may also contain requirements that the developer considers are necessary to ensure the product is fit for its purpose (e.g. product assurance standards and interfaces to test equipment).

The main outputs of the SR phase are the:
- Software Requirements Document (SRD);
- Software Project Management Plan for the AD phase (SPMP/AD);
- Software Configuration Management Plan for the AD phase(SCMP/AD);
- Software Verification and Validation Plan for the AD Phase (SVVP/AD);
- Software Quality Assurance Plan for the AD phase (SQAP/AD);
- System Test Plan (SVVP/ST).

Progress reports, configuration status accounts, and audit reports are also outputs of the phase. These should always be archived by the project.

Defining the software requirements is the developer's responsibility. Besides the developer, participants in the SR phase should include users, systems engineers, hardware engineers and operations personnel. Project management should ensure that all parties can review the requirements, to minimise incompleteness and error.

SR phase activities must be carried out according to the plans defined in the UR phase (SR01). Progress against plans should be continuously monitored by project management and documented at regular intervals in progress reports.

Figure 2.1 summarises activities and document flow in the SR phase. The following subsections describe the activities of the SR phase in more detail.

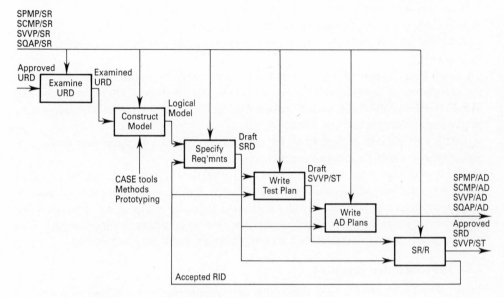

Figure 2.1: SR phase activities

2.2 EXAMINATION OF THE URD

If the developers have not taken part in the User Requirements Review, they should examine the URD and confirm that it is understandable. The *Guide to the User Requirements Definition Phase* contains material that should assist in making the URD understandable. Developers should also confirm that adequate technical skills are available for the SR phase.

2.3 CONSTRUCTION OF THE LOGICAL MODEL

A software model is:
- a simplified description of a system;
- hierarchical, with consistent decomposition criteria;
- composed of symbols organised according to some convention;
- built using recognised methods and tools;
- used for reasoning about the software.

A software model should be a 'simplified description' in the sense that it describes the high-level essentials. A hierarchical presentation also makes the description simpler to understand, evaluate at various levels of detail, and maintain. A recognised method, not an undocumented ad-hoc assembly of 'common sense ideas', should be used to construct a software model (SR03). A method, however, does not substitute for the experience and insight of developers, but helps developers apply those abilities better.

In the SR phase, the developers construct an implementation-independent model of what is needed by the user (SR02). This is called a 'logical model' and it:
- shows what the system must do;

- is organised as a hierarchy, progressing through levels of abstraction;
- avoids using implementation terminology (e.g. workstation);
- permits reasoning from cause-to-effect and vice-versa.

A logical model makes the software requirements understandable as a whole, not just individually.

A logical model should be built iteratively. Some tasks may need to be repeated until the description of each level is clear and consistent. Walkthroughs, inspections and technical reviews should be used to ensure that each level of the model is agreed before proceeding to the next level of detail.

CASE tools should be used in all but the smallest projects, because they make clear and consistent models easier to construct and modify.

The type of logical model built depends on the method selected. The method selected depends on the type of software required. Chapter 3 summarises the methods suitable for constructing a logical model. In the following sections, functional decomposition concepts and terminology are used to describe how to construct a logical model. This does not imply that this method shall be used, but only that it may be suitable.

2.3.1 Functional decomposition

The first step in building a logical model is to break the system down into a set of basic functions with a few simple inputs and outputs. This is called 'functional decomposition'.

Functional decomposition is called a 'top-down' method because it starts from a single high-level function and results in a set of low-level functions that combine to perform the high-level function. Each level therefore models the system at different levels of abstraction. The top-down approach produces the most general functions first, leaving the detail to be defined only when necessary.

Consistent criteria should be established for decomposing functions into subfunctions. The criteria should not have any 'implementation bias' (i.e. include design and production considerations). Examples of implementation bias are: 'by programming language', 'by memory requirements' or 'by existing software'.

Software Engineering Standards defines the guidelines for building a good logical model. These are repeated below.

(1) Functions should have a single definite purpose.
(2) Functions should be appropriate to the level they appear at (e.g. 'Calculate Checksum' should not appear at the same level as 'Verify Telecommands').
(3) Interfaces should be minimised. This allows design components with weak coupling to be easily derived.
(4) Each function should be decomposed into no more than seven lower-level functions.
(5) Implementation terminology should be absent (e.g. file, record, task, module, workstation).
(6) Performance attributes of each function (capacity, speed etc) should be stated wherever possible.
(7) Critical functions should be identified.

(8) Function names should reflect the purpose and say 'what' is to be done, not 'how' it must be done.

(9) Function names should have a declarative structure (e.g. 'Validate Telecommands').

The recommendation to minimise interfaces needs further qualification. The number of interfaces can be measured by the number of:

- inputs and outputs;
- different functions that interface with it.

High-level functions may have many inputs and outputs. In the first iteration of the logical model, the goal is a set of low-level functions that have a few simple interfaces. The processing of the low-level functions should be briefly described.

In the second and subsequent iterations, functions and data are restructured to reduce the number of interfaces at all levels. Data structures should match the functional decomposition. The data a function deals with should be appropriate to its level.

A logical model should initially cope with routine behaviour. Additional functions may be added later to handle non-routine behaviour, such as startup, shutdown and error handling.

Functional decomposition has reached a sufficient level of detail when the model:

- provides all the capabilities required by the user;
- follows the nine guidelines describe above.

When the use of commercial software looks feasible, developers should ensure that it meets all the user requirements. For example, suppose a high-level database management function is identified. The developer decides that decomposition of the function 'Manage Database' can be stopped because a constraint requirement demands that a particular DBMS is used. This would be wrong if there is a user requirement to select objects from the database. Decomposition should be continued until the user requirement has been included in the model. The designer then has to ensure that a DBMS with the select function is chosen.

2.3.2 Performance analysis

User requirements may contain performance attributes (e.g. capacity, speed and accuracy). These attributes define the performance requirements for a function or group of functions. The logical model should be checked to ensure that no performance requirements conflict; this is done by studying pathways through the data flow.

Decisions about how to partition the performance attributes between a set of functions may involve implementation considerations. Such decisions are best left to the designer and should be avoided in the SR phase.

2.3.3 Criticality analysis

Capability requirements in the URD may have their availability specified in terms of 'Hazard Consequence Severity Category' (HCSC). This can range from 'Catastrophic' through 'Critical' and 'Marginal' to 'Negligible'. If this has been done, the logical model should be analysed to propagate the HCSC to all the requirements related to the capability that have the HCSC attached. Reference 24 describes three criticality analysis techniques:

- Software Failure Modes, Effects and Criticality Analysis (software FMECA);
- Software Common Mode Failure Analysis (Software CFMA);
- Software Fault Tree Analysis (Software FTA).

2.3.4 Prototyping

Models are usually static. However it may be useful to make parts of the model executable to verify them. Such an animated, dynamic model is a kind of prototype.

Prototyping can clarify requirements. The precise details of a user interface may not be clear from the URD, for example. The construction of a prototype for verification by the user is the most effective method of clarifying such requirements.

Data and control flows can be decomposed in numerous ways. For example a URD may say 'enter data into a form and produce a report'.

Only after some analysis does it become apparent what the contents of the form or report should be, and this ought to be confirmed with the user. The best way to do this to make an example of the form or report, and this may require prototype software to be written.

The development team may identify some requirements as containing a high degree of risk (i.e. there is a large amount of uncertainty whether they can be satisfied). The production of a prototype to assess the feasibility or necessity of such requirements can be very effective in deciding whether they ought to be included in the SRD.

2.4 SPECIFICATION OF THE SOFTWARE REQUIREMENTS

Software Engineering Standards defines the following types of software requirements:

Functional Requirements	Documentation Requirements
Performance Requirements	Security Requirements
Interface Requirements	Portability Requirements
Operational Requirements	Quality Requirements
Resource Requirements	Reliability Requirements
Verification Requirements	Maintainability Requirements
Acceptance-Testing Requirements	Safety Requirements

Functional requirements should be organised top-down, according to the structure of the logical model. Non-functional requirements should be attached to functional requirements and can therefore appear at all levels in the hierarchy, and apply to all functional requirements below them. They may be organised as a separate set and cross-referenced, where this is simpler.

2.4.1 Functional requirements

A function is a 'defined objective or characteristic action of a system or component' and a functional requirement 'specifies a function that a system or system component must be able to perform [Ref. 2]. Functional requirements are matched one-to-one to nodes of the logical model. A functional requirement should:

- define 'what' a process must do, not 'how' to implement it;
- define the transformation to be performed on specified inputs to generate specified outputs;
- have performance requirements attached;
- be stated rigourously.

Functional requirements can be stated rigourously by using short, simple sentences. Several styles are possible, for example Structured English and Precondition-Postcondition style [Ref. 7, 12].

Examples of functional requirements are:

- 'Calibrate the instrument data'
- 'Select all calibration stars brighter than the 6th magnitude'

2.4.2 Performance requirements

Performance requirements specify numerical values for measurable variables used to define a function (e.g. rate, frequency, capacity, speed and accuracy). Performance requirements may be included in the quantitative statement of each function, or included as separate requirements. For example the requirements:

'Calibrate the instrument data'

'Calibration accuracy shall be 10%'

can be combined to make a single requirement:

'Calibrate the instrument data to an accuracy of 10%'

The approach chosen has to trade-off modifiability against duplication.

Performance requirements may be represented as a range of values [Ref. 21], for example the:

- acceptable value;
- nominal value;
- ideal value.

The acceptable value defines the minimum level of performance allowed; the nominal value defines a safe margin of performance above the acceptable value, and the ideal value defines the most desirable level of performance.

2.4.3 Interface requirements

Interface requirements specify hardware, software or database elements that the system, or system component, must interact or communicate with. Accordingly, interface requirements should be classified into software, hardware and communications interfaces.

Interface requirements should also be classified into 'internal' and 'external' interface requirements, depending upon whether or not the interface coincides with the system boundary. Whereas the former should always be described in the SRD, the latter may be described in separate 'Interface Control Documents' (ICDs).

This ensures a common, self-contained definition of the interface.

An interface requirement may be stated by:

- describing the data flow or control flow across the interface;
- describing the protocol that governs the exchanges across the interface;

- referencing the specification of the component in another system that is to be used and describing:
    - when the external function is utilised;
    - what is transferred when the external function is utilised.
- defining a constraint on an external function;
- defining a constraint imposed by an external function.

Unless it is present as a constraint, an interface requirement should only define the logical aspects of an interface (e.g. the number and type of items that have to be exchanged), and not the physical details (e.g. byte location of fields in a record, ASCII or binary format etc.). The physical description of data structures should be deferred to the design phase.

Examples of interface requirements are:

- 'Functions X and Y shall exchange instrument data';
- 'Communications between the computer and remote instruments shall be via the IEEE-488 protocol'.
- 'Transmit the amount of fuel remaining to the ground control system every fifteen seconds'.

2.4.4 Operational requirements

Operational requirements specify how the system will run (i.e. when it is to be operated) and how it will communicate with human operators (e.g. screen and keyboards etc.).

Operational requirements may describe physical aspects of the user interface. Descriptions of the dialogue, screen layouts, command language style are all types of operational requirements.

Operational requirements may define ergonomic aspects, e.g. the levels of efficiency that users should be able to attain.

The user may have constrained the user interface in the URD. A function may require the input of some data, for example, and this may be implemented by a keyboard or a speech interface. The user may demand that a speech interface be employed, and this should be stated as an operational requirement.

2.4.5 Resource requirements

Resource requirements specify the upper limits on physical resources such as processing power, main memory, disk space etc. They may describe any requirements that the development or operational environment place upon the software. A resource requirement should state the facts about the resources, and not constrain how they are deployed.

At a system design level, specific allocations of computer resources may have been allocated to software subsystems. Software developers must be aware of resource constraints when they design the software. In some cases (e.g. embedded systems) resource constraints cannot be relaxed.

Examples of resource requirements are:

- 'All programs shall execute with standard user quotas.'
- '5 Mbytes of disk space are available.'

2.4.6 Verification requirements

Verification requirements constrain the design of the product. They may do this by requiring features that facilitate verification of system functions, or by saying how the product is to be verified.

Verification requirements may include specifications of any:

- simulations to be performed;
- requirements imposed by the test environment;
- diagnostic facilities.

Simulation is 'a model that behaves or operates like a given system when provided a set of controlled inputs' [Ref. 2]. A simulator is needed when a system cannot be exercised in the operational environment prior to delivery. The simulator reproduces the behaviour of the operational environment.

2.4.7 Acceptance-testing requirements

Acceptance-testing requirements constrain the design of the product. They are a type of verification requirement, and apply specifically to the TR phase.

2.4.8 Documentation requirements

Documentation requirements state project-specific requirements for documentation, in addition to those contained in *Software Engineering Standards*. The format and style of the Interface Control Documents may be described in the documentation requirements, for example.

Documentation should be designed for the target readers (i.e. users and maintenance personnel). The URD contains a section called 'User Characteristics' that may help profile the readership.

2.4.9 Security requirements

Security requirements specify the requirements for securing the system against threats to confidentiality, integrity and availability. They should describe the level and frequency of access allowed to authorised users of the software. If prevention against unauthorised use is required, the type of unauthorised user should be described. The level of physical protection of the computer facilities may be stated (e.g. backups are to be kept in a fire-proof safe off-site).

Examples of security requirements are protection against:

- accidental destruction of the software;
- accidental loss of data;
- unauthorised use of the software;
- computer viruses.

2.4.10 Portability requirements

Portability requirements specify how easy it should be to move the software from one environment to another. Possible computer and operating systems, other than those of the target system, should be stated.

Examples of the portability requirements are:
- 'it shall be possible to recompile this software to run on computer X without modifying more than 2% of the source code';
- 'no part of the software shall be written in assembler'.

Portability requirements can reduce performance of the software and increase the effort required to build it. For example, asking that the software be made portable between operating systems may require that operating system service routines be called from dedicated modules. This can affect performance, since the number of calls to execute a specific operation is increased. Further, use of computer-specific extensions to a programming language may be precluded.

Portability requirements should therefore be formulated after taking careful consideration of the probable life-time of the software, operating system and hardware.

The portability requirements may reflect a difference in the development and target environment.

2.4.11 Quality requirements

Quality requirements specify the attributes of the software that make it fit for its purpose. The major quality attributes of reliability, maintainability and safety should always be stated separately. Where appropriate, software quality attributes should be specified in measurable terms (i.e. with the use of metrics). For example requirements for the:
- use of specific procedures, standards and regulations;
- use of external software quality assurance personnel;
- qualifications of suppliers.

Any quality-related requirements stated by the user in the UR phase may be supplemented in the SR phase by the in-house standards of the development organisation. Such standards attempt to guarantee the quality of a product by using proper procedures for its production.

2.4.12 Reliability requirements

Software reliability is 'the ability of a system or component to perform its required functions under stated conditions for a specified period of time' [Ref. 2]. The reliability metric, 'Mean Time Between Failure' (MTBF), measures reliability according to this definition.

Reliability requirements should specify the acceptable Mean Time Between Failures of the software, averaged over a significant period. They may also specify the minimum time between failures that is ever acceptable. Reliability requirements may have to be derived from the user's availability requirements. This can be done from the relation:

$$\text{Availability} = \text{MTBF} / (\text{MTBF} + \text{MTTR}).$$

MTTR is the Mean Time To Repair (see Section 2.4.13). MTBF is the average time the software is available, whereas the sum of MTBF and MTTR is the average time it should be operational.

Adequate margins should be added to the availability requirements when deriving the reliability requirements. The specification of the Reliability Requirements should provide a classification of failures based on their severity. Table 2.3.12 provides an example classification, based on the 'able-to-continue?' criterion.

Failure Class	Definition
SEVERE	Operations cannot be continued
WARNING	Operations can be continued, with reduced capability
INFORMATION	Operations can be continued

Table 2.3.12: Failure classification example

Two Examples of reliability requirements are:
- 'the MTBF for severe failures shall be 4 weeks, averaged over 6 months.'
- 'the minimum time between severe failures shall be in excess of 5 days.'

2.4.13 Maintainability requirements

Maintainability is 'the ease with which a software system or component can be modified to correct faults, improve performance or other attributes, or adapt to a changed environment' [Ref. 2]. All aspects of maintainability should be covered in the specification of the maintainability requirements, and should be specified, where appropriate, in quantitative terms.

The idea of fault repair is used to formulate the more restricted definition of maintainability commonly used in software engineering, i.e. 'the ability of an item under stated conditions of use to be retained in, or restored to, within a given period of time, a specified state in which it can perform its required functions'. The maintainability metric, Mean Time To Repair (MTTR), measures maintainability according to this second definition.

Maintainability requirements should specify the acceptable MTTR, averaged over a significant period. They may also specify the maximum time to repair faults ever acceptable. Maintainability requirements may have to be derived from the user's availability requirements (see Section 2.4.12).

Adaptability requirements can effect the software design by ensuring that parameters that are likely to vary do not get 'hard-wired' into the code, or that certain objects are made generic.

Examples of maintainability requirements are:
- 'the MTTR shall be 1 day averaged over a 1 year.'
- 'the time to repair shall never exceed 1 week.'

2.4.14 Safety requirements

Safety requirements specify any requirements to reduce the possibility of damage that can follow from software failure. Safety requirements may identify critical functions whose failure may be hazardous to people or property. Software should be considered safety-critical if the hardware it controls can cause injury to people or damage to property.

While reliability requirements should be used to specify the acceptable frequency of failures, safety requirements should be used to specify what should happen when failures of a critical piece of software actually do occur. In the safety category are requirements for:

- graceful degradation after a failure (e.g. warnings are issued to users before system shutdown and measures are taken to protect property and lives);
- continuation of system availability after a single-point failure.

2.5 SYSTEM TEST PLANNING

System Test Plans must be generated in the SR phase and documented in the System Test section of the Software Verification and Validation Plan (SVVP/ST). See Chapter 6 of this document. The System Test Plan should describe the scope, approach and resources required for the system tests, and address the verification requirements in the SRD.

2.6 THE SOFTWARE REQUIREMENTS REVIEW

The SRD and SVVP/ST are produced iteratively. Walkthroughs and internal reviews should be held before a formal review.

The outputs of the SR phase must be formally reviewed during the Software Requirements Review (SR09). This should be a technical review. The recommended procedure, described in the *Guide to Software Verification and Validation*, is based closely on the IEEE standard for Technical Reviews [Ref. 8].

Normally, only the SRD and System Test Plans undergo the full technical review procedure involving users, developers, management and quality assurance staff. The Software Project Management Plan (SPMP/AD), Software Configuration Management Plan (SCMP/AD), Software Verification and Validation Plan (SVVP/AD), and Software Quality Assurance Plan (SQAP/AD) are usually reviewed by management and quality assurance staff only.

In summary, the objective of the SR/R is to verify that the:

- SRD states the software requirements clearly, completely and in sufficient detail to enable the design process to be started;
- SVVP/ST is an adequate plan for system testing the software in the DD phase.

The documents are distributed to the participants in the formal review process for examination. A problem with a document is described in a 'Review Item Discrepancy' (RID) form that may be prepared by any participant in the review. Review meetings are then held which have the documents and RIDs as input. A review meeting should discuss all the RIDs and either accept or reject them. The review meeting may also discuss possible solutions to the problems raised by the RIDs.

The output of a formal review meeting includes a set of accepted RIDs. Each review meeting should end with a decision whether another review meeting is necessary. It is quite possible to proceed to the AD phase with some actions outstanding, which should be relatively minor or have agreed solutions already defined.

2.7 PLANNING THE ARCHITECTURAL DESIGN PHASE

Plans of AD phase activities must be drawn up in the SR phase. Generation of the plans for the AD phase is discussed in chapter 6 of this document. These plans should cover project management, configuration management, verification and validation and quality assurance. Outputs are the:

- Software Project Management Plan for the AD phase (SPMP/AD);
- Software Configuration Management Plan for the AD phase (SCMP/AD);
- Software Verification and Validation Plan for the AD phase (SVVP/AD);
- Software Quality Assurance Plan for the AD phase (SQAP/AD).

CHAPTER 3
METHODS FOR SOFTWARE REQUIREMENTS DEFINITION

3.1 INTRODUCTION

Analysis is the study of a problem, prior to taking some action. The SR phase may be called the 'analysis phase' of the *Software Engineering Standards* life cycle. The analysis should be carried out using a recognised method, or combination of methods, suitable for the project. The method selected should define techniques for:

- constructing a logical model;
- specifying the software requirements.

This guide does not provide an exhaustive, authoritative description of any particular method. The references should be consulted to obtain that information. This guide seeks neither to make any particular method a standard nor to define a complete set of acceptable methods. Each project should examine its needs, choose a method and define and justify the selection in the SRD. To assist in making this choice, this chapter summarises some well-known methods and indicates how they can be applied in the SR phase. Possible methods are:

- functional decomposition;
- structured analysis;
- object-oriented analysis;
- formal methods;
- Jackson System Development;
- rapid prototyping.

Although the authors of any particular method will argue for its general applicability, all of the methods appear to have been developed with a particular type of system in mind. It is necessary to look at the examples and case histories to decide whether a method is suitable.

3.2 FUNCTIONAL DECOMPOSITION

Functional decomposition is the traditional method of analysis. The emphasis is on 'what' functionality must be available, not 'how' it is to be implemented. The functional breakdown is constructed top-down, producing a set of functions, subfunctions and functional interfaces. See Section 2.3.1.

The functional decomposition method was incorporated into the structured analysis method in the late 1970's.

3.3 STRUCTURED ANALYSIS

Structured analysis is a name for a class of methods that analyse a problem by constructing data flow models. Members of this class are:

- Yourdon methods (DeMarco and Ward/Mellor);
- Structured Systems Analysis and Design Methodology (SSADM);
- Structured Analysis and Design Technique (SADT™).

Structured analysis includes all the concepts of functional decomposition, but produces a better functional specification by rigourously defining the functional interfaces, i.e. the data and control flow between the processes that perform the required functions. The ubiquitous 'Data Flow Diagram' is characteristic of structured analysis methods.

Yourdon methods [Ref. 7, 12] are widely used in the USA and Europe. SSADM [Ref. 4, 9] is recommended by the UK government for 'data processing systems'. It is now under the control of the British Standards Institute (BSI) and will therefore become a British Standard. SADT has been successfully used by the European Space Agency for some time [Ref. 17, 20].

According to its early operational definition by DeMarco, structured analysis is the use of the following techniques to produce a specification of the system required:

- Data Flow Diagrams;
- Data Dictionary;
- Structured English;
- Decision Tables;
- Decision Trees.

These techniques are adequate for the analysis of 'information systems'. Developments of structured analysis for 'real-time' or 'embedded systems', have supplemented this list with:

- Transformation Schema;
- State-Transition Diagrams;
- Event Lists;
- Data Schema;
- Precondition-Postcondition Specifications.

SSADM, with its emphasis on data modelling, also includes:

- Entity-Relationship Diagrams (or Entity Models);
- Entity Life Histories.

The methods of structured analysis fall into the groups shown in Table 3.3 according to whether they identify, organise or specify functions or entities.

Activity	Technique
Function Identification	Event Lists
	Entity Life Histories
Function Organisation	Data Flow Diagrams
	Transformation Schema
	Actigrams
Function Specification	Structured English
	Decision Tables
	Decision Trees
	State-Transition Diagrams
	Transition Tables
	Precondition-Postconditions
Entity Identification	"Spot the nouns in the description"
Entity Organisation	Data Structure Diagrams
	Data Schema
	Entity-Relationship Diagrams
Entity Specification	Data Dictionary

Table 3.3: Structured Analysis Techniques

Structured analysis aims to produce a 'Structured Specification' containing a systematic, rigourous description of a system. This description is in terms of system models. Analysis and design of the system is a model-making process.

3.3.1 DeMarco/SSADM modelling approach

The DeMarco and SSADM methods create and refine the system model through four stages:
- current physical model;
- current logical model;
- required logical model;
- required physical model.

The goal of the SR phase should be to build a required logical model. The required physical model incorporates implementation considerations and its construction should be deferred to the AD phase.

The DeMarco/SSADM modelling approach assumes that a system is being replaced. The current physical model describes the present way of doing things. This must be rationalised, to make the current logical model, and then combined with the 'problems and requirements list' of the users to construct the required logical model.

This evolutionary concept can be applied quite often. Most systems have a clear ancestry, and much can be learned by studying their predecessors. This prevents people from 'reinventing wheels'. The URD should always describe or reference similar systems so that the developer can best understand the context of the user requirements. *Software Engineering Standards* explicitly demands that the relationship to predecessor projects be documented in the SRD. If a system is being replaced and a data processing system is required, then the DeMarco/SSADM approach is recommended.

The DeMarco/SSADM modelling approach is difficult to apply directly when the predecessor system was retired some time previously or does not exist. In such cases the developer of a data processing system should look at the DeMarco/SSADM approach in terms of the activities that must be done in each modelling stage. Each activity uses one or more of the techniques described in Table 3.3. When it makes no sense to think in terms of 'current physical models' and 'current logical models', the developer should define an approach that is suitable for the project. Such a tailored approach should include activities used in the standard modelling stages.

3.3.2 Ward/Mellor modelling approach

Ward and Mellor describe an iterative modelling process that first defines the top levels of an 'essential model'. Instead of proceeding immediately to the lower levels of the essential model, Ward and Mellor recommend that the top levels of an 'implementation model' are built. The cycle continues with definition of the next lower level of the essential model. This stops the essential model diverging too far from reality and prevents the implementation model losing coherence and structure.

The essential model is a kind of logical model. It describes what the system must do to be successful, regardless of the technology chosen to implement it. The essential model is built by first defining the system's environment and identifying the inputs, outputs, stimuli and responses it must handle. This is called 'environmental modelling'. Once the environment is defined, the innards of the system are defined, in progressive detail, by relating inputs to outputs and stimuli to responses. This is called 'behavioural modelling' and supersedes the top-down functional decomposition modelling approach.

Real-time software projects should consider using the Ward/Mellor method in the SR phase. The developer should not, however, attempt to construct the definitive implementation model in the SR phase. This task should be done in the AD phase. Instead, predefined design constraints should be used to outline the implementation model and steer the development of the essential model.

3.3.3 SADT modelling approach

There are two stages of requirements definition in SADT:
- context analysis;
- functional specification.

The purpose of context analysis is to define the boundary conditions of the system. 'Functional specification' defines what the system has to do. The output of the functional specification stage is a 'functional architecture', which should be expressed using SADT diagrams.

The functional architecture is a kind of logical model. It is derived from a top-down functional decomposition of the system, starting from the context diagram, which shows all the external interfaces of the system. Data should be decomposed in parallel with the functions.

In the SR phase, SADT diagrams can be used to illustrate the data flow between functions. Mechanism flows should be suppressed. Control flows may be necessary to depict real-time processing.

3.4 OBJECT-ORIENTED ANALYSIS

Object-Oriented Analysis (OOA) is the name for a class of methods that analyse a problem by studying the objects in the problem domain. An object is 'an abstraction of something in the domain of a problem or its implementation, reflecting the capabilities of a system to keep information about it, interact with it or both; an encapsulation of attribute values and their exclusive services' [Ref. 29]. A class describes a set of objects with common attributes and services. An object is an 'instance' of a class and the act of creating an object is called 'instantiation'.

Classes can be decomposed into subclasses. There might be several types of Telemetry Packet for example, and subclasses of Telemetry Packet such as 'Photometer Packet' and 'Spectrometer Packet' may be created. Subclasses share family characteristics, and OOA provides for this by permitting subclasses to inherit operations and attributes from their parents.

Object-oriented analysis can be viewed as a synthesis of the object concepts pioneered in the Simula67 and Smalltalk programming languages, and the techniques of structured analysis, particularly data modelling. Object-oriented analysis differs from structured analysis by:

- building an object model first, instead of the functional model (i.e. hierarchy of data flow diagrams);
- integrating objects, attributes and operations, instead of separating them between the data model and the functional model.

OOA has been quite successful in tackling problems that are resistant to structured analysis, such as user interfaces. OOA provides a seamless transition to OOD and programming in languages such as Smalltalk, Ada and C++, and is the preferred analysis method when object-oriented methods are going to be used later in the life cycle. Further, the proponents of OOA argue that the objects in a system are more fundamental to its nature than the functions it provides. Specifications based on objects will be more adaptable than specifications based on functions.

The leading OOA methods are:

- Coad-Yourdon;
- Rumbaugh et al's Object Modelling Technique (OMT);
- Shlaer-Mellor;
- Booch.

OOA methods are evolving, and analysts often combine the techniques of different methods when analysing problems. Users of OOA methods are recommended to adopt such a pragmatic approach.

3.4.1 Coad and Yourdon

Coad and Yourdon [Ref. 18] describe an Object-Oriented Analysis method based on five major activities:

- finding classes and objects;
- identifying structures;
- identifying subjects;
- defining attributes;

- defining services.

These activities are used to construct each layer of a 'five-layer' object model.

Objects exist in the problem domain. Classes are abstractions of the objects. Objects are instances of classes. The first task of the method is to identify classes and objects.

The second task of the method is to identify structures. Two kinds of structures are recognised: 'generalisation- specialisation structures' and 'whole-part structures'. The former type of structure is like a family tree, and inheritance is possible between members of the structure. The latter kind of structure is used to model entity relationships (e.g. each motor contains one armature).

Large, complex models may need to be organised into 'subjects', with each subject supporting a particular view of the problem. For example the object model of a motor vehicle might have a mechanical view and an electrical view.

Attributes characterise each class. For example an attribute of an engine might be 'number of cylinders'. Each object will have a value for the attribute.

Services define what the objects do. Defining the services is equivalent to defining system functions.

The strengths of Coad and Yourdon's method are its brief, concise description and its use of general texts as sources of definitions, so that the definitions fit common sense and jargon is minimised. The main weakness of the method is its complex notation, which is difficult to use without tool support. Some users of the Coad-Yourdon method have used the OMT diagramming notation instead.

3.4.2 OMT

Rumbaugh et al's Object Modelling Technique (OMT) [Ref 25] transforms the users' problem statement (such as that documented in a User Requirement Document) into three models:

- object model;
- dynamic model;
- functional model.

The three models collectively make the logical model required by *Software Engineering Standards*.

The object model shows the static structure in the real world. The procedure for constructing it is:

- identify objects;
- identify classes of objects;
- identify associations (i.e. relationships) between objects;
- identify object attributes;
- use inheritance to organise and simplify class structure;
- organise tightly coupled classes and associations into modules;
- supply brief textual descriptions on each object.

Important types of association are 'aggregation' (i.e. is a part of) and 'generalisation' (i.e. is a type of).

The dynamic model shows the behaviour of the system, especially the sequencing of interactions. The procedure for constructing it is:

- identify sequences of events in the problem domain and document them in 'event traces';
- build a state-transition diagram for each object that is affected by the events, showing the messages that flow, actions that are performed and object state changes that take place when events occur.

The functional model shows how values are derived, without regard for when they are computed. The procedure for constructing it is not to use functional decomposition, but to:

- identify input and output values that the system receives and produces;
- construct data flow diagrams showing how the output values are computed from the input values;
- identify objects that are used as 'data stores';
- identify the object operations that comprise each process.

The functional model is synthesised from object operations, rather than decomposed from a top level function. The operations of objects may be defined at any stage in modelling.

The strengths of OMT are its simple yet powerful notation capabilities and its maturity. It was applied in several projects by its authors before it was published. The main weakness is the lack of techniques for integrating the object, dynamic and functional models.

3.4.3 Shlaer-Mellor

Shlaer and Mellor begin analysis by identifying the problem domains of the system. Each domain 'is a separate world inhabited by its own conceptual entities, or objects' [Ref 26, 27]. Large domains are partitioned into subsystems. Each domain or subsystem is then separately analysed in three steps:

- information modelling;
- state modelling;
- process modelling.

The three modelling activities collectively make the logical model required by *Software Engineering Standards*.

The goal of information modelling is to identify the:

- objects in the subsystem
- attributes of each object;
- relationships between each object.

The information model is documented by means of diagrams and definitions of the objects, attributes and relationships.

The goal of state modelling is to identify the:

- states of each object, and the actions that are performed in them;
- events that cause objects to move from one state to another;
- sequences of states that form the life cycle of each object;

- sequences of messages communicating events that flow between objects and subsystems.

State models are documented by means of state model diagrams, showing the sequences of states, object communication model diagrams, showing the message flows between states, and event lists.

The goal of process modelling is to identify the:

- operations of each object required in each action;
- attributes of each object that are stored in each action.

Process models are documented by means of action data flow diagrams, showing operations and data flows that occur in each action, an object access model diagrams, showing interobject data access. Complex processes should also be described.

The strengths of the Shlaer-Mellor method are its maturity (its authors claim to have been developing it since 1979) and existence of techniques for integrating the information, state and process models. The main weakness of the method is its complexity.

3.4.4 Booch

Booch models an object-oriented design in terms of a logical view, which defines the classes, objects, and their relationships, and a physical view, which defines the module and process architecture [Ref. 28]. The logical view corresponds to the logical model that *Software Engineering Standards* requires software engineers to construct in the SR phase. The Booch object-oriented method has four steps:

- identify the classes and objects at a given level of abstraction;
- identify the semantics of these classes and objects;
- identify the relationships among these classes and objects;
- implement the classes and objects.

The first three steps should be completed in the SR phase. The last stage is performed in the AD and DD phases. Booch asserts that the process of object-oriented design is neither top-down nor bottom-up but something he calls 'round-trip gestalt design'. The process develops a system incrementally and iteratively. Users of the Booch method are advised to bundle the SR and AD phases together into single 'modelling phase'.

Booch provides four diagramming techniques for documenting the logical view:

- class diagrams, which are used to show the existence of classes and their relationships;
- object diagrams, which are used to show the existence of objects and their behaviour, especially with regard to message communication;
- state-transition diagrams, which show the possible states of each class, and the events that cause transitions from one state to another;
- timing diagrams, which show the sequence of the objects' operations.

Booch's books on object-oriented methods have been described by Stroustrup, the inventor of C++, as the only books worth reading on the subject. This compliment reflects the many insights into good analysis and design practise in his writings. However Booch's notation is cumbersome and few tools are available.

3.5 FORMAL METHODS

A Formal Method should be used when it is necessary to be able to prove that certain consequences will follow specified actions. Formal Methods must have a calculus, to allow proofs to be constructed. This makes rigorous verification possible.

Formal Methods have been criticised for making specifications unintelligible to users. In the *Software Engineering Standards* life cycle, the URD provides the user view of the specification. While the primary user of the SRD is the developer, it does have to be reviewed by other people, and so explanatory notes should be added to ensure that the SRD can be understood by its readership.

Like mathematical treatises, formal specifications contain theorems stating truths about the system to be built. Verification of each theorem is done by proving it from the axioms of the specification. This can, unfortunately, lead to a large number of statements. To avoid this problem, the 'rigourous' approach can be adopted where shorter, intuitive demonstrations of correctness are used [Ref. 11]. Only critical or problematical statements are explicitly proved.

Formal Methods should be considered for the specification of safety-critical systems, or where there are severe availability or security constraints. There are several Formal Methods available, some of that are summarised in the table below. Z, VDM and LOTOS are discussed in more detail. Table 3.5 lists the more common formal methods.

Method	Reference	Summary
Z	10	Functional specification method for sequential programs
VDM Vienna Development Method	11	Functional specification and development method for sequential programs.
LOTOS Language Of Temporal Ordering Specification	IS 8807	Formal Method with an International Standard. Combination of CCS, CSP and the abstract data typing language ACT ONE. Tools are available.
CSP Communicating Sequential Processes	14	Design language for asynchronous parallelism with synchronous communication. Influenced by JSD and CCS.
OBJ	15	Functional specification language and prototyping tool for sequential programs. Objects (i.e. abstract data types) are the main components of OBJ specifications.
CCS Calculus for Communicating Systems	16	Specification and design of concurrent behaviour of systems. Calculus for asynchronous parallelism with synchronous communication. Used in protocol and communications work. See CSP.
Petri Nets	19	Modelling of concurrent behaviour of systems

Table 3.5: Summary of Formal Methods

3.5.1 Z

Z is a model-oriented specification method based on set theory and first order predicate calculus. The set theory is used to define and organise the entities the software deals with. The predicate calculus is used to define and organise the activities the entities take part in, by stating truths about their behaviour.

Z can be used in the SR phase to permit mathematical modelling the functional behaviour of software. Z is suitable for the specification of sequential programs. Its inability to model concurrent processes makes it unsuitable for use in real-time software projects. To overcome this deficiency Z is being combined with another Formal Method, CSP.

Z specifications can be easily adapted to the requirements of an SRD. Z specifications contain:

- an English language description of all parts of the system;
- a mathematical definition of the system's components;
- consistency theorems;
- other theorems stating important consequences.

3.5.2 VDM

The 'Vienna Development Method' (VDM) is a model-oriented specification and design method based on set theory and Precondition-Postcondition specifications. The set theory is used to define and organise the entities the software deals with. The condition specifications are used to define and organise the activities the entities take part in by stating truths about their behaviour.

VDM uses a top-down method to develop a system model from a high-level definition, using abstract data types and descriptions of external operations, to a low-level definition in implementation-oriented terms. This 'contractual' process, whereby a given level is the implementation of the level above and the requirements for the level below, is called 'reification'. The ability to reason from specification through to implementation is a major feature of VDM.

VDM can be used in the SR phase to permit mathematical modelling the functional behaviour of software. VDM specifications can be easily adapted to the requirements of an SRD.

- VDM specifications contain a:
- description of the state of the system (a mathematical definition of the system components);
- list of data types and invariants;
- list of Precondition-Postcondition specifications.

VDM is generally considered to be deficient in some areas, specifically:

- it is not possible to define explicitly operations (i.e the precondition-postcondition technique does not describe how state variables are changed);
- it is not possible to specify concurrency (making it unsuitable for real-time applications);
- the underlying structure is not modular;
- the specification language lacks abstract and generic features.

3.5.3 LOTOS

LOTOS (Language Of Temporal Ordering Specification) is a formal description technique defined by the International Standardisation Organisation (ISO). It is the only analysis method that is an ISO standard. It was originally developed for use on the Open Systems Interconnection (OSI) standards, but is especially suitable for the specification of distributed processing systems.

LOTOS has two integrated components:

- a 'process algebra' component, which is based on a combination of Calculus of Communicating Systems (CCS, ref 16) and Communicating Sequential Processes (CSP, ref 14);
- a 'data type' component that is based on the algebraic specification language ACT ONE.

LOTOS is both 'executable' (i.e., the specified behaviour may be simulated), and amenable to proof techniques (due to its algebraic properties).

LOTOS encourages developers to work in a structured manner (either top-down or bottom-up), and may be used in several different fashions. Various 'LOTOS specification styles' have been identified and documented, ranging from 'constraint-oriented' where constraints on, or properties of, the system are specified in isolation from any internal processing mechanisms, to 'monolithic' where the system's behaviour is captured as a tree of alternatives.

Each style has its own strengths; the 'constraint-oriented' style provides a high-level specification of the system and is a powerful way to impose separation of concerns. The 'monolithic' style may be viewed as a much lower level system description that can be transformed into an implementation with relative ease. Two or more styles are often applied in concert, and a LOTOS specification may be refined in much the same way as an English language system requirements specification would be refined into an architectural design and then a detailed design. An obvious benefit of using LOTOS in this way is that each refinement may be verified (i.e. preservation of system properties from a high-level specification to a lower-level specification may be proven).

3.6   JACKSON SYSTEM DEVELOPMENT

Jackson System Development (JSD) analysis techniques are [Ref.13]:
- Structure Diagrams;
- Structure Text;
- System Specification Diagrams.

Unlike structured analysis, which is generally known by its techniques, JSD is best characterised by:

- emphasis on the need to develop software that models the behaviour of the things in the real world it is concerned with;
- emphasis on the need to build in adaptability by devising a model that defines the possible system functions;
- avoidance of the top-down approach in favour of a subject-matter based approach.

The term 'model' has a specific meaning in JSD. A model is 'a realisation, in the computer, of an abstract description of the real world' [Ref. 13]. Since the real world has a time dimension it follows that the model will be composed of one or more 'sequential' processes. Each process is identified by the entities that it is concerned with. The steps in each process describe the (sequential) events in the life cycle of the entity.

A JSD model is described in a 'System Specification' and is, in principle, directly executable. However this will only be the case if each process can be directly mapped to a processor. For example there may be a one-to-one relationship between a telescope and the computer that controls it, but there is a many-to-one relationship between a bank customer and the computer that processes customer transactions (many customers, one computer). JSD implementations employ a 'scheduling' process to coordinate many concurrent processes running on a single processor.

Structured analysis concentrates on devising a 'data model' (hence Data Flow Diagrams and Data Dictionaries). While this may be quite proper for information systems it is sometimes not very helpful when building real-time systems. The JSD method attempts to correct this deficiency by concentrating on devising a 'process model' that is more suited to real-time applications. Application of JSD to information systems is likely to be more difficult than with structured methods, but should be considered where adaptability is a very high priority constraint requirement.

Table 3.6 shows what JSD development activities should take place in the SR phase.

JSD Activity			
Level 0	Level 1	Level 2	Level 3
Specification	Specify Model of Reality	Develop	Write Entity-Action List
		Model Abstractly	Draw Entity-Structure Diagrams
		Define initial versions of model processes	
	Specify System Functions	Add functions to model processes	
		Add timing constr.	

Table 3.6: SR phase JSD development activities

3.7 RAPID PROTOTYPING

A prototype is a 'executable model of selected aspects of a proposed system' [Ref. 5]. If the requirements are not clear, or suspected to be incomplete, it can be useful to develop a prototype based on tentative requirements to explore what the software requirements really are. This is called 'exploratory prototyping'. Prototypes can help define user interface requirements.

Rapid Prototyping is 'the process of quickly building and evaluating a series of prototypes' [Ref. 6]. Specification and development are iterative.

Rapid Prototyping can be incorporated within the *Software Engineering Standards* life cycle if the iteration loop is contained within a phase.

The development of an information system using 4GLs would contain the loop:
repeat until the user signs off the SRD
    analyse requirements

create data base
create user interface
add selected functions
review execution of prototype with user

Requirements should be analysed using a recognised method, such as structured analysis, and properly documented in an SRD. Rapid Prototyping needs tool support, otherwise the prototyping may not be rapid enough to be worthwhile.

The prototype's operation should be reviewed with the user and the results used to formulate the requirements in the SRD. The review of the execution of a prototype with a user is not a substitute for the SR review.

Rapid Prototyping can also be used with an Evolutionary Development life cycle approach. A Rapid Prototyping project could consist of several short-period life cycles. Rapid Prototyping tools would be used extensively in the early life cycles, permitting the speedy development of the first prototypes. In later life cycles the product is optimised, which may require new system-specific code to be written.

Software written to support the prototyping activity should not be reused in later phases - the prototypes are 'throwaways'. To allow prototypes to be built quickly, design standards and software requirements can be relaxed. Since quality should be built into deliverable software from its inception, it is bad practice to reuse prototype modules in later phases. Such modules are likely to have interfaces inconsistent with the rest of the design. It is permissible, of course, to use ideas present in prototype code in the DD phase.

CHAPTER 4
TOOLS FOR SOFTWARE REQUIREMENTS DEFINITION

4.1 INTRODUCTION

This chapter discusses the tools for constructing a logical model and specifying the software requirements. Tools can be combined to suit the needs of a particular project.

4.2 TOOLS FOR LOGICAL MODEL CONSTRUCTION

In all but the smallest projects, CASE tools should be used during the SR phase. Like many general purpose tools, such as word processors and drawing packages, a CASE tool should provide:

- a windows, icons, menu and pointer (WIMP) style interface for the easy creation and editing of diagrams;
- a what you see is what you get (WYSIWYG) style interface that ensures that what is created on the display screen is an exact image of what will appear in the document.

Method-specific CASE tools offer the following advantages over general purpose tools:

- enforcement of the rules of the methods;
- consistency checking;
- ease of modification;
- automatic traceability of user requirements through to the software requirements;
- built-in configuration management.

Tools should be selected that have an integrated data dictionary or 'repository' for consistency checking. Developers should check that a tool supports the method that they intend to use. Appendix E contains a more detailed list of desirable tool capabilities.

Configuration management of the model description is essential. The model should evolve from baseline to baseline during the SR phase, and the specification and enforcement of procedures for the identification, change control and status accounting of the model description are necessary. In large projects, configuration management tools should be used.

4.3 TOOLS FOR SOFTWARE REQUIREMENTS SPECIFICATION

4.3.1 Software requirements management

For large systems, a database management system (DBMS) for storing the software requirements becomes invaluable for maintaining consistency and accessibility.

Desirable capabilities of a requirements DBMS are:
- insertion of new requirements;
- modification of existing requirements;
- deletion of requirements;
- storage of attributes (e.g. identifier) with the text;
- selecting by requirement attributes and text strings;
- sorting by requirement attributes and text strings;
- cross-referencing;
- change history recording;
- access control;
- display;
- printing, in a variety formats.

4.3.2 Document production

A word processor or text processor should be used for producing a document. Tools for the creation of paragraphs, sections, headers, footers, tables of contents and indexes all facilitate the production of a document. A spell checker is desirable. An outliner may be found useful for creation of subheadings, for viewing the document at different levels of detail and for rearranging the document. The ability to handle diagrams is very important.

Documents invariably go through many drafts as they are created, reviewed and modified. Revised drafts should include change bars. Document comparison programs, which can mark changed text automatically, are invaluable for easing the review process.

Tools for communal preparation of documents are now beginning to be available, allowing many authors to comment and add to a single document in a controlled manner.

CHAPTER 5
THE SOFTWARE REQUIREMENTS DOCUMENT

5.1 INTRODUCTION

The purpose of an SRD is to be an authoritative statement of 'what' the software is to do. An SRD must be complete (SR11) and cover all the requirements stated in the URD (SR12).

The SRD should be detailed enough to allow the implementation of the software without user involvement. The size and content of the SRD should, however, reflect the size and complexity of the software product. It does not, however, need to cover any implementation aspects, and, provided that it is complete, the smaller the SRD, the more readable and reviewable it is.

The SRD is a mandatory output (SR10) of the SR phase and has a definite role to play in the *Software Engineering Standards* documentation scheme. SRD authors should not go beyond the bounds of that role. This means that:

- the SRD must not include implementation details or terminology, unless it has to be present as a constraint (SR15);
- descriptions of functions must say what the software is to do,
- and must avoid saying how it is to be done (SR16);
- the SRD must avoid specifying the hardware or equipment, unless it is a constraint placed by the user (SR17).

5.2 STYLE

The SRD should be systematic, rigourous, clear, consistent and modifiable. Wherever possible, software requirements should be stated in quantitative terms to increase their verifiability.

5.2.1 Clarity

An SRD is 'clear' if each requirement is unambiguous and its meaning is clear to all readers.

If a requirements specification language is used, explanatory text, written in natural language, should be included in the SRD to make it understandable to those not familiar with the specification language.

5.2.2 Consistency

The SRD must be consistent (SR14). There are several types of inconsistency:

- different terms used for the same thing;

- the same term used for different things;
- incompatible activities happening at the same time;
- activities happening in the wrong order.

Where a term could have multiple meanings, a single meaning for the term should be defined in a glossary, and only that meaning should be used throughout.

An SRD is consistent if no set of individual requirements conflict. Methods and tools help consistency to be achieved.

5.2.3 Modifiability

Modifiability enables changes to be made easily, completely, and consistently.

When requirements duplicate or overlap one another, cross-references should be included to preserve modifiability.

5.3 EVOLUTION

The SRD should be put under formal change control by the developer as soon as it is approved. New requirements may need to be added and old requirements may have to be modified or deleted. If the SRD is being developed by a team of people, the control of the document may need to be started at the beginning of the SR phase.

The Software Configuration Management Plan for the SR phase should have defined a formal change process to identify, control, track and report projected changes as soon as they are initially identified. Approved changes in requirements must be recorded in the SRD by inserting document change records and a document status sheet at the start of the SRD.

5.4 RESPONSIBILITY

Whoever actually writes the SRD, the responsibility for it lies with the developer. The developer should nominate people with proven analytical skills to write the SRD. Members of the design and implementation team may take part in the SR/R as they can advise on the technical feasibility of requirements.

5.5 MEDIUM

It is usually assumed that the SRD is a paper document. It may be distributed electronically to participants who have access to the necessary equipment.

5.6 CONTENT

The SRD must be compiled according to the table of contents provided in Appendix C of *Software Engineering Standards* (SR18). This table of contents is derived from ANSI/IEEE Std 830-1993 'Recommended Practice for Software Requirements Specifications'[Ref. 3]. The description of the model is the only significant addition.

Section 1 should briefly describe the purpose of both the SRD and the product. Section 2 should provide a general description of the project and the product. Section 3 should contain the definitive material about what is required. Appendix A should contain a glossary of terms. Large SRDs (forty pages or more) should also contain an index.

References should be given where appropriate. An SRD should not refer to documents that follow it in the *Software Engineering Standards* life cycle. An SRD should contain no TBCs or TBDs by the time of the Software Requirements Review.

Service Information:
- a - Abstract
- b - Table of Contents
- c - Document Status Sheet
- d - Document Change Records made since last issue

1 INTRODUCTION[1]
- 1.1 Purpose
- 1.2 Scope
- 1.3 Definitions, acronyms and abbreviations
- 1.4 References
- 1.5 Overview

2 GENERAL DESCRIPTION
- 2.1 Relation to current projects
- 2.2 Relation to predecessor and successor projects
- 2.3 Function and purpose
- 2.4 Environmental considerations
- 2.5 Relation to other systems
- 2.6 General constraints
- 2.7 Model description

3 SPECIFIC REQUIREMENTS
(The subsections may be regrouped around high-level functions)
- 3.1 Functional requirements
- 3.2 Performance requirements
- 3.3 Interface requirements
- 3.4 Operational requirements
- 3.5 Resource requirements
- 3.6 Verification requirements
- 3.7 Acceptance testing requirements
- 3.8 Documentation requirements
- 3.9 Security requirements
- 3.10 Portability requirements
- 3.11 Quality requirements
- 3.12 Reliability requirements
- 3.13 Maintainability requirements
- 3.14 Safety requirements

---

[1]   The Software Requirements Document contents lists is based upon extracts from IEEE Std 830-1993, IEEE Recommended Practice for Software Requirements Specifications, copyright © 1993 by the Institute for Electrical and Electronic Engineers Inc. The IEEE disclaims any responsibility or liability resulting from the placement and use in this publication. Information is reprinted with the permission of the IEEE.

    3.14 Safety requirements

4 REQUIREMENTS TRACEABILITY MATRIX

Relevant material unsuitable for inclusion in the above contents list should be inserted in additional appendices. If there is no material for a section then the phrase 'Not Applicable' should be inserted and the section numbering preserved.

5.6.1 SRD/1 Introduction

5.6.1.1 SRD/1.1 Purpose (of the document)

This section should:
    (1) define the purpose of the particular SRD;
    (2) specify the intended readership of the SRD.

5.6.1.2 SRD/1.2 Scope (of the software)

This section should:
    (1) identify the software product(s) to be produced by name;
    (2) explain what the proposed software will do (and will not do, if necessary);
    (3) describe the relevant benefits, objectives and goals as precisely as possible;
    (4) be consistent with similar statements in higher-level specifications, if they exist.

5.6.1.3 SRD/1.3 Definitions, acronyms and abbreviations

This section should provide definitions of all terms, acronyms, and abbreviations needed for the SRD, or refer to other documents where the definitions can be found.

5.6.1.4 SRD/1.4 References

This section should provide a complete list of all the applicable and reference documents. Each document should be identified by its title, author and date. Each document should be marked as applicable or reference. If appropriate, report number, journal name and publishing organisation should be included.

5.6.1.5 SRD/1.5 Overview (of the document)

This section should:
    (1) describe what the rest of the SRD contains;
    (2) explain how the SRD is organised.

5.6.2 SRD/2 General Description

This chapter should describe the general factors that affect the product and its requirements. It does not state specific requirements; it only makes those requirements easier to understand.

5.6.2.1 SRD/2.1 Relationship to current projects

This section should describe the context of the project in relation to current projects. This section should identify any other relevant projects the developer is carrying out for the initiator. The project may be independent of other projects or part of a larger project.

Any parent projects should be identified. A detailed description of the interface of the product to the larger system should, however, be deferred until Section 2.5.

5.6.2.2 SRD/2.2 Relationship to predecessor and successor projects

This section should describe the context of the project in relation to past and future projects. This section should identify projects that the developer has carried out for the initiator in the past and also any projects the developer may be expected to carry out in the future, if known.

If the product is to replace an existing product, the reasons for replacing that system should be summarised in this section.

5.6.2.3 SRD/2.3 Function and purpose

This section should discuss the purpose of the product. It should expand upon the points made in Section 1.2.

5.6.2.4 SRD/2.4 Environmental considerations

This section should summarise:
- the physical environment of the target system, i.e. where is the system going to be used and by whom? The URD section called 'User Characteristics' may provide useful material on this topic.
- the hardware environment in the target system, i.e. what computer(s) does the software have to run on?
- the operating environment in the target system, i.e. what operating systems are used?
- the hardware environment in the development system, i.e. what computer(s) does the software have to be developed on?
- the operating environment in the development system, i.e. what software development environment is to be used? or what software tools are to be used?

5.6.2.5 SRD/2.5 Relation to other systems

This section should describe in detail the product's relationship to other systems, for example is the product:
- an independent system?
- a subsystem of a larger system?
- replacing another system?

If the product is a subsystem then this section should:
- summarise the essential characteristics of the larger system;
- identify the other subsystems this subsystem will interface with;
- summarise the computer hardware and peripheral equipment to be used.

A block diagram may be presented showing the major components of the larger system or project, interconnections, and external interfaces.

The URD contains a section 'Product Perspective' that may provide relevant material for this section.

5.6.2.6 SRD/2.6 General constraints

This section should describe any items that will limit the developer's options for building the software. It should provide background information and seek to justify the constraints. The URD contains a section called 'General Constraints' that may provide relevant material for this section.

5.6.2.7 SRD/2.7 Model description

This section should include a top-down description of the logical model. Diagrams, tables and explanatory text may be included.

The functionality at each level should be described, to enable the reader to 'walkthrough' the model level-by-level, function-by-function, flow-by-flow. A bare-bones description of a system in terms of data flow diagrams and low-level functional specifications needs supplementary commentary. Natural language is recommended.

5.6.3 SRD/3 Specific Requirements

The software requirements are detailed in this section. Each requirement must include an identifier (SR04). Essential requirements must be marked as such (SR05). For incremental delivery, each software requirement must include a measure of priority so that the developer can decide the production schedule (SR06). References that trace the software requirements back to the URD must accompany each software requirement (SR07). Any other sources should be stated. Each software requirement must be verifiable (SR08).

The functional requirements should be structured top-down in this section. Non-functional requirements can appear at all levels of the hierarchy of functions, and, by the inheritance principle, apply to all the functional requirements below them. Non-functional requirements may be attached to functional requirements by cross-references or by physically grouping them together in the document.

If a non-functional requirement appears at a lower level, it supersedes any requirement of that type that appears at a higher level. Critical functions, for example, may have more stringent reliability and safety requirements than those of non-critical functions.

Specific requirements may be written in natural language. This makes them understandable to non-specialists, but permits inconsistencies, ambiguity and imprecision to arise. These undesirable properties can be avoided by using requirements specification languages. Such languages range in rigour from Structured English to Z, VDM and LOTOS.

Each software requirement must have a unique identifier (SR04). Forward traceability to subsequent phases in the life cycle depends upon each requirement having a unique identifier.

Essential software requirements have to be met for the software to be acceptable. If a software requirement is essential, it must be clearly flagged (SR05). Non-essential software requirements should be marked with a measure of desirability (e.g. scale of 1, 2, 3).

The priority of a requirement measures the order, or the timing, of the related functionality becoming available. If the transfer is to be phased, so that some parts come into operation before others, each requirement must be marked with a measure of priority (SR06).

Unstable requirements should be flagged. These requirements may be dependent on feedback from the UR, SR and AD phases. The usual method for flagging unstable requirements is to attach the marker 'TBC'.

The source of each software requirement must be stated (SR07), using the identifier of a user requirement, a document cross-reference, or even the name of a person or group. Backwards traceability depends upon each requirement explicitly referencing its source in the URD or elsewhere.

Each software requirement must be verifiable (SR08). Clarity increases verifiability. Clarity is enhanced by ensuring that each software requirement is well separated from the others. A software requirement is verifiable if some method can be devised for objectively demonstrating that the software implements it correctly.

5.6.4 SRD/Appendix A Requirements Traceability matrix

This section should contain a table summarising how each user requirement is met in the SRD (SR13). See Appendix D.

CHAPTER 6
LIFE CYCLE MANAGEMENT ACTIVITIES

6.1 INTRODUCTION

SR phase activities must be carried out according to the plans defined in the UR phase (SR01). These are:
- Software Project Management Plan for the SR phase (SPMP/SR);
- Software Configuration Management Plan for the SR phase (SCMP/SR);
- Software Verification and Validation Plan for the SR phase (SVVP/SR);
- Software Quality Assurance Plan for the SR phase (SQAP/SR).

Progress against plans should be continuously monitored by project management and documented at regular intervals in progress reports.

Plans for AD phase activities must be drawn up in the SR phase. These plans cover project management, configuration management, verification and validation, quality assurance and system tests.

6.2 PROJECT MANAGEMENT PLAN FOR THE AD PHASE

During the SR phase, the AD phase section of the SPMP (SPMP/AD) must be produced (SPM05). The SPMP/AD describes, in detail, the project activities to be carried out in the AD phase.

An estimate of the total project cost must be included in the SPMP/AD (SPM06). Every effort should be made to arrive at a total project cost estimate with an accuracy better than 30%. In addition, a precise estimate of the effort involved in the AD phase must be included in the SPMP/AD (SPM07).

Technical knowledge and experience gained on similar projects should be used to produce the cost estimate. Specific factors affecting estimates for the work required in the AD phase are the:
- number of software requirements;
- level of software requirements;
- complexity of the software requirements;
- stability of software requirements;
- level of definition of external interfaces;
- quality of the SRD.

The function-point analysis method may be of use in the SR phase for costing data-processing systems [Ref. 23].

If an evolutionary software development or incremental delivery life cycle is to be used, the SPMP/AD should say so.

Guidance on writing the SPMP/AD is provided in the *Guide to Software Project Management Planning*.

6.3 CONFIGURATION MANAGEMENT PLAN FOR THE AD PHASE

During the SR phase, the AD phase section of the SCMP (SCMP/AD) must be produced (SCM44). The SCMP/AD must cover the configuration management procedures for documentation, and any CASE tool outputs or prototype code, to be produced in the AD phase (SCM45).

Guidance on writing the SCMP/AD is provided in the *Guide to Software Configuration Management Planning*.

6.4 VERIFICATION AND VALIDATION PLAN FOR THE AD PHASE

During the AD phase, the AD phase section of the SVVP (SVVP/AD) must be produced (SVV12). The SVVP/AD must define how to trace software requirements to components, so that each software component can be justified (SVV13). It should describe how the ADD is to be evaluated by defining the review procedures. It may include specifications of the tests to be performed with prototypes.

During the SR phase, the developer analyses the user requirements and may insert 'acceptance-testing requirements' in the SRD. These requirements constrain the design of the acceptance tests. This must be recognised in the design of the acceptance tests.

The planning of the system tests should proceed in parallel with the definition of the software requirements. The developer may identify 'verification requirements' for the software. These are additional constraints on the verification activities. These requirements are also stated in the SRD.

Guidance on writing the SVVP/AD is provided in the *Guide to Software Verification and Validation*.

6.5   QUALITY ASSURANCE PLAN FOR THE AD PHASE

During the SR phase, the AD phase section of the SQAP (SQAP/AD) must be produced (SQA06). The SQAP/AD must describe, in detail, the quality assurance activities to be carried out in the AD phase (SQA07).

SQA activities include monitoring the following activities:
- management;
- documentation;
- standards, practices, conventions, and metrics;
- reviews and audits;
- testing activities;
- problem reporting and corrective action;
- tools, techniques and methods;
- code and media control;
- supplier control;
- records collection maintenance and retention;
- training;
- risk management.

Guidance on writing the SQAP/AD is provided in the *Guide to Software Quality Assurance*.

The SQAP/AD should take account of all the software requirements related to quality, in particular:

- quality requirements;
- reliability requirements;
- maintainability requirements;
- safety requirements;
- standards requirements;
- verification requirements;
- acceptance-testing requirements.

The level of monitoring planned for the AD phase should be appropriate to the requirements and the criticality of the software. Risk analysis should be used to target areas for detailed scrutiny.

6.6 SYSTEM TEST PLANS

The developer must plan the system tests in the SR phase and document it in the SVVP (SVV14). This plan should define the scope, approach, resources and schedule of system testing activities.

Specific tests for each software requirement are not formulated until the DD phase. The System Test Plan should deal with the general issues, for example:

- where will the system tests be done?
- who will attend?
- who will carry them out?
- are tests needed for all software requirements?
- must any special test equipment be used?
- how long is the system testing programme expected to last?
- are simulations necessary?

Guidance on writing the SVVP/ST is provided in the *Guide to Software Verification and Validation*.

APPENDIX A
GLOSSARY

A.1 LIST OF ACRONYMS

AD	Architectural Design
ANSI	American National Standards Institute
BSSC	Board for Software Standardisation and Control
CASE	Computer Aided Software Engineering
CCS	Calculus of Communicating Systems
CSP	Communicating Sequential Processes
DBMS	Database Management System
ESA	European Space Agency
IEEE	Institute of Electrical and Electronics Engineers
ISO	International Standards Organisation
ICD	Interface Control Document
LOTOS	Language Of Temporal Ordering Specification
OOA	Object-Oriented Analysis
OSI	Open Systems Interconnection
PA	Product Assurance
PSS	Procedures, Specifications and Standards
QA	Quality Assurance
RID	Review Item Discrepancy
SADT	Structured Analysis and Design Technique
SCM	Software Configuration Management
SCMP	Software Configuration Management Plan
SPM	Software Project Management
SPMP	Software Project Management Plan
SQA	Software Quality Assurance
SQAP	Software Quality Assurance Plan
SR	Software Requirements
SRD	Software Requirements Document
SR/R	Software Requirements Review
SSADM	Structured Systems Analysis and Design Methodology
ST	System Test
SUM	Software User Manual
SVVP	Software Verification and Validation Plan
TBC	To Be Confirmed

TBD	To Be Defined
UR	User Requirements
URD	User Requirements Document
VDM	Vienna Development Method

APPENDIX B
REFERENCES

1. Software Engineering Standards, C.Mazza, J.Fairclough, B.Melton, D.dePablo, A.Scheffer, R.Stevens, Prentice-Hall 1994.
2. IEEE Standard Glossary for Software Engineering Terminology, ANSI/IEEE Std 610.12-1990.
3. IEEE Guide to Software Requirements Specifications, ANSI/IEEE Std 830-1984.
4. SSADM Version 4, NCC Blackwell Publications, 1991
5. Software Evolution Through Rapid Prototyping, Luqi, in COMPUTER, May 1989
6. Structured Rapid Prototyping, J.Connell and L.Shafer, Yourdon Press, 1989.
7. Structured Analysis and System Specification, T.DeMarco, Yourdon Press, 1978.
8. IEEE Standard for Software Reviews and Audits, IEEE Std 1028-1988.
9. Structured Systems Analysis and Design Methodology, G.Cutts, Paradigm, 1987.
10. The Z Notation - a reference manual, J.M.Spivey, Prentice-Hall, 1989.
11. Systematic Software Development Using VDM, C.B.Jones, Prentice-Hall, 1986.
12. Structured Development for Real-Time Systems, P.T.Ward & S.J.Mellor, Yourdon Press, 1985. (Three Volumes).
13. System Development, M.Jackson, Prentice-Hall, 1983.
14. Communicating Sequential Processes, C.A.R.Hoare, Prentice Hall International, 1985.
15. Programming with parameterised abstract objects in OBJ, Goguen J A, Meseguer J and Plaisted D, in Theory and Practice of Software Technology, North Holland, 1982.
16. A Calculus for Communicating Systems, R.Milner, in Lecture Notes in Computer Science, No 192, Springer-Verlag.
17. Structured Analysis for Requirements Definition, D.T.Ross and K.E.Schoman, IEEE Transactions on Software Engineering, Vol SE-3, No 1, January 1977.
18. Object-Oriented Analysis, P.Coad and E.Yourdon, Second Edition, Yourdon Press, 1991.
19. Petri Nets, J.L.Petersen, in ACM Computing Surveys, 9(3) Sept 1977.
20. Structured Analysis (SA): A Language for Communicating Ideas, D.T.Ross, IEEE Transactions on Software Engineering, Vol SE-3, No 1, January 1977.
21. Principles of Software Engineering Management, T.Gilb, Addison-Wesley.
22. The STARTs Guide - a guide to methods and software tools for the construction of large real-time systems, NCC Publications, 1987.
23. Software function, source lines of code, and development effort prediction: a software science validation, A.J.Albrecht and J.E.Gaffney, IEEE Transactions on Software Engineering, vol SE-9, No 6, November 1983.

24. Software Reliability Assurance for ESA space systems, ESA PSS-01-230 Issue 1 Draft 8, October 1991.

25. Object-Oriented Modeling and Design, J.Rumbaugh, M.Blaha, W.Premerlani, F.Eddy and W.Lorensen, Prentice-Hall, 1991

26. Object-Oriented Systems Analysis - Modeling the World in Data, S.Shlaer and S.J.Mellor, Yourdon Press, 1988

27. Object Lifecycles - Modeling the World in States, S.Shlaer and S.J.Mellor, Yourdon Press, 1992.

28. Object-Oriented Design with Applications, G.Booch, Benjamin Cummings, 1991.

29. Object-Oriented Design, P.Coad and E.Yourdon, Prentice-Hall, 1991.

APPENDIX C
MANDATORY PRACTICES

This appendix is repeated from *Software Engineering Standards*, Appendix D.3

SR01   SR phase activities shall be carried out according to the plans defined in the UR phase.

SR02   The developer shall construct an implementation-independent model of what is needed by the user.

SR03   A recognised method for software requirements analysis shall be adopted and applied consistently in the SR phase.

SR04   Each software requirement shall include an identifier.

SR05   Essential software requirements shall be marked as such.

SR06   For incremental delivery, each software requirement shall include a measure of priority so that the developer can decide the production schedule.

SR07   References that trace software requirements back to the URD shall accompany each software requirement.

SR08   Each software requirement shall be verifiable.

SR09   The outputs of the SR phase shall be formally reviewed during the Software Requirements Review.

SR10   An output of the SR phase shall be the Software Requirements Document (SRD).

SR11   The SRD shall be complete.

SR12   The SRD shall cover all the requirements stated in the URD.

SR13   A table showing how user requirements correspond to software requirements shall be placed in the SRD.

SR14   The SRD shall be consistent.

SR15   The SRD shall not include implementation details or terminology, unless it has to be present as a constraint.

SR16   Descriptions of functions ... shall say what the software is to do, and must avoid saying how it is to be done.

SR17   The SRD shall avoid specifying the hardware or equipment, unless it is a constraint placed by the user.

SR18   The SRD shall be compiled according to the table of contents provided in Appendix C.

APPENDIX D
REQUIREMENTS TRACEABILITY MATRIX

REQUIREMENTS TRACEABILITY MATRIX SRD TRACED TO URD		DATE: <YY-MM-DD> PAGE 1 OF <nn>
PROJECT: <TITLE OF PROJECT>		
URD IDENTIFIER	SRD IDENTIFIER	SUMMARY OF USER REQUIREMENT

APPENDIX E
CASE TOOL SELECTION CRITERIA

This appendix lists selection criteria for the evaluation of CASE tools for building a logical model.

The tool should:

1. enforce the rules of each method it supports;
2. allow the user to construct diagrams according to the conventions of the selected method;
3. support consistency checking (e.g. balancing a DFD set);
4. store the model description;
5. be able to store multiple model descriptions;
6. support top-down decomposition (e.g. by allowing the user to create and edit lower-level DFDs by 'exploding' processes in a higher-level diagram);
7. minimise line-crossing in a diagram;
8. minimise the number of keystrokes required to add a symbol;
9. allow the user to 'tune' a method by adding and deleting rules;
10. support concurrent access by multiple users;
11. permit controlled access to the model database (usually called a repository);
12. permit reuse of all or part of existing model descriptions, to allow the bottom-up integration of models (e.g. rather than decompose a high-level function such as 'Calculate Orbit', it should be possible to import a specification of this function from another model);
13. support document generation according to user-defined templates and formats;
14. support traceability of user requirements to software requirements (and software requirements through to components and code);
15. support conversion of a diagram from one style to another (e.g. Yourdon to SADT and vice-versa);
16. allow the user to execute the model (to verify real-time behaviour by animation and simulation);
17. support all configuration management functions (e.g. to identify items, control changes to them, storage of baselines etc);
18. keep the users informed of changes when part of a design is concurrently accessed;
19. support consistency checking in any of 3 checking modes, selectable by the user:
    - interpretative, i.e. check each change as it is made; reject any illegal changes;
    - compiler, i.e. accept all changes and check them all at once at the end of the session;
    - monitor, i.e. check each change as it is made; issue warnings about illegal changes;

20. link the checking mode with the access mode when there are multiple users, so that local changes can be done in any checking mode, but changes that have non-local effects are checked immediately and rejected if they are in error;
21. support scoping and overloading of data item names;
22. provide context-dependent help facilities;
23. make effective use of colour to allow parts of a display to be easily distinguished;
24. have a consistent user interface;
25. permit direct hardcopy output;
26. permit data to be imported from other CASE tools;
27. permit the exporting of data in standard graphics file formats (e.g. CGM);
28. provide standard word processing functions;
29. permit the exporting of data to external word-processing applications and editors;
30. describe the format of tool database (i.e. repository) in the user documentation, so that users can manipulate the database using external software and packages (e.g. tables of ASCII data).

APPENDIX F
INDEX

Guide to the software architectural design phase

TABLE OF CONTENTS

CHAPTER 1
INTRODUCTION

1.1 PURPOSE

Software Engineering Standards [Ref. 1] defines the third phase of the software life cycle to be the 'Architectural Design Phase' (AD phase). Activities and products are examined in the 'AD review' (AD/R) at the end of the phase.

The AD phase can be called the 'solution phase' of the life cycle because it defines the software in terms of the major software components and interfaces. The 'Architectural Design' must cover all the requirements in the SRD.

This document provides guidance on how to produce the architectural design. This document should be read by all active participants in the AD phase, e.g. initiators, user representatives, analysts, designers, project managers and product assurance personnel.

1.2 OVERVIEW

Chapter 2 discusses the AD phase. Chapters 3 and 4 discuss methods and tools for architectural design definition. Chapter 5 describes how to write the ADD, starting from the template. Chapter 6 summarises the life cycle management activities, which are discussed at greater length in other guides.

All the mandatory practices in *Software Engineering Standards* relevant to the AD phase are repeated in this document. The identifier of the practice is added in parentheses to mark a repetition. No new mandatory practices are defined.

CHAPTER 2
THE ARCHITECTURAL DESIGN PHASE

2.1 INTRODUCTION

In the AD phase, the software requirements are transformed into definitions of software components and their interfaces, to establish the framework of the software. This is done by examining the SRD and building a 'physical model' using recognised software engineering methods. The physical model should describe the solution in concrete, implementation terms. Just as the logical model produced in the SR phase structures the problem and makes it manageable, the physical model does the same for the solution.

The physical model is used to produce a structured set of component specifications that are consistent, coherent and complete. Each specification defines the functions, inputs and outputs of the component (see Section 2.4).

The major software components are documented in the Architectural Design Document (ADD). The ADD gives the developer's solution to the problem stated in the SRD. The ADD must cover all the requirements stated in the SRD (AD20), but avoid the detailed consideration of software requirements that do not affect the structure.

The main outputs of the AD phase are the:
- Architectural Design Document (ADD);
- Software Project Management Plan for the DD phase (SPMP/DD);
- Software Configuration Management Plan for the DD phase(SCMP/DD);
- Software Verification and Validation Plan for the DD Phase (SVVP/DD);
- Software Quality Assurance Plan for the DD phase (SQAP/DD);
- Integration Test Plan (SVVP/IT).

Progress reports, configuration status accounts and audit reports are also outputs of the phase.

While the architectural design is a responsibility of the developer, participants in the AD phase also should include user representatives, systems engineers, hardware engineers and operations personnel. In reviewing the architectural design, project management should ensure that all parties are consulted, to minimise the risk of incompleteness and error.

AD phase activities must be carried out according to the plans defined in the SR phase (AD01). Progress against plans should be continuously monitored by project management and documented at regular intervals in progress reports.

Figure 2.1 summarises activities and document flow in the AD phase. The following subsections describe the activities of the AD phase in more detail.

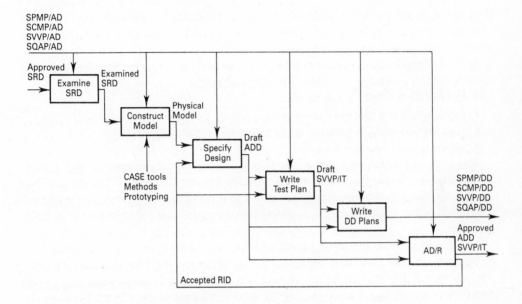

Figure 2.1: AD phase activities

2.2 EXAMINATION OF THE SRD

Normally the developers will have taken part in the SR/R, but if not, they should examine the SRD and confirm that it is understandable. *Guide to the Software Requirements Definition Phase*, contains material that should assist this. In particular, if a specific method has been used for the specification of the requirements, the development organisation should ensure that the examination is carried out by staff familiar with that method.

The developers should also confirm that adequate technical skill is available to produce the outputs of the AD phase.

2.3 CONSTRUCTION OF THE PHYSICAL MODEL

A software model is:
- a simplified description of a system;
- hierarchical, with consistent decomposition criteria;
- composed of symbols organised according to some convention;
- built with the aid of recognised methods and tools;
- used for reasoning about the software.

A 'simplified description' is obtained by abstracting the essentials and ignoring non-essentials. A hierarchical presentation makes the model simpler to understand.

A recognised method for software design must be adopted and used consistently in the AD phase (AD02). The criteria for 'recognition' are the availability of documentation and tools. The availability of training courses is also important.

A method does not substitute for the experience and insight of the developer but helps to apply those abilities more effectively.

In the AD phase, the developer constructs a 'physical model' describing the design in implementation terminology (AD03). The physical model:

- defines the software components;
- is presented as a hierarchy of control;
- uses implementation terminology (e.g. computer, file , record);
- shows control and data flow.

The physical model provides a framework for software development that allows independent work on the low-level components in the DD phase. The framework defines interfaces that programmers need to know to build their part of the software. Programmers can work in parallel, knowing that their part of the system will fit in with the others.

The logical model is the starting point for the construction of the physical model. The design method may provide a technique for transforming the logical model into the physical model. Design constraints, such as the need to reuse components, may cause departure from the structure of the logical model. The effect on adaptability of each modification of the structure should be assessed. A minor new requirement should not cause a major design change. The designer's goal is to produce an efficient design that has the structure of the logical model and meets all the software requirements.

The method used to decompose the software into its component parts shall permit the top-down approach (AD04). Top-down design starts by defining the top level software components and then proceeds to the definition of the lower-level components. The top-down approach is vital for controlling complexity because it enforces 'information hiding' by demanding that lower-level components behave as 'black boxes'. Even if a design method allows other approaches (e.g. bottom-up), the presentation of the design in the ADD must always be top-down.

The construction of the physical model should be an iterative process where some or all of the tasks are repeated until a clear, consistent definition has been formulated. Walkthroughs, inspections and technical reviews should be used to agree each level of the physical model before descending to the next level of detail.

In all but the smallest projects, CASE tools should be used for building a physical model. They make consistent models that are easier to construct and modify.

The type of physical model that is built depends upon the method selected. Chapter 3 summarises the methods for constructing a physical model. In the following subsections, concepts and terminology of structured methods are used to show how to define the architecture. This does not imply that these methods shall be used, but only that they may be suitable.

2.3.1 Decomposition of the software into components

The design process starts by decomposing the software into components. The decomposition should be done top-down, based on the functional decomposition in the logical model.

The correspondence between functional requirements in the SRD and components in the ADD is not necessarily one-to-one and frequently isn't. This is because of the need to work within the constraints forced by the non-functional requirements (see Section 2.3.2) and the capabilities of the software and hardware technology. Designs that meet these constraints are said to be 'feasible'. When there are two or more feasible solutions to a design problem, the designer should choose the most cost-effective one.

Correctness at each level can only be confirmed after demonstrating feasibility of the next level down. Such demonstrations may require prototyping. Designers rely on their knowledge of the technology, and experience of similar systems, to achieve a good design in just a few iterations.

The decomposition of the software into components should proceed until the architectural design is detailed enough to allow:
- individual groups or team members to commence the DD phase;
- the schedule and cost of the DD and TR phases to be estimated.

In a multitasking real-time system, the appropriate level to stop architectural design is when the processing has become purely sequential. This is the lowest level of the task hierarchy, and is the stage at which the control flow has been fully defined.

It is usually unnecessary to describe the architecture down to the module level. However some consideration of module level processing is usually necessary if the functionality at higher levels is to be allocated correctly.

2.3.2 Implementation of non-functional requirements

The SRD contains several categories of requirements that are non-functional. Such requirements can be found under the headings of:

Performance Requirements
Interface Requirements
Operational Requirements
Resource Requirements
Verification Requirements
Acceptance-Testing Requirements
Documentation Requirements
Security Requirements
Portability Requirements
Quality Requirements
Reliability Requirements
Maintainability Requirements
Safety Requirements

The specification of each component should be compared with all the requirements. This task is made easier if the requirements are grouped with their related functions in the SRD. Some kinds of non-functional requirements do not influence the architecture and their implementation can be deferred to the DD phase. Nevertheless, each requirement must be accounted for, even if this only involves including the non-functional requirement in a component's specification.

2.3.2.1 Performance requirements

Performance requirements may be stated for the whole system, or be attached to high-level functions. Whatever the approach, the designer should identify the components that are used to provide the service implied by the performance requirements and specify the performance of each component.

Performance attributes may be incorporated in the functional requirements in the SRD. Where there is a one-to-one correspondence between a component and a function, definition of the performance of the component is straightforward.

The performance of a component that has not yet been built can only be estimated from knowledge of the underlying technology upon which it is based. The designer may have to confirm the feasibility of the performance specification by prototyping. As an example, the execution time of an i/o routine can be predicted from knowledge of the required data flow volume and i/o rate to a peripheral. This prediction should be confirmed by prototyping the routine.

2.3.2.2 Interface requirements

A component design should satisfy all the interface requirements associated with a functional requirement.

Interface requirements may define internal or external control and data flows. The developer has to design the physical mechanism for the control and data flows. Mechanisms may include protocols, subroutine calls, interrupts, file and record formats, and so on.

The interfaces to a component should match its level of abstraction. A component that processes files should have files flowing in and out. Processing of records, fields, bits and bytes should be delegated to lower-level components.

Interfaces should be implemented in such a way as to minimise the coupling. This can be done in several ways:
- minimise the number of separate items flowing into and out of the component;
- minimise the number of separate routes into and out of the component.

Minimisation of the number of separate items flowing into the component should not reduce the understandability of the interface. Data items should be aggregated into structures that have the appropriate level of abstraction, but not arbitrarily bunched together to reduce the numbers (e.g. by using an array).

Ideally, a single entry point for both the control and data flows should be provided. For a subroutine, this means providing all the external data the routine needs in the call argument list. Separating the control and data flow routes (e.g. by routing the data into a component via a common area) greatly increases the coupling between components.

External interface requirements may be referenced by the SRD in an Interface Control Document (ICD). The physical mechanism of the interface may be predefined, and may constrain the software design. Distorting effects should be minimised by providing dedicated components to handle external interfaces. Incidentally, this approach enhances portability and maintainability.

Where an interface standard has to be used, software components that provide the interface can be reused from existing libraries or systems. The repercussions of reusing a component should be considered before making the decision to do it.

2.3.2.3 Operational requirements

The operational requirements of the software should be considered in the AD phase. This should result in a definition of the:

- ergonomic aspects;
- screen layouts;
- user interface language;
- help system.

2.3.2.4 Resource requirements

Resource requirements should be an important consideration in the AD phase, as they may affect the choice of programming language and the high-level architecture. For example the design of the software for a single processor system can be quite different from that of a multiple processor system.

2.3.2.5 Verification requirements

Verification requirements may call for test harnesses or even a 'simulator'. The developer must consider the interfaces to external software used for verification.

A simulator may be used to exercise the system under development, and is external to it. The architectural design of a simulator should be entirely separate from the main design.

2.3.2.6 Acceptance-testing requirements

Like verification requirements, acceptance-testing requirements may call for test harnesses or even a 'simulator' (see Section 2.3.2.5).

2.3.2.7 Documentation requirements

Documentation requirements seldom affect the Architectural Design.

2.3.2.8 Security requirements

Security requirements may affect the selection of hardware, the operating system, the design of the interfaces among components, and the design of database components. Decisions about access to capabilities of the system may have to be made in the AD phase.

2.3.2.9 Portability requirements

Portability requirements can severely constrain the architectural design by forcing the isolation of machine-dependent features. Portability requirements can restrict the options for meeting performance requirements and make them more difficult to meet.

The designer must study the portability requirements carefully and isolate the features common to all the intended environments, and then design the software to use only these features. This may not always be possible, so the designer must explicitly define components to implement features not available in all the intended environments.

2.3.2.10 Quality requirements

Quality requirements can affect:
- the choice of design methods;
- the decisions about reuse, e.g: has the reused software been specified, designed and tested properly?
- the choice of tools;
- the type of design review, e.g. walkthroughs or inspections?

2.3.2.11 Reliability requirements

Reliability requirements can only be directly verified after the software has been written. The key to designing a system having a specified level of reliability is to:
- be aware of the design quality factors that are predictive of eventual software reliability (e.g. complexity);
- calibrate the relationship between predictive metrics and the indicative metrics of reliability (e.g. MTBF);
- ensure that the design scores well in terms of the predictive metrics.

For small projects, careful adherence to the design quality guidelines will be sufficient. This is the 'qualitative' approach to satisfying the reliability requirements. For larger projects, or projects with stringent reliability requirements, a 'quantitative' approach should measure adherence to design quality guidelines with reliability metrics. Metrics have been devised (e.g. 39 metrics are listed in Reference 17) to measure reliability at all phases in the life cycle.

An obvious way of meeting reliability requirements is to reuse software whose operational reliability has already been proven.

Engineering features specifically designed to enhance reliability include:
- fault tolerance;
- redundancy;
- voting.

Fault tolerance allows continued operation of a system after the occurrence of a fault, perhaps with a reduced level of capability or performance. Fault tolerance can be widely applied in software (e.g. software will frequently fail if it does not check its input).

Redundancy achieves fault tolerance with no reduction of capability because systems are replicated. There are two types of redundancy:
- passive;
- active.

Passive redundancy is characterised by one system being 'online' at a time. The remaining systems are on standby. If the online system fails, a standby is brought into operation. This is the 'backup' concept.

Active redundancy is characterised by multiple systems being 'online' simultaneously. Voting is required to control an active redundant system. An odd number of different implementations of the system each meeting the same requirements are developed and installed by different teams. Control flow is a majority decision between the different systems. The systems may have:

- identical software and hardware;
- identical hardware and different software;
- different hardware and software.

2.3.2.12 Maintainability requirements

Maintainability requirements should be considered throughout the architectural design phase. However it is only possible to verify directly the Mean Time To Repair (MTTR) in the operations phase. MTTR can be verified indirectly in the architectural design phase by relating it to design metrics, such as complexity.

The techniques used for increasing software reliability also tend to increase its maintainability. Smaller projects should follow the design quality guidelines to assure maintainability. Larger projects should adopt a quantitative approach based on metrics. Maintainability is also enhanced by:

- selecting a high-level programming language;
- minimising the volume of code that has to be maintained;
- providing software engineering tools that allow modifications to be made easily;
- assigning values to parameters at runtime;
- building in features that allow faults to be located quickly;
- provision of remote maintenance facilities.

Some software engineering tools may be for configuration management. The Software Configuration Management Plan should take account of the maintainability requirements, since the efficiency of these procedures can have a marked effect on maintainability.

Binding is 'the assignment of a value or referent to an identifier' [Ref. 2]. An example is the assignment of a value to a parameter. Static binding is 'binding performed prior to the execution of a program and not subject to change during program execution' [Ref. 2]. Contrast with dynamic binding, which is 'binding performed during the execution of a computer program' [Ref. 2]. Increasing dynamic binding and reducing static binding makes the software more adaptable and maintainable, usually at the expense of complexity and performance. The designer should examine these trade-offs in deciding when to bind values to parameters.

Features that allow errors to be located quickly and easily should be built into the software. Examples are tracebacks, error reporting systems and routines that check their input and report anomalies. The policy and procedures for error reporting should be formulated in the AD phase and applied consistently by the whole project from the start of the DD phase.

Remote maintenance facilities can enhance maintainability in two ways. Firstly, operations can be monitored and the occurrence of faults prevented. Secondly, faults can be cured more quickly because it is not always necessary to travel to the site.

2.3.2.13 Safety requirements

Designing for safety ensures that people and property are not endangered:
- during normal operations;
- following a failure.

It would be unsafe, for example, to design a control system that opens and closes a lift door and omit a mechanism to detect and respond to people or property blocking the door.

A system may be very reliable and maintainable yet may still be unsafe when a fault occurs. The designer should include features to ensure safe behaviour after a fault, for example:
- transfer of control to an identical redundant system;
- transfer of control to a reduced capability backup system;
- graceful degradation, either to a useful, but reduced level of capability, or even to complete shutdown.

Systems which behave safely when faults occur are said to be 'fail safe'.

Prevention of accidents is achieved by adding 'active safety' features, such as the capability to monitor obstructions in the lift door control system example. Prevention of damage following an accident is achieved by adding 'passive safety' features, such as an error handling mechanism.

If safety requirements have been omitted from the SRD, the designer should alert management. Analysts and designers share the responsibility for the development of safe systems.

2.3.3 Design quality

Designs should be adaptable, efficient and understandable. Adaptable designs are easy to modify and maintain. Efficient designs make minimal use of available resources. Designs must be understandable if they are to be built, operated and maintained effectively.

Attaining these goals is assisted by aiming for simplicity. Metrics should be used for measuring simplicity/complexity (e.g. number of interfaces per component and cyclomatic complexity).

Simple components are made by maximising the degree to which the activities internal to the component are related to one another (i.e. 'cohesion'). Simple structures can be made by:
- minimising the number of distinct items that are passed between components (i.e. 'coupling');
- ensuring that the function a component performs is appropriate to its place in the hierarchy (i.e. 'system shape');
- ensuring the structure of the software follows the structure of the data it deals with (i.e. 'data structure match');

- designing components so that their use by other components can be maximised (i.e. 'fan-in');
- restricting the number of child components to seven or less (i.e. 'fan-out');
- removing duplication between components by making new components (i.e. 'factoring').

Designs should be 'modular', with minimal coupling between components and maximum cohesion within each component. Modular designs are more understandable, reusable and maintainable than designs consisting of components with complicated interfaces and poorly matched groupings of functions.

Each level of a design should include only the essential aspects and omit inessential detail. This means they should have the appropriate degree of 'abstraction'. This enhances understandability, adaptability and maintainability.

Understandable designs employ terminology in a consistent way and always use the same solution to the same problem. Where teams of designers collaborate to produce a design, understandability can be considerably impaired by permitting unnecessary variety. CASE tools, designs standards and design reviews all help to enforce consistency and uniformity.

As each layer is defined, the design should be refined to increase the quality, reliability, maintainability and safety of the software. When the next lower layer is designed, unforeseen consequences of earlier design decisions are often spotted. The developer must be prepared to revise all levels of a design during its development. However if the guidelines described in this section are applied throughout the design process, the need for major revisions in the design will be minimised.

2.3.3.1 Design metrics

2.3.3.1.1 Cohesion

The parts of a component should all relate to a single purpose. Cohesion measures the degree to which activities within a component are related to one another. The cohesion of each component should be maximised. High cohesion leads to robust, adaptable, maintainable software.

Cohesion should be evaluated externally (does the name signify a specific purpose?) and internally (does it contain unrelated pieces of logic?). Reference 15 identifies seven types of cohesion:
- functional cohesion;
- sequential cohesion;
- communicational cohesion;
- procedural cohesion;
- temporal cohesion;
- logical cohesion;
- coincidental cohesion.

Functional cohesion is most desirable and coincidental cohesion should definitely be avoided. The other types of cohesion are acceptable under certain conditions. The seven types are discussed below with reference to typical components that might be found in a statistics package.

Functionally cohesive components contain elements that all contribute to the execution of one and only one problem-related task. Names carry a clear idea of purpose (e.g. CALCULATE_MEAN). Functionally cohesive components should be easy to reuse. All the components at the bottom of a structure should be functionally cohesive.

Sequentially cohesive components contain chains of activities, with the output of an activity being the input to the next. Names consist of specific verbs and composite objects (e.g. CALCULATE_TOTAL_AND_MEAN). Sequentially cohesive components should be split into functionally cohesive components.

Communicationally cohesive components contain activities that share the same input data. Names have over-general verbs but specific objects (e.g. ANALYSE_CENSUS_DATA), showing that the object is used for a range of activities. Communicationally cohesive components should be split into functionally cohesive components.

Procedurally cohesive components contain chains of activities, with control passing from one activity to the next. Individual activities are only related to the overall goal rather than to one another. Names of procedurally cohesive components are often 'high level', because they convey an idea of their possible activities, rather than their actual activities (e.g. PROCESS_CENSUS_DATA). Procedurally cohesive components are acceptable at the highest levels of the structure.

Temporally cohesive components contain activities that all take place simultaneously. The names define a stage in the processing (e.g. INITIALISE, TERMINATE). Bundling unrelated activities together on a temporal basis is bad practice because it reduces modularity. An initialisation component may have to be related to other components by a global data area, for example, and this increases coupling and reduces the possibilities for reuse. Temporal cohesion should be avoided.

Logically cohesive components perform a range of similar activities. Much of the processing is shared, but special effects are controlled by means of flags or 'control couples'. The names of logically cohesive components can be quite general, but the results can be quite specialised (e.g. PROCESS_STATISTICS). Logical cohesion causes general sounding names to appear at the bottom levels of the structure, and this can make the design less understandable. Logical cohesion should be avoided, but this may require significant restructuring.

Coincidentally cohesive components contain wholly unrelated activities. Names give no idea of the purpose of the component (e.g. MISCELLANEOUS_ROUTINE). Coincidentally cohesive components are often invented at the end of the design process to contain miscellaneous activities that do not neatly fit with any others. Coincidental cohesion severely reduces understandability and maintainability, and should be avoided, even if the penalty is substantial redesign.

Practical methods for increasing cohesion are to:
- make sure that each component has a single clearly defined function;
- make sure that every part of the component contributes to that function;
- keep the internal processing short and simple.

2.3.3.1.2 Coupling

A 'couple' is an item of information passed between two components. The 'coupling' between two components can be measured by the number of couples passed. The number of couples flowing into and out of a component should be minimised.

The term 'coupling' is also frequently used to describe the relative independence of a component. 'Tightly' coupled components have a high level of interdependence and 'loosely' coupled components have a low level of interdependence. Dependencies between components should be minimised to maximise reusability and maintainability.

Reducing coupling also simplifies interfaces. The information passed between components should be the minimum necessary to do the job.

High-level components can have high coupling when low-level information items are passed in and out. Low-level items should be grouped into data structures to reduce the coupling. The component can then refer to the data structure.

Reference 15 describes five types of coupling:
- data coupling;
- stamp coupling;
- control coupling;
- common coupling;
- content coupling.

Data coupling is most desirable and content coupling should be avoided. The other types of coupling are all acceptable under certain conditions, which are discussed below.

Data coupling is passing only the data needed. The couple name is a noun or noun phrase. The couple name can be the object in the component name. For example a component called 'CALCULATE_MEAN' might have an output data couple called 'MEAN'.

Stamp coupling is passing more data than is needed. The couple name is a noun or noun phrase. Stamp coupling should be avoided. Components should only be given the data that is relevant to their task. An example of stamp coupling is to pass a data structure called 'CENSUS_DATA' to a component that only requires the ages of the people in the census to calculate the average age.

Control coupling is communication by flags. The couple name may contain a verb. It is bad practice to use control coupling for the primary control flow; this should be implied by the component hierarchy. It is acceptable to use control coupling for secondary control flows such as in error handling.

Common coupling is communication by means of global data, and causes data to be less secure because faults in components that have access to the data area may corrupt it. Common coupling should normally be avoided, although it is sometimes necessary to provide access to data by components that do not have a direct call connection (e.g. if A calls B calls C, and A has to pass data to C).

Content coupling is communication by changing the instructions and internal data in another component. Content coupling is bad because it prevents information hiding. Only older languages and assembler allow this type of coupling.

Practical methods of reducing coupling are to:
- structure the data;

- avoid using flags or semaphores for primary control flow and use messages or component calls;
- avoid passing data through components that do not use it;
- provide access to global or shared data by dedicated components.
- make sure that each component has a single entry point and exit point.

2.3.3.1.3 System shape

System shape, also called 'data abstraction', describes the degree to which:
- the top components in a system are divorced from the physical aspects of the data they deal with;
- physical characteristics of the input and output data are independent.

If the system achieves these criteria to a high degree then the shape is said to be 'balanced'.

The system shape rule is: 'separate logical and physical functionality'.

2.3.3.1.4 Data structure match

In administrative data processing systems, the structure of the system should follow the structure of the data it deals with [Ref. 21]. A pay-roll package should deal with files at the highest levels, records at the middle levels and fields at the lowest levels.

The data structure match rule is: 'when appropriate, match the system structure to the data structure'.

2.3.3.1.5 Fan-in

The number of components that call a component measures its 'fan-in'. Reusability increases as fan-in increases.

Simple fan-in rules are: 'maximise fan-in' and 'reuse components as often as possible'.

2.3.3.1.6 Fan-out

The number of components that a component calls measures its 'fan-out'. Fan-out should usually be small, not more than seven. However some kinds of constructs force much higher fan-out values (e.g. case statements) and this is often acceptable.

Simple fan-out rules are: 'make the average fan-out seven or less' or 'make components depend on as few others as possible'.

2.3.3.1.7 Factoring

Factoring measures lack of duplication in software. A component may be factorised to increase cohesiveness and reduce size. Factoring creates reusable components with high fan-in. Factoring should be performed in the AD phase to identify utility software common to all components.

2.3.3.2 Complexity metrics

Suitable metrics for the design phases are listed in Table 2.3.3.2. This list has been compiled from ANSI/IEEE Std 982.1-1988 and 982.2-1988 [Ref. 17 and 18]. For a detailed discussion, the reader should consult the references.

	Metric	Definition
1.	Number of Entries and Exits	measures the complexity by counting the entry and exit points in each component [Ref. 17, Section 4.13]
2	Software Science Measures	measures the complexity using the counts of operators and operands [Ref. 17, Section 4.14]
3.	Graph Theoretic Complexity	measures the design complexity in terms of numbers of components, interfaces and resources [Ref. 17, Section 4.15, and Ref. 23]. Similar to Cyclomatic Complexity.
4.	Cyclomatic Complexity	measures the component complexity from: Number of program flows between groups of program statements - Number of sequential groups of program statements + 2. A component with sequential flow from entry to exit has a cyclomatic complexity of 1-2+1=1 [Ref. 17, Section 4.16, and Ref. 23]
5.	Minimal Unit Test Case Determination	measures the complexity of a component from the number of independent paths through it, so that a minimal number of covering test cases can be generated for unit test [Ref. 17, Section 4.17]
6.	Design Structure	measures the design complexity in terms of its top-down profile, component dependence, component requirements for prior processing, database size and modularity and number of entry and exit points per component [Ref. 17, Section 4.19]
7.	Data Flow Complexity	measures the structural and procedural complexity in terms of component length, fan-in and fan-out [Ref. 17, Section 4.25]

Table 2.3.3.2: Complexity metrics

2.3.3.3 Abstraction

An abstraction is 'a view of an object that focuses on the information relevant to a particular purpose and ignores the remainder of the information' [Ref. 2]. Design methods and tools should support abstraction by providing techniques for encapsulating functions and data in ways best suited to the view required. It should be possible to view a hierarchical design at various levels of detail.

The level of abstraction of a component should be related to its place within the structure of a system. For example a component that deals with files should delegate record handling operations to lower-level modules, as shown in Figures 2.3.3.3.A and B.

Figure 2.3.3.3A: Incorrectly layered abstractions

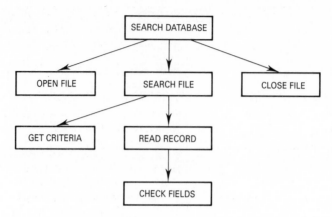

Figure 2.3.3.3B: Correctly layered abstractions.

2.3.3.4 Information hiding

Information hiding is 'the technique of encapsulating software design decisions in components so that the interfaces to the component reveal as little as possible about its inner working' (adapted from Reference 2). Components that hide information about their inner workings are 'black boxes'.

Information hiding is needed to enable developers to view the system at different layers of abstraction. Therefore it should not be necessary to understand any low-level processing to understand the high-level processing.

Sometimes information needs to be shared among components and this goes against the 'information hiding' principle. The 'information clustering' technique restricts access to information to as few components as possible. A library of components is often built to provide the sole means of access to information clusters such as common blocks.

2.3.3.5 Modularity

Modularity is 'the degree to which a system or computer program is composed of discrete components such that a change in one component has minimal impact on other components' [Ref. 2]. Component coupling is low in a modular design.

2.3.4 Prototyping

'Experimental prototypes' may be built to verify the correctness of a technical solution. If different designs meet the same requirements, prototypes can help identify the best choice. High risk, critical technologies should be prototyped in the AD phase. This is essential if a workable design is to be selected. Just as in the requirements phases, prototyping in the AD phase can avoid expensive redesign and recoding in later phases.

Two types of experimental prototypes can be distinguished: 'partial-system' prototypes and 'whole-system' prototypes. Partial-system prototypes are built to demonstrate the feasibility of a particular feature of the design. They are usually programmed in the language to be used in the DD phase. Whole-system prototypes are built to test the complete design. They may be built with CASE tools that permit execution of the design, or off-the-shelf tools that can be adapted for the application. Whole-system prototypes can help identify behavioural problems, such as resource contention.

2.3.5 Choosing a design approach

There is no unique design for any software system. Studies of the different options may be necessary. Alternative designs should be outlined and the trade-off between promising candidates discussed. The choice depends upon the type of system. In a real-time situation, performance and response time could be important, whereas in an administrative system stability of the data base might be more important.

The designer should consider the two major kinds of implementation for each software component:

- generating new components from scratch;
- reusing a component from another system or library.

New components are likely to need most maintenance. The expertise needed to maintain old components might not be available at all, and this can be an equally difficult problem.

Reuse generally leads to increased reliability because software failures peak at time of first release and decline thereafter. Unfortunately the logic of a system often has to be distorted to accommodate components not designed specifically for it, and this reduces adaptability. The structure of the system becomes over-strained and cannot stand the stresses imposed by additional features.

Developers should consider the requirements for maintainability, reliability, portability and adaptability in deciding whether to create new components or reuse old ones.

Only the selected design approach should be reflected in the ADD (and DDD). However the reasons for each major design decision should be recorded in the Project History Document. Modification of the software in later phases may require design decisions to be re-examined.

2.4 SPECIFICATION OF THE ARCHITECTURAL DESIGN

The architectural design is specified by identifying the components, defining the control and data flow between them, and stating for each of them the:

- functions to be performed;
- data input;
- data output;
- resource utilisation.

2.4.1 Assigning functions to components

The function of a component is defined by stating its objective or characteristic actions [Ref. 2].

The functional definition of a component should be derived from the functional requirements in the SRD, and references should be added to the component definition to record this.

When the architectural design is terminated at the task level, each task may be associated with many functional requirements. Nevertheless, there should be a strong association between the functions carried out by a component (i.e. each component should have high cohesion).

Internal processing should be described in terms of the control and data flow to lower-level components. The control flow may be described diagrammatically, using structure charts, transformation schemas or object diagrams. It should describe both nominal and non-nominal behaviour.

At the lowest design level, the processing done by each component should be defined. This may be done in natural language, Structured English or pseudo code. Parts of the functional specification may be reproduced or referenced to define what processing is required (e.g. state-transition diagrams, decision trees etc).

The data processing of each component can be defined by listing the data that the component deals with, and the operations that the component performs (e.g. create, read, update, delete). This information can be gathered from entity life histories [Ref. 4, 9]. The job of functional definition is then to describe how data processing operations are to be done. This approach ensures that no data processing functions are accidentally omitted.

2.4.2 Definition of data structures

Data structure definitions must include the:
- characteristics of each part (e.g. name, type, dimension) (AD10);
- relationships between parts (i.e. structure) (AD11);
- range of possible values of each part (AD12);
- initial values of each part (AD13).

The names of the parts of a data structure should be meaningful and unambiguous. They should leave no doubt about what the part is. Acronyms and obscure coding systems should be avoided in the architectural design.

The data type of each part of the data structure must be stated. Similarly the dimensionality of each item must be defined. Effort should be taken to keep the dimensionality of each part of the data structure as low as possible. Arrays should be homogeneous, with all the cells storing similar information.

The range of possible values of each part of the data structure should be stated. Knowledge about the possible values helps define the storage requirements. In the DD phase, defensive programming techniques use knowledge about the possible values to check the input to components.

The designer must define how data structures are initialised. Inputs that may change should be accessible to the user or operator (e.g. as in 'table-driven' software). Parameters that will never change (e.g.) need to be stored so that all components use the same value (e.g. FORTRAN include files of PARAMETER statements).

The accessibility of the data structures to components is an important consideration in architectural design, and has a crucial effect on the component coupling. Access to a data structure should be granted only on a 'need-to-know' basis and the temptation to define global data should be resisted.

Global data implies some form of data sharing, and even if access to the global data is controlled (e.g. by semaphores), a single component may corrupt the data area. Such failures are usually irrecoverable. It is, however, acceptable to make data global if it is the only way of achieving the necessary performance.

Data structures shared between a component and its immediate subordinates should be passed. When components are separated from one another in the hierarchy this technique becomes clumsy, and leads to the occurrence of 'tramp data', i.e. data that passes through components without being used. The best solution to the 'tramp data' problem is to make an 'information cluster' (see Section 2.3.3.4).

2.4.3 Definition of control flow

Control flow should always be described from initialisation to termination. It should be related to the system state, perhaps by the use of state-transition diagrams [Ref. 11].

The precise control flow mechanism should be described, for example:

- calls;
- interrupts;
- messages.

Control flow defines the component hierarchy. When control and data couples are removed from a structure chart, for example, the tree diagram that is left defines the component hierarchy.

2.4.3.1 Sequential and parallel control flow

Control flow may be sequential, parallel or a combination of the two. Decisions about sequential and parallel control flow are a crucial activity in architectural design. They should be based on the logical model. Functions that exchange data, even indirectly, must be arranged in sequence, whereas functions that have no such interface can execute in parallel.

Observations about sequential and parallel activities can affect how functions are allocated to components. For example, all the functions that execute in sequence may be allocated to a single task (or program) whereas functions that can execute in parallel may be allocated to different tasks.

2.4.3.2 Synchronous and asynchronous control flow

Control flow may be synchronous or asynchronous. The execution of two components is synchronous if, at any stage in the operation of one component, the state of the other is precisely determined. Sequential processing is always synchronous (when one component is doing something, the other must be doing nothing). Parallel control flow may also be synchronised, as in an array processor where multiple processors, each handling a different array element, are all synchronised by the same clock.

'Polling' is a synchronous activity. A component interrogates other lower-level components (which may be external) for information and takes appropriate action. Polling is a robust, easy-to-program mechanism but it can cause performance problems.

Tasks running on separate computers run asynchronously, as do tasks running on a single processor under a multi-tasking operating system. Operations must be controlled by some type of handshake, such as a rendezvous. A 'scheduler' type task is usually necessary to coordinate all the other tasks.

An interrupt is an example of an asynchronous control flow. Interrupts force components to suspend their operation and pass control to other components. The exact component state when the interruption occurs cannot be predicted. Such non-deterministic behaviour makes verification and maintenance more difficult.

Another example of an asynchronous control flow is a 'one-way' message. A component sends a message and proceeds with its own processing without waiting for confirmation of reception. There is no handshake. Designers should only introduce this type of control flow if the rest of the processing of the sender makes no assumptions about the receiver state.

Asynchronous control flows can cause improvements in software performance; this advantage should be carefully traded-off against the extra complexity they may add.

2.4.4 Definition of the computer resource utilisation

The computer resources (e.g. CPU speed, memory, storage, system software) needed for development and operations must be estimated in the AD phase and defined in the ADD (AD15). For many software projects, the development and operational environments will be the same. Any resource requirements in the SRD will constrain the design.

Virtual memory systems have reduced the problem of main memory utilisation. Even so, the packaging of the components into units that execute together may still be necessary in some systems. These issues may have to be addressed in the AD phase, as they influence the division of work and how the software is integrated.

2.4.5 Selection of the programming language

The chosen programming languages should support top-down decomposition, structured programming and concurrent production and documentation. The programming language and the AD method should be compatible.

The relation between the AD method and programming language means that the choice should be made when the AD method is selected, at the beginning of the AD phase. However the process of design may lead to this initial choice of programming language being revised.

The selection of the programming languages to be used should be reviewed when the architectural design is complete.

Other considerations will affect the choice of programming language. Portability and maintenance considerations imply that assembler should be avoided. Portability considerations argue against using FORTRAN for real-time software because operating system services have to be called. The system services are not standard language features. Programming languages that allow meaningful names rather than terse, abbreviated names should be favoured since readable software is easier to maintain. Standardised languages and high-quality compilers, debuggers, static and dynamic analysis tools are important considerations.

While it may be necessary to use more than one programming language (e.g a mixed microprocessor and minicomputer configuration), maintenance is easier if a single programming language is used.

It is not sufficient just to define the language to be used. The particular language standard and compiler should also be defined during the AD phase. The rules for using non-standard features allowed by a compiler should be formulated. Language extensions should be avoided as this makes the software less portable. However, performance and maintenance requirements may sometimes outweigh those of portability and make some non-standard features acceptable.

2.5 INTEGRATION TEST PLANNING

Integration Test Plans must be generated in the AD phase and documented in the Integration Test section of the Software Verification and Validation Plan (SVVP/IT). The Integration Test Plan should describe the scope, approach and resources required for the integration tests, and take account of the verification requirements in the SRD. See Chapter 6.

2.6 PLANNING THE DETAILED DESIGN PHASE

Plans of DD phase activities must be drawn up in the AD phase. Generation of DD phase plans is discussed in Chapter 6. These plans cover project management, configuration management, verification and validation and quality assurance. Outputs are the:
- Software Project Management Plan for the AD phase (SPMP/DD);
- Software Configuration Management Plan for the DD phase (SCMP/DD);
- Software Verification and Validation Plan for the DD phase (SVVP/DD);
- Software Quality Assurance Plan for the DD phase (SQAP/DD).

2.7 THE ARCHITECTURAL DESIGN PHASE REVIEW

Production of the ADD and SVVP/IT is an iterative process. The development team should hold walkthroughs and internal reviews of a document before its formal review.

The outputs of the AD phase shall be formally reviewed during the Architectural Design Review (AD16). This should be a technical review. The recommended procedure is described in the *Guide to Software Verification and Validation*, and is based closely on the IEEE standard for Technical Reviews [Ref. 8].

Normally, only the ADD and Integration Test Plans undergo the full technical review procedure involving users, developers, management and quality assurance staff. The Software Project Management Plan (SPMP/DD), Software Configuration Management Plan (SCMP/DD), Software Verification and Validation Plan (SVVP/DD), and Software Quality Assurance Plan (SQAP/DD) are usually reviewed by management and quality assurance staff only.

In summary, the objective of the AD/R is to verify that the:
- ADD describes the optimal solution to the problem stated in the SRD;
- ADD describes the architectural design clearly, completely and in sufficient detail to enable the detailed design process to be started;

- SVVP/IT is an adequate plan for integration testing of the software in the DD phase.

An AD/R begins when the documents are distributed to participants for review. A problem with a document is described in a 'Review Item Discrepancy' (RID) form that may be prepared by any participant. Review meetings are then held that have the documents and RIDs as input. A review meeting should discuss all the RIDs and either accept or reject them. The review meeting may also discuss possible solutions to the problems raised by them. The output of the meeting includes the processed RIDs.

An AD/R terminates when a disposition has been agreed for all the RIDs. Each AD/R must decide whether another review cycle is necessary, or whether the DD phase can begin.

CHAPTER 3
METHODS FOR ARCHITECTURAL DESIGN

3.1 INTRODUCTION

An architectural design method should provide a systematic way of defining the software components. Any method should facilitate the production of a high-quality, efficient design that meets all the requirements.

This guide summarises a range of design methods to enable the designer to make a choice. The details about each method should be obtained from the references. This guide does not seek either to make any particular method a standard or to define a set of acceptable methods. Each project should examine its needs, choose a method (or combination of methods) and justify the selection in the ADD. To help make this choice, this guide summarises some well-known methods and discusses how they can be applied in the AD phase.

Methods that may prove useful for architectural design are:
- Structured Design;
- Object-Oriented Design;
- Jackson System Development;
- Formal Methods.

The AD method can affect the choice of programming language. Early versions of Structured Design, for example, decompose the software to fit a control flow concept based on the call structure of a third generation programming language such as FORTRAN, C and COBOL. Similarly, the use of object-oriented design implies the use of an object-oriented programming language such as C++ and Smalltalk.

3.2 STRUCTURED DESIGN

Structured Design is not a single method, but a name for a class of methods. Members of this class are:
- Yourdon methods (Yourdon/Constantine and Ward/Mellor);
- Structured Analysis and Design Technique (SADT™)[1];
- Structured Systems Analysis and Design Methodology (SSADM).

Yourdon methods are widely used in the USA and Europe. SSADM is recommended by the UK government for 'data processing systems'. It is now under the control of the British Standards Institute (BSI). SADT has been successfully used by the European Space Agency (ESA) in many projects.

---

[1] Trademark of SoftTech Inc, Waltham, Mass, USA

3.2.1 Yourdon methods

Structured Design is 'a disciplined approach to software design that adheres to a specified set of rules based on principles such as top-down design, stepwise refinement and data flow analysis' [Ref. 1]. In the Yourdon approach [Ref. 11, 16, 20], the technique can be characterised by the use of:

- Structure Charts to show hierarchy and control and data flow;
- Pseudo Code to describe the processing.

The well-defined path between the analysis and design phases is a major advantage of structured methods. DeMarco's version of structured analysis defines four kinds of model. Table 3.2.1 relates the models to the *Software Engineering Standards* life cycle phase in which they should be built.

Model No	Model Name	*Software Engineering Standards* phase
1	current physical model	SR phase
2	current logical model	SR phase
3	required logical model	SR phase
4	required physical model	AD phase

Table 3.2.1: Structured Analysis Models

The required physical model should be defined at the beginning the AD phase since it is input to the Structured Design process.

Structured Design defines concepts for assessing the quality of design produced by any method. It has also pioneered concepts, now found in more recent methods, such as:

- allowing the form of the problem to guide the solution;
- attempting to reduce complexity via partitioning and hierarchical organisation;
- making systems understandable through rigorous diagramming techniques.

Structured Design methods arose out of experience of building 'data processing' systems and so early methods could only describe sequential control flow. A more recent extension of structured methods developed by Ward and Mellor catered for real-time systems [Ref. 11] by adding extra features such as:

- control transformations and event flows in DFDs;
- time-continuous and time-discrete behaviour in DFDs;
- Petri Nets, to verify the executability of DFDs [Ref. 13];
- State-Transition Diagrams to describe control transformations.

Ward and Mellor define the purpose of the analysis phase as the creation of an 'essential model'. In the design phase the 'essential model' is transformed to a computer 'implementation model'. The implementation model is progressively designed in a top-down manner by allocating functions to processors, tasks and modules.

Transformation Schemas are used to describe the design at the processor level, where there may be parallelism. Structure Charts are used at the task level and below, where the control flow is sequential.

3.2.2 SADT

Structured Analysis and Design Technique (SADT) uses the same diagramming techniques for both analysis and design [Ref. 3]. Unlike the early versions of Yourdon,

SADT has always catered for real-time systems modelling, because it permits the representation of control flows. However SADT diagrams need to be supplemented with State-Transition Diagrams to define behaviour.

SADT diagram boxes should represent components. Each box should be labelled with the component identifier. Control flows should represent calls, interrupts and loading operations. Input and output data flows should represent the files, messages and calling arguments passed between components. Mechanism flows should carry special information about the implementation of the component.

3.2.3 SSADM

SSADM is a detailed methodology with six activities [Ref. 4, 9]:
1. analysis of the current situation;
2. specification of requirements;
3. selection of system option;
4. logical data design;
5. logical process design;
6. physical design.

Activities 1 and 2 should take place in the UR and SR phases respectively. The output of 2 is a required logical model of the software, which should be described in the SRD. Activities 3 to 6 should take place in the AD phase. The ADD should describe the physical design.

SSADM results in a process model and a data model. The models are built in parallel and each is used to check the consistency of the other. This built-in consistency checking approach is the major advantage that SSADM offers. Data modelling is treated more thoroughly by SSADM than by the other methods. SSADM does not support the design of real-time systems.

3.3 OBJECT-ORIENTED DESIGN

Object-Oriented Design (OOD) is an approach to software design based on objects and classes. An object is 'an abstraction of something in the domain of a problem or its implementation, reflecting the capabilities of a system to keep information about it, interact with it or both; an encapsulation of attribute values and their exclusive services' [Ref. 24]. A class describes a set of objects with common attributes and services. An object is an 'instance' of a class and the act of creating an object is called 'instantiation'.

Classes may be entities with abstract data types, such as 'Telemetry Packet' and 'Spectrum', as well as simpler entities with primitive data types such as real numbers, integers and character strings. A class is defined by its attributes and services. For example the 'Spectrum' class would have attributes such as 'minimum frequency', 'centre frequency', 'maximum frequency' and services such as 'calibrate'.

Classes can be decomposed into subclasses. There might be several types of Telemetry Packet for example, and subclasses of Telemetry Packet such as 'Photometer Packet' and 'Spectrometer Packet' may be created. Subclasses share family characteristics, and OOD provides for this by permitting subclasses to inherit operations and attributes from their parents. This leads to modular, structured systems that require less code to implement. Common code is automatically localised in a top-down way.

Object-oriented design methods offer better support for reuse than other methods. The traditional bottom-up reuse mechanism where an application module calls a library module is of course possible. In addition, the inheritance feature permits top-down reuse of superclass attributes and operations.

OOD combines information and services, leading to increased modularity. Control and data structures can be defined in an integrated way.

Other features of the object-oriented approach besides classes, objects and inheritance are message passing and polymorphism. Objects send messages to other objects to command their services. Messages are also used to pass information. Polymorphism is the capability, at runtime, to refer to instances of various classes. Polymorphism is often implemented by allowing 'dynamic binding'.

The object-oriented features such as polymorphism rely on dynamic memory allocation. This can make the performance of object-oriented software unpredictable. Care should be taken when programming real-time applications to ensure that functions that must complete by a defined deadline have their processing fully defined at compile-time, not run-time.

OOD is most effective when implemented through an object-oriented programming language that supports object definition, inheritance, message passing and polymorphism. Smalltalk, C++, Eiffel and Object Pascal support all these features.

Object-oriented techniques have been shown to be much more suitable for implementing event-driven software, such as Graphical User Interfaces (GUIs), than structured methods. Many CASE tools for structured methods are implemented by means of object-oriented techniques.

If object-oriented methods are to be used, they should be used throughout the life cycle. This means that OOD should only be selected for the AD phase if Object-Oriented Analysis (OOA) have been used in the SR phase. The seamless transition from analysis to design to programming is a major advantage of the object-oriented methods, as it facilitates iteration. An early paper by Booch [Ref. 13] describes a technique for transforming a logical model built using structured analysis to a physical model using object-oriented design. In practice the results have not been satisfactory. The structured analysis view is based on functions and data and the object-oriented view is based on classes, objects, attributes and services. The views are quite different, and it is difficult to hold both in mind simultaneously.

Like Structured Design, Object-Oriented Design is not a single method, but a name for a class of methods. Members of this class include:

- Booch;
- Hierarchical Object-Oriented Design (HOOD).
- Coad-Yourdon;
- Object Modelling Technique (OMT) from Rumbaugh et al;
- Shlaer-Mellor.

These methods are discussed below.

3.3.1 Booch

Booch originated object-oriented design [Ref. 22], and continues to play a leading role in the development of the method [Ref. 26].

Booch models an object-oriented design in terms of a logical view, which defines the classes, objects, and their relationships, and a physical view, which defines the module and process architecture. The logical view corresponds to the logical model that *Software Engineering Standards* requires software engineers to construct in the SR phase (see *Guide to the Software Requirements Definition Phase*). The physical view corresponds to the physical model that *Software Engineering Standards* requires software engineers to construct in the AD phase.

Booch provides two diagramming techniques for documenting the physical view:
- module diagrams, which are used to show the allocation of classes and objects to modules such as programs, packages and tasks in the physical design (the term 'module' in Booch's method is used to describe any design component);
- process diagrams, which show the allocation of modules to hardware processors.

Booch's books on Object-Oriented Design contain many insights into good design practise. However Booch's notation is cumbersome and few tools are available.

3.3.2 HOOD

Hierarchical Object-Oriented Design (HOOD) [Ref. 14] is one of a family of object-oriented methods that try to marry object-orientation with structured design methods (see Reference 25 for another example). Hierarchy follows naturally from decomposition of the top-level 'root' object. As in structured design, data couples flow between software components. The main difference between HOOD and structured methods is that software components get their identity from their correspondence to things in the real world, rather than to functions that the system has to perform.

HOOD was originally designed to be used with Ada, although Ada does not support inheritance, and is not an object-oriented programming language. This is not serious problem for the HOOD designer, because the method does not use classes to structure systems.

HOOD does not have a complementary analysis method. The logical model is normally built using structured analysis. Transformation of the logical model to the physical model is difficult, making it hard to construct a coherent design.

HOOD has been used embedded Ada applications. It has a niche, but is unlikely to become as widespread and well supported by tools as, say, OMT.

3.3.3 Coad and Yourdon

Coad and Yourdon have published an integrated approach to object-oriented analysis and design [Ref. 24]. An object-oriented design is constructed from four components:
- problem domain component;
- human interaction component;
- task management component;
- data management component.

Each component is composed of classes and objects. The problem domain component is based on the (logical) model built with OOA in the analysis phase. It defines the subject matter of the system and its responsibilities. If the system is to be implemented in an object-oriented language, the correspondence between problem domain classes and objects will be one to one, and the problem domain component can be directly programmed. However substantial refinement of the logical model is normally required, resulting in the addition of more attributes and services. Reuse considerations, and the non-availability of a fully object-oriented programming language, may make the design of the problem domain component depart from ideal represented by the OOA model.

The human interaction component handles sending and receiving messages to and from the user. The classes and objects in the human interaction component have names taken from the user interface language, e.g. window and menu.

Many systems will have multiple threads of execution, and the designer must construct a task management component to organise the processing. The designer needs to define tasks as event-driven or clock-driven, as well as their priority and criticality.

The data management component provides the infrastructure to store and retrieve objects. It may be a simple file system, a relational database management system, or even an object-oriented database management system.

The four components together make the physical model of the system. At the top level, all Coad and Yourdon Object-Oriented Designs have the same structure.

Classes and objects are organised into 'generalisation-specialisation' and 'whole-part' structures. Generalisation-specialisation structures are 'family trees', with children inheriting the attributes of their parents. Whole-part structures are formed when an object is decomposed.

The strengths of Coad and Yourdon's method are its brief, concise description and its use of general texts as sources of definitions, so that the definitions fit common sense and jargon is minimised. The main weakness of the method is its complex notation, which is difficult to use without tool support. Some users of the Coad-Yourdon method have used the OMT diagramming notation instead.

3.3.4 OMT

The Object Modelling Technique (OMT) of Rumbaugh et al [Ref 26] contains two design activities:
- system design;
- object design.

System design should be performed in the AD phase. The object design should be performed in the DD phase.

The steps of system design are conventional and are:
- organise the system into subsystems and arrange them in layers and partitions;
- identify concurrency inherent in the problem;
- allocate subsystems to processors;
- define the data management implementation strategy;
- identify global resources and define the mechanism for controlling access to them;
- choose an approach to implementing software control;

- consider boundary conditions;
- establish trade-off priorities.

Many systems are quite similar, and Rumbaugh suggests that system designs be based on one of several frameworks or 'canonical architectures'. The ones they propose are:

- batch transformation - a data transformation performed once on an entire input set;
- continuous transformation - a data transformation performed continuously as inputs change;
- interactive interface - a system dominated by external interactions;
- dynamic simulation - a system that simulates evolving real world objects;
- real-time system - a system dominated by strict timing constraints;
- transaction manager - a system concerned with storing and updating data.

The OMT system design approach contains many design ideas that are generally applicable.

3.3.5 Shlaer-Mellor

Shlaer and Mellor [Ref 28] describe an Object-Oriented Design Language (OODLE), derived from the Booch and Buhr notation. There are four types of diagram:

- class diagram;
- class structure chart;
- dependency diagram;
- inheritance diagram.

There is a class diagram for each class. The class diagram defines the operations and attributes of the class.

The class structure chart defines the module structure of the class, and the control and data flow between the modules of the class. There is a class structure chart for each class.

Dependency diagrams illustrate the dependencies between classes, which may be:

- client-server;
- friends.

A client server dependency exists when a class (the client) calls upon the operations of another class (the server).

A friendship dependency exists when one class access the internal data of another class. This is an information-hiding violation.

Inheritance diagrams show the inheritance relationships between classes.

Shlaer and Mellor define a 'recursive design' method that uses the OODLE notation as follows:

- define how the generic computing processes will be implemented;
- implement the object model classes using the generic computing processes.

The Shlaer-Mellor design approach is more complex than that of other object-oriented methods.

3.4 JACKSON SYSTEM DEVELOPMENT

Jackson System Development method should only be used in the AD phase if it has been used in the SR phase [Ref. 12]. In this case the SRD will contain:

- definitions of the real-world entities with which the software is to be concerned;
- definitions of the actions of these entities in the real world;
- a description of that part of the real world that is to be simulated in software;
- specifications of the functions that the software will perform, i.e. a selection of real-world actions that the software will emulate.

Table 3.4 shows how the JSD activities map to the *Software Engineering Standards* life cycle.

The first JSD task in the AD phase is matching processes to processors, i.e. deciding what computer runs each process. In JSD there may be a process for each instance of an entity type. The designer must make sure that the computer has enough performance to run all the instances of the process type.

The second JSD task in the AD phase is to transform process specifications. Unless there is one computer available for each process described in the SRD (e.g. a dedicated control system), it will be necessary to transform the specification of each process into a form capable of execution on a computer. Rather than having many individual processes that run once, it is necessary to have a single generic process that runs many times. A computer program consists of data and instructions. To transform a process into a program, the instruction and data components of each process must be separated. In JSD, the data component of a process is called the 'state-vector'. The state-vector also retains information on the stage that processing has got to, so that individual processes can be resumed at the correct point. The state-vector of a process should be specified in the AD phase. A state-vector should reside in permanent storage. The executable portion of a process should be specified in the AD phase in pseudo code. This may be carried over from the SRD without major modification; introduction of detailed implementation considerations should be deferred until the DD phase.

The other major JSD task in the AD phase is to schedule processing. The execution of the processing has to be coordinated. In JSD this is done by introducing a 'scheduling' process that activates and deactivates other processes and controls their execution.

JSD Activity			
Level 0	Level 1	Level 2	Level 3
Specification (SR Phase)	Specify Model of Reality	Develop Model Abstractly	Write Entity-Action List
			Draw Entity-Structure Diagrams
		Define Initial versions of Model processes	
	Specify System Functions	Add functions to model processes	
		Add timing constraints	
Implementation (AD Phase)	Match processes to processors		
	Transform processes		
	Devise Scheduler		
Implementation (DD Phase)	Define Database		

Table 3.4: JSD activities and the *Software Engineering Standards* life cycle

3.5 FORMAL METHODS

Formal methods aim to produce a rigorous specification of the software in terms of an agreed notation with well-defined semantics. Formal methods should only be applied in the AD phase if they have been used in the SR phase. See *Guide to the Software Requirements Definition Phase*, for a discussion of Formal Methods. Formal methods may be used when the software is safety-critical, or when the availability and security requirements are very demanding.

Development of a formal specification should proceed by increasing the detail until direct realisation of the specification in a programming language is possible. This procedure is sometimes called 'reification' [Ref. 10].

The AD phase of a software development using a formal method is marked by the taking of the first implementation decisions about the software. Relevant questions are: 'how are the abstract data types to be represented? and 'how are operations to be implemented? These decisions may constrain subsequent iterations of the specification. When a Formal Method is being used, the AD phase should end when the specification can be coded in a high-level programming language.

CHAPTER 4
TOOLS FOR ARCHITECTURAL DESIGN

4.1 INTRODUCTION

This chapter discusses the tools for constructing a physical model and specifying the architectural design. Tools can be combined to suit the needs of a particular project.

4.2 TOOLS FOR PHYSICAL MODEL CONSTRUCTION

In all but the smallest projects, CASE tools should be used during the AD phase. Like many general purpose tools (e.g. such as word processors and drawing packages), CASE tools should provide:

- windows, icons, menu and pointer (WIMP) style interface for the easy creation and editing of diagrams;
- what you see is what you get (WYSIWYG) style interface that ensures that what is created on the display screen is an exact image of what will appear in the document.

Method-specific CASE tools offer the following features not offered by general-purpose tools:

- enforcement of the rules of the methods;
- consistency checking;
- easy modification;
- automatic traceability of components to software requirements;
- built-in configuration management;
- support for abstraction and information hiding;
- support for simulation.

CASE Tools should have an integrated data dictionary or another kind or 'repository'. This is necessary for consistency checking. Developers should check that a tool supports the parts of the method that they intend to use. Appendix E contains a more detailed list of desirable tool capabilities.

Configuration management of the model is essential. The model should evolve from baseline to baseline as it develops in the AD phase, and enforcement of procedures for the identification, change control and status accounting of the model are necessary. In large projects, configuration management tools should be used for the management of the model database.

4.3 TOOLS FOR ARCHITECTURAL DESIGN SPECIFICATION

A word processor or text processor should be used. Tools for the creation of paragraphs, sections, headers, footers, tables of contents and indexes all ease the production of a document. A spelling checker is desirable. An outliner may be found useful for creation of sub-headings, for viewing the document at different levels of detail and for rearranging the document. The ability to handle diagrams is very important.

Documents invariably go through many drafts as they are created, reviewed and modified. Revised drafts should include change bars. Document-comparison programs, which can mark changed text automatically, are invaluable for easing the review process.

Tools for communal preparation of documents are now beginning to be available, allowing many authors to comment and add to a single document.

CHAPTER 5
THE ARCHITECTURAL DESIGN DOCUMENT

5.1 INTRODUCTION

The ADD defines the framework of the solution. The ADD must be an output from the AD phase (AD19). The ADD must be sufficiently detailed to allow the project leader to draw up a detailed implementation plan and to control the overall project during the remaining development phases (AD23). It should be detailed enough to define the integration tests. Components (especially interfaces) should be defined in sufficient detail so that programmers, or teams of programmers, can work independently. The ADD is incomplete if programmers have to make decisions that affect programmers working on other components. Provided it meets these goals, the smaller the ADD, the more readable and reviewable it is.

The ADD should:
- avoid extensive specification of module processing (this is done in the DD phase);
- not cover the project management, configuration management, verification and quality assurance aspects (which are covered by the SPMP, SCMP, SVVP and SQAP).

Only the selected design approach should be reflected in the ADD (AD05). Descriptions of options and analyses of trade-offs should be archived by the project and reviewed in the Project History Document (PHD).

5.2 STYLE

The style of an ADD should be systematic and rigorous. The ADD should be clear, consistent and modifiable.

5.2.1 Clarity

An ADD is clear if each component has definite inputs, outputs, function and relationships to other components. The natural language used in an ADD should be shared by all members of the development team.

Explanatory text, written in natural language, should be included to enable review by those not familiar with the design method.

5.2.2 Consistency

The ADD must be consistent (AD22). There are several types of inconsistency:
- different terms used for the same thing;
- the same term used for different things;

- incompatible activities happening simultaneously;
- activities happening in the wrong order;
- using two different components to perform the same function.

Where a term could have multiple meanings, a single meaning for the term should be defined in a glossary, and only that meaning should be used throughout.

Duplication and overlap lead to inconsistency. If the same functional requirement can be traced to more than one component, this will be a clue to inconsistency. Methods and tools help consistency to be achieved.

5.2.3 Modifiability

An ADD is modifiable if design changes can be documented easily, completely and consistently.

5.3 EVOLUTION

The ADD should be put under change control by the developer at the start of the Detailed Design Phase. New components may need to be added and old components modified or deleted. If the ADD is being developed by a team of people, the control of the document may be started at the beginning of the AD phase.

The Software Configuration Management Plan defines a formal change process to identify, control, track and report projected changes, as soon as they are identified. Approved changes in components must be recorded in the ADD by inserting document change records and a document status sheet at the start of the ADD.

5.4 RESPONSIBILITY

The developer is responsible for producing the ADD. The developer should nominate people with proven design and implementation skills to write it.

5.5 MEDIUM

The ADD is usually a paper document. It may be distributed electronically when participants have access to the necessary equipment.

5.6 CONTENT

The ADD must define the major software components and the interfaces between them (AD17). Components may be systems, subsystems, data stores, components, programs and processes. The types of software components will reflect the AD method used. At the end of the AD phase the descriptions of the components are assembled into an ADD.

The ADD must be compiled according to the table of contents provided in Appendix C of *Software Engineering Standards* (AD24). This table of contents is derived from ANSI/IEEE Std 1016-1987 'Recommended Practice for Software Design Descriptions' [Ref. 17]. This standard defines a Software Design Description as a 'representation or model of the software system to be created. The model should provide the precise design information needed for the planning, analysis and implementation of the software system'. The ADD should be such a Software Design Description.

References should be given where appropriate, but an ADD should not refer to documents that follow it in the *Software Engineering Standards* life cycle. An ADD should contain no TBCs or TBDs by the time of the Architectural Design Review.

Relevant material unsuitable for inclusion in the contents list should be inserted in additional appendices. If there is no material for a section then the phrase 'Not Applicable' should be inserted and the section numbering preserved.

Service Information:
a - Abstract
b - Table of Contents
c - Document Status Sheet
d - Document Change Records made since last issue

1 INTRODUCTION[2]
    1.1 Purpose
    1.2 Scope
    1.3 Definitions, acronyms and abbreviations
    1.4 References
    1.5 Overview

2 SYSTEM OVERVIEW

3 SYSTEM CONTEXT
    3.n External interface definition

4 SYSTEM DESIGN
    4.1 Design method
    4.2 Decomposition description

5 COMPONENT DESCRIPTION
    5.n [Component identifier]
        5.n.1 Type
        5.n.2 Purpose
        5.n.3 Function
        5.n.4 Subordinates
        5.n.5 Dependencies
        5.n.6 Interfaces
        5.n.7 Resources
        5.n.8 References
        5.n.9 Processing
        5.n.10 Data

---

[2] The Architectural Design Document contents lists is based upon extracts from IEEE Std 1016-1987, IEEE Recommended Practice for Software Design Descriptions, copyright © 1987 by the Institute for Electrical and Electronic Engineers Inc. The IEEE disclaims any responsibility or liability resulting from the placement and use in this publication. Information is reprinted with the permission of the IEEE.

6 FEASIBILITY AND RESOURCE ESTIMATES

7 SOFTWARE REQUIREMENTS VS COMPONENTS TRACEABILITY MATRIX

5.6.1 ADD/1 INTRODUCTION

This section should provide an overview of the entire document and a description of the scope of the software.

5.6.1.1 ADD/1.1 Purpose (of the document)

This section should:
   (1) describe the purpose of the particular ADD;
   (2) specify the intended readership of the ADD.

5.6.1.2 ADD/1.2 Scope (of the software)

This section should:
   (1) identify the software products to be produced;
   (2) explain what the proposed software will do (and will not do, if necessary);
   (3) define relevant benefits, objectives and goals as precisely as possible;
   (4) be consistent with similar statements in higher-level specifications, if they exist.

5.6.1.3 ADD/1.3 Definitions, acronyms and abbreviations

This section should define all terms, acronyms and abbreviations used in the ADD, or refer to other documents where the definitions can be found.

5.6.1.4 ADD/1.4 References

This section should list all the applicable and reference documents, identified by title, author and date. Each document should be marked as applicable or reference. If appropriate, report number, journal name and publishing organisation should be included.

5.6.1.5 ADD/1.5 Overview (of the document)

This section should:
   (1) describe what the rest of the ADD contains;
   (2) explain how the ADD is organised.
   This section is not included in the table of contents provided in *Software Engineering Standards*, and is therefore optional.

5.6.2 ADD/2 SYSTEM OVERVIEW

This section should briefly introduce to the system context and design, and discuss the background to the project.
   This section may summarise the costs and benefits of the selected architecture, and may refer to trade-off studies and prototyping exercises.

5.6.3 ADD/3 SYSTEM CONTEXT

This section should define all the external interfaces (AD18). This discussion should be based on a system block diagram or context diagram to illustrate the relationship between this system and other systems.

5.6.4 ADD/4 SYSTEM DESIGN

5.6.4.1 ADD/4.1 Design Method

The design method used should be named and referenced. A brief description may be added to aid readers not familiar with the method. Any deviations and extensions of the method should be explained and justified.

5.6.4.2 ADD/4.2 Decomposition description

The software components should be summarised. This should be presented as structure charts or object diagrams showing the hierarchy, control flow (AD14) and data flow between the components.

Components can be organised in various ways to provide the views needed by different members of the development organisation. ANSI/IEEE 1016-1987 describes three possible ways of presenting the software design. They are the 'Decomposition View', the 'Dependency View' and the 'Interface View'. Ideally, all views should be provided.

The Decomposition View shows the component breakdown. It defines the system using one or more of the identity, type, purpose, function and subordinate parts of the component description. Suitable methods are tables listing component identities with a one-line summary of their purpose. The intended readership consists of managers, for work package definition, and development personnel, to trace or cross-reference components and functions.

The Dependency View emphasises the relationships among the components. It should define the system using one or more of the identity, type, purpose, dependency and resource parts of the component description. Suitable methods of presentation are Structure Charts and Object Diagrams. The intended readership of this description consists of managers, for the formulation of the order of implementation of work packages, and maintenance personnel, who need to assess the impact of design changes.

The Interface View emphasises the functionality of the components and their interfaces. It should define the system using one or more of the identity, functions and interface parts of the component description. Suitable methods of presentation are interface files and parameter tables. The intended readership of this description comprises designers, programmers and testers, who need to know how to use the components in the system.

5.6.5 ADD/3 COMPONENT DESCRIPTION

The descriptions of the components should be laid out hierarchically. There should be subsections dealing with the following aspects of each component:

5.n Component identifier
    5.n.1 Type
    5.n.2 Purpose
    5.n.3 Function
    5.n.4 Subordinates
    5.n.5 Dependencies
    5.n.6 Interfaces
    5.n.7 Resources
    5.n.8 References
    5.n.9 Processing
    5.n.10 Data

The number 'n' should relate to the place of the component in the hierarchy.

5.6.5.1 ADD/5.n Component Identifier

Each component should have a unique identifier (SCM06) for effective configuration management. The component should be named according to the rules of the programming language or operating system to be used. Where possible, a hierarchical naming scheme should be used that identifies the parent of the component (e.g. ParentName_ChildName)

The identifier should reflect the purpose and function of the component and be brief yet be meaningful. If abbreviation is necessary, abbreviations should be applied consistently and without ambiguity. Abbreviations should be documented. Component identifiers should be mutually consistent (e.g. if there is a routine called READ_RECORD then one might expect a routine called WRITE_RECORD, not RECORD_WRITING_ROUTINE).

5.6.5.1.1 ADD/5.n.1 Type

Component type should be defined by stating its logical and physical characteristics. The logical characteristics should be defined by stating the package, library or class that the component belongs to. The physical characteristics should be defined by stating the type of component, using the implementation terminology (e.g. task, subroutine, subprogram, package, file).

The contents of some component description sections depend on the component type. For the purpose of this guide the categories: executable (i.e. contains computer instructions) or non-executable (i.e. contains only data) are used.

5.6.5.1.2 ADD/5.n.2 Purpose

The purpose of a component should be defined by tracing it to the software requirements that it implements.

Backwards traceability depends upon each component description explicitly referencing the requirements that justify its existence.

5.6.5.1.3 ADD/5.n.3 Function

The function of a component must be defined in the ADD (AD07). This should be done by stating what the component does.

The function description depends upon the component type. Therefore it may be a description of:

- the process;
- the information stored or transmitted.

Process descriptions may use such techniques as Structured English, Precondition-Postcondition specifications and State-Transition Diagrams.

5.6.5.1.4 ADD/5.n.4 Subordinates

The subordinates of a component should be defined by listing the immediate children. The subordinates of a module are the modules that are 'called by' it. The subordinates of a database could be the files that 'compose' it. The subordinates of an object are the objects that are 'used by' it.

5.6.5.1.5 ADD/5.n.5 Dependencies

The dependencies of a component should be defined by listing the constraints placed upon its use by other components. For example:

- 'what operations have to have taken place before this component is called?'
- 'what operations are excluded when this operation is taking place?'
- 'what components have to be executed after this one?'.

5.6.5.1.6 ADD/5.n.6 Interfaces

Both control flow and data flow aspects of an interface need to be specified in the ADD for each 'executable' component. Data aspects of 'non-executable' components should be defined in Subsection 10.

The control flow to and from a component should be defined in terms of how execution of the component is to be started (e.g. subroutine call) and how it is to be terminated (e.g. return). This may be implicit in the definition of the type of component, and a description may not be necessary. Control flows may also take place during execution (e.g. interrupt) and these should be defined, if they exist.

The data flow input to and output from each component must be detailed in the ADD (AD06, AD08, AD09). Data structures should be identified that:

- are associated with the control flow (e.g. call argument list);
- interface components through common data areas and files.

One component's input may be another's output and to avoid duplication of interface definitions, specific data components should be defined and described separately (e.g. files, messages). The interface definition should only identify the data component and not define its contents.

The interfaces of a component should be defined by explaining 'how' the component interacts with the components that use it. This can be done by describing the mechanisms for:

- invoking or interrupting the component's execution;
- communicating through parameters, common data areas or messages.

If a component interfaces to components in the same system then the interface description should be defined in the ADD. If a component interfaces to components in other systems, the interface description should be defined in an Interface Control Document (ICD).

5.6.5.1.7 ADD/5.n.7 Resources

The resources a component requires should be defined by itemising what the component needs from its environment to perform its function. Items that are part of the component interface are excluded. Examples of resources that might be needed by a component are displays, printers and buffers.

5.6.5.1.8 ADD/5.n.8 References

Explicit references should be inserted where a component description uses or implies material from another document.

5.6.5.1.9 ADD/5.n.9 Processing

The processing a component needs to do should be defined by summarising the control and data flow within it. For some kinds of component (e.g. files) there is no such flow. In practice it is often difficult to separate the description of function from the description of processing. Therefore a detailed description of function can compensate for a lack of detail in the specification of the processing. Techniques of process specification more oriented towards software design are Program Design Language, Pseudo Code and Flow Charts.

The ADD should not provide a complete, exhaustive specification of the processing to be done by bottom-level components; this should be done in the Detailed Design and Production Phase. The processing of higher-level components, especially the control flow, data flow and state transitions should be specified.

Software constraints may specify that the processing be performed by means of a particular algorithm (which should be stated or referenced).

5.6.5.1.10 ADD/5.n.10 Data

The data internal to a component should be defined. The amount of detail required depends strongly on the type of component. The logical and physical data structure of files that interface major components should be defined in detail. The specification of the data internal to a major component should be postponed to the DD phase.

Data structure definitions must include the:
- description of each element (e.g. name, type, dimension) (AD10);
- relationships between the elements (i.e. the structure, AD11);
- range of possible values of each element (AD12);
- initial values of each element (AD13).

5.6.6 ADD/6 FEASIBILITY AND RESOURCE ESTIMATES

This section should contain a summary of the computer resources required to build, operate and maintain the software (AD15).

5.6.7 ADD/7 SOFTWARE REQUIREMENTS TRACEABILITY MATRIX

This section should contain a table that summarises how each software requirement has been met in the ADD (AD21). The tabular format permits one-to-one and one-to-many relationships to be shown. A template is provided in Appendix D.

CHAPTER 6
LIFE CYCLE MANAGEMENT ACTIVITIES

6.1 INTRODUCTION

AD phase activities must be carried out according to the plans defined in the SR phase (AD01). These are:

- Software Project Management Plan for the AD phase (SPMP/AD);
- Software Configuration Management Plan for the AD phase (SCMP/AD);
- Software Verification and Validation Plan for the AD phase (SVVP/AD);
- Software Quality Assurance Plan for the AD phase (SQAP/AD).

Progress against plans should be continuously monitored by project management and documented at regular intervals in progress reports.

Plans of DD phase activities must be drawn up in the AD phase. These plans should cover project management, configuration management, verification and validation, quality assurance and integration tests.

6.2 PROJECT MANAGEMENT PLAN FOR THE DD PHASE

By the end of the AD review, the DD phase section of the SPMP (SPMP/DD) must be produced (SPM08). The SPMP/DD describes, in detail, the project activities to be carried out in the DD phase.

An estimate of the total project cost must be included in the SPMP/DD (SPM09). Every effort should be made to arrive at a total project cost estimates with an accuracy better than 10%. The SPMP/DD must contain a Work-Breakdown Structure (WBS) that is directly related to the breakdown of the software into components (SPM10).

The SPMP/DD must contain a planning network showing the relationships between the coding testing and integration activities (SPM11). No software production packages in the SPMP/DD must last longer than 1 man-month (SPM12).

Cost estimation methods can be used to estimate the total number of man-months and the implementation schedule needed for the DD phase. Estimates of the number of lines of code, supplemented by many other parameters, are the usual input. When properly calibrated (using data collected from previous projects done by the same organisation), such models can yield predictions that are 20% accurate 68% of the time (TRW's initial calibration of the COCOMO model). Even if cost models are used, technical knowledge and experience gained on similar projects need to be used to arrive at the desired 10% accurate cost estimate.

Guidance on writing the SPMP/DD is provided in the *Guide to Software Project Management.*

6.3 CONFIGURATION MANAGEMENT PLAN FOR THE DD PHASE

During the AD phase, the DD phase section of the SCMP (SCMP/DD) must be produced (SCM46). The SCMP/DD must cover the configuration management procedures for documentation, deliverable code, and any CASE tool outputs or prototype code, to be produced in the DD phase (SCM47).

Guidance on writing the SCMP/DD is provided in the *Guide to Software Configuration Management*.

6.4 VERIFICATION AND VALIDATION PLAN FOR THE DD PHASE

During the AD phase, the DD phase section of the SVVP (SVVP/DD) must be produced (SVV15). The SVVP/DD must define how the DDD and the code are evaluated by defining the review and traceability procedures. It may include specifications of the tests to be performed with prototypes.

The planning of the integration tests should proceed in parallel with the definition of the architectural design.

Guidance on writing the SVVP/DD is provided in the *Guide to Software Verification and Validation*.

6.5 QUALITY ASSURANCE PLAN FOR THE DD PHASE

During the AD phase, the DD phase section of the SQAP (SQAP/DD) must be produced (SQA08). The SQAP/DD must describe, in detail, the quality assurance activities to be carried out in the DD phase (SQA09).

SQA activities include monitoring the following activities:

- management;
- documentation;
- standards, practices, conventions and metrics;
- reviews and audits;
- testing activities;
- problem reporting and corrective action;
- tools, techniques and methods;
- code and media control;
- supplier control;
- record collection, maintenance and retention;
- training;
- risk management.

Guidance on writing the SQAP/AD is provided in *Guide to Software Quality Assurance*.

The SQAP/DD should take account of all the software requirements related to quality, in particular:

- quality requirements;
- reliability requirements;
- maintainability requirements;
- safety requirements;
- verification requirements;

- acceptance-testing requirements.

The level of monitoring planned for the AD phase should be appropriate to the requirements and the criticality of the software. Risk analysis should be used to target areas for detailed scrutiny.

6.6 INTEGRATION TEST PLANS

The developer must construct an integration test plan in the AD phase and document it in the SVVP (SVV17). This plan should define the scope, approach, resources and schedule of integration testing activities.

Specific tests for each software requirement are not formulated until the DD phase. The Integration Test Plan should deal with the general issues, for example:

- where will the integration tests be done?
- who will attend?
- who will carry them out?
- are tests needed for all software requirements?
- must any special test software be used?
- how long is the integration testing programme expected to last?
- are simulations necessary?

Guidance on writing the SVVP/IT is provided in the *Guide to Software Verification and Validation*.

APPENDIX A
GLOSSARY

A.1 LIST OF ACRONYMS

Terms used in this document are consistent with *Software Engineering Standards* [Ref. 1] and ANSI/IEEE Std 610.12-1990 [Ref. 2].

AD	Architectural Design
ADD	Architectural Design Document
AD/R	Architectural Design Review
ANSI	American National Standards Institute
BSSC	Board for Software Standardisation and Control
CASE	Computer Aided Software Engineering
DD	Detailed Design and production
DFD	Data Flow Diagram
ESA	European Space Agency
GUI	Graphical User Interface
HOOD	Hierarchical Object Oriented Design
IEEE	Institute of Electrical and Electronics Engineers
ISO	International Standards Organisation
ICD	Interface Control Document
JSD	Jackson System Development
MTBF	Mean Time Between Failures
MTTR	Mean Time To Repair
OOA	Object-Oriented Analysis
OOD	Object-Oriented Design
OSI	Open Systems Interconnection
PA	Product Assurance
PSS	Procedures, Specifications and Standards
QA	Quality Assurance
RID	Review Item Discrepancy
SADT	Structured Analysis and Design Technique
SCM	Software Configuration Management
SCMP	Software Configuration Management Plan
SPM	Software Project Management
SPMP	Software Project Management Plan
SQA	Software Quality Assurance
SQAP	Software Quality Assurance Plan

SR	Software Requirements
SRD	Software Requirements Document
SR/R	Software Requirements Review
SSADM	Structured Systems Analysis and Design Methodology
ST	System Test
SUM	Software User Manual
SVVP	Software Verification and Validation Plan
TBC	To Be Confirmed
TBD	To Be Defined
UR	User Requirements
URD	User Requirements Document
UR/R	User Requirements Review

APPENDIX B
REFERENCES

1. Software Engineering Standards, C.Mazza, J.Fairclough, B.Melton, D.dePablo, A.Scheffer, R.Stevens, 1994.
2. IEEE Standard Glossary for Software Engineering Terminology, ANSI/IEEE Std 610.12-1990.
3. Structured Analysis (SA): A Language for Communicating Ideas, D.T.Ross, IEEE Transactions on Software Engineering, Vol SE-3, No 1, January 1977.
4. SSADM Version 4, NCC Blackwell Publications, 1991
5. The STARTs Guide - a guide to methods and software tools for the construction of large real-time systems, NCC Publications, 1987.
6. Structured Rapid Prototyping, J.Connell and L.Shafer, Yourdon Press, 1989.
7. Structured Analysis and System Specification, T.DeMarco, Yourdon Press, 1978.
8. IEEE Standard for Software Reviews and Audits, IEEE Std 1028-1988.
9. Structured Systems Analysis and Design Methodology, G.Cutts, Paradigm, 1987.
10. Systematic Software Development Using VDM, C.B.Jones, Prentice-Hall, 1986.
11. Structured Development for Real-Time Systems, P.T.Ward & S.J.Mellor, Yourdon Press, 1985. (Three Volumes).
12. System Development, M.Jackson, Prentice-Hall, 1983.
13. Object Oriented Development, G.Booch, in IEEE Transactions on Software Engineering, VOL SE-12, February 1986.
14. Hood Reference Manual, Issue 3, Draft C, Reference WME/89-173/JB HOOD Working Group, ESTEC, 1989.
15. The Practical Guide to Structured Systems Design, M.Page-Jones, Yourdon Press, 1980.
16. IEEE Recommended Practice for Software Design Descriptions, ANSI/IEEE Std 1016-1987.
17. IEEE Standard Dictionary of Measures to Produce Reliable Software, IEEE Std 982.1-1988.
18. IEEE Guide for the Use of IEEE Standard Dictionary of Measures to Produce Reliable Software, IEEE Std 982.2-1988.
19. Structured Design: Fundamentals of a Discipline of Computer Program and Systems Design, E. Yourdon and L. Constantine, Yourdon Press, 1978.
20. Structured Analysis and System Specification, T. DeMarco, Yourdon Press, 1978.
21. Principles of Program Design, M. Jackson, Academic Press, 1975.
22. Software Engineering with Ada, second edition, G.Booch, Benjamin/Cummings Publishing Company Inc, 1986.

23. A complexity Measure, T.J.McCabe, IEEE Transactions on Software Engineering, Vol. SE-2, No. 4, December 1976.

24. Object-Oriented Design, P. Coad and E. Yourdon, Prentice-Hall, 1991.

25. The Object-Oriented Structured Design Notation for Software Design Representation, A.I. Wasserman, P.A. Pircher and R.J. Muller, Computer, March 1990.

26. Object-Oriented Design with Applications, G. Booch, Benjamin- Cummings, 1991.

27. Object-Oriented Modeling and Design, J.Rumbaugh, M.Blaha, W.Premerlani, F.Eddy and W.Lorensen, Prentice-Hall, 1991

28. Object-Oriented Systems Analysis - Modeling the World in Data, S.Shlaer and S.J.Mellor, Yourdon Press, 1988

29. Object Lifecycles - Modeling the World in States, S.Shlaer and S.J.Mellor, Yourdon Press, 1992.

APPENDIX C
MANDATORY PRACTICES

This appendix is repeated from *Software Engineering Standards*, appendix D.4

AD01   AD phase activities shall be carried out according to the plans defined in the SR phase.

AD02   A recognised method for software design shall be adopted and applied consistently in the AD phase.

AD03   The developer shall construct a 'physical model', which describes the design of the software using implementation terminology.

AD04   The method used to decompose the software into its component parts shall permit a top-down approach.

AD05   Only the selected design approach shall be reflected in the ADD.
        For each component the following information shall be detailed in the ADD:

AD06   •   data input;

AD07   •   functions to be performed;

AD08   •   data output.

AD09   Data structures that interface components shall be defined in the ADD.
        Data structure definitions shall include the:

AD10   •   description of each element (e.g. name, type, dimension);

AD11   •   relationships between the elements (i.e. the structure);

AD12   •   range of possible values of each element;

AD13   •   initial values of each element.

AD14   The control flow between the components shall be defined in the ADD.

AD15   The computer resources (e.g. CPU speed, memory, storage, system software) needed in the development environment and the operational environment shall be estimated in the AD phase and defined in the ADD.

AD16   The outputs of the AD phase shall be formally reviewed during the Architectural Design Review.

AD17   The ADD shall define the major components of the software and the interfaces between them.

AD18   The ADD shall define or reference all external interfaces.

AD19   The ADD shall be an output from the AD phase.

AD20   The ADD shall be complete, covering all the software requirements described in the SRD.

AD21   A table cross-referencing software requirements to parts of the architectural design shall be placed in the ADD.

AD22   The ADD shall be consistent.

AD23   The ADD shall be sufficiently detailed to allow the project leader to draw up a detailed implementation plan and to control the overall project during the remaining development phases.

AD24   The ADD shall be compiled according to the table of contents provided in Appendix C.

APPENDIX D
REQUIREMENTS TRACEABILITY MATRIX

REQUIREMENTS TRACEABILITY MATRIX **ADD TRACED TO SRD**		DATE: <YY-MM-DD> PAGE 1 OF <nn>
PROJECT: <TITLE OF PROJECT>		
SRD IDENTIFIER	ADD IDENTIFIER	SOFTWARE REQUIREMENT

APPENDIX E
CASE TOOL SELECTION CRITERIA

This appendix lists selection criteria for the evaluation of CASE tools for building a physical model.

The tool should:

1. enforce the rules of each method it supports;
2. allow the user to construct diagrams according to the conventions of the selected method;
3. support consistency checking (e.g. balancing);
4. store the model description;
5. be able to store multiple model descriptions;
6. support top-down decomposition (e.g. by allowing the user to create and edit lower-level component designs by 'exploding' those in a higher-level diagram);
7. minimise line-crossing in a diagram;
8. minimise the number of keystrokes required to add a symbol;
9. allow the user to 'tune' a method by adding and deleting rules;
10. support concurrent access by multiple users;
11. permit access to the model database (usually called a repository) to be controlled;
12. permit reuse of all or part of existing model descriptions, to allow the bottom-up integration of models (e.g. rather than decompose a component such as 'READ_ORBIT_FILE', it should be possible to import a specification of this component from another model);
13. support document generation according to user-defined templates and formats;
14. support traceability of software requirements to components and code;
15. support conversion of a diagram from one style to another (e.g. Yourdon to SADT and vice-versa);
16. allow the user to execute the model (to verify real-time behaviour by animation and simulation);
17. support all configuration management functions (e.g. to identify items, control changes to them, storage of baselines etc);
18. keep the users informed of changes when part of a design is concurrently accessed;
19. support consistency checking in any of three checking modes, selectable by the user:
    - interpreter, i.e. check each change as it is made; reject any illegal changes;
    - compiler, i.e. accept all changes and check them all at once at the end of the session;

- monitor, i.e. check each change as it is made; issue warnings about illegal changes.

20. link the checking mode with the access mode when there are multiple users, so that local changes can be done in any checking mode, but changes that have non-local effects are checked immediately and rejected if they are in error;

21. support scoping and overloading of data item names;

22. support the production of module shells from component specifications;

23. support the insertion and editing of a description of the processing in the module shell;

24. provide context-dependent help facilities;

25. make effective use of colour to allow parts of a display to be easily distinguished;

26. have a consistent user interface;

27. permit direct hardcopy output;

28. permit data to be imported from other CASE tools;

29. permit the exporting of data in standard graphics file formats (e.g. CGM);

30. permit the exporting of data to external word-processing applications and editors;

31. describe the format of the tool database or repository in the user documentation, so that users can manipulate the database by means of external software and packages (e.g. tables of ASCII data).

APPENDIX F
INDEX

Guide
to the software
detailed design and
production
phase

TABLE OF CONTENTS

CHAPTER 1
INTRODUCTION

1.1 PURPOSE

Software Engineering Standards [Ref 1] defines the fourth phase of the software life cycle to be the 'Detailed Design and Production Phase' (DD phase). Activities, products and readiness for delivery are examined in the 'DD review' (DD/R) at the end of the phase.

The DD phase can be called the 'implementation phase' of the life cycle because the developers code, document and test the software after detailing the design specified in the ADD.

This document provides guidance on how to produce the Detailed Design Document (DDD), the code and the Software User Manual (SUM). This document should be read by all active participants in the DD phase, e.g. designers, programmers, project managers and product assurance personnel.

1.2 OVERVIEW

Chapter 2 discusses the DD phase. Chapters 3 and 4 discuss methods and tools for detailed design and production. Chapter 5 and 6 describe how to write the DDD and SUM, starting from the templates. Chapter 7 summarises the life cycle management activities, which are discussed at greater length in other guides.

All the mandatory practices in *Software Engineering Standards* relevant to the DD phase are repeated in this document. The identifier of the practice is added in parentheses to mark a repetition. No new mandatory practices are defined.

CHAPTER 2
THE DETAILED DESIGN AND PRODUCTION PHASE

2.1 INTRODUCTION

Software design is the 'process of defining the architecture, components, interfaces, and other characteristics of a system or component' [Ref 2]. Detailed design is the process of defining the lower-level components, modules and interfaces. Production is the process of:

- programming - coding the components;
- integrating - assembling the components;
- verifying - testing modules, subsystems and the full system.

The physical model outlined in the AD phase is extended to produce a structured set of component specifications that are consistent, coherent and complete. Each specification defines the functions, inputs, outputs and internal processing of the component.

The software components are documented in the Detailed Design Document (DDD). The DDD is a comprehensive specification of the code. It is the primary reference for maintenance staff in the Transfer phase (TR phase) and the Operations and Maintenance phase (OM phase).

The main outputs of the DD phase are the:

- source and object code;
- Detailed Design Document (DDD);
- Software User Manual (SUM);
- Software Project Management Plan for the TR phase (SPMP/TR);
- Software Configuration Management Plan for the TR phase (SCMP/TR);
- Software Quality Assurance Plan for the TR phase (SQAP/TR);
- Acceptance Test specification (SVVP/AT).

Progress reports, configuration status accounts, and audit reports are also outputs of the phase. These should always be archived.

The detailed design and production of the code is the responsibility of the developer. Engineers developing systems with which the software interfaces may be consulted during this phase. User representatives and operations personnel may observe system tests.

DD phase activities must be carried out according to the plans defined in the AD phase (DD01). Progress against plans should be continuously monitored by project management and documented at regular intervals in progress reports.

Figure 2.1 is an ideal representation of the flow of software products in the DD phase. The reader should be aware that some DD phase activities can occur in parallel as separate teams build the major components and integrate them. Teams may progress at different rates; some may be engaged in coding and testing while others are designing. The following subsections discuss the activities shown in Figure 2.1.

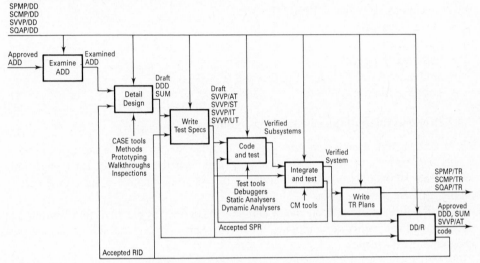

Figure 2.1: DD phase activities

2.2 EXAMINATION OF THE ADD

If the developers have not taken part in the AD/R they should examine the ADD and confirm that it is understandable. Developers should consult the *Guide to the Software Architectural Design Phase* for help on ADDs. The examination should be carried out by staff familiar with the architectural design method. The developers should also confirm that adequate technical skill is available to produce the outputs of the DD phase.

2.3 DETAILED DESIGN

Design standards must be set at the start of the DD phase by project management to coordinate the collective efforts of the team. This is especially necessary when development team members are working in parallel.

The developers must first complete the top-down decomposition of the software started in the AD phase (DD02) and then outline the processing to be carried out by each component. Developers must continue the structured approach and not introduce unnecessary complexity. They must build defences against likely problems.

Developers should verify detailed designs in design reviews, level by level. Review of the design by walkthrough or inspection before coding is a more efficient way of eliminating design errors than testing.

The developer should start the production of the user documentation early in the DD phase. This is especially important when the HCI component is significantly large: writing the SUM forces the developer to keep the user's view continuously in mind.

The following subsections discuss these activities in more detail.

2.3.1 Definition of design standards

Wherever possible, standards and conventions used in the AD phase should be carried over into the DD phase. They should be documented in part one of the DDD. Standards and conventions should be defined for:

- design methods;
- documentation;
- naming components;
- Computer Aided Software Engineering (CASE) tools;
- error handling.

2.3.2 Decomposition of the software into modules

As in architectural design, the first stage of detailed design is to define the functions, inputs and outputs of each software component. Whereas architectural design only considered the major, top-level components, this stage of detailed design must specify all the software components.

The developer starts with the major components defined in the ADD and continues to decompose them until the components can be expressed as modules in the selected programming languages.

Decomposition should be carried out using the same methods and tools employed in the AD phase. Modelling tools and graphical methods employed in architectural design can still be used.

Component processing is only specified to the level of detail necessary to answer the question: 'is further decomposition necessary?'. Decomposition criteria are:

- will the module have too many statements?
- will the module be too complex?
- does the module have low cohesion?
- does the module have high coupling?
- does the module contain similar processing to other modules?

The *Guide to the Software Architectural Design Phase* discusses complexity, cohesion and coupling.

2.3.3 Reuse of the software

Software reuse questions can arise at all stages of design. In the AD phase decisions may have been taken to reuse software for all or some major components, such as:

- application generators;
- database management systems;
- human-computer interaction utilities;
- mathematical utilities;
- graphical utilities.

In the DD phase developers may have to:

- decide which library modules to use;
- build shells around the library modules to standardise interfaces (e.g. for error handling) and enhance portability;

Defensive design principles have influenced the design of most modern languages. Strong type-checking languages automatically check that the calling data type matches the called data type, for example. Ada goes further and builds range checking into the language. The degree to which a language supports defensive design can be a major factor in its favour.

2.3.6 Optimisation

Conventionally, optimisation means to make the best compromise between opposing tendencies. Improvement in one area is often associated with degradation in another. Software performance is often traded-off against maintainability and portability, for example.

The optimisation process is to:
- define the attributes to change (e.g. execution time);
- measure the attribute values before modifying the software;
- measure the attribute values after modifying the software;
- analyse the change in attribute values before deciding whether to modify the software again.

Optimisation can stop when the goals set in the SRD have been met. Every change has some risk, and the costs and benefits of each change should be clearly defined.

The 'law of diminishing returns' can also be used to decide when to stop optimisation. If there are only slight improvements in the values of attribute values after optimisation, the developers should stop trying to seek improvements.

Failure to get a group of people to agree about the solution to an optimisation problem is itself significant. It means that the attribute is probably optimised, and any improvement in one attribute results in an unacceptable degradation in another.

The structured programming method discourages optimisation because of its effect on reliability and maintainability. Code should be clear and simple, and its optimisation should be left to the compiler. Compilers are more likely to do a better job of optimisation than programmers, because compilers incorporate detailed knowledge of the machine. Often the actual causes of inefficiency are quite different from what programmers might suspect, and can only be revealed with a dynamic analysis tool (see Section 4.3.9).

In summary, developers should define what they are trying to optimise and why, before starting to do it. If in doubt, remember Jackson's two rules of optimisation [Ref. 6]:
- don't do it, but if you must:
- don't do it yet.

2.3.7 Prototyping

Experimental prototyping can be useful for:
- comparing alternative designs;
- checking the feasibility of the design.

The high-level design will normally have been identified during the AD phase. Detailed designs may have to be prototyped in the DD phase to find out which designs best meet the requirements.

The feasibility of a novel design idea should be checked by prototyping. This ensures that an idea not only works, but also that it works well enough to meet non-functional requirements for quality and performance.

2.3.8 Design reviews

Detailed designs should be reviewed top-down, level by level, as they are generated during the DD phase. Reviews may take the form of walkthroughs or inspections. Walkthroughs are useful on all projects for informing and passing on expertise. Inspections are efficient methods for eliminating defects before production begins.

Two types of walkthrough are useful:
- code reading;
- 'what-if?' analysis.

In a code reading, reviews trace the logic of a module from beginning to end. In 'what-if?' analysis, component behaviour is examined for specific inputs.

Static analysis tools evaluate modules without executing them. Static analysis functions are built in to some compilers. Output from static analysis tools may be input to a code review.

When the detailed design of a major component is complete, a critical design review must certify its readiness for implementation (DD10). The project leader should participate in these reviews, with the team leader and team members concerned.

2.3.9 Documentation

The developers must produce the DDD and the SUM. While the ADD specifies tasks, files and programs, the DDD specifies modules. The SUM describes how to use the software, and may be affected by documentation requirements in the SRD.

The recommended approach to module documentation is:
- create the module template to contain headings for the standard DDD entries:

    n Component identifier

    n.1 Type
    n.2 Purpose
    n.3 Function
    n.4 Subordinates
    n.5 Dependencies
    n.6 Interfaces
    n.7 Resources
    n.8 References
    n.9 Processing
    n.10 Data
- detail the design by filling in the sections, with the processing section containing the high-level definition of the processing in a PDL or pseudo-code;
- assemble the completed templates for insertion in the DDD.

A standard module template enables the DDD component specifications to be generated automatically. Tools to extract the module header from the source code and create an entry for the DDD greatly simplify maintenance. When a module is modified, the programmer edits, compiles and verifies the source module, and then runs the tool to generate the new DDD entry.

The SUM contains the information needed by the users of the software to operate it. The SUM should be gradually prepared during the DD phase. The developers should exercise the procedures described in the SUM when testing the software.

2.4 TEST SPECIFICATIONS

The purpose of testing is to prove empirically that the system, or component under test, meets specified requirements. Normally it is not possible to prove by testing that a component contains no errors.

According to Myers, an important aspect of testing is to execute a program with the intention of finding errors [Ref. 14]. Testers should adopt this 'falsificationist' approach because it encourages testers to devise tests that the software fails, not passes. This idea originates from Karl Popper, the influential philosopher who first proposed the 'falsificationist' approach as a scientific method.

Testers must be critical and objective for testing to be effective. On large projects, system and acceptance test specifications should not be written by the analysts, designers and programmers responsible for the SRD, ADD, DDD and code. On small and medium-size projects, it is acceptable for the developer to write the test specifications and for the user or product assurance representatives to review them. Users should run the acceptance tests, not the developers.

2.4.1 Unit test planning

Unit test plans must be generated in the DD phase and documented in the Unit Test section of the Software Verification and Validation Plan (SVVP/UT). The Unit Test Plan should describe the scope, approach and resources required for the unit tests, and take account of the verification requirements in the SRD (see Section 2.5.3 and Chapter 7).

2.4.2 Test designs, test cases and test procedures

The developer must write specifications for the:
- acceptance tests,
- system tests,
- integration tests,
- unit tests

in the DD phase and document them in the SVVP. The specifications should be based on the test plans, and comply with the verification and acceptance testing requirements in the SRD. The specifications should define the:
- test designs (SVV19);
- test cases (SVV20);
- test procedures (SVV21);

see Section 2.6 below and Chapter 7.

When individual modules have been coded and unit tested, developers have to integrate them into larger components, test the larger components, integrate the larger components and so on. Integration is therefore inextricably linked with testing.

The Software Project Management Plan for the DD phase (SPMP/DD) should contain a delivery plan for the software based on the life cycle approach adopted. The delivery plan influences the integration tests defined in the Software Verification and Validation Plan (SVVP/IT). For a given delivery plan, the SVVP/IT should make integration testing efficient by minimising the number of test aids (e.g. drivers and stubs) and test data files required.

2.5 CODING AND UNIT TESTING

Coding is both the final stage of the design process and also the first stage of production. Coding produces modules, which must be unit tested. Unit testing is the second stage of the production process.

2.5.1 Coding

The transition from the detailed design stage to the coding stage comes when the developer begins to write modules that compile in the programming language. This transition is obvious when detailed design has been performed with flowcharts, but is less so when the developer has used a PDL or pseudo-code.

Coding must be based on the principles of:
- structured programming (DD03);
- concurrent production and documentation (DD04).

Every module should be understandable to a reviewer or maintenance programmer, moderately familiar with the programming language and unfamiliar with the program, the compiler and operating system. Understandability can be achieved in a variety of ways:
- including an introductory header for each module;
- declaring all variables;
- documenting all variables;
- using meaningful, unambiguous names;
- avoiding mixing data types;
- avoiding temporary variables;
- using parentheses in expressions;
- laying out code legibly;
- adding helpful comments;
- avoiding obscuring the module logic with diagnostic code;
- adhering to structured programming rules;
- being consistent in the use of the programming language;
- keeping modules short;
- keeping the code simple.

2.5.1.1 Module headers

Each module should have a header that introduces the module. This should include:

- title;
- configuration item identifier (SCM15);
- original author (SCM16);
- creation date (SCM17);
- change history (SCM18).

If tools to support consistency between source code and DDD are available, the introduction should be followed by explanatory comments from the component description in the DDD part 2.

The header usually comes after the module title statement (e.g. SUBROUTINE) and before the variable declarations.

The standard header should be made available so that it can be edited, completed and inserted at the head of each module.

2.5.1.2 Declarations of variables

Programmers should declare the type of all variables, whatever the programming language. The possible values of variables should either be stated in the variable declaration (as in Ada), or documented. Some languages, such as FORTRAN and Prolog, allow variables to be used without explicit declaration of their type.

Programmers using weakly typed languages should declare all variables. Where strong typing is a compiler option, it should always be used (e.g. IMPLICIT NONE in some FORTRAN compilers). Declarations should be grouped, with argument list variables, global variables and local variable declarations clearly separated.

2.5.1.3 Documentation of variables

Programmers should document the meaning of all variables. Documentation should be integrated with the code (e.g. as a comment to the declaration). The possible values of variables should either be stated in the variable declaration (as in Ada), or documented.

2.5.1.4 Names of variables

Finding meaningful names for variables exercises the imagination of every programmer, but it is effort well worth spending. Names should reflect the purpose of the variable. Natural language words should be used wherever possible. Abbreviations and acronyms, if used, should be defined, perhaps as part of the comment to a variable's declaration.

Similar names should be avoided so that a single typing error in the name of a variable does not identify another variable. Another reason not to use similar names is to avoid ambiguity.

2.5.1.5 Mixing data types

Some programming languages prevent the mixing of data types by the strong type checking feature (e.g. Ada). Mixing data types in expressions should always be avoided, even if the programming language allows it (e.g. FORTRAN). Examples of mixing data types include:

- mixing data types in expressions;
- mismatching data types in an argument list;
- equivalencing different data types.

2.5.1.6 Temporary variables

The temptation to define temporary variables to optimise code should be avoided. Although the use of temporary variables can simplify a statement, more statements are required, and more variables have to be declared. The net effect is that the module as a whole appears more complex.

2.5.1.7 Parentheses

Parentheses should be used in programming language expressions to avoid ambiguity, and to help the reader identify the sequences of operations to be performed. They should not be used solely to override the precedence rules of the language.

2.5.1.8 Layout and presentation

The layout of the code should allow the control logic to be easily appreciated. The usual technique is to separate blocks of sequential code from other statements by blank lines, and to indent statements in condition or iteration blocks. Statements that begin and end sequence, iteration and condition constructs should be aligned vertically (e.g. BEGIN... END, DO... ENDDO, and IF... ELSEIF... ELSE... ENDIF). Long statements should be broken and continued on the next line at a clause in the logic, not at the end of the line. There should never be more than one statement on a line.

2.5.1.9 Comments

Comments increase understandability, but they are no substitute for well-designed, well-presented and intelligible code. Comments should be used to explain difficult or unusual parts of the code. Trivial comments should be avoided.

PDL statements and pseudo-code may be preserved in the code as comments to help reviewers. Comments should be clearly distinguishable from code. It is not adequate only to use a language keyword; comments should be well separated from code by means of blank lines, and perhaps written in mixed case (if upper case is used for the code).

2.5.1.10 Diagnostic code

Diagnostic code is often inserted into a module to:

- make assertions about the state of the program;
- display the contents of variables.

Care should be taken to prevent diagnostic code obscuring the module logic. There is often a temptation to remove diagnostic code to present a clean 'final' version of the source code. However routine diagnostic code that allows verification of correct execution can be invaluable in the maintenance phase. It is therefore recommended that routine diagnostic code be commented out or conditionally compiled (e.g. included as 'debug lines'). Ad hoc diagnostic code added to help discover the cause of a particular problem should be removed after the problem has been solved.

2.5.1.11 Structured programming

The rules of structured programming are given in section 3.2.3. These rules should always be followed when a procedural language is used (such as FORTRAN, COBOL, Pascal or Ada). It is easy to break the rules of structured programming when the older procedural languages (e.g. FORTRAN, COBOL) are used, but less so with the more modern ones (Pascal, Ada).

2.5.1.12 Consistent programming

Language constructs should be used consistently. Inconsistency often occurs when modules are developed and maintained by different people. Coding standards can help achieve consistency, but it is not realistic for them to cover every situation. Modifications to the code should preserve the style of the original.

2.5.1.13 Module size

Modules should be so short that the entire module can be seen at once. This allows the structure, and the control logic, to be appreciated easily. The recommended maximum size of modules is about 50 lines, excluding the header and diagnostic code.

2.5.1.14 Code simplicity

Modules should be 'simple'. The principle of 'Occam's razor', (i.e. that an idea should be expressed by means of the minimum number of entities), should be observed in programming. Simplicity can be checked formally by applying complexity measures [Ref. 11]. Simplicity can be checked informally using the rule of seven: the number of separate things that have to be held in mind when examining a part of the module should not exceed seven. Whatever method of evaluation is used, all measurements of simplicity should be confirmed by peer review.

2.5.2 Coding standards

Coding standards should be established for all the languages used, and documented or referenced in the DDD. They should provide rules for:
- presentation, (e.g. header information and comment layout);
- naming programs, subprograms, files, variables and data;
- limiting the size of modules;
- using library routines, especially:
  - operating system routines;
  - commercial library routines (e.g. numerical analysis);
  - project-specific utility routines;
- defining constants;
- defining data types;
- using global data;

- using compiler specific features not in the language standard;
- error handling.

2.5.3 Unit testing

Unit tests verify the design and implementation of all components from the lowest level defined in the detailed design up to the lowest level in the architectural design (normally the task level). Test harnesses, composed of a collection of drivers and stubs, need to be constructed to enable unit testing of modules below the top level.

Unit tests verify that a module is doing what it is supposed to do ('black box' testing), and that it is doing it in the way it was intended ('white box' testing). The traditional technique for white box testing is to insert diagnostic code. Although this may still be necessary for testing real-time behaviour, debuggers are now the preferred tool for white box testing. The usual way to test a new module is to step through a few test cases with the debugger and then to run black box tests for the rest. Later, black box tests are run to fully exercise the module. The input test data should be realistic and sample the range of possibilities. Programmers revert to 'white box' testing mode when they have to debug a problem found in a black box test.

Before a module can be accepted, every statement shall be successfully executed at least once (DD06). Coverage data should be collected during unit tests. Tools and techniques for collecting coverage data are:

- debuggers;
- dynamic analysers;
- diagnostic code.

The inclusion of diagnostics can clutter up the code (see Section 2.5.1.10) and debuggers and dynamic analysers are much preferable. Coverage should be documented in a debug log, a coverage report, or a printout produced by the diagnostic code.

Unit testing is normally carried out by individuals or teams responsible for producing the component.

Unit test plans, test designs, test cases, test procedures and test reports are documented in the Unit Test section of the Software Verification and Validation Plan (SVVP/UT).

2.6 INTEGRATION AND SYSTEM TESTING

The third stage of the production process is to integrate major components resulting from coding and unit testing into the system. In the fourth stage of production, the fully integrated system is tested.

2.6.1 Integration

Integration is the process of building a software system by combining components into a working entity. Integration of components should proceed in an orderly function-by-function sequence. This allows the operational capabilities of the software to be demonstrated early, and thus gives visible evidence that the project is progressing.

Normally, the first components to be integrated support input and output. Once these components have been integrated and tested, they can be used to test others. Whatever sequence of functions is used, it should minimise the resources required for testing (e.g. testing effort and test tools), while ensuring that all source statements are verified. The Software Verification and Validation Plan section for the integration tests (SVVP/IT) should define the assembly sequence for integration.

Within the functional groupings, components may be integrated and tested top-down or bottom-up. In top-down integration, 'stubs' simulate lower-level modules. In bottom-up integration, 'drivers' simulate the higher-level modules. Stubs and drivers can be used to implement test cases, not just enable the software to be linked and loaded.

The integration process must be controlled by the software configuration management procedures defined in the SCMP (DD05). Good SCM procedures are essential for correct integration. All deliverable code must be identified in a configuration item list (DD12).

2.6.2 Integration testing

Integration testing is done in the DD phase when the major components defined in the ADD are assembled. Integration tests should verify that major components interface correctly.

Integration testing must check that all the data exchanged across an interface comply with the data structure specifications in the ADD (DD07). Integration testing must confirm that the control flows defined in the ADD have been implemented (DD08).

Integration test designs, test cases, test procedures and test reports are documented in the Integration Test section of the Software Verification and Validation Plan (SVVP/IT).

2.6.3 System testing

System testing is the process of testing an integrated software system. This testing can be done in the development or target environment, or a combination of the two. System testing must verify compliance with system objectives, as stated in the SRD (DD09). System testing should include such activities as:

- passing data into the system, correctly processing and outputting it (i.e. end-to-end system tests);
- practice for acceptance tests (i.e. verification that user requirements will be met);
- stress tests (i.e. measurement of performance limits);
- preliminary estimation of reliability and maintainability;
- verification of the Software User Manual.

Trends in the occurrence of defects should be monitored in system tests; the behaviour of such trends is important for the estimation of potential acceptability.

For most embedded systems, as well as systems using special peripherals, it is often useful or necessary to build simulators for the systems with which the software will interface. Such simulators are often required because of:

- late availability of the other systems;
- limited test time with the other systems;
- desire to avoid damaging delicate and/or expensive systems.

Simulators are normally a separate project in themselves. They should be available on time, and certified as identical, from an interface point of view, with the systems they simulate.

System test designs, test cases, test procedures and test reports are documented in the System Test section of the Software Verification and Validation Plan (SVVP/ST).

The SUM is a key document during system (and acceptance) testing. The developers should verify it when testing the system.

2.7 PLANNING THE TRANSFER PHASE

Plans of TR phase activities must be drawn up in the DD phase. Generation of TR phase plans is discussed in Chapter 7. These plans cover project management, configuration management, verification and validation and quality assurance. Outputs are the:

- Software Project Management Plan for the TR phase (SPMP/TR);
- Software Configuration Management Plan for the TR phase (SCMP/TR);
- Software Quality Assurance Plan for the TR phase (SQAP/TR).

2.8 THE DETAILED DESIGN PHASE REVIEW

The development team should hold walkthroughs and internal reviews of a product before its formal review. After production, the DD Review (DD/R) must consider the results of the verification activities and decide whether to transfer the software (DD11). This should be a technical review. The recommended procedure is described in the *Guide to Software Verification and Validation*, which is based closely on the IEEE standard for Technical Reviews [Ref. 4].

Normally, only the code, DDD, SUM and SVVP/AT undergo the full technical review procedure involving users, developers, management and quality assurance staff. The Software Project Management Plan (SPMP/TR), Software Configuration Management Plan (SCMP/TR), and Software Quality Assurance Plan (SQAP/TR) are usually reviewed by management and quality assurance staff only.

In summary, the objective of the DD/R is to verify that:

- the DDD describes the detailed design clearly, completely and in sufficient detail to enable maintenance and development of the software by qualified software engineers not involved in the project;
- modules have been coded according to the DDD;
- modules have been verified according to the unit test specifications in the SVVP/UT;
- major components have been integrated according to the ADD;
- major components have been verified according to the integration test specifications in the SVVP/IT;
- the software has been verified against the SRD according to the system test specifications in the SVVP/ST;
- the SUM explains what the software does and instructs the users how to operate the software correctly;
- the SVVP/AT specifies the test designs, test cases and test procedures so that all the user requirements can be validated.

The DD/R begins when the DDD, SUM, and SVVP, including the test results, are distributed to participants for review. A problem with a document is described in a 'Review Item Discrepancy' (RID) form. A problem with code is described in a Software Problem Report (SPR). Review meetings are then held that have the documents, RIDs and SPRs as input. A review meeting should discuss all the RIDs and SPRs and decide an action for each. The review meeting may also discuss possible solutions to the problems raised by them. The output of the meeting includes the processed RIDs, SPRs and Software Change Requests (SCR).

The DD/R terminates when a disposition has been agreed for all the RIDs. Each DD/R must decide whether another review cycle is necessary, or whether the TR phase can begin.

CHAPTER 3
METHODS FOR DETAILED DESIGN AND PRODUCTION

3.1 INTRODUCTION

This chapter summarises a range of design methods and programming languages. The details about each method and programming language should be obtained from the references. This guide does not make any particular method or language a standard, nor does it define a set of acceptable methods and languages. Each project should examine its needs, choose appropriate methods and programming languages, and justify the selection in the DDD.

3.2 DETAILED DESIGN METHODS

Detailed design first extends the architectural design to the bottom level components. Developers should use the same design method that they employed in the AD phase. The *Guide to the Software Architectural Design Phase*, discusses:
- Structured Design;
- Object Oriented Design;
- Jackson System Development;
- Formal Methods.

The next stage of design is to define module processing. This is done by methods such as:
- flowcharts;
- stepwise refinement;
- structured programming;
- program design languages (PDLs);
- pseudo coding;
- Jackson Structured Programming (JSP).

3.2.1 Flowcharts

A flowchart is 'a control flow diagram in which suitably annotated geometrical figures are used to represent operations, data, equipment, and arrows are used to indicate the sequential flow from one to another' [Ref. 2]. It should represent the processing.

Flowcharts are an old software design method, dating from a time when the only tools available to a software designer were a pencil, paper, and stencil. A box is used to represent process steps and diamonds are used to represent decisions. Arrows are used to represent control flow.

Flowcharts predate structured programming and they are difficult to combine with a stepwise refinement approach. Flowcharts are not well supported by tools and so their maintenance can be a burden. Although directly related to module internals, they cannot be integrated with the code, unlike PDLs and pseudo-code. For all these reasons, flowcharts are no longer a recommended technique for detailed design.

3.2.2 Stepwise refinement

Stepwise refinement is the most common method of detailed design. The guidelines for stepwise refinement are:
- start from functional and interface specifications;
- concentrate on the control flow;
- defer data declarations until the coding phase;
- keep steps of refinement small to ease verification;
- review each step as it is made.

Stepwise refinement is closely associated with structured programming (see Section 3.2.3).

3.2.3 Structured programming

Structured programming is commonly associated with the name of E.W. Dijkstra [Ref. 10]. It is the original 'structured method' and proposed:
- hierarchical decomposition;
- the use of only sequence, selection and iteration constructs;
- avoiding jumps in the program.

Myers emphasises the importance of writing code with the intention of communicating with people instead of machines [Ref.14].

The Structured Programming method emphasises that simplicity is the key to achieving correctness, reliability, maintainability and adaptability. Simplicity is achieved through using only three constructs: sequence, selection and iteration. Other constructs are unnecessary.

Structured programming and stepwise refinement (see Section 3.2.3) are inextricably linked. The goal of refinement is to define a procedure that can be encoded in the sequence, selection and iteration constructs of the selected programming language.

Structured programming also lays down the following rules for module construction:
- each module should have a single entry and exit point;
- control flow should proceed from the beginning to the end;
- related code should be blocked together, not dispersed around the module;
- branching should only be performed under prescribed conditions (e.g. on error).

The use of control structures other than sequence, selection and iteration introduces unnecessary complexity. The whole point about banning 'GOTO' was to prevent the definition of complex control structures. Jumping out of loops causes control structures only to be partially contained within others and makes the code fragile.

Modern block-structured languages, such as Pascal and Ada, implement the principles of structured programming, and enforce the three basic control structures.

Ada supports branching only at the same logical level and not to arbitrary points in the program.

The basic rules of structured programming can lead to control structures being nested too deeply. It can be quite difficult to follow the logic of a module when the control structures are nested more than three or four levels. Three common ways to minimise this problem are to:

- define more lower-level modules;
- put the error-handling code in blocks separate to the main code.
- branching to the end of the module on detecting an error.

3.2.4 Program Design Languages

Program Design Languages (PDL) are used to develop, analyse and document a program design [from Ref. 7]. A PDL is often obtained from the essential features of a high-level programming language. A PDL may contain special constructs and verification protocols.

It is possible to use a complete programming language (e.g. Smalltalk, Ada) as a PDL [Ref. 7]. ANSI/IEEE Std 990-1987 'IEEE Recommended Practice for Ada As a Program Design Language', provides recommendations 'reflecting the state of the art and alternative approaches to good practice for characteristics of PDLs based on the syntax and semantics of Ada' [Ref. 9]. Using Ada as a model, it says that a PDL should provide support for:

- abstraction;
- decomposition;
- information hiding;
- stepwise refinement;
- modularity;
- algorithm design;
- data structure design;
- connectivity;
- adaptability.

Adoption of a standard PDL makes it possible to define interfaces to modelling tools and programming languages. The ability to generate executable statements from a PDL is desirable.

Using an entire language as a PDL increases the likelihood of tool support. However, it is important that a PDL be simple. Developers should establish conventions for the features of a language that are to be used in detailed design.

PDLs are the preferred detailed design method on larger projects, where the existence of standards and the possibility of tool support makes them more attractive than pseudo-code.

3.2.5 Pseudo-code

Pseudo-code is a combination of programming language constructs and natural language used to express a computer program design [Ref. 2]. Pseudo-code is distinguished from the code proper by the presence of statements that do not compile. Such statements only indicate what needs to be coded. They do not affect the module logic.

Pseudo-code is an informal PDL (see Section 3.2.4) that gives the designer greater freedom of expression than a PDL, at the sacrifice of tool support. Pseudo-code is acceptable for small projects and in prototyping, but on larger projects a PDL is definitely preferable.

3.2.6 Jackson Structured Programming

Jackson Structured Programming (JSP) is a program design technique that derives a program's structure from the structures of its input and output data [Ref. 6]. The JSP dictum is that 'the program structure should match the data structure'.

In JSP, the basic procedure is to:
- consider the problem environment and define the structures for the data to be processed;
- form a program structure based on these data structures;
- define the tasks to be performed in terms of the elementary operations available, and allocate each of those operations to suitable components in the program structure.

The elementary operations (i.e. statements in the programming language) must be grouped into one of the three composite operations: sequence, iteration and selection. These are the standard structured programming constructs, giving the technique its name.

JSP is suitable for the detailed design of software that processes sequential streams of data whose structure can be described hierarchically. JSP has been quite successful for information systems applications.

Jackson System Development (JSD) is a descendant of JSP. If used, JSD should be started in the SR phase (see the *Guide to the Software Requirements Definition Phase*).

3.3 PRODUCTION METHODS

Software production involves writing code in a programming language, verifying the code and integrating it with other code to make a working system. This section therefore discusses programming languages and integration methods.

3.3.1 Programming languages

Programming languages are best classified by their features and application domains. Classification by 'generation' (e.g. 3GL, 4GL) can be very misleading because the generation of a language can be completely unrelated to its age (e.g. Ada, LISP). Even so, study of the history of programming languages can give useful insights into the applicability and features of particular languages [Ref. 13].

3.3.1.1 Feature classification

The following classes of programming languages are widely recognised:
- procedural languages;
- object-oriented languages;

- functional languages;
- logic programming languages.

Application-specific languages based on database management systems are not discussed here because of their lack of generality. Control languages, such as those used to command operating systems, are also not discussed for similar reasons.

Procedural languages are sometimes called 'imperative languages' or 'algorithmic languages'. Functional and logic programming languages are often collectively called 'declarative languages' because they allow programmers to declare 'what' is to be done rather than 'how'.

3.3.1.1.1 Procedural languages

A 'procedural language' should support the following features:
- sequence (composition);
- selection (alternation);
- iteration;
- division into modules.

The traditional procedural languages such as COBOL and FORTRAN support these features.

The sequence construct, also known as the composition construct, allows programmers to specify the order of execution. This is trivially done by placing one statement after another, but can imply the ability to branch (e.g. GOTO).

The sequence construct is used to express the dependencies between operations. Statements that come later in the sequence depend on the results of previous statements. The sequence construct is the most important feature of procedural languages, because the program logic is embedded in the sequence of operations, instead of in a data model (e.g. the trees of Prolog, the lists of LISP and the tables of RDBMS languages).

The selection construct, also known as the condition or alternation construct, allows programmers to evaluate a condition and take appropriate action (e.g. IF... THEN and CASE statements).

The iteration construct allows programmers to construct loops (e.g. DO...). This saves repetition of instructions.

The module construct allows programmers to identify a group of instructions and utilise them elsewhere (e.g. CALL...). It saves repetition of instructions and permits hierarchical decomposition.

Some procedural languages also support:
- block structuring;
- strong typing;
- recursion.

Block structuring enforces the structured programming principle that modules should have only one entry point and one exit point. Pascal, Ada and C support block structuring.

Strong typing requires the data type of each data object to be declared [Ref. 2]. This stops operators being applied to inappropriate data objects and the interaction of data objects of incompatible data types (e.g. when the data type of a calling argument does not match the data type of a called argument). Ada and Pascal are strongly typed languages. Strong typing helps a compiler to find errors and to compile efficiently.

Recursion allows a module to call itself (e.g. module A calls module A), permitting greater economy in programming. Pascal, Ada and C support recursion.

3.3.1.1.2 Object-oriented languages

An object-oriented programming language should support all structured programming language features plus:
- inheritance;
- polymorphism;
- messages.

Examples of object-oriented languages are Smalltalk and C++. Reference 14 provides a useful review of object-oriented programming languages.

Inheritance is the technique by which modules can acquire capabilities from higher-level modules, i.e. simply by being declared as members of a class, they have all the attributes and services of that class.

Polymorphism is the ability of a process to work on different data types, or for an entity to refer at runtime to instances of specific classes. Polymorphism cuts down the amount of source code required. Ideally, a language should be completely polymorphic, so the need to formulate sections of code for each data type is unnecessary. Polymorphism implies support for dynamic binding.

Object-oriented programming languages use 'messages' to implement interfaces. A message encapsulates the details of an action to be performed. A message is sent from a 'sender object' to a 'receiver object' to invoke the services of the latter.

3.3.1.1.3 Functional languages

Functional languages, such as LISP and ML, support declarative structuring. Declarative structuring allows programmers to specify only 'what' is required, without stating how it is to be done. It is an important feature, because it means standard processing capabilities are built into the language (e.g. information retrieval) .

With declarative structuring, procedural constructs are unnecessary. In particular, the sequence construct is not used for the program logic. An underlying information model (e.g. a tree or a list) is used to define the logic. If some information is required for an operation, it is automatically obtained from the information model. Although it is possible to make one operation depend on the result of a previous one, this is not the usual style of programming.

Functional languages work by applying operators (functions) to arguments (parameters). The arguments themselves may be functional expressions, so that a functional program can be thought of as a single expression applying one function to another. For example if DOUBLE is the function defined as DOUBLE(X) = X + X, and APPLY is the function that executes another function on each member of a list, then the expression APPLY(DOUBLE, [1, 2, 3]) returns [2, 4, 6].

Programs written in functional languages appear very different from those written in procedural languages, because assignment statements are absent. Assignment is unnecessary in a functional language, because all relationships are implied by the information model.

Functional programs are typically short, clear, and specification-like, and are suitable both for specification and for rapid implementation, typically of design prototypes. Modern compilers have reduced the performance problems of functional languages.

A special feature of functional languages is their inherent suitability for parallel implementation, but in practice this has been slow to materialise.

3.3.1.1.4 Logic programming languages

Logic programming languages implement some form of classical logic. Like functional languages, they have a declarative structure. In addition they support:
- backtracking;
- backward chaining;
- forward chaining.

Prolog is the foremost logic programming language.

Backtracking is the ability to return to an earlier point in a chain of reasoning when an earlier conclusion is subsequently found to be false. It is especially useful when traversing a knowledge tree. Backtracking is incompatible with assignment, since assignment cannot be undone because it erases the contents of variables. Languages which support backtracking are, of necessity, non-procedural.

Backward chaining starts from a hypothesis and reasons backwards to the facts that cause the hypothesis to be true. For example if the fact A and hypothesis B are chained in the expression IF A THEN B, backwards chaining enables the truth of A to be deduced from the truth of B (note that A may be only one of a number of reasons for B to be true).

Forward chaining is the opposite of backward chaining. Forward chaining starts from a collection of facts and reasons forward to a conclusion. For example if the fact X and conclusion Y are chained in the expression IF X THEN Y, forward chaining enables the truth of Y to be deduced from the truth of X.

Forward chaining means that a change to a data item is automatically propagated to all the dependent items. It can be used to support 'data-driven' reasoning.

3.3.1.2 Applications

Commonly recognised application categories for programming languages are:
- real-time systems, including control systems and embedded systems;
- transaction processing, including business and information systems;
- numerical analysis;
- simulation;
- human-computer interaction toolkits (HCI);
- artificial intelligence (AI);
- operating systems.

The application area of language strongly influences the features that are built into it. There is no true 'general purpose language', although some languages are suitable for more than one of the application categories listed above.

3.3.1.3 FORTRAN

FORTRAN was the first widely-used high-level programming language. Its structuring concepts include the now-familiar IF... THEN alternation, DO iteration, primitive data types such as integer, and procedure composition. FORTRAN does not support recursion.

FORTRAN is familiar to generations of programmers who have learned to use it safely. It is a simple language, compared with Ada, and can be compiled rapidly into efficient object code. Compilers are available for most hardware, but these are not always compatible, both because of the addition of machine-dependent features, especially input/output, and because of successive versions of FORTRAN itself. However, good standards exist.

The language includes some features now generally considered risky, such as:

- the GOTO statement, which allows the rules of structured programming to be easily broken;
- the EQUIVALENCE statement, which permits different names to be used for the same storage location;
- local storage, which permits possibly undesired values to be used from a previous call;
- multiple entry and exit points.

FORTRAN remains the primary language for scientific software. Most compilers allow access to operating system features, which, at the expense of portability, allows FORTRAN to be used for developing real-time control systems.

3.3.1.4 COBOL

COBOL remains the most widely used programming language for business and administration systems. As a procedural language it provides the usual sequence, selection (IF... OTHERWISE...) and iteration constructs (PERFORM...). COBOL has powerful data structuring and file handling mechanisms (e.g. hierarchically arranged records, direct access and indexed files). Although its limited data manipulation facilities severely restricts the programmers' ability to construct complex arithmetic expressions, it does allow fixed point arithmetic, necessary for accurate accounting.

COBOL was conceived as the first 'end-user' programming language. It relies on verbal expressions, not symbols (e.g. ADD, SUBTRACT, MULTIPLY, DIVIDE instead of +, -, x and). It has therefore been criticised as forcing a verbose programming style. While this does help make COBOL programs self-explanatory, COBOL programs can still be difficult to understand if they are not well-structured. Jackson's Principles of Program Design are explained with the aid of examples of good and bad COBOL programming [Ref. 6].

3.3.1.5 Pascal

Pascal was conceived by a single designer (Niklaus Wirth) to teach the principles of structured programming. It is accordingly simple and direct, though perhaps idiosyncratic. It contains very clear constructs: IF... THEN... ELSE, WHILE... DO, REPEAT... UNTIL, CASE... OF, and so on. Sets, procedures, functions, arrays, records and other constructs are matched by a versatile and safe data typing system, which permits the compiler to detect many kinds of error.

Wirth omitted several powerful features to make Pascal compile efficiently. For example, functions may not return more than one argument, and this must be a primitive type (although some extensions permit records to be returned). String handling and input/output functions are simplistic and have been the source of portability problems.

Pascal handles recursive data structures, such as lists and trees by means of explicit pointers and (sometimes) variant records. These defeat the type checking mechanism and are awkward to handle.

Pascal is now well-defined in an ISO standard, and is very widely available with good compilers and supporting tools. To a considerable extent the language enforces good programming practice.

3.3.1.6 C

C is a language in the same family as Pascal, with its roots in Algol. The language is less strongly typed than Pascal or Algol. It is easy and efficient to compile, and because of its low-level features, such as bit manipulation, can exploit machine-dependent facilities.

C has a rich variety of operators that allow programmers to adopt a very terse style. This can unfortunately make programs difficult to read and understand. Discipline is required to produce code that is portable and maintainable. Coding standards are especially necessary to make C code consistent and readable.

One advantage of C is its close connection with the Unix operating system, which guarantees C a place as a (or the) major systems programming language. A very wide range of tools and library modules are available for the language.

3.3.1.7 Modula-2

Modula-2 is derived from Pascal. It offers a few new constructs and considerably more power and generality. Two important features are modularity, including incremental compilation, and simulation of concurrency and inter-process communication (via co-routining).

Niklaus Wirth, the inventor of both Pascal and Modula-2, intended that Modula-2 replace Pascal. However Modula-2 is not widely used because of the scarcity of development tools for popular platforms. In contrast to Ada, its main competitor, it is a 'small' language (its compiler is only about 5000 lines, as opposed to Ada's several hundred thousand lines [Ref. 13]).

3.3.1.8 Ada

Ada is a powerful language well suited for the creation of large, reliable and maintainable systems. Unlike most languages it was systematically developed (from a US Department of Defense specification [Ref. 7]). Its many features include tasks (processes) able to communicate asynchronously with each other, strong typing and type checking, and generic programming.

Ada derives ideas from many sources, including several of the languages mentioned here. Although it is a 'large' language, and therefore difficult to master, it can seem relatively familiar to C and Pascal programmers. Applications written in Ada may often be slower than comparable applications written in other languages, perhaps largely due to the immaturity of the compilers. This may become less of a problem in time (as has been seen with other languages).

Ada provides features normally called from the operating system by other languages, providing a valuable degree of device independence and portability for Ada programs. However Ada real time control features may not be adequate for some applications, and direct access to operating system services may be necessary.

Ada does not support inheritance, so it is not an object-oriented language. Ada allows programmers to create 'generic packages' which act as classes. However it is not possible to structure generic packages and inherit package attributes and services.

3.3.1.9 Smalltalk

Smalltalk is the leading member of the family of object-oriented languages. The language is based on the idea of classes of object, which communicate by passing messages, and inherit attributes from classes to which they belong.

Smalltalk is inherently modular and extensible; indeed, every Smalltalk program is an extension of the core language. Large libraries are available offering a wide range of predefined classes for graphics, data handling, arithmetic, communications and so on. Programs can often be created by minor additions to, or modifications of, existing objects.

The language is thus very suitable for rapid iterative development and prototyping, but it is also efficient enough for many applications. It is the language of choice for educating software engineers in object-oriented programming.

Smalltalk differs from other programming languages in being a complete programming environment. This feature is also the language's Achilles heel: using Smalltalk is very much an 'all or nothing' decision. Interfacing to software written in other languages is not usually possible.

3.3.1.10 C++

C++ is an object-oriented and more strongly typed version of C. It therefore enforces greater discipline in programming than C. It is a noticeably more modern language, exploiting the strongest concepts of Pascal and Smalltalk, while providing all the features of its parent language C. The rapid emergence of C++ has been helped by the appearance of tools and standards.

3.3.1.11 LISP

LISP was the first list processing language. It is mostly a functional language but with some procedural features. Because a program is itself a list, it can readily be treated as data by another program. Hence, LISP is an excellent language for writing interpreters and expert systems, and much pioneering work in artificial intelligence has been done in the language.

LISP is now a mature language and accordingly has a rich set of predefined tools (functions) and environments available for it. LISP compilers are available on most architectures, but these are not well standardised; so-called Common LISP is a widespread dialect with commercial backing. LISP is often run on specialised workstations with language-sensitive editors, interpreters and debuggers, and sometimes with dedicated hardware. Interfaces to C and Prolog, and to procedural components like graphics packages, are frequently provided.

The language was once heavily criticised for inefficiency and illegibility. List manipulation is inherently more costly than, say, array manipulation, but careful optimisation and good compilers have greatly reduced the overheads. The style of LISP programs is more verbose and less legible than that of modern functional languages such as ML. However, recent versions of LISP have again become more purely functional and have updated their syntax. The problem of understanding heavily bracketed expressions (lists of lists) has largely been solved with pretty-printers and automatic bracket checkers.

3.3.1.12 ML

ML (short for Meta-Language) is the most widely used of a family of functional (i.e. non-procedural) programming languages that include Hope and Miranda. Like Prolog, it is declarative and admirably free of side-effects. Functions are similar to those in Pascal, except that they may take any desired form and return essentially any type of result as a structure. ML is notably modular and polymorphic, permitting creation of reusable components in a style analogous to that of Ada. ML lacks the quirkiness of some functional languages, and permits procedural constructs for efficiency.

3.3.1.13 Prolog

Prolog was the first of a family of logic programming languages. Full predicate logic is too complex to implement efficiently, so Prolog compromises by implementing a restricted but useful subset, namely Horn Clause logic. This permits a single affirmative conclusion, but from any number of premises. If a conclusion can be reached in more than one way, more than one clause is provided for it. Thus, groups of clauses act as the analogues of IF... THEN or CASE statements, while a single clause is effectively a procedure or function.

Because a conclusion may fail to be reached by one route, but the same, or another conclusion may be reached by another route, Prolog permits backtracking. This provides a powerful search mechanism. The need to maintain an extensive stack means, however, that Prolog requires a lot of run-time storage.

The language is essentially declarative, not procedural, as the clauses relate one fact or conclusion to another: thus, if something is true then it is always true. Prolog is very well suited to systems embodying rules, deduction, and knowledge (including databases), though it is capable of graphics, arithmetic and device control on a range of machines. It is not ideally suited for highly numerical applications. Prolog itself is (virtually) typeless and freely polymorphic, making it insecure; many of its daughter languages embody varieties of type checking. The language is inherently extensible.

With its interactive environment, it is very suitable for prototyping; it has also been used for specification. Most Prolog compilers permit modules of C to be called, typically as if they were built-in predicates.

3.3.1.14 Summary

Table 3.3.1.14 lists the programming languages, their types, primary applications and standards.

Language	Type	Primary Applications	Standard
FORTRAN	Procedural	Numerical analysis Real-time systems	ISO 1539
COBOL	Procedural	Transaction processing	ISO 1989
Pascal	Procedural	Numerical analysis Real-time systems	ISO 7185
C	Procedural	Real-time systems Operating systems	ANSI
Modula-2	Procedural	Real-time systems Numerical analysis	
Ada	Procedural	Real-time systems Simulation	MIL STD 1815A-1983
Smalltalk	Object-oriented	Simulation HCI toolkits	Smalltalk-80
C++	Object-oriented	Real-time systems Simulation HCI toolkits	AT&T
LISP	Functional	AI	Common LISP
ML	Functional	AI	
Prolog	Logic programming	AI	Edinburgh syntax

Table 3.3.1.14 Summary of Programming Languages

3.3.2 Integration methods

A function-by-function integration method should be used that:
- establishes the infrastructure functions first;
- harmonises with the delivery plan.

It is necessary to establish the infrastructure functions to minimise the amount of test software needed. Examples of infrastructure functions are those that provide data input and output. Building the infrastructure saves the effort of providing drivers and stubs for the components that use it. The infrastructure provides the kernel system from which the rest of the system can grow.

In an incremental development, the delivery plan can constrain the integration method by forcing functions to be delivered in a user-specified order, not one that minimises the integration effort.

Each function will be provided by a group of components that may be integrated 'top-down' and 'bottom-up'. The idea of integrating all the components at one level before proceeding to the next is common to both methods. In top-down integration, the next level to integrate is always the next lower one, while in bottom-up integration the next higher level is integrated.

The integration methods are described in more detail below.

3.3.2.1 Function-by-function

The steps in the function-by-function method are to:
1) select the functions to be integrated;
2) identify the components that carry out the functions;
3) identify the component dependencies (i.e. input data flows or control flows).
4) order the components by the number of dependencies (i.e. fewest dependencies first);
5) when a component depends on another later in the order, create a driver to simulate the input of the component later in the order;
6) introduce the components with the fewest dependencies first.

This approach minimises the number of stubs and drivers required. Stubs and drivers simulate the input to a component, so if the 'real' tested components provide the input, effort does not need to be expended on producing stubs and drivers.

Data flow diagrams are useful for representing component dependencies. Output flows that are not input to any other component should be omitted from the diagram.

When the incremental delivery life cycle approach is being used, the basic procedure above must be modified:
a) define the functions;
b) define when the functions are required;
c) for each release;
do steps 1) to 6) above.

Dependencies with components in a previous or a future release are not counted. If one component depends upon another in a previous release, the existing software can satisfy the dependency. If the component depends upon a component in a future release then a driver to simulate the input must be provided.

3.3.2.2 Top-down integration

The top-down approach to integration is to use 'stub' modules to represent lower-level modules. As modules are completed and tested, they replace the stubs. Stubs can be used to implement test cases.

3.3.2.3 Bottom-up integration

The bottom-up approach to integration is to use 'driver' modules to represent higher-level modules. As modules are completed and tested, they replace the drivers. Drivers can be used to implement test cases.

CHAPTER 4
TOOLS FOR DETAILED DESIGN AND PRODUCTION

4.1 INTRODUCTION

This chapter discusses the tools for detailing the design and producing the software. Tools can be combined to suit the needs of a particular project.

4.2 DETAILED DESIGN

4.2.1 Modelling tools

In all but the smallest projects,modelling tools should be used during the DD phase. Like many general purpose tools (e.g. such as word processors and drawing packages),modelling tools should provide:
- windows, icons, menu and pointer (WIMP) style interface for the easy creation and editing of diagrams;
- what you see is what you get (WYSIWYG) style interface that ensures that what is created on the display screen closely resembles what will appear in the document.

Method-specificmodelling tools offer the following features not offered by general purpose tools:
- enforcement of the rules of the methods;
- consistency checking;
- easy modification;
- automatic traceability of components to software requirements;
- configuration management of the design information;
- support for abstraction and information hiding;
- support for simulation.

Modelling tools should have an integrated data dictionary or another kind or 'repository'. This is necessary for consistency checking. Developers should check that a tool supports the parts of the method that they intend to use. The *Guide to the Software Architectural Design Phase* contains a more detailed list of desirable tool capabilities.

4.2.2 Configuration management tools

Configuration management of the physical model is essential. The model should evolve from baseline to baseline as it develops in the DD phase, and enforcement of procedures for the identification, change control and status accounting of the model are necessary.

In large projects, configuration management tools should be used for the management of the model database.

4.2.3 Precompilers

A precompiler generates code from PDL specifications. This is useful in design, but less so in later stages of development unless software faults can be easily traced back to PDL statements.

4.3 PRODUCTION

A range of production tools are available to help programmers develop, debug, build and test software. Table 4.3 lists the tools in order of their appearance in the production process.

Tool	Purpose
Modelling tools	generate module shells
code generators	translate formal relationships into source code
editors	create and modify source code and documentation
language-sensitive editors	create syntactically correct source code
static analysers	examine source code
compilers	translate source code to object code
linkers	join object modules into executable programs
debuggers	locate errors during execution
dynamic analysers	examine running programs
test tools	test modules and programs
word processors	document production
documentation generators	derive user documentation from the source code
configuration management tools	store and track versions of modules and files, and record the constituents of each build

Table 4.3: Production tools

4.3.1 Modelling tools

Many modelling tools automatically generate constant, type, and variable declarations for inclusion in the source code of every module. Some modelling tools can translate diagrams showing the calling tree of modules into fully commented function or procedure calls, though these may lack values for actual parameters.

If modelling tools are used, coding begins by completing the skeleton of the module. All the calls are completed; then iteration constructs (WHILE, REPEAT, LOOP, etc) are entered; then alternation constructs (IF, CASE, etc) are inserted. Finally, low-level details such as arithmetic, input/output, and other system calls are filled in.

4.3.2 Code generators

Numerous code generator packages are now available, claiming to take the work out of design and coding. They can help reduce the workload in some areas, such as database management and human-computer interaction. These areas are characterised by repetitive code, and the need to perform numerous trivial but essential operations in set sequences. Such tasks are best automated for accuracy and efficiency.

As code generators become more closely integrated with design methods, it will be possible to code a larger proportion of the components of any given system automatically. Current design methods generally provide limited code generation, for example creating the data declarations and module skeletons; module bodies must then be coded by hand.

Even if parts of the system are to be coded manually, there are still advantages in using a code generator. Changes in software requirements can result in automatic changes to data and module declarations, preserving and checking consistency across the phases of the life-cycle.

4.3.3 Editors

Largely replaced by the word processor for documentation, basic text editors are still widely used for source code creation and modification. Although language-sensitive editors (see Section 4.3.4) offer greater functionality, basic text editors provide all the facilities that many programmers require.

4.3.4 Language-sensitive editors

Language-sensitive editors are now available for many programming languages. They contain an interpreter that helps the user to write syntactically correct code. For example, if the user selects 'open a file', a menu appears of the known files of the right type. Language-sensitive editors are not ideal for some programming languages, because of the richness of their syntax. Skilled programmers often find them restrictive.

Another approach provides the reserved words of a language from a keypad, which may be real (on a keyboard or tablet), or virtual (on a screen panel). The selection of a keyword like WHILE with a single action is a convenience; the editor may also insert associated syntactic items, such as brackets and comments such as /* END WHILE */ . This does not prevent errors, but is at least a useful guide and the freedom of the programmer is not sacrificed.

The simplest language-sensitive editors do little more than recognise brackets and provide indentation to match. For example, the Pascal reserved words BEGIN and END bracket blocks in IF... THEN... ELSE statements. Automatic indentation after these words have been typed helps to make programs readable and reduces mistakes.

It is also possible to provide templates for program construction, containing standard headers, the obligatory sections for constant and type declarations, and so on. These may be generated automatically by modelling tools. Editors which recognise these templates (and the general form of a legal module), can speed development and help prevent errors. There is considerable scope for the further integration with modelling tools and code generators.

4.3.5 Static analysers

Static analysis is the process of scanning the text of a program to check for faults of construction, dangerous or undesirable features, and the application of software standards. They are especially useful for relatively unstructured languages such as assembler and FORTRAN.

Static analysers may:

- check for variables that are not used, or are used before being assigned a value;
- check that the ranges of variables stay within bounds;
- provide a view of the structure of an application;
- provide a view of the internal logical structure of each module;
- measure the complexity of the code with respect to a metric, such as cyclomatic complexity [Ref. 11];
- translate the source code to an intermediate language for formal verification;
- symbolically execute the code by substituting algebraic symbols for program variables;
- measure simple attributes of the code, such as the number of lines of code, and the maximum level of nesting.

Although they can be used to expose poorly structured code, static analysers should not be relied upon to improve poor programming. Structuring should be done in architectural and detailed design, not after implementation.

Most compilers provide some simple static analysis features, such as checking for variables that are not used (see Section 4.3.6). Dedicated static analysis tools usually provide advanced static analysis functions, such as analysis of code structure.

Static analysis tools are no substitute for code review. They just support the review process. Some bad programming practices, such as the choice of meaningful identifiers, evade all known static analysis tools, for example.

4.3.6 Compilers

The choice of compiler on a given computer or operating system may be limited. However, compilers vary widely in speed, thoroughness of checking, ease of use, handling of standard syntax and of language extensions, quality of listings and code output, and programming support features. The choice of compiler is therefore crucial. Trade-offs can become complex, leading to selection by reputation and not by analysis. Users should assess their compilation needs and compare the available options on this basis.

Speed of compilation affects the ease and cost of developing, debugging, and maintaining the product, whereas code quality affects the runtime performance of the product itself. Benchmark source code should therefore reflect the type of code likely to be found in the product to be developed. Compilers should be compared on such data by measuring compilation time, execution time, and object code size. Runtime stack and heap sizes may also be critical where memory is scarce.

Full checking of compiler compliance with language standards is beyond the means of essentially all software projects. Standards organisations such as ISO, ANSI and BSI certify compilers for a few languages including FORTRAN, COBOL and Pascal. The US Department of Defense certifies Ada compilers. Manufacturers' documentation should be scanned for extensions to, or omissions from, the standards.

Compilers vary widely in programming support features. Good compilers offer much help to the developer, for example:

- full listings;
- cross-reference;

- data on module sizes;
- diagnostics;
- thorough checking;
- switches (e.g. array bounds checking; strict language or extensions).

Some compilers now offer many of the features of development environments, including built-in editors and debuggers, trace tools, version control, linkers, and incremental compilation (with a built-in interpreter). These can substantially speed development.

Where there are switchable checks, project programming standards (DDD, section 2.4) should state which options are applicable.

The most advanced compilers perform a range of optimisations for sequential and parallel machines, attempting to discover and eliminate source code inefficiencies. These may be switchable, for example by directives in the source code. Ada explicitly provides for such directives with the 'pragma' statement. Users should investigate whether the optimisations they require are implemented in candidate compilers.

4.3.7 Linkers

The linker may be provided with the machine, operating system, or compiler; or, as with Ada, may be integrated with the compiler/interpreter and runtime system. The user therefore has little control over the choice of linker. When there is a choice, it should be considered carefully, as modern linkers vary considerably in performance, affecting especially the speed of debugging and maintenance.

It is convenient if the linker can automatically discover the appropriate libraries and directories to use, and which modules or components to link. Most linkers can be controlled by parameters, which can be created by a build or make utility; some are closely integrated with such utilities, or indeed with compilers.

In a large system, linking can take significantly longer than compilation, so users should compare linker performance on realistic benchmarks before selecting one for a project. Speed is not the only parameter to consider: some linkers may generate better quality executable code than others.

4.3.8 Debuggers

The use of interactive symbolic debuggers is strongly encouraged, especially for verification. A good debugger is integrated with an editor as well as a compiler/interpreter, and permits a range of investigative modes. Convenient debugging modes include step-by-step execution, breakpoint (spypoint) tracing, variable value reporting, watch condition setting (e.g. a variable beyond a limit value), and interaction.

For graphics, windows, menus, and other software involving cursor control, the debugger must be properly windowed to avoid confusion with the software being debugged. On some devices, illegal calls, e.g. graphics calls outside the frame area, cause processes to abort; debuggers should be able to trap such calls and permit interactive recovery action, or at least diagnosis.

The debugging of real-time software, where it is not possible to step through code, is a special challenge. The traditional diagnostic log is still useful here. The requirement is, as with all debugging, to view the software in a realistic environment. This may be possible with a simulator; if not, hardware-style techniques, in which bus or circuit signals are monitored in real time, may be necessary. Implementers of real-time projects should consider how they may debug and verify their software, and should allocate resources for this purpose.

4.3.9 Dynamic analysers

Dynamic analysis is the process of measuring how much machine resources (e.g. CPU time, i/o time, memory) each module, and line of code, consumes. In contrast to static analysis (see Section 4.3.5), dynamic analysis is performed on a running program.

Dynamic analysis tools, also called 'profilers' can be used for measuring test coverage, since lines of code that are not executed consume no resources. The verification of test coverage, i.e. that all statements have been executed during testing, is a requirement of *Software Engineering Standards*. Test coverage is best measured automatically.

Some dynamic analysers check that the program utilises memory correctly. For example they will verify that calls to allocate memory are properly matched with calls to release it, they can detect 'memory leaks'.

Dynamic analysis enables a variety of optimisations to be carried out to 'tune' the system. Optimisation can be a very inefficient process without detailed knowledge of the system performance. Dynamic analysis tools can locate the parts of the system that are causing performance problems. Source-level modifications can often yield the desired performance gains.

Where there are precise performance requirements, developers should use a dynamic analyser to verify that the system is satisfactorily tuned, and to direct optimisation effort. If there are no precise performance requirements, and a system runs satisfactorily, dynamic analysis can still help detect some types of coding errors (e.g. unnecessary initialisations).

If a dynamic analyser is not available, resource consumption can be measured by means of timing routines. An interactive debugger can be used to observe coverage.

4.3.10 Test tools

Test tools may support one or more of the following functions:
- test data generation;
- test driving and harnessing;
- automated results checking;
- fault diagnosis and debugging;
- test data management.

General purpose test tools can sometimes generate large quantities of input based on simple assumptions. System-specific simulators and modelling tools are needed if realistic test data is required.

Test drivers and harnesses normally have to be provided by the developers. The integration plan should identify what test drivers and stubs are required for testing, and these normally have to be specially developed.

Interpreter systems permit test drivers and harnesses to be created interactively. Short test drivers, consisting of little more than such a call, can be prepared and called as interpreted commands. Such test drivers do not need to be compiled into the final version. Of the languages mentioned in Section 3.3.1, Pascal, ML, Prolog, LISP and Smalltalk are known to be runnable interpretatively.

Tools that provide automated results checking can greatly increase the efficiency of regression testing, and thereby its depth and scope.

If the comparison reveals a discrepancy between past and present results, support for fault diagnosis, via tracebacks of the execution, reports of the contents of variables, can ease the solution of the problem identified in the test.

Perhaps of all the functions, support for the management of test data is the most important. Management of the input and output test data is required if regression testing is to be meaningful.

4.3.11 Word processors

A word processor or text processor should be used. Tools for the creation of paragraphs, sections, headers, footers, tables of contents and indexes all ease the production of a document. A spelling checker is essential, and a grammar checker is desirable. An outliner may be found useful for creation of sub-headings, for viewing the document at different levels of detail and for rearranging the document. The ability to handle diagrams is very important.

Documents invariably go through many drafts as they are created, reviewed and modified. Revised drafts should include change bars. Document comparison programs, which can mark changed text automatically, are invaluable for easing the review process.

Tools for communal preparation of documents are now beginning to be available, allowing many authors to comment and add to a single document.

4.3.12 Documentation generators

Documentation generators allow the automatic production of help and documentation from the information in the code. They help maintain consistency between code and documentation, and make the process of documentation truly concurrent with the coding.

Code generators (see Section 4.3.2) may include tools for automatically generating documentation about the screens, windows and reports that the programmer creates.

4.3.13 Configuration management tools

Configuration management is covered in the *Guide to Software Configuration Management*. Implementers should consider the use of an automated configuration management tool in the circumstances of each project.

A variety of tools, often centred on a database, is available to assist in controlling the development of software when many modules may exist in many versions. Some tools allow the developer to specify a configuration (m modules in n versions), and then automatically compile, link, and archive it. The use of configuration management tools becomes essential when the number of modules or versions becomes large.

4.3.14 Class browsers

Class browsers are tools that permit software engineers to examine libraries of code written in an object-oriented language such as C++. They provide facilities for searching the source code library for modules with the required functionality. Class browsers are an essential tool for reuse.

CHAPTER 5
THE DETAILED DESIGN DOCUMENT

5.1 INTRODUCTION

The purpose of a DDD is to describe the detailed solution to the problem stated in the SRD. The DDD must be an output of the DD phase (DD13). The DDD must be complete, accounting for all the software requirements in the SRD (DD15). The DDD should be sufficiently detailed to allow the code to be implemented and maintained. Components (especially interfaces) should be described in sufficient detail to be fully understood.

5.2 STYLE

The style of a DDD should be systematic and rigorous. The language and diagrams used in a DDD should be clear and constructed to a consistent plan. The document as a whole must be modifiable.

5.2.1 Clarity

A DDD is clear if it is easy to understand. The structure of the DDD must reflect the structure of the software design, in terms of the levels and components of the software (DD14). The natural language used in a DDD must be shared by all the development team.

The DDD should not introduce ambiguity. Terms should be used accurately.

A diagram is clear if it is constructed from consistently used symbols, icons, or labels, and is well arranged. Important visual principles are to:
- emphasise important information;
- align symbols regularly;
- allow diagrams to be read left-to-right or top-to-bottom;
- arrange similar items in a row, in the same style;
- exploit visual symmetry to express functional symmetry;
- avoid crossing lines and overlaps;
- avoid crowding.

Diagrams should have a brief title, and be referenced by the text which they illustrate.

Diagrams and text should complement one another and be as closely integrated as possible. The purpose of each diagram should be explained in the text, and each diagram should explain aspects that cannot be expressed in a few words. Diagrams can be used to structure the discussion in the text.

5.2.2 Consistency

The DDD must be consistent. There are several types of inconsistency:
- different terms used for the same thing;
- the same term used for different things;
- incompatible activities happening simultaneously;
- activities happening in the wrong order.

Where a term could have multiple meanings, a single meaning should be defined in a glossary, and only that meaning should be used in the DDD.

Duplication and overlap lead to inconsistency. Clues to inconsistency are a single functional requirement tracing to more than one component. Methods and tools help consistency to be achieved.

Consistency should be preserved both within diagrams and between diagrams in the same document. Diagrams of different kinds should be immediately distinguishable.

5.2.3 Modifiability

A DDD is modifiable if changes to the document can be made easily, completely, and consistently. Good tools make modification easier, although it is always necessary to check for unpredictable side-effects of changes. For example a global string search and replace capability can be very useful, but developers should always guard against unintended changes.

Diagrams, tables, spreadsheets, charts and graphs are modifiable if they are held in a form which can readily be changed. Such items should be prepared either within the word processor, or by a tool compatible with the word processor. For example, diagrams may be imported automatically into a document: typically, the print process scans the document for symbolic markers indicating graphics and other files.

Where graphics or other data are prepared on the same hardware as the code, it may be necessary to import them by other means. For example, a screen capture utility may create bitmap files ready for printing. These may be numbered and included as an annex. Projects using methods of this kind should define conventions for handling and configuration management of such data.

5.3 EVOLUTION

The DDD should be put under change control by the developer at the start of the Transfer Phase. New components may need to be added and old components modified or deleted. If the DDD is being developed by a team of people, the control of the document may be started at the beginning of the DD phase.

The Software Configuration Management Plan defines a formal change process to identify, control, track and report projected changes, as soon as they are first identified. Approved changes in components must be recorded in the DDD by inserting document change records and a document status sheet at the start of the DDD.

5.4 RESPONSIBILITY

Whoever writes the DDD, the responsibility for it lies with the developer. The developer should nominate people with proven design and implementation skills to write the DDD.

5.5 MEDIUM

The DDD is usually a paper document. The DDD may be distributed electronically when participants have access to the necessary equipment.

5.6 CONTENT

The DDD is the authoritative reference document on how the software works. Part 2 of the DDD must have the same structure and identification scheme as the code itself, with a 1:1 correspondence between sections of the documentation and the software components (DD14). The DDD must be complete, accounting for all the software requirements in the SRD (DD15).

The DDD should be compiled according to the table of contents provided in Appendix C of *Software Engineering Standards*. This table of contents is derived from ANSI/IEEE Std 1016-1987 'IEEE Recommended Practice for Software Design Descriptions' [Ref. 5]. This standard defines a Software Design Description as a 'representation or model of the software system to be created. The model should provide the precise design information needed for the planning, analysis and implementation of the software system'. The DDD should be such a Software Design Description.

The table of contents is reproduced below. Relevant material unsuitable for inclusion in the contents list should be inserted in additional appendices. If there is no material for a section then the phrase 'Not Applicable' should be inserted and the section numbering preserved.

Service Information:
a - Abstract
b - Table of Contents
c - Document Status Sheet
d - Document Change Records made since last issue

PART 1 - GENERAL DESCRIPTION[1]
   1 INTRODUCTION
        1.1 Purpose
        1.2 Scope
        1.3 Definitions, acronyms and abbreviations
        1.4 References
        1.5 Overview

---

[1] The Detailed Design Document contents lists is based upon extracts from IEEE Std 1016-1987, IEEE Recommended Practice for Software Design Descriptions, copyright © 1987 by the Institute for Electrical and Electronic Engineers Inc. The IEEE disclaims any responsibility or liability resulting from the placement and use in this publication. Information is reprinted with the permission of the IEEE.

2 PROJECT STANDARDS, CONVENTIONS AND PROCEDURES
    2.1 Design standards
    2.2 Documentation standards
    2.3 Naming conventions
    2.4 Programming standards
    2.5 Software development tools

PART 2 - COMPONENT DESIGN SPECIFICATIONS

N [COMPONENT IDENTIFIER]
    n.1 Type
    n.2 Purpose
    n.3 Function
    n.4 Subordinates
    n.5 Dependencies
    n.6 Interfaces
    n.7 Resources
    n.8 References
    n.9 Processing
    n.10 Data

    Appendix A Source code listings
    Appendix B Software Requirements vs Components Traceability matrix

A component may belong to a class of components that share characteristics. To avoid repeatedly describing shared characteristics, a sensible approach is to reference the description of the class.

References should be given where appropriate, but a DDD should not refer to documents that follow it in the *Software Engineering Standards* life cycle.

Part 1 of the DDD must be completed before any coding is started. The component design specification in Part 2 must be complete (i.e. no TBCs or TBDs) before coding is started.

5.6.1 DDD/Part 1 - General description

5.6.1.1 DDD/Part 1/1 Introduction

This section should describe the purpose and scope, and provide a glossary, list of references and document overview.

5.6.1.1.1 DDD/Part 1/1.1 Purpose (of the document)

This section should:
    (1) describe the purpose of the particular DDD;
    (2) specify the intended readership of the DDD.

5.6.1.1.2 DDD/Part 1/1.2 Scope (of the software)

This section should:
(1) identify the software products to be produced;
(2) explain what the proposed software will do (and will not do, if necessary);
(3) define relevant benefits, objectives, and goals as precisely as possible;
(4) be consistent with similar statements in higher-level specifications, if they exist.

5.6.1.1.3 DDD/Part 1/1.3 Definitions, acronyms and abbreviations

This section should define all terms, acronyms, and abbreviations used in the DDD, or refer to other documents where the definitions can be found.

5.6.1.1.4 DDD/Part 1/1.4 References

This section should list all the applicable and reference documents, identified by title, author and date. Each document should be marked as applicable or reference. If appropriate, report number, journal name and publishing organisation should be included.

5.6.1.1.5 DDD/Part 1/1.5 Overview (of the document)

This section should:
(1) describe what the rest of the DDD contains;
(2) explain how the DDD is organised.

5.6.1.2 DDD/Part 1/2 Project standards, conventions and procedures

5.6.1.2.1 DDD/Part 1/2.1 Design standards

These should usually reference methods carried over from the AD phase and only describe DD phase specific methods.

The Detailed Design Standard might need to be different if more than one method or programming language is involved: for example, if some C language design and programming takes place in an Ada project.

5.6.1.2.2 DDD/Part 1/2.2 Documentation standards

This section should describe the format, style, and tools adopted by the project for DD and code documentation. Headers, footers, section formats and typefaces should be specified. They may be prepared as word processor template files, for automatic inclusion in all project documents. If the formats are new, they should be prototyped and reviewed (with users in the case of the SUM).

This section should contain the standard module header and contain instructions for its completion (see Section 2.3.9).

5.6.1.2.3 DDD/Part 1/2.3 Naming conventions

This section should explain all naming conventions used, and draw attention to any points a maintenance programmer would not expect. A table of the file types and the permitted names or extensions for each is recommended for quick reference. See the examples in Table 5.6.1.2.3 and Section 5.6.2.1.

File Type	Name	Extension
document	<<mnemonic>>	.DOC
Ada source code	IDENTIFIER	.ADA
Fortran source code	IDENTIFIER	.FOR
diagram	<<mnemonic>>	.PIC

Table 5.6.1.2.3: Names and extensions

Conventions for naming files, programs, modules, and possibly other structures such as variables and messages, should all be documented here.

5.6.1.2.4 DDD/Part 1/2.4 Programming standards

This section should define the project programming standards. Whatever languages or standards are chosen, the aim should be to create a convenient and easily usable method for writing good-quality software. Note especially the guidelines in Section 2.3.

When programming in any other language, a standard for its use should be written to provide guidance for programmers. This standard may be referenced or included here.

In general, the programming standard should define a consistent and uniform programming style. Specific points to cover are:
- modularity and structuring;
- headers and commenting;
- indenting and layout;
- library routines to be used;
- language constructs to use;
- language constructs to avoid.

5.6.1.2.5 DDD/Part 1/2.5 Software development tools

This section should list the tools chosen to assist software development. Normally the list will include:
- a modelling tool;
- a source code editor;
- a compiler;
- a debugger;
- a linker;
- a configuration management tool / builder;
- a word processor for documentation;
- a tool for drawing diagrams.

Many projects will also use a configuration management system to store configuration items, such as documentation, code and test data.

Prototyping projects might make use of an interpretative tool, such as an incremental compiler/interpreter/debugger.

Other tools that may be helpful to many projects include:
- static analysers;
- dynamic analysers;
- network and data communication tools;
- graphics packages;
- statistics and mathematical packages.

Real-time and embedded systems may require special development tools, including:
- cross-compilers;
- diagnostic, logging, and probe tools.

5.6.2 DDD/Part 2 - Component design specifications

The descriptions of the components should be laid out hierarchically. There should be subsections dealing with the following aspects of each component:

N COMPONENT IDENTIFIER
   n.1 Type
   n.2 Purpose
   n.3 Function
   n.4 Subordinates
   n.5 Dependencies
   n.6 Interfaces
   n.7 Resources
   n.8 References
   n.9 Processing
   n.10 Data

The number 'n' should relate to the place of the component in the hierarchy.

5.6.2.1 DDD/Part 2/5.n Component Identifier

Each component should have a unique identifier (SCM06) for effective configuration management. The component should be named according to the rules of the programming language or operating system to be used. Where possible, a hierarchical naming scheme should be used that identifies the parent of the component (e.g. ParentName_ChildName)

The identifier should reflect the purpose and function of the component and be brief yet meaningful. If abbreviation is necessary, abbreviations should be applied consistently and without ambiguity.

Abbreviations should be documented. Component identifiers should be mutually consistent (e.g. if there is a routine called READ_RECORD then one might expect a routine called WRITE_RECORD, not RECORD_WRITING_ROUTINE).

A naming style that clearly distinguishes objects of different classes is good programming practice. In Pascal, for instance, it is traditional to use upper case for user-defined types, mixed case for modules, and lower case for variables, giving the following appearance:
- procedure Count_Chars; {a module}
- type SMALL_INT = 1..255; {a type}
- var count: SMALL_INT; {a variable}

Other styles may be appropriate in other languages. The naming style should be consistent throughout a project. It is wise to avoid styles that might confuse maintenance programmers accustomed to standard industrial practices.

5.6.2.1.1 DDD/Part 2/5.n.1 Type

Component type should be defined by stating its logical and physical characteristics. The logical characteristics should be defined by stating the package, library or class that the component belongs to. The physical characteristics should be defined by stating the type of component, using the implementation terminology (e.g. task, subroutine, subprogram, package, file).

The contents of some component-description sections depend on the component type. For this guide the categories: executable (i.e. contains computer instructions) or non-executable (i.e. contains only data) are used.

5.6.2.1.2 DDD/Part 2/5.n.2 Purpose

The purpose of a component should be defined by tracing it to the software requirements that it implements.

Backward traceability depends upon each component description explicitly referencing the requirements that justify its existence.

5.6.2.1.3 DDD/Part 2/5.n.3 Function

The function of a component must be defined in the DDD. This should be done by stating what the component does.

The function description depends upon the component type. Therefore it may be a description of the:
- process;
- information stored or transmitted.

Process descriptions may use such techniques as Structured English, Precondition-Postcondition specifications and State-Transition Diagrams.

5.6.2.1.4 DDD/Part 2/5.n.4 Subordinates

The subordinates of a component should be defined by listing the immediate children. The subordinates of a program are the subroutines that are 'called by' it. The subordinates of a database could be the files that 'compose' it. The subordinates of an object are the objects that are 'used by' it.

5.6.2.1.5 DDD/Part 2/5.n.5 Dependencies

The dependencies of a component should be defined by listing the constraints placed upon its use by other components. For example:
- 'what operations must have taken place before this component is called?'
- 'what operations are excluded while this operation is taking place?'
- 'what operations have to be carried out after this one?'.

5.6.2.1.6 DDD/Part 2/5.n.6 Interfaces

Both control flow and data flow aspects of each interface need to be specified in the DDD for each 'executable' component. Data aspects of 'non-executable' components should be defined in Subsection 10.

The control flow to and from a component should be defined in terms of how execution of the component is to be started (e.g. subroutine call) and how it is to be terminated (e.g. return). This may be implicit in the definition of the type of component, and a description may not be necessary. Control flows may also take place during execution (e.g. interrupt) and these should be defined, if they exist.

The data flow input to and output from each component must be detailed in the DDD. Data structures should be identified that:

- are associated with the control flow (e.g. call argument list);
- interface components through common data areas and files.

One component's input may be another's output and to avoid duplication of interface definitions, specific data components should be defined and described separately (e.g. files, messages). The interface definition should only identify the data component and not define its contents.

The interfaces of a component should be defined by explaining 'how' the component interacts with the components that use it. This can be done by describing the mechanisms for:

- invoking or interrupting the component's execution;
- communicating through parameters, common data areas or messages.

If a component interfaces to components in the same system, the interface description should be defined in the DDD (if not already in the ADD). If a component interfaces to components in other systems, the interface description should be defined in an Interface Control Document (ICD).

5.6.2.1.7 DDD/Part 2/5.n.7 Resources

The resources a component requires should be defined by itemising what the component needs from its environment to perform its function. Items that are part of the component interface are excluded. Examples of resources that might be needed by a component are displays, printers and buffers.

5.6.2.1.8 DDD/Part 2/5.n.8 References

Explicit references should be inserted where a component description uses or implies material from another document.

5.6.2.1.9 DDD/Part 2/5.n.9 Processing

The DDD should describe in detail how processing is carried out. Algorithms that are fully described elsewhere may be summarised briefly, provided their sources are properly referenced.

The processing a component needs to do should be defined by defining the control and data flow within it. For some kinds of component (e.g. files) there is no such flow. In practice it is often difficult to separate the description of function from the description of processing. Therefore a detailed description of function can compensate for a lack of detail in the specification of the processing. Techniques of process specification more oriented towards software design are Program Design Language, Pseudo-code and Flow Charts.

Software constraints may specify that the processing be performed using a particular algorithm (which should be stated or referenced).

5.6.2.1.10 DDD/Part 2/5.n.10 Data

The data internal to a component should be defined. The amount of detail required depends strongly on the type of component. The logical and physical data structure of files that interface components should have been defined in the DDD (files and data structures that interface major components will have been defined in the ADD). The data structures internal to a program or subroutine should also be specified (contrast the ADD, where it is omitted).

Data structure definitions must include the:
- description of each element (e.g. name, type, dimension);
- relationships between the elements (i.e. the structure);
- range of possible values of each element;
- initial values of each element.

5.6.3 DDD/Appendix A: Source code listings

This section must contain either:
- listings of the source code, or
- a configuration item list identifying where the source code can be found (DD12).

5.6.4 DDD/Appendix B: Software requirements traceability matrix

This section should contain a table that summarises how each software requirement has been met in the DDD (DD16). The tabular format permits one-to-one and one-to-many relationships to be shown. A template is provided in Appendix D.

CHAPTER 6
THE SOFTWARE USER MANUAL

6.1 INTRODUCTION

The purpose of the Software User Manual (SUM) is to describe how to use the software. It should both educate users about what the software does, and instruct them how to do it. The SUM should combine tutorials and reference information to meet the needs of both novices and experts. A Software User Manual (SUM) must be an output of the DD phase (DD17).

The rules for the style and content of the Software User Manual are based on ANSI/IEEE Std 1063-1987, 'Standard for Software User Documentation'.

6.2 STYLE

The author of the SUM needs to be aware of the basic rules of clear writing:
- keep sentences short (e.g. 20 words or less);
- avoid using long words (e.g. 10 letters or more);
- keep paragraphs short (e.g. 10 sentences or less);
- avoid using the passive tense;
- use correct grammar;
- make each paragraph express one point;
- tell the reader what you going to say, say it, and then tell the reader what you have said.

A grammar checker can help the author obey the first five rules.

The concepts of clarity, consistency and modifiability apply to the SUM just as much as to the DDD (see Section 5.2). The rest of this section presents some other considerations that should influence the style of the SUM.

The SUM should reflect the characteristics of the users. Different types of users, e.g. end users and operators, will have different needs. Further, the user's view may change from that of a trainee to expert. The authors of the SUM should study the characteristics of the users. The URD normally contains a summary.

The SUM should reflect the characteristics of the interface between he system and the user. Embedded software for controlling an instrument on board a satellite might have no interface to humans. At the opposite extreme, a data reduction package might require a large amount of user interaction, and the SUM might be absolutely critical to the success of the package.

6.2.1 Matching the style to the user characteristics

Different viewpoints that may need to be addressed are:
- the end user's view;
- the operator's view;
- the trainee's view.

An individual user may hold more than one view.

6.2.1.1 The end user's view

The end user's view takes in every aspect of the use of the system. The SUM should describe the purpose of the system and should reference the URD.

The SUM should contain an overview of the process to be supported, perhaps making reference to technical information, such as the underlying physics and algorithms employed. Information should be presented from the end user's view, not the developer's. Algorithms should be represented in mathematical form, not in a programming language, for example. Descriptions should not stray into the workings of the system; they are in the SUM only to help the end user understand the intention of the system.

The end user's view is an external view, unconcerned with details of the implementation. Accordingly, the SUM should give an external view of the system, with examples of input required from end users, and the results that would occur (e.g. output). The SUM should place the system in its working context.

6.2.1.2 The operator's view

The operator's view focuses on successfully controlling the software, whether in normal conditions, or when recovering from errors.

From the point of view of the operator, the SUM should contain clear instructions about each task that has to be performed. In particular:
- instructions should be easy to find;
- instructions should be easy to understand.

Ease of location and understanding are important in emergencies. Instructions will be easy to find and understand if a regular structure is adopted for the description of each task.

Writers should ensure that wrong actions are not accidentally selected, and that correct or undo actions are possible if the operator makes a mistake. The SUM should document such corrective actions with examples.

Any irreversible actions must be clearly distinguished in the SUM (and in the system). Typically, the operator will be asked to confirm that an irreversible action is to be selected. All confirmation procedures must be explained with examples in the SUM.

6.2.1.3 The trainee's view

A particularly important view is that of the trainee. There are always users who are not familiar with a system, and they are especially likely to need the support of a well-written guide or tutorial. Since the first experience with a system is often decisive, it is just as vital to write a helpful tutorial for the trainee.

Every SUM should contain a tutorial section, which should provide a welcoming introduction to the software (e.g. 'Getting Started').

6.2.2 Matching the style to the HCI characteristics

The SUM should reflect the Human Computer Interaction (HCI) characteristics of the software. This section presents some guidelines for:

- command-driven systems;
- menu-driven systems;
- GUI, WIMPs and WYSIWYG systems;
- natural language and speech interface systems;
- embedded systems.

6.2.2.1 Command-driven systems

Command-driven systems require the user to type in commands. The keyboard input is echoed on a screen. Command driven systems are simple to implement, and are often preferred by expert users.

Command-driven systems can take some time to learn, and the SUM has a critical role to play in educating the users of the software. A well thought-out SUM can compensate for a difficult user interface.

The alphanumeric nature of the interaction can be directly represented in the SUM. For example:
Commentary and instructions,

```
> user input
  system output
```

should be clearly distinguished from each other.

6.2.2.2 Menu-driven systems

Traditional menu-driven systems present the user with a fixed hierarchy of menus. The user starts at the top of the tree and moves up and down the tree. The structure of the menus normally follows the natural sequence of operations (e.g. OPEN the file first, then EDIT it). Often the left-most or the top-most item on the menu is what is usually done first. Sometimes this temporal logic is abandoned in favour of ergonomic considerations (e.g. putting the most frequently used command first).

The SUM should describe the standard paths for traversing the menus. The structure of the SUM should follow the natural sequence of operations, which is normally the menu structure. An index should be provided to give alphabetical access.

6.2.2.3 Graphical User Interface systems

Graphical User Interfaces (GUI) include Windows, Icons, Mouse and Pointer (WIMP) and What You See Is What You Get (WYSIWYG) style interfaces. An aim of their inventors was to make the operation of a system so simple and intuitive that the reading of a user manual is unnecessary. Unfortunately, making information about the system only available through the system can be very restrictive, and may not support the mode of inquiry of the user. SUMs separate to the software are always required, no matter how sophisticated the interface.

SUMs for a GUI should not assume basic GUI skills. They should instruct the user how to operate the interface and should describe what the user looks at and 'feels'. Pictures and diagrams of the behaviour should be given, so that the reader is left in no doubt about what the intended behaviour is. This is especially important when the user does not have access to the system when reading the tutorial.

6.2.2.4 Natural-language and speech interface systems

Natural-language and speech interfaces are coming into use. Unlike menu-driven systems and WIMPs, WYSIWYG and GUI type systems, the options are not normally defined on a screen. There may be many options.

For natural language and speech interface systems, the SUM should provide:
- a full list of facilities, explaining their purposes and use;
- examples showing how the facilities relate to each other;
- a list of useful command verbs and auxiliary words for each facility;
- a clear statement of types of sentence that are NOT recognised.

6.2.2.5 Embedded systems

Software that is embedded within a system may not require any human interaction at the software level. Nevertheless a SUM must be supplied with the software and provide at least:
- an overview;
- error messages;
- recovery procedures.

6.3 EVOLUTION

The development of the SUM should start as early as possible. Establishing the potential readership for the SUM should be the first step. This information is critical for establishing the style of the document. Useful information may be found in the section 'User Characteristics' in the URD.

The Software Configuration Management Plan defines a formal change process to identify, control, track and report projected changes when they are first identified. Approved changes to the SUM must be recorded by inserting document change records and a document status sheet at the start of the document.

The SUM is an integral part of the software. The SUM and the rest of the software must evolve in step. The completeness and accuracy of the SUM should be reviewed whenever a new release of the software is made.

6.4 RESPONSIBILITY

Whoever writes the SUM, the responsibility for it must be the developer's. The developer should nominate people with proven authorship skills to write the SUM.

6.5 MEDIUM

Traditionally, manuals have been printed as books. There are substantial advantages to be gained from issuing manuals in machine-readable form. Implementers should consider whether their system would benefit from such treatment. Two possibilities are:
- online help;
- hypertext.

There should be specific requirements in the URD and SRD for online help and hypertext, since their implementation can absorb both computer resources (e.g. storage) and development effort.

6.5.1 Online help

Information in the SUM may be used to construct an 'online help' system. Online help has the advantages of always being available with the system, whereas paper manuals may be mislaid. Three possibilities, in order of increasing desirability are:
- a standalone help system, not accessible from inside the
- application;
- an integrated help system, accessible from within the application;
- an integrated, context-sensitive help system, that gives the help information about the task being carried out.

In the last option, the user should be able to continue the search for help outside the current context (e.g. to get background information).

6.5.2 Hypertext

A hypertext is a structure of pages of text or graphics (and sometimes of other media). Pages are linked by keywords or phrases. For example, the word 'file' might give access to a page containing the words 'store', 'search', and 'retrieve'; in turn, each of these might give access to a page explaining a command within the documented system. Keywords may be displayed as text (usually highlighted), or may be indicated by icons or regions of a diagram which respond to a pointing device (such as a mouse).

Hypertext readily accommodates the hierarchical structure of most programs, but it can equally represent a network of topics linked by arbitrary connections.

This gives hypertext the advantage of a richer pattern of access than printed text, which is inherently linear (despite hypertext-like helps, such as indexes).

Hypertext is also good for guided tours, which simulate the operation of the program, while pointing out interesting features and setting exercises.

The quality of graphics within a hypertext must enable tables, charts, graphs and diagrams to be read quickly and without strain. Older terminals and personal computers may not be suitable for this purpose. Modern bit-mapped workstations, and personal computers with higher-resolution graphics cards, rarely cause legibility problems.

Stand-alone hypertext has the advantage of being simple and safe; it does not increase the complexity or risk of system software, because it is not connected directly to it.

A disadvantage of stand-alone hypertext is that it is not automatically context-sensitive. On a multitasking operating system, it can be made context-sensitive by issuing a message from the (documented) system to the hypertext mechanism, naming the entry point (for example, 'file names' or 'data display').

Reliable proprietary hypertext packages are available on many processors; alternatively, simple hypertext mechanisms can be implemented by means of a database, a specialised tool, or if necessary a programming language.

6.6 CONTENT

The recommended table of contents for a SUM is given below. If it is felt necessary to depart from this structure, implementers should justify any differences briefly, and if possible preserve the standard section numbering for easy reference.

Service Information:
  a - Abstract
  b - Table of Contents
  c - Document Status Sheet
  d - Document Change Records made since last issue.

1 INTRODUCTION[2]
    1.1 Intended readership
    1.2 Applicability statement
    1.3 Purpose
    1.4 How to use this document
    1.5 Related documents (including applicable documents)
    1.6 Conventions
    1.7 Problem reporting instructions

2 [OVERVIEW SECTION]
(The section ought to give the user a general understanding of what parts of software provide the capabilities needed)

3 [INSTRUCTION SECTION]
(For each operation, provide...
    (a) Functional description
    (b) Cautions and warnings
    (c) Procedures, including,
        - Set-up and initialisation
        - Input operations
        - What results to expect
    (d) Probable errors and possible causes

---

[2] The Software User Manual contents list is based upon extracts from IEEE Std 1063-1987, IEEE Standard for Software User Documentation, copyright © 1987 by the Institute for Electrical and Electronic Engineers Inc. The IEEE disclaims any responsibility or liability resulting from the placement and use in this publication. Information is reprinted with the permission of the IEEE.

4 [REFERENCE SECTION]
(Describe each operation, including:
- (a) Functional description
- (b) Cautions and warnings
- (c) Formal description, including as appropriate:
    - required parameters
    - optional parameters
    - default options
    - order and syntax
- (d) Examples
- (e) Possible error messages and causes
- (f) Cross references to other operations)

Appendix A Error messages and recovery procedures
Appendix B Glossary
Appendix C Index (for manuals of 40 pages or more)

In the instruction section of the SUM, material is ordered according to the learning path, with the simplest, most necessary operations appearing first and more advanced, complicated operations appearing later. The size of this section depends on the intended readership. Some users may understand the software after a few examples (and can switch to using the reference section) while other users may require many worked examples.

The reference section of the SUM presents the basic operations, ordered for easy reference (e.g. alphabetically). Reference documentation should be more formal, rigorous and exhaustive than the instructional section. For example a command may be described in the instruction section in concrete terms, with a specific worked example. The description in the reference section should describe all the parameters, qualifiers and keywords, with several examples.

The overview, instruction, and reference sections should be given appropriate names by the SUM authors. For example, an orbit modelling system might have sections separately bound and titled:
- Orbit Modelling System Overview;
- Orbit Modelling System Tutorial;
- Orbit Modelling System Reference Manual.

At lower levels within the SUM, authors are free to define a structure suited to the readership and subject matter. Particular attention should be paid to:
- ordering subjects (e.g. commands, procedures);
- providing visual aids.

'Alphabetical' ordering of subjects acts as a built-in index and speeds access. It has the disadvantage of separating related items, such as 'INSERT' and 'RETRIEVE'. Implementers should consider which method of structuring is most appropriate to an individual document. Where a body of information can be accessed in several ways, it should be indexed and cross-referenced to facilitate the major access methods.

Another possible method is 'procedural' or 'step-by-step' ordering, in which subjects are described in the order the user will execute them. This style is appropriate for the instruction section.

Visual aids in the form of diagrams, graphs, charts, tables, screen dumps and photographs should be given wherever they materially assist the user. These may illustrate the software or hardware, procedures to be followed by the user, data, or the structure of the SUM itself.

Implementers may also include illustrations for other purposes. For example, instructional material may contain cartoons to facilitate understanding or to maintain interest.

Icons may be used to mark differing types of section, such as definitions and procedures. All icons should be explained at the start of the SUM.

6.6.1 SUM\Table of Contents

A table of contents is an important help and should be provided in every SUM. Short manuals may have a simple list of sections. Manuals over 40 pages should provide a fuller list, down to at least the third level of subsections (1.2.3, etc). Where the SUM is issued in several volumes, the first volume should contain a simple table of contents for the entire SUM, and each volume should contain its own table of contents.

There is no fixed style for tables of contents, but they should reference page as well as section numbers. Section headings should be quoted exactly as they appear in the body of the manual. Subsections may be indented to group them visually by containing a section.

A convenient style is to link the title to the page number with a leader string of dots:
1.2.3 Section Title 29

Lists of figures and tables should be provided in manuals with many of them (e.g. more than twenty).

6.6.2 SUM\1 Introduction

6.6.2.1 SUM\1.1 Intended readership

This section should define the categories of user (e.g. end user and operator) and, for each category:
- define the level of experience assumed;
- state which sections of SUM are most relevant to their needs.

6.6.2.2 SUM\1.2 Applicability statement

This section should define the software releases that the issue of the SUM applies to.

6.6.2.3 SUM\1.3 Purpose

This section should define both the purpose of the SUM and the purpose of the software. It should name the process to be supported by software and the role of the SUM in supporting that process.

6.6.2.4 SUM\1.4 How to use this document

This section should describe what each section of the document contains, its intended use, and the relationship between sections.

6.6.2.5 SUM\1.5 Related documents

This section should list related documents and define the relationship of each document to the others. All document trees that the SUM belongs to should be defined in this section. If the SUM is a multivolume set, each member of the set should be separately identified.

6.6.2.6 SUM\1.6 Conventions

This section should summarise symbols, stylistic conventions, and command syntax conventions used in the document.

Examples of stylistic conventions are boldface and Courier Font to distinguish user input. Examples of syntax conventions are the rules for combining commands, keywords and parameters, or how to operate a WIMP interface.

6.6.2.7 SUM\1.7 Problem Reporting Instructions

This section should summarise the procedures for reporting software problems. *Software Engineering Standards* specifies the problem reporting procedure [Ref. 1, part 2, section 3.2.3.2.2]. The SUM should not refer users to *Software Engineering Standards*.

6.6.3 SUM\2 Overview Section

This section should give an overview of the software to all users and summarises:
- the process to be supported to by software;
- the fundamental principles of the process;
- what the software does to support the process;
- what the user needs to supply to the software.

The description of the process to be supported, and its fundamental principles, may be derived from the URD. It should not use software terminology.

The software should be described from an external 'black box' point of view. The discussion should be limited to functions, inputs and outputs that the user sees.

The overview can often become much clearer if a good metaphor is used for the system. Some GUIs, for example, use the 'office system' metaphor of desk, filing cabinets, folders, indexes etc. Often a metaphor will have been defined very early in the system development, to help capture the requirements. The same metaphor can be very useful in explaining the system to new users.

6.6.4 SUM\3 Instruction Section

This section should aim to teach new users how to operate the software. The viewpoint is that of the trainee.

The section should begin by taking the user through short and simple sessions. Each session should have a single purpose, such as 'to enable the user to edit a data description record'. The sessions should be designed to accompany actual use of the system, and should contain explicit references to the user's actions and the system's behaviour. The trainee should derive a sense of achievement by controlling a practical session that achieves a result.

Diagrams, plans, tables, drawings, and other illustrations should be used to show what the software is doing, and to enable the novice to form a clear and accurate mental model of the system.

The tutorial may be structured in any convenient style. It is wise to divide it into sessions lasting 30-40 minutes. Longer sessions are difficult to absorb.

A session could have the goal of introducing the user to a set of 'advanced' facilities in a system. It may not be practical or desirable to present a whole session. It may be more appropriate to give a 'tutorial tour'. Even so, it is still helpful to fit all the examples into a single framework (e.g. how to store, search and retrieve).

For each session, this section should provide:

(a) Functional description

A description of what the session is supposed to achieve, in the user's terms.

(b) Cautions and warnings

A list of precautions that may need to be taken; the user is not concerned with all possibilities at this stage, but with gaining a working understanding of some aspect of the system.

(c) Procedures

> **- set-up and initialisation operations**
>
> A description of how to prepare for and start the task;
>
> **- input operations**
>
> > A step-by-step description what the user must do and a description of the screens or windows that the system shows in response;
>
> **- what results to expect**
>
> > A description of the final results that are expected.

(d) Likely errors and possible causes

An informal description of the major errors that are possible in this task, and how to avoid them. The aim is to give the trainee user the confidence to carry on when problems arise. This section should not simply provide a list of errors, but should set them in their context.

6.6.5 SUM\4 Reference Section

This section should give comprehensive information about all the software capabilities. The viewpoint is that of the operator or expert user.

The section should contain a list of operations ordered for easy access. The order may be alphabetical (e.g. for command-driven systems) or correspond directly to the structure of the user interface (e.g. for menu-driven systems).

In contrast to the informal style of the instruction section, the reference section should be formal, rigorous and exhaustive.

For each operation, this section should provide:

(a) Functional description

A concise description of what the operation achieves.

(b) Cautions and warnings

A list of cautions and warnings that apply to the operation.

(c) Formal description, including as appropriate:

> - required parameters
> - optional parameters
> - defaults
> - syntax & semantics

Describe precisely what the operation does and how it is used. The means of doing this should be decided in advance. Syntax may be defined formally using the Backus-Naur Form (BNF). Semantics may be described by means of tables, diagrams, equations, or formal language.

(d) Examples

Give one or more worked examples to enable operators to understand the format at a glance. Commands should be illustrated with several short examples, giving the exact form of the most common permutations of parameters and qualifiers in full, and stating what they achieve.

(e) Possible errors and their causes

List all the errors that are possible for this operation and state what causes each one. If error numbers are used, explain what each one means.

(f) References to related operations

Give references to other operations which the operator may need to complete a task, and to logically related operations (e.g. refer to RETRIEVE and DELETE when describing the INSERT operation).

The operations should be described in a convenient order for quick reference: for example, alphabetically, or in functionally related groups. If the section is separately bound, then it should contain its own tables of error messages, glossary, and index; otherwise they should be provided as appendices to the body of the SUM. These appendices are described below.

6.6.6 SUM\Appendix A - Error messages and recovery procedures

This section should list all the error messages. It should not simply repeat the error message: referral to this section means that the user requires help. For each error message the section should give a diagnosis, and suggest recovery procedures. For example:

file 'TEST.DOC' does not exist.

> There is no file called 'TEST.DOC' in the current directory and drive. Check that you are in the correct directory to access this file.

If recovery action is likely to involve loss of data, remind the user about possible backup or archiving procedures.

6.6.7 SUM\Appendix B - Glossary

A glossary should be provided if the manual contains terms that operators are unlikely to know, or that are ambiguous.

Care should be taken to avoid redefining terms that operators usually employ in a different sense in a similar context. References may be provided to fuller definitions of terms, either in the SUM itself or in other sources.

Pairs of terms with opposite meanings, or groups of terms with associated meanings, should be cross-referenced within the glossary. Cross-references may be indicated with a highlight, such as italic type.

List any words used in other than their plain dictionary sense, and define their specialised meanings.

All the acronyms used in the SUM should be listed with brief explanations of what they mean.

6.6.8 SUM\Appendix C - Index

An index helps to make manuals easier to use. Manuals over 40 pages should have an index, containing a systematic list of topics from the user's viewpoint.

Indexes should contain major synonyms and variants, especially if these are well known to users but are not employed in the SUM for technical reasons. Such entries may point to primary index entries.

Index entries should point to topics in the body of the manual by:

- page number;
- section number;
- illustration number;
- primary index entry (one level of reference only).

Index entries can usefully contain auxiliary information, especially cross-references to contrasting or related terms. For example, the entry for INSERT could say 'see also DELETE'.

Indexes can provide the most help to users if attention is drawn primarily to important keywords, and to important locations in the body of the manual. This may be achieved by highlighting such entries, and by grouping minor entries under major headings. Indexes should not contain more than two levels of entry.

If a single index points to different kinds of location, such as pages and illustration numbers, these should be unambiguously distinguished, e.g.

- page 35
- figure 7

as the use of highlighting (35, 7) is not sufficient to prevent confusion in this case.

CHAPTER 7
LIFE CYCLE MANAGEMENT ACTIVITIES

7.1 INTRODUCTION

DD phase activities must be carried out according to the plans defined in the AD phase (DD01). These are:
- Software Project Management Plan for the DD phase (SPMP/DD);
- Software Configuration Management Plan for the DD phase (SCMP/DD);
- Software Verification and Validation Plan for the DD phase (SVVP/DD);
- Software Quality Assurance Plan for the DD phase (SQAP/DD).

Progress against plans should be continuously monitored by project management and documented at regular intervals in progress reports.

Plans of TR phase activities must be drawn up in the DD phase. These plans should cover project management, configuration management, quality assurance and acceptance tests.

7.2 PROJECT MANAGEMENT PLAN FOR THE TR PHASE

By the end of the DD review, the TR phase section of the SPMP (SPMP/TR) must be profduced (SPM13). The SPMP/TR describes, in detail, the project activities to be carried out in the TR phase.

Guidance on writing the SPMP/TR is provided in the *Guide to Software Project Management*.

7.3 CONFIGURATION MANAGEMENT PLAN FOR THE TR PHASE

During the DD phase, the TR phase section of the SCMP (SCMP/TR) must be produced (SCM48). The SCMP/TR must cover the configuration management procedures for deliverables in the operational environment (SCM49).

Guidance on writing the SCMP/TR is provided in *Guide to Software Configuration Management*.

7.4 QUALITY ASSURANCE PLAN FOR THE TR PHASE

During the DD phase, the TR phase section of the SQAP (SQAP/TR) must be produced (SQA10). The SQAP/TR must describe, in detail, the quality assurance activities to be carried out in the TR phase until final acceptance in the OM phase (SQA11).

SQA activities include monitoring the following activities:
- management;
- documentation;

- standards, practices, conventions, and metrics;
- reviews and audits;
- testing activities;
- problem reporting and corrective action;
- tools, techniques and methods;
- code and media control;
- supplier control;
- record collection, maintenance and retention;
- training;
- risk management.

Guidance on writing the SQAP/TR is provided in *Guide to Software Quality Assurance*.

The SQAP/TR should take account of all the software requirements related to quality, in particular:

- quality requirements;
- reliability requirements;
- maintainability requirements;
- safety requirements;
- verification requirements;
- acceptance-testing requirements.

The level of monitoring planned for the TR phase should be appropriate to the requirements and the criticality of the software. Risk analysis should be used to target areas for detailed scrutiny.

7.5 ACCEPTANCE TEST SPECIFICATION

The developer must construct an acceptance test specification in the DD phase and document it in the SVVP (SVV17). The specification should be based on the acceptance test plan produced in the UR phase. This specification should define the acceptance test:

- designs (SVV19);
- cases (SVV20);
- procedures (SVV21).

Guidance on writing the SVVP/AT is provided in *Guide to Software Verification and Validation*.

APPENDIX A
GLOSSARY

Terms used in this document are consistent with *Software Engineering Standards* [Ref. 1] and ANSI/IEEE Std 610.12-1990 [Ref. 2].

A.1 LIST OF ACRONYMS

AD	Architectural Design
ADD	Architectural Design Document
AD/R	Architectural Design Review
ANSI	American National Standards Institute
AT	Acceptance Test
BSI	British Standards Institute
BSSC	Board for Software Standardisation and Control
CASE	Computer Aided Software Engineering
DD	Detailed Design and production
DDD	Detailed Design Document
DD/R	Detailed Design and production Review
ESA	European Space Agency
HCI	Human-Computer Interaction
IEEE	Institute of Electrical and Electronics Engineers
ISO	International Standards Organisation
IT	Integration Test
ICD	Interface Control Document
JSD	Jackson System Development
JSP	Jackson Structured Programming
OOA	Object-Oriented Analysis
OOD	Object-Oriented Design
PA	Product Assurance
PDL	Program Design Language
PERT	Program Evaluation and Review Technique
PSS	Procedures, Specifications and Standards
RID	Review Item Discrepancy
SADT	Structured Analysis and Design Technique
SCM	Software Configuration Management
SCMP	Software Configuration Management Plan
SCR	Software Change Request
SPM	Software Project Management
SPMP	Software Project Management Plan

SPR	Software Problem Report
SQA	Software Quality Assurance
SQAP	Software Quality Assurance Plan
SRD	Software Requirements Document
ST	System Test
SUM	Software User Manual
SVVP	Software Verification and Validation Plan
TBC	To Be Confirmed
TBD	To Be Defined
TR	Transfer
URD	User Requirements Document
UT	Unit Test

APPENDIX B
REFERENCES

1. Software Engineering Standards, C.Mazza, J.Fairclough, B.Melton, D.dePablo, A.Scheffer, R.Stevens, Prentice-Hall, 1994.
2. IEEE Standard Glossary for Software Engineering Terminology, ANSI/IEEE Std 610.12-1990.
3. The STARTs Guide - a guide to methods and software tools for the construction of large real-time systems, NCC Publications, 1987.
4. IEEE Standard for Software Reviews and Audits, IEEE Std 1028-1988.
5. IEEE Recommended Practice for Software Design Descriptions, ANSI/IEEE Std 1016-1987.
6. Principles of Program Design, M. Jackson, Academic Press, 1975.
7. Software Engineering with Ada, second edition, G.Booch, Benjamin/Cummings Publishing Company Inc, 1986.
8. Petri Nets, J.L.Petersen, in ACM Computing Surveys, 9(3) Sept 1977.
9. IEEE Recommended Practice for Ada as Program Design Language, ANSI/IEEE Std 990-1987.
10. Structured Programming, O.-J. Dahl, E.W. Dijkstra and C.A.R.Hoare, Academic Press, 1972.
11. T.J.McCabe, A Complexity Measure, IEEE Transactions on Software Engineering, VOL SE-2, No 4, December 1976.
12. Structured Development for Real-Time Systems, P.T.Ward and S.J.Mellor, Yourdon Press, 1985 (Three Volumes).
13. Computer Languages, N.S.Baron, Penguin Books, 1986.
14. Software Reliability, G.J.Myers, Wiley, 1976
15. Object-Oriented Design, P.Coad and E.Yourdon, Prentice-Hall, 1991.

APPENDIX C
MANDATORY PRACTICES

This appendix is repeated from *Software Engineering Standards* appendix D.5.

DD01   DD phase activities shall be carried out according to the plans defined in the AD phase.

The detailed design and production of software shall be based on the following three principles:

DD02   •   top-down decomposition;

DD03   •   structured programming;

DD04   •   concurrent production and documentation.

DD05   The integration process shall be controlled by the software configuration management procedures defined in the SCMP.

DD06   Before a module can be accepted, every statement in a module shall be executed successfully at least once.

DD07   Integration testing shall check that all the data exchanged across an interface agrees with the data structure specifications in the ADD.

DD08   Integration testing shall confirm that the control flows defined in the ADD have been implemented.

DD09   System testing shall verify compliance with system objectives, as stated in the SRD.

DD10   When the design of a major component is finished, a critical design review shall be convened to certify its readiness for implementation.

DD11   After production, the DD Review (DD/R) shall consider the results of the verification activities and decide whether to transfer the software.

DD12   All deliverable code shall be identified in a configuration item list.

DD13   The DDD shall be an output of the DD phase.

DD14   Part 2 of the DDD shall have the same structure and identification scheme as the code itself, with a 1:1 correspondence between sections of the documentation and the software components.

DD15   The DDD shall be complete, accounting for all the software requirements in the SRD.

DD16   A table cross-referencing software requirements to the detailed design components shall be placed in the DDD.

DD17   A Software User Manual (SUM) shall be an output of the DD phase.

APPENDIX D
REQUIREMENTS TRACEABILITY MATRIX

REQUIREMENTS TRACEABILITY MATRIX DDD TRACED TO SRD		DATE: \<YY-MM-DD> PAGE 1 OF \<nn>
PROJECT: \<TITLE OF PROJECT>		
SRD IDENTIFIER	DDD IDENTIFIER	SOFTWARE REQUIREMENT

APPENDIX E
INDEX

Guide
to the software
transfer
phase

TABLE OF CONTENTS

CHAPTER 1
INTRODUCTION

1.1 PURPOSE

Software Engineering Standards [Ref 1] defines the fifth phase of the software life cycle to be the 'Transfer' (TR) phase.

The Transfer Phase can be called the 'handover phase' of the life cycle because the developers release the software to the users. The software is installed on the target computer system and acceptance tests are run to validate it. Activities, products and readiness for operations are reviewed by the Software Review Board (SRB) at the end of the phase.

This document provides guidance on how to transfer the software and write the Software Transfer Document (STD). This document should be read by everyone who participates in the Transfer Phase, such as the software project manager, software engineers, software quality assurance staff, maintenance staff and users.

1.2 OVERVIEW

Chapter 2 discusses the Transfer Phase. Chapter 3 describes how to write the Software Transfer Document.

All the mandatory practices in *Software Engineering Standards* relevant to the software Transfer Phase are repeated in this document. The identifier of the practice is added in parentheses to mark a repetition. This document contains no new mandatory practices.

CHAPTER 2
THE TRANSFER PHASE

2.1 INTRODUCTION

Software transfer is the process of handing-over the software to the users. This process requires the participation of both developers and users. It should be controlled and monitored by a test manager, who represents the users.

The Transfer Phase starts when the DD Phase Review Board has decided that the software is ready for transfer. The phase ends when the software be provisionally accepted.

The software should have been system tested in an environment representative of the target environment before the DD phase review. These system tests should include rehearsals of the acceptance tests. Such rehearsals are often referred to as 'Factory Acceptance Tests' (FATs).

The primary inputs to the phase are the code, Detailed Design Document (DDD) and the Software User Manual (SUM). Four plans are also required:
- Software Project Management Plan for the Transfer Phase (SPMP/TR);
- Software Configuration Management Plan for the Transfer Phase (SCMP/TR);
- Software Verification and Validation Plan, Acceptance Test section (SVVP/AT);
- Software Quality Assurance Plan for the Transfer Phase (SQAP/TR).

The Transfer Phase must be carried out according to these plans (TR03). Figure 2.1 overleaf shows the information flows into and out of the phase, and between each activity.

The first activity of Transfer Phase is to build and install the software in the target environment. The build procedures should be described in the DDD and the installation procedures should be described in the SUM. Tool support should be provided for build and installation.

The users then run the acceptance tests, as defined by the SVVP/AT. Some members of the development team should observe the tests. Test reports are completed for each execution of a test procedure. Software Problem Reports (SPRs) are completed for each problem that occurs. Tools may be employed for running the acceptance tests.

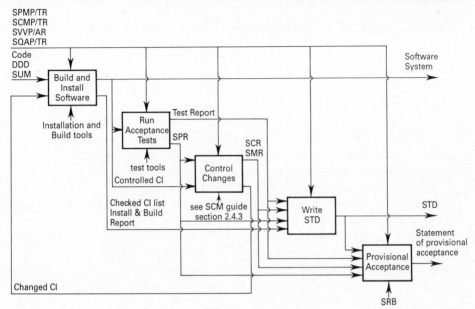

Figure 2.1: Transfer Phase activities

Problems that arise during the Transfer Phase may have to be solved before the software can be provisionally accepted. This requires the use of the change control process defined in the SCMP/TR. Software Change Requests (SCRs), Software Modification Reports (SMRs), and new versions of configuration items are produced by this process. Changed configuration items are included in a rebuild of a software. The software is then reinstalled and acceptance tests are rerun.

When problems occur, the sequence of activities of build and install software, run acceptance tests and control changes must be repeated. Software project managers should reserve enough resources to ensure that the cost of repeating these activities can be contained within the project budget.

When the acceptance tests have been completed the developer writes the Software Transfer Document (STD). This document should summarise the build and installation, acceptance test and change control activities.

When the STD is ready, the Software Review Board (SRB) meets to review the installation and acceptance test reports and any outstanding problems with the software. If the SRB is satisfied with the results, and sure that no outstanding problems are severe enough to prevent safe operation, it recommends that the initiator provisionally accepts the software. The initiator then issues a statement of provisional acceptance.

The following sections discuss in more detail the activities of software build and installation, acceptance testing, writing the STD and provisional acceptance. The change control process is discussed in section 2.3.3 and 2.4.3 of the *Guide to Software Configuration Management*.

2.2 BUILD AND INSTALL SOFTWARE

Building and installing the software consists of checking the deliverables, compiling all the source files, linking the object files, and copying the resulting executable files into the target environment for acceptance tests.

The deliverables should be listed in a 'configuration item list' . A configuration item may be any type of software or hardware element, such as a document, a source file, an object file, an executable file, a disk, or a tape. The first action upon delivery is to compare the deliverables with the configuration item list. This is done by:
- checking that all the necessary media have been supplied;
- checking that the media contain the necessary files.

After the configuration check, the software is copied to where it is to be built for the target environment.

Building the software consists of compiling the source files and linking the resulting object files into executable programs. Two kinds of builds are possible:
- a complete build, in which all sources are compiled;
- a partial build, in which only selected sources are compiled (e.g those that have changed since the last build).

Partial builds often rely on the use of procedures (e.g. 'make' files) that contain knowledge of the dependencies between files.

Software Engineering Standards requires that the capability of building the system from the components that are directly modifiable by the maintenance team be established (TR04). This means that the Transfer Phase must begin with a complete build of the software for the target environment. A complete build checks that all sources in the system are present, and is part of the process of checking that all the necessary configuration items are present.

The procedures for building the software should be contained in the DDD[1]. Tools should be provided for building the software, and the build procedures should describe how to operate them.

The build tools should allow both complete builds and partial builds. The ability to rapidly modify the software during the TR and OM phases may depend upon the ability to perform partial builds.

Installation consists of copying the 'as-built' software system to the target environment and configuring the target environment so that the software can be run as described in the Software User Manual.

The installation procedures should be described in the Software User Manual, or an annex to it.

Installation should be supported by tools that automate the process as much as possible. Instructions issued by the tools should be simple and clear. Complicated installation procedures requiring extensive manual input should be avoided.

Any changes to the existing environment should be minimal and clearly documented. Installation software should prompt the user for permission before making any changes to the system configuration (e.g. modifying the CONFIG.SYS file of a DOS-based PC).

---

[1]   *Software Engineering Standards* omitted this section from part one of the DDD. This section will be added to the DDD template in the next issue of Software Engineering Standards.

Procedures should be provided for deinstallation, so that rollback of the system to the state before installation is possible.

2.3 RUN ACCEPTANCE TESTS

The purpose of the acceptance tests is to show that the software meets the user requirements specified in the URD. This is called 'validation'. The acceptance tests are performed on the software system installed in the previous stage of the Transfer Phase.

This section addresses the following questions that have to be considered when validating the software:
- where are the acceptance tests specified?
- who should participate?
- what tools are suitable?
- what criteria should be used for passing the tests?
- what criteria should be used for suspending the tests?

2.3.1 The Acceptance Test Specification

The acceptance tests are specified in the acceptance test section of the Software Verification and Validation Plan (SVVP/AT). The SVVP/AT contains five subsections, the first four of which are prepared before the Transfer Phase:
- test plan;
- test designs;
- test cases;
- test procedures;
- test reports.

The test plan is prepared as soon as the User Requirements Document (URD) is completed at the end of the UR phase (SVV11). The test plan outlines the scope, approach, resources and schedule of the acceptance tests.

In the DD phase, tests are designed for the user requirements (SVV19), although some acceptance test design may be done earlier. Test cases and procedures are defined in the DD phase when the detailed design of the software has sufficiently stabilised (SVV20, SVV21).

The acceptance tests necessary for provisional acceptance (see Section 2.5) must be indicated in the SVVP (TR05). Some of the tests (e.g. of reliability) often require an extended period of operations, and can only be completed by final acceptance. Such tests should be clearly identified.

Personnel that carry out the tests should be familiar with the SUM and the operational environment. Instructions in the SUM need not be repeated in the SVVP.

Acceptance test reports are prepared in the Transfer Phase as each acceptance test is performed. They should be added to the SVVP/AT (SVV22). Possible formats include:
- acceptance test report forms recording the date and outcome of the test cases executed by the procedure;
- execution log file.

Guidance on the preparation of the SVVP/AT is contained in the *Guide to Software Verification and Validation*. These guidelines will be of interest to developers, who have to prepare the SVVP/AT. The following sections deal with acceptance test issues relevant to both users and developers.

2.3.2 Participation in Acceptance Tests

Users may be end users (i.e. a person who utilises the products or services of the system) or operators (i.e. a person who controls and monitors the hardware and software of a system). Both end users and operators must participate in the acceptance tests (TR01). A test manager should be appointed to control and monitor the acceptance tests and represent the users.

Members of the development team and an SQA representative should participate in the acceptance tests.

Acceptance testing is not a substitute for a training programme, which should be scheduled separately.

2.3.3 Acceptance Test Tools

Acceptance test procedures should be automated as far as possible. Tools that may be useful for acceptance testing are:
- test harnesses for running test procedures;
- performance analysers for measuring resource usage;
- comparators for comparing actual results with expected results;
- test management tools for organising the test data and scripts.

Simulators should be used when other parts of the system are not available or would be put at risk.

2.3.4 Acceptance Test Pass and Fail Criteria

The acceptance test plan (SVVP/AT/Plan) defines the test pass and fail criteria. These should be as objective as possible. The criterion that is normally used is 'the software will be judged to have passed an acceptance test if no critical software problems that relate to the test occur during the Transfer Phase'. Projects should define criteria for criticality, for example:
- critical: crash, incorrect result, unsafe behaviour;
- non-critical: typing error, failure to meet a non-essential requirement.

2.3.5 Acceptance Test Suspension and Resumption Criteria

The acceptance test plan defines the test suspension and resumption criteria. The suspension criteria should define the events that cause the abandonment of an acceptance test case, an acceptance test procedure and the acceptance test run. Criteria may, for example, be based upon test duration, percentage of tests failed, or failure of specific tests.

Flexibility in the application of the suspension criteria is usually necessary. For example a single critical software problem might cause a test procedure or even a whole test run to be abandoned. In other cases it may be possible to continue after experiencing problems, although it may not be an efficient use of resources to do so. In some situations, it may be possible to complete the acceptance tests even if there are several problems, because the problems lie within a subsystem that can be tested independently of the rest of the system.

When the problems that have caused the abandonment of an acceptance test procedure have been corrected, the entire test procedure should be repeated. All the acceptance test procedures should normally be repeated if acceptance tests are resumed after the abandonment of a test run. The decision about which acceptance tests are rerun lies with the users, in consultation with the developers.

2.4   WRITE SOFTWARE TRANSFER DOCUMENT

The purpose of the Software Transfer Document (STD) is to present the results of the Transfer Phase in a concise form, so that the Software Review Board can readily decide upon the acceptability of the software. The STD is prepared by the developer. Further information about the STD is contained in Chapter 3.

2.5   PROVISIONAL ACCEPTANCE

When the acceptance tests have been completed, the software is reviewed by the SRB. Inputs to the review are the:
- Software Transfer Document (STD);
- acceptance test results;
- Software Problem Reports made during the Transfer Phase;
- Software Change Requests made during the Transfer Phase;
- Software Modification Reports made during the Transfer Phase.

The Software Review Board (SRB) reviews these inputs and recommends, to the initiator, whether the software can be provisionally accepted or not (TR02).

The responsibilities and constitution of the SRB are defined in Section 2.2.1.3 of the *Guide to Software Configuration Management*. The software review should be a formal technical review. The procedures for a technical review are described in Section 2.3.1 of the *Guide to Software Verification and Validation*.

The SRB should confirm that the deliverables are complete and up to date by reviewing the checked configuration item list, which is part of the Software Transfer Document. The SRB should then evaluate the degree of compliance of the software with the user requirements by considering the number and nature of:
- failed test cases;
- tests cases not attempted or not completed;
- critical software problems reported;
- critical software problems not solved.

Solution of a problem means that a change request has been approved, modification has been done, and all tests repeated and passed.

The number of test cases, critical software problems and non-critical software problems should be evaluated for the whole system and for each subsystem. The SRB might, for example, decide that some subsystems are acceptable and others are not.

When the number of problems encountered in acceptance tests is low, the SRB should check the thoroughness of the acceptance tests. Experience has indicated that the existence of faults in delivered software is the rule rather than the exception (typically 1 to 4 defects per 1000 lines of code [Ref 3]).

Where appropriate, the SRB should examine the trends in the number of critical software problems reported and solved. There should be a downward trend in the number of critical problems reported. An upward trend is a cause for concern.

If the SRB decides that the degree of compliance of the software with the user requirements is acceptable, it should recommend to the initiator that the software is provisionally accepted.

The statement of provisional acceptance is produced by the initiator, on behalf of the users, and sent to the developer (TR06). The provisionally accepted software system consists of the outputs of all previous phases and the modifications found necessary in the Transfer Phase (TR07). Before it can be finally accepted, the software must enter the Operations and Maintenance phase and undergo a period of operations to prove its reliability.

CHAPTER 3
THE SOFTWARE TRANSFER DOCUMENT

3.1 INTRODUCTION

Software Engineering Standards states that the Software Transfer Document (STD) shall be an output of the Transfer Phase (TR08). The purpose of the STD is to summarise:
- the software that has been delivered;
- the build of the software;
- the installation of the software;
- the acceptance test results;
- the problems that occurred during the Transfer Phase;
- the changes requested during the Transfer Phase;
- the modifications done during the Transfer Phase.

3.2 STYLE

The STD should be concise, clear and consistent.

3.3 EVOLUTION

The developer should prepare the STD after the acceptance tests and before the software review.

If the software is provisionally accepted, the completed STD must be handed over by the developer to the maintenance organisation at the end of the Transfer Phase (TR09).

After the Transfer Phase the STD should not be modified. New releases of the software in the Operations and Maintenance Phase are documented in Software Release Notes (SRNs), rather than in new issues of the STD.

3.4 RESPONSIBILITY

The developer is responsible for the production of the STD. The software librarian or software quality assurance engineer are suitable people for writing it.

3.5 MEDIUM

The STD is normally a paper document.

3.6 CONTENT

Software Engineering Standards recommends the following table of contents for the Software Transfer Document:

```
1 INTRODUCTION
    1.1 Purpose
    1.2 Scope
    1.3 Definitions, acronyms and abbreviations
    1.4 References
2 BUILD PROCEDURES²
3 INSTALLATION PROCEDURES
4 CONFIGURATION ITEM LIST
5 ACCEPTANCE TEST REPORT SUMMARY
6 SOFTWARE PROBLEM REPORTS
7 SOFTWARE CHANGE REQUESTS
8 SOFTWARE MODIFICATION REPORTS
```

3.6.1 STD/1 INTRODUCTION

3.6.1.1 STD/1.1 Purpose

This section should define the purpose of the STD, for example: 'This Software Transfer Document (STD) reports in summary form the Transfer Phase activities for the [insert the name of the project here]'.

3.6.1.2 STD/1.2 Scope

This section should summarise the software that is being transferred.

Projects that adopt incremental delivery or evolutionary life cycle approaches will have multiple Transfer Phases. Each Transfer Phase must produce an STD. Each STD should define the scope of the software being transferred in that particular Transfer Phase.

3.6.1.3 STD/1.3 Definitions, acronyms and abbreviations

This section should define all the terms, acronyms, and abbreviations used in the STD, or refer to other documents where the definitions can be found.

3.6.1.4 STD/1.4 References

This section should provide a complete list of all the applicable or reference documents, identified by title, author and date. Each document should be marked as applicable or reference. If appropriate, report number, journal name and publishing organisation should be included.

---

² *Software Engineering Standards* states that Build Procedures must be section 3 and Installation Procedures must be section 2. This order will be reversed in the next issue of Software Engineering Standards.

3.6.2 STD/2 BUILD PROCEDURES

This section should report what happened when the software system was built. For example this section may report:

- when the software was built;
- where the software was built;
- the hardware and software environment in which the software was built;
- which version of the software was built;
- any problems encountered during the build;
- the CPU time and elapsed time required for building the system;
- the elapsed time required for building the system.

This section should reference the build procedures, which should have been defined in the Detailed Design Document[3].

3.6.3 STD/3 INSTALLATION PROCEDURES

This section should report what happened when the software was installed. For example this section may report:

- when the software was installed;
- where the software was installed;
- the hardware and software environment in which the software was installed;
- which version of the software was installed;
- any problems encountered during the installation;
- the elapsed time required for installing the system;
- the disk space used;
- the system parameters modified.

The organisation of the software files in the target environment should be described (e.g. root directory, subdirectories etc).

This section should reference the installation procedures, which should have been defined in the Software User Manual, or an annex to it.

3.6.4 STD/4 CONFIGURATION ITEM LIST

This section should contain the list of the configuration items transferred. There should be evidence that the transferral of each configuration item has been verified (e.g. a completed checklist).

3.6.5 STD/5 ACCEPTANCE TEST REPORT SUMMARY

This section must contain a summary of the acceptance test reports (TR10). An overall statement of pass or fail for each subsystem should be provided. Specific test failures should be identified and discussed.

This section should identify all the user requirements that the software does not comply with. The list should include the value of the need attribute of the requirement (e.g. essential, desirable).

---

[3] *Software Engineering Standards* omitted this section from part one of the DDD. This section will be added to the DDD template in the next issue of Software Engineering Standards.

This section should present data for the following metrics:
- number of acceptance test cases passed;
- number of acceptance test cases failed;
- number acceptance test cases not attempted or completed.

Data should be presented for the whole system and individually for each subsystem.

3.6.6 STD/6 SOFTWARE PROBLEM REPORTS

This section should list the Software Problem Reports (SPRs) raised during the Transfer Phase and their status at STD issue. Information about software problems should be present in the project configuration status accounts.

This section should present data for the following metrics:
- number of software problems reported;
- number of software problems closed;
- number of software problems open (i.e. status is action or update).

Data should be presented for all the SPRs, critical SPRs and non-critical SPRs.

3.6.7 STD/7 SOFTWARE CHANGE REQUESTS

This section should list the Software Change Requests (SCRs) raised during the Transfer Phase and their status at STD issue. Information about software changes should be present in the project configuration status accounts.

This section should present data for the following metrics:
- number of software change requests closed;
- number of software change requests open (i.e. status is action or update).

Data should be presented for all the SCRs, critical SCRs and non-critical SCRs.

3.6.8 STD/8 SOFTWARE MODIFICATION REPORTS

This section must list the Software Modification Reports (SMRs) completed during the Transfer Phase (TR10). Information about software modifications should be present in the project configuration status accounts.

This section should present data for the following metrics:
- number of software modifications closed;
- number of software modifications in progress.

Data should be presented for all the SMRs, critical SMRs and non-critical SMRs. An SMR is critical if it relates to a critical SCR.

APPENDIX A
GLOSSARY

A.1 LIST OF TERMS

Terms used in this document are consistent with *Software Engineering Standards* [Ref 1] and ANSI/IEEE Std 610.12 [Ref 2]. Additional terms not defined in these standards are listed below.

complete build
The process of compiling all the source files written by the developers and linking the object files produced with each other, and external object files.

development environment
The environment of computer hardware, operating software and test software in which the software system is developed.

end user
A person who utilises the products or services of a system.

installation
The process of copying a software system into the target environment and configuring the target environment to make the software system usable.

operational environment
The target environment, external software and users.

operator
A person who controls and monitors the hardware and software of a system.

partial build
The process of compiling selected source files (e.g those that have changed since the last build) and linking the object files produced with each other, and pre-existing object files.

target environment
The environment of computer hardware and operating software in which the software system is used.

user
A person who utilises the products or services of a system, or a person who controls and monitors the hardware and software of a system (i.e. an end user, an operator, or both).

A.2 LIST OF ACRONYMS

ANSI	American National Standards Institute
AT	Acceptance Test
BSSC	Board for Software Standardisation and Control
CASE	Computer Aided Software Engineering
DD	Detailed Design and production
FAT	Factory Acceptance Test
SCMP	Software Configuration Management Plan
SCR	Software Change Request
SMR	Software Modification Report
SPMP	Software Project Management Plan
SPR	Software Problem Report
SQAP	Software Quality Assurance Plan
SR	Software Requirements definition
SRD	Software Requirements Document
SRN	Software Release Note
STD	Software Transfer Document
SVVP	Software Verification and Validation Plan
TR	Transfer
UR	User Requirements definition
URD	User Requirements Document

APPENDIX B
REFERENCES

1. Software Engineering Standards, C.Mazza, J.Fairclough, B.Melton, D.dePablo, A.Scheffer, R.Stevens, Prentice-Hall, 1994.
2. IEEE Standard Glossary of Software Engineering Terminology, ANSI/IEEE Std 610.12-1990
3. Managing Computer Projects, R. Gibson, Prentice-Hall, 1992.

APPENDIX C
MANDATORY PRACTICES

This appendix is repeated from *Software Engineering Standards* appendix D.6

TR01   Representatives of users and operations personnel shall participate in acceptance tests.

TR02   The Software Review Board (SRB) shall review the software's performance in the acceptance tests and recommend, to the initiator, whether the software can be provisionally accepted or not.

TR03   Transfer Phase activities shall be carried out according to the plans defined in the DD phase.

TR04   The capability of building the system from the components that are directly modifiable by the maintenance team shall be established.

TR05   Acceptance tests necessary for provisional acceptance shall be indicated in the SVVP.

TR06   The statement of provisional acceptance shall be produced by the initiator, on behalf of the users, and sent to the developer.

TR07   The provisionally accepted software system shall consist of the outputs of all previous phases and modifications found necessary in the Transfer Phase.

TR08   An output of the Transfer Phase shall be the STD.

TR09   The STD shall be handed over from the developer to the maintenance organisation at provisional acceptance.

TR10   The STD shall contain the summary of the acceptance test reports, and all documentation about software changes performed during the Transfer Phase.

APPENDIX D
INDEX

Guide
to the software
operations and
maintenance
phase

TABLE OF CONTENTS

CHAPTER 1
INTRODUCTION

1.1 PURPOSE

Software Engineering Standards [Ref 1] defines the sixth and last phase of the software life cycle to be the 'Operations and Maintenance' (OM) phase.

The OM Phase is the 'operational' phase of the life cycle in which users operate the software and utilise the end products and services it provides. The developers provide maintenance and user support until the software is finally accepted, after which a maintenance organisation becomes responsible for it.

This document describes how to maintain the software, support operations, and how to produce the 'Project History Document' (PHD). This document should be read by everyone involved with software maintenance or software operations support. The software project manager of the development organisation should read the chapter on the Project History Document.

1.2 OVERVIEW

Chapter 2 discusses the OM phase. Chapters 3 and 4 discuss methods and tools for software maintenance. Chapter 5 describes how to write the PHD. Chapter 6 discusses life cycle management activities.

All the mandatory practices in *Software Engineering Standards* relevant to the software operations and maintenance phase are repeated in this document. The identifier of the practice is added in parentheses to mark a repetition. This document contains no new mandatory practices.

CHAPTER 2
THE OPERATIONS AND MAINTENANCE PHASE

2.1 INTRODUCTION

Operations provide a product or a service to end users. This guide discusses operations from the point of view of their interactions with software maintenance activities and the support activities needed to use the software efficiently and effectively.

Software maintenance is 'the process of modifying a software system or component after delivery to correct faults, improve performance or other attributes, or adapt to a changed environment' [Ref 2]. Maintenance is always necessary to keep software usable and useful. Often there are very tight constraints on changing software and optimum solutions can be difficult to find. Such constraints make maintenance a challenge; contrast to the development phase, when designers have considerably more freedom in the type of solution they can adopt.

Software maintenance activities can be classified as:

- corrective;
- perfective;
- adaptive.

Corrective maintenance removes software faults. Corrective maintenance should be the overriding priority of the software maintenance team.

Perfective maintenance improves the system without changing its functionality. The objective of perfective maintenance should be to prevent failures and optimise the software. This might be done, for example, by modifying the components that have the highest failure rate, or components whose performance can be cost-effectively improved [Ref 6].

Adaptive maintenance modifies the software to keep it up to date with its environment. Users, hardware platforms and other systems all make up the environment of a software system. Adaptive maintenance may be needed because of changes in the user requirements, changes in the target platform, or changes in external interfaces.

Minor adaptive changes (e.g. addition of a new command parameter) may be handled by the normal maintenance process. Major adaptive changes (e.g. addition of costly new user requirements, or porting the software to a new platform) should be carried out as a separate development project (See Chapter 5).

The operations and maintenance phase starts when the initiator provisionally accepts the software. The phase ends when the software is taken out of use. The phase is divided into two periods by the final acceptance milestone (OM03). All the acceptance tests must have been successfully completed before final acceptance (OM02).

There must be a maintenance organisation for every software product in operational use (OM04). The developers are responsible for software maintenance and user support until final acceptance. Responsibility for these activities passes to a maintenance team upon final acceptance. The software project manager leads the developers. Similarly, the 'software maintenance manager' leads the maintenance team. Software project managers and software maintenance managers are collectively called 'software managers'.

The mandatory inputs to the operations and maintenance phase are the provisionally accepted software system, the statement of provisional acceptance and the Software Transfer Document (STD). Some of the plans from the development phases may also be input.

The developer writes the Project History Document (PHD) during the warranty period. This gives an overview of the whole project and a summary account of the problems and performance of the software during the warranty period. This document should be input to the Software Review Board (SRB) that recommends about final acceptance. The PHD is delivered to the initiator at final acceptance (OM10).

Before final acceptance, the activities of the development team are controlled by the SPMP/TR (OM01). The development team will normally continue to use the SCMP, SVVP and SQAP from the earlier phases. After final acceptance, the maintenance team works according to its own plans. The new plans may reuse plans that the development team made, if appropriate. The maintenance team may have a different configuration management system, for example, but continue to employ the test tools and test software used by the developers.

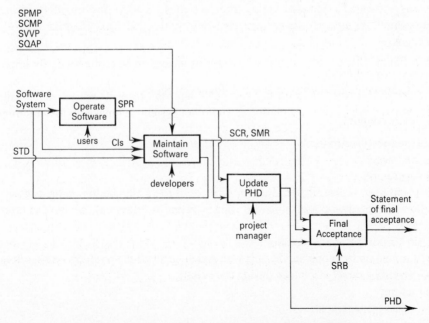

Figure 2.1A: OM phase activities before final acceptance

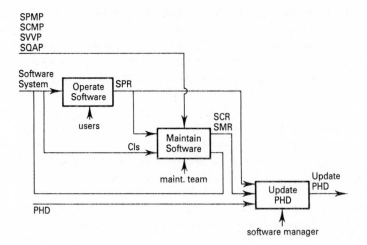

Figure 2.1B: OM phase activities after final acceptance

Figures 2.1A and 2.1B show the activities, inputs and outputs of the phase, and the information flows between them. The arrows into the bottom of each box indicate the group responsible for each activity. The following sections discuss in more detail the activities of operate software, maintain software, update Project History Document and final acceptance.

2.2 OPERATE SOFTWARE

The way software is operated varies from system to system and therefore cannot be discussed in this guide. However there are two activities that occur during most software operations:

- user support;
- problem reporting.

These activities are discussed in the following sections.

2.2.1 User support

There are two types of user:

- end user;
- operator.

An 'end user' utilises the products or services of a system. An 'operator' controls and monitors the hardware and software of a system. A user may be an end user, an operator, or both.

User support activities include:

- training users to operate the software and understand the products and services;
- providing direct assistance during operations;
- set-up;
- data management.

Users should receive training. The amount of training depends upon the experience of the users and the complexity or novelty of the software. The training may range from allowing the users time to read the SUM and familiarise themselves with the software, to a course provided by experts, possibly from the development or maintenance teams.

Software User Manuals and training are often insufficient to enable users to operate the software in all situations and deal with problems. Users may require:

- direct assistance from experts in the development or maintenance teams;
- help desks.

Full-time direct assistance from experts is normally required to support critical activities. Part-time direct assistance from experts is often sufficient for software that is not critical and has few users.

When the number of users becomes too large for the experts to be able to combine user support activities with their software maintenance activities, a help desk is normally established to:

- provide users with advice, news and other information about the software;
- receive problem reports and decide how they should be handled.

While help desk staff do not need to have expert knowledge of the design and code, they should have detailed knowledge of how to operate it and how to solve simple problems.

The set-up of a software system may be a user support activity when the software set-up is complex, shared by multiple users, or requires experts to change it to minimise the risk of error.

Data management is a common user support activity, and may include:

- configuring data files for users;
- managing disk storage resources;
- backup and archiving.

2.2.2 Problem reporting

Users should document problems in Software Problem Reports (SPRs). These should be genuine problems that the user believes lie in the software, not problems arising from unfamiliarity with it.

Each SPR should report one and only one problem and contain:

- software configuration item title or name;
- software configuration item version or release number;
- priority of the problem with respect to other problems;
- a description of the problem;
- operating environment;
- recommended solution (if possible).

The priority of a problem has two dimensions:

- criticality (critical/non-critical);
- urgency (urgent/routine).

The person reporting the problem should decide whether it is critical or non-critical. A problem is critical if the software or an essential feature of the software is unavailable. The person should also decide whether the solution is required as soon as possible (urgent) or when the Software Review Board decides is best (routine).

Users should attempt to describe the problem and the operating environment as accurately as possible to help the software engineers to reproduce the problem. Printouts and log files may be attached to the Software Problem Report to assist problem diagnosis.

Problems may occur because the software does not have specific capabilities or comply with some constraints. Users should document such omissions in SPRs, not in a modification to the User Requirements Document. The URD may be modified at a later stage when and if the Software Review Board (SRB) approves the new user requirement.

Figure 2.2 shows the life cycle of a software problem report. An SPR is prepared and submitted to the maintenance team for diagnosis. The maintenance team prepares a Software Change Request (SCR) if they decide that a software change is required to solve the problem. The SPR and related SCR are then considered at a Software Review Board meeting.

The Software Review Board decides upon one of four possible outcomes for the SPR:

- reject the SPR;
- update the software based upon the related SCR;
- action someone to carry out further diagnosis;
- close the SPR because the update has been completed.

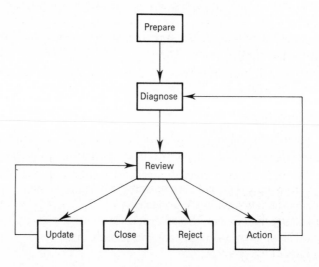

Figure 2.2: The life cycle of an SPR

2.3 MAINTAIN SOFTWARE

Software maintenance should be a controlled process that ensures that the software continues to meet the needs of the end user. This process consists of the following activities:

- change software;
- release software;
- install release;
- validate release.

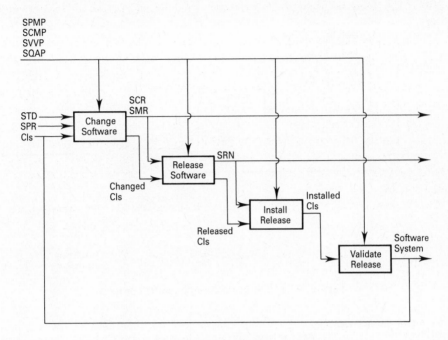

Figure 2.3: The software maintenance process

Figure 2.3 shows the inputs and outputs of each activity, which are discussed in more detail in the following sections.

2.3.1 Change Software

Software change should be governed by a change control process defined in the Software Configuration Management Plan. All change control processes should be based upon the code change control process described in the *Guide to Software Configuration Management,* shown in Figure 2.3.1. Configuration management tools should be used to control software change. These are described in the Guide to Software Configuration Management.

Software change is a four stage process:

- diagnose problems;
- review change requests;
- modify software;
- verify software.

The following sections describe each stage.

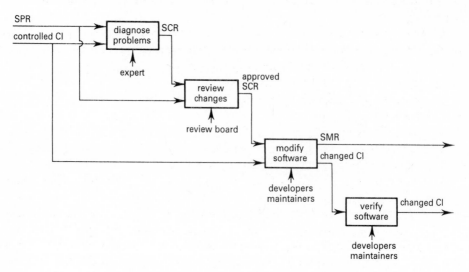

Figure 2.3.1: The basic change control process

2.3.1.1 Diagnose Problems

Software Problem Reports (SPRs) arising from software operations are collected and assigned to an expert software engineer from the maintenance team, who examines software configuration items and diagnoses the cause of the problem. The software engineer may recommend software changes in a Software Change Request (SCR).

The steps in problem diagnosis are:

- examine SPR;
- reproduce the problem, if possible;
- examine code and/or documentation;
- identify the fault;
- identify the cause;
- write a Software Change Request, if necessary.

Examination of code and documentation may require backtracking from code and Software User Manual through the Detailed Design Document, the Architectural Design Document, the Software Requirements Document and ultimately the User Requirements Document.

Software engineers often diagnose a problem by building a variant configuration item that:

- is able to work with debugging tools;
- contains diagnostic code.

The software engineers run the variant and attempt to reproduce the problem and understand why it happened. When they have made a diagnosis they may insert prototype code to solve the problem. They then test that the problem does not recur. If it does not, the person responsible for modifying the software may user the prototype code as a starting point. The maintenance team should be wary of the first solution that works.

When the cause of a problem has been found, the software engineer should request a change to the software to prevent the problem recurring. Every Software Change Request (SCR) should contain the following information:

- software configuration item title or name;
- software configuration item version or release number;
- changes required;
- priority of the request;
- responsible staff;
- estimated start date, end date and manpower effort.

The software engineer provides the first three pieces of information. The software manager should define the last three.

The specification of the changes should be detailed enough to allow management to decide upon their necessity and practicality. The SCR does not need to contain the detailed design of the change. Any changes identified by the person who diagnosed the problem, such as marked-up listings of source code and pages of documentation, should be attached to the SCR.

Like software problems, the priority of a software change request has two dimensions:

- criticality (critical/non-critical);
- urgency (urgent/routine).

The software manager should decide whether the change request is critical or non-critical. A change is critical if it has a major impact on either the software behaviour or the maintenance budget. The criticality of a software change request is evaluated differently from the criticality of a software problem. For example an SPR may be classified as critical because an essential feature of the software is not available. The corresponding SCR may be non-critical because a single line of code is diagnosed as causing the problem, and this can be easily modified.

The software manager should decide whether the change is urgent or routine. A change is urgent if it has to be implemented and released to the user as soon as possible. Routine changes are released in convenient groups according to the release schedule in the software project management plan. The software manager normally gives the same urgency rating as the user, although he or she has the right to award a different rating.

The SCR is normally presented as a form, but it may be a document. A change request document should contain sections on:

- user requirements document changes;
- software requirements document changes;
- architectural design document changes;
- detailed design document changes;
- software project management plan update;
- software verification and validation plan for the change;
- software quality assurance plan for the change.

Each section should include or reference the corresponding development documents as appropriate. For example a change to the code to remedy a detailed design fault might:

- put 'no change' in the URD, SRD and ADD change sections;
- contain a new version of the DDD component description;
- contain a listing of the code with a prototype modification suggested by the expert who made the change request;
- contain a unit test design, unit test case and unit test procedure for verifying the code change;
- identify the integration, system and acceptance test cases that should be rerun;
- contain a work package description for the change;
- identify the software release that will contain the change.

Investigation of a software problem may reveal the need to implement a temporary 'workaround' solution to a problem pending the implementation of a complete solution. The workaround and the complete solution should have a separate SCR.

2.3.1.2 Review Changes

The Software Review Board (SRB) must authorise all changes to the software (OM08). The SRB should consist of people who have sufficient authority to resolve any problems with the software. The software manager and software quality assurance engineer should always be members. Users are normally members unless the software is part of a larger system. In this case the system manager is a member, and represents the interests of the whole system and the users.

The SRB should delegate responsibility for filtering SPRs and SCRs to the software manager. The order of filtering is:

- criticality (critical/non-critical);
- urgency (urgent/routine).

The decision tree shown in Figure 2.3.1.2 illustrates the four possible combinations of urgency and criticality, and defines what action should be taken.

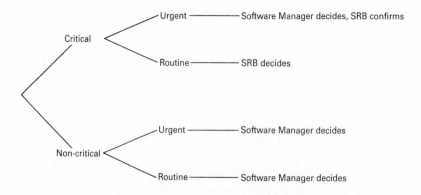

Figure 2.3.1.2: SPR and SCR filtering

The three possible actions are:

1. **critical and urgent:** the software manager decides upon the implementation of the change and passes the SCR and associated SPRs to the SRB for confirmation;
2. **critical and routine:** the software manager passes the SCR and associated SPRs to the SRB for review and decision;
3. **non-critical:** the software manager decides upon the implementation of the change and passes the SCR and associated SPRs to the SRB for information.

Software Review Board meetings should use the technical review process described in the *Guide to Software Verification and Validation*, with the following modifications:

- the objective of an SRB review is to decide what software changes will be implemented;
- the inputs to the SRB review are the SCRs, SPRs and attachments such as part of a document, a source code listing, a program traceback or a log file;
- the preparation activity is to examine the SPRs and SCRs, not RIDs;
- SRB review meetings are concerned with the SPRs and SCRs, not RIDs, and follow the typical agenda described below.

A typical SRB review meeting agenda consists of:

1. introduction;
2. review actions from the previous meeting;
3. review of the SPR and SCR criticality and urgency classification;
4. review of the critical SPRs;
5. review of the critical SCRs;
6. decision on the SPRs and SCRs;
7. conclusion.

Actions from the previous meeting may have included software change requests. The SRB should close SPRs that are associated with satisfied change requests. Every closed SPR must have one or more associated Software Modification Reports (SMRs) that describe what has been done to solve the problem.

The criticality and urgency of SPRs and SCRs should be reviewed. Members may request that they be reclassified.

Critical SPRs that have not been closed are then discussed. The discussion should confine itself to describing the seriousness and extent of the problem. The Software Review Board decisions should be one of 'update', 'action or 'reject' (See Figure 2.2). The status should become 'update' when the SRB is satisfied that the problem exists and requires a change to the software. The status should become 'action' when there is no satisfactory diagnosis. The status should become 'reject' if the SRB decides that the problem does not exist or that no update or action is necessary.

Critical SCRs are then discussed. The discussion should confine itself to reviewing the effects of the requested changes and the risks involved. Detailed design issues should be avoided. The SRB may discuss the recommendations of the software manager as to:

- who should be the responsible staff;
- how much effort should be allocated;
- when the changes should be implemented and released.

Any part of the SCR may be modified by the SRB. After discussion, the SRB should decide upon whether to approve the change request.

2.3.1.3 Modify Software

When the software change request has been approved, the maintenance team implement the change. The remaining tasks are to:
- modify the documents and code;
- review the modified documents and code;
- test the modified code.

The outputs of these tasks are a Software Modification Report (SMR) and modified configuration items. The SMR defines the:
- names of configuration items that have been modified;
- version or release numbers of the modified configuration items;
- changes that have been implemented;
- actual start date, end date and manpower effort.

Attachments to the SMR should include unit, integration and system test results, as appropriate.

Software systems can be ruined by poor maintenance, and people responsible for it should:
- evaluate the effects of every change;
- verify all software modifications thoroughly;
- keep documentation up to date.

2.3.1.3.1 Evaluating the effects of a change

Software engineers should evaluate the effect of a modification on:
a. performance;
b. resource consumption.
c. cohesion;
d. coupling;
e. complexity;
f. consistency;
g. portability;
h. reliability;
i. maintainability;
j. safety;
k. security.

The effect of changes may be evaluated with the aid of reverse engineering tools and librarian tools. Reverse engineering tools can identify the modules affected by a change at program design level (e.g. identify each module that uses a particular global variable). Librarian tools with cross reference facilities can track dependencies at the source file level (e.g. identify every file that includes a specific file).

There is often more than one way of changing the software to solve a problem, and software engineers should examine the options, compare their effects on the software, and select the best solution. The following sections provide guidance on the evaluation of the software in terms of the attributes listed above.

a. Performance

Performance requirements specify the capacity and speed of the operations the software has to perform. Design specifications may specify how fast a component has to execute.

The effects of a change on software performance should be predicted and later measured in tests. Performance analysis tools may assist measurement. Prototyping may be useful.

b. Resource Consumption

Resource requirements specify the maximum amount of computer resources the software can use. Design specifications may specify the maximum resources available.

The effects of a change on resource consumption should be predicted when it is designed and later measured in tests. Performance analysis tools and system monitoring tools should be used to measure resource consumption. Again, prototyping may be useful.

c. Cohesion

Cohesion measures the degree to which the activities within a component relate to one another. The cohesion of a software component should not be reduced by a change. Cohesion effects should be evaluated when changes are designed.

The *Guide to the Software Architectural Design Phase* identifies seven types of cohesion ranging from functional (good) to coincidental (bad). This scale can be used to evaluate the effect of a change on the cohesion of a software component.

d. Coupling

Coupling measures the interdependence of two or more components. Changes that increase coupling should be avoided, as they reduce information hiding. Coupling effects should be evaluated when changes are designed.

The *Guide to the Software Architectural Design Phase* identifies five types of coupling ranging from 'data coupling' (good) to 'content coupling' (bad). This scale can be used to evaluate the effect of a change on the coupling of a software component.

e. Complexity

During the operations and maintenance phase the complexity of software naturally tends to grow because its control structures have to be extended to meet new requirements [Ref 7]. Software engineers should contain this natural growth of complexity because more complex software requires more testing, and more testing requires more effort. Eventually changes become infeasible because they require more effort than is available to implement them. Reduced complexity means greater reliability and maintainability.

Software complexity can be measured by several metrics, the best known metric being cyclomatic complexity [Ref 3]. Procedures for measuring cyclomatic complexity and other important metrics are contained in the *Guide to the Software Architectural Design Phase* and the *Guide to Software Verification and Validation*. McCabe has proposed an 'essential complexity metric' for measuring the distortion of the control structure of a module caused by a software change [Ref 8].

f. Consistency

Coding standards define the style in which a programming language should be used. They may enforce or ban the use of language features and define rules for layout and presentation. Changes to software should conform to the coding standards and should be seamless

Polymorphism means that a function will perform the same operation on a variety of data types. Programmers extending the range of data types can easily create inconsistent variations of the same function. This can cause a polymorphic function to behave in unexpected ways. Programmers modifying a polymorphic function should fully understand what the variations of the function do.

g. Portability

Portability is measured by the ease of moving software from one environment to another. Portability can be achieved by adhering to language and coding standards. A common way to make software portable is to encapsulate platform-specific code in 'interface modules'. Only the interface modules need to be modified when the software is ported.

Software engineers should evaluate the effect of a modification on the portability of the software when it is designed. Changes that reduce portability should be avoided.

h. Reliability

Reliability is most commonly measured by the Mean Time Between Failures (MTBF). Changes that reduce reliability should be avoided.

Changes that introduce defects into the software make it less reliable. The software verification process aims to detect and remove defects (see Section 2.3.1.). Walkthroughs and inspections should be used to verify that defects are not introduced when the change is designed. Tests should be used to verify that no defects have been introduced by the change after it has been implemented.

The effect of a modification on software reliability can be estimated indirectly by measuring its effect on the complexity of the software. This effect can be measured when the change is designed.

Reliability can be reduced by reusing components that have not been developed to the same standards as the rest of the software. Software engineers should find out how reliable a software component is before reusing it.

i. Maintainability

Maintainability measures the ease with which software can be maintained. The most common maintainability metric is 'Mean Time To Repair'. Changes that make software less maintainable should be avoided.

Examples of changes that make software less maintainable are those that:
- violate coding standards;
- reduce cohesion;
- increase coupling;
- increase essential complexity [Ref 8].

The costs and benefits of changes that make software more maintainable should be evaluated before such changes are made. All modified code must be tested, and the cost of retesting the new code may outweigh the reduced effort required to make future changes.

j. Safety

Changes to the software should not endanger people or property during operations or following a failure. The effect on the safety of the software should first be evaluated when the change is designed and later during the verification process. The behaviour of the software after a failure should be analysed from the safety point of view.

k. Security

Changes to the software should not expose the system to threats to its confidentiality, integrity and availability. The effect of a change on the security of the software should first be evaluated when the change is designed and later during the verification process.

2.3.1.3.2 Keeping documentation up to date

Consistency between code and documentation must be maintained (OM06). This is achieved by:

- thorough analysis of the impact of every change before it is made, to ensure that no inconsistencies are introduced;
- concurrent update of code and documentation;
- verification of the changes by peer review or independent review.

Tools for deriving detailed design information from source code are invaluable for keeping documentation up to date. The detailed design component specification is placed in the module header. When making a change, programmers:

- modify the detailed design specification in the header;
- modify the module code;
- compile the module;
- review the module modifications;
- unit test the module;
- run a tool to derive the corresponding detailed design document section.

Programmers should use the traceability matrices to check for consistency between the code, DDD, ADD, SRD and URD. Traceability matrices are important navigational aids and should be kept up to date. Tools that support traceability are very useful in the maintenance phase.

2.3.1.4 Verify software modifications

Software modifications should be verified by:

- a. review of the detailed design and code;
- b. testing.

a. Detailed design and code reviews

The detailed design and code of all changes should be reviewed before they are tested. These reviews should be distinguished from earlier reviews done by the software manager or Software Review Board (SRB) that examine and approve the change request. The detailed design and code are normally not available when the change request is approved.

The detailed design and code of all changes should be examined by someone other than the software engineer who implemented them. The walkthrough or inspection process should be used.

b. Tests

Modified software must be retested before release (SCM39). This is normally done by:

- unit, integration and system testing each change;
- running regression tests at unit, integration and system level to verify that there are no side-effects.

Changes that do not alter the control flow should be tested by rerunning the white box tests that execute the part of the software that changed. Changes that do alter the control flow should be tested by designing white box tests to execute every new branch in the control flow that has been created. Black box tests should be designed to verify any new functionality.

Ideally system tests should be run after each change. This may be a very costly exercise for a large system, and an alternative less costly approach often adopted for large systems is to accumulate changes and then run the system tests (including regression tests) just before release. The disadvantage of this approach is that it may be difficult to identify which change, if any, is the cause of a problem in the system tests.

2.3.2 Release Software

Changed configuration items are made available to users through the software release process. This consists of:

- defining the release;
- documenting the release;
- auditing the release;
- delivering the release.

2.3.2.1 Define release

Software managers should define the content and timing of a software release according to the needs of users. This means that:

- solutions to urgent problems are released as soon as possible only to the people experiencing the problem, or who are likely to experience the problem;
- other changes are released when the users are ready to accommodate them.

Software managers, in consultation with the Software Review Board, should allocate changes to one of three types of release:

- major release;
- minor release;
- emergency release (also called a 'patch').

Table 2.3.2.1 shows how they differ according to whether:

- adaptive changes have been made;
- perfective changes have been made;
- corrective changes have been made;
- all or selected software configuration items are included in the release;
- all or selected users will receive the release.

	Adaptive Changes	Perfective Changes	Corrective Changes	CIs	Users
Major Release	Yes	Yes	Yes	All	All
Minor Release	Small	Yes	Yes	All	All
Emergency Release	No	No	Yes	Selected	Selected

Table 2.3.2.1: Major, minor and emergency releases

The purpose of a major release of a software system is to provide new capabilities. These require adaptive changes. Major releases also correct outstanding faults and perfect the existing software. Operations may have to be interrupted for some time after a major release has been installed because training is required. Major releases should therefore not be made too frequently because of the disruption they can cause. A typical time interval between major releases is one year. Projects using evolutionary and incremental delivery life cycle approaches would normally make a major release in each transfer phase.

The purpose of a minor release is to provide corrections to a group of problems. Some low-risk perfective maintenance changes may be included. A minor release of a software system may also provide small extensions to existing capabilities. Such changes can be easily assimilated by users without training.

The frequency of minor releases depends upon:
- the rate at which software problems are reported;
- the urgency of solving the software problems.

The purpose of an emergency release is to get a modification to the users who need it as fast as possible. Only the configuration items directly affected by the fault are released. Changes are nearly always corrective.

2.3.2.2 Document release

Every software release must be accompanied by a Software Release Note (SRN) (SCM14). Software Release Notes should describe the:
- software item title/name;
- software item version/release number;
- changes in the release;
- list of configuration items included in the release;
- installation instructions.

Forms are used for simple releases and documents for complex releases.

2.3.2.2.1 Release number

The SRN should define the version number of the release. The structure of the version number should reflect the number of different types of releases used. A common structure used is two or three integers separated by a full stop:

major release number.minor release number[.emergency release number]

The square brackets indicate that the emergency release number is optional because it is only included when it is not zero. When any release number is incremented the succeeding numbers are set to zero.

2.3.2.2.2 Changes in the release

The section of the SRN should list all the changes in the release. For each change:
- give a paragraph summarising the effects that the users will see resulting from the change;
- enumerate the related SPRs and SCRs (SCM36).

2.3.2.2.3 List of configuration items included in the release

This section of the SRN should list the configuration identifiers of all the configuration items in the release.

2.3.2.2.4 Installation instructions

This section of the SRN should describe how to install the release. This is normally done by referencing the installation instructions in the Software User Manual[1], or providing updated instructions, or both.

2.3.2.3 Audit release

Functional and physical audits shall be performed before the release of the software (SVV03). The purpose of the audits is to verify that all the necessary software configuration items are present, consistent and correct.

A functional audit verifies that the development of a configuration item has been completed satisfactorily, that the item has achieved the performance and functional characteristics specified in the software requirements and design documents [Ref 2]. This is normally done by checking the test reports for the software release. A functional audit also verifies that the operational and support documents are complete and satisfactory.

A physical audit verifies that an as-built configuration conforms to its documentation. This is done by checking that:
- all the configuration items listed in the SRN are actually present;
- documentation and code in a software release are consistent (SCM37).

---

[1] *Software Engineering Standards* states that Installation Instructions should be placed in the STD. The SUM is a normally a more suitable place to put them.

2.3.2.4 Deliver release

The software can be delivered when the audits have been done. The maintenance team are responsible for copying the software onto the release media, packaging the media with the software documentation and delivering the package.

The maintenance team must archive every release (SCM38). This is best done by keeping a copy of the delivered package. Although users may wish to retain old releases for reference, the responsibility for retaining a copy of every release lies with the maintenance team.

2.3.3 Install Release

Upon delivery, the contents of the release are checked against the configuration item list in the Software Release Note (SRN) and then the software is installed. The installation procedures are also described or identified in the SRN.

Installation should be supported by tools that
- automate the installation process as much as possible;
- issue simple and clear instructions;
- reuse configuration information from the existing system and not require users to reenter it;
- make minimal changes to the system configuration (e.g. modifying the CONFIG.SYS and AUTOEXEC.BAT files of a PC);
- always get permission before making any changes to the system configuration;

The installation process should be reversible, so that rollback of the system to the state before the installation process was started is always possible. One way to do this is to make a backup copy of the existing system before starting the installation.

The installation software should remove obsolete configuration items from the directories where the new version of the system is installed.

2.3.4 Validate release

After installation, users should run some or all of the acceptance tests to validate the software. The acceptance test specification should have been updated to include tests of any new user requirements that have been implemented.

2.4 UPDATE PROJECT HISTORY DOCUMENT

The purpose of the Project History Document (PHD) is to provide a summary critical account of the project. The PHD should:
- describe the objectives of the project;
- summarise how the project was managed;
- state the cost of the project and compare it with predictions;
- discuss how the standards were applied;
- describe the performance of the system in OM phase;
- describe any lessons learned.

The benefits of the PHD are:
- the maintenance team is informed about what the development team did, so they can avoid repeating mistakes or trying out inappropriate solutions;

- the maintenance team is told how well the system performs, as they may have to make good any shortfall;
- managers of future projects will know how much a similar project is likely to cost, and problems and pitfalls they are likely to experience.

The software manager should write the PHD. Information should be collected throughout the project. Work on the PHD should start early in the project, with updates at every major milestone. Detailed guidance on writing the PHD is provided in Chapter 4.

2.5 FINAL ACCEPTANCE

A review of the software should be held at the end of the warranty period in order to decide whether the software is ready for final acceptance. All the acceptance tests must have been completed before the software can be finally accepted (OM02).

The review team should consist of the Software Review Board (SRB) members. The responsibilities and constitution of the Software Review Board are defined in the *Guide to Software Configuration Management* Section 2.2.1.3.

The software review should be a formal technical review. The procedures for a technical review are described in Section 2.3.1 of the *Guide to Software Verification and Validation*.

The final acceptance review meeting may coincide with an ordinary SRB meeting. The decision upon final acceptance is added to the agenda described in Section 2.3.1.2.

Inputs to the review are the:
- Project History Document (PHD);
- results of acceptance tests held over to the OM phase;
- Software Problem Reports made during the OM phase;
- Software Change Requests made during the OM phase;
- Software Modification Reports made during the OM phase.

The Software Review Board reviews these inputs and recommends, to the initiator, whether the software can be finally accepted.

The SRB should evaluate the degree of compliance of the software with the user requirements by considering the number and nature of:
- acceptance test cases failed;
- acceptance tests cases not attempted or completed;
- critical software problems reported;
- critical software problems not solved.

Solution of a problem means that a change request has been approved, modification has been made, and all tests repeated and passed.

The number of test cases, critical software problems and non-critical software problems should be evaluated for the whole system and for each subsystem. The SRB might, for example, decide that some subsystems are acceptable and others are not.

The SRB should study the trends in the number of critical software problems reported and solved. Although there are likely to be 'spikes' in the trend charts associated with software releases, there should be a downward trend in the number of critical problems during the OM phase. An upward trend should be cause for concern.

Sufficient data should have accumulated to evaluate the Mean Time Between Failures (MTBF) and Mean Time To Repair (MTTR). The MTBF may be estimated by dividing the total number of critical software problems raised during the phase by the total time spent operating the software during the phase. The MTTR may be estimated by averaging the difference between the start and end dates of the modifications completed.

If the SRB decides that the degree of compliance of the software with the user requirements is acceptable, it should recommend to the initiator that the software be finally accepted.

The statement of final acceptance is produced by the initiator, on behalf of the users, and sent to the developer (OM09). The finally accepted software system consists of one or more sets of documentation, source, object and executable code corresponding to the current versions and releases of the product.

CHAPTER 3
TOOLS FOR SOFTWARE MAINTENANCE

3.1 INTRODUCTION

Tools used during software development will continue to be used during the operations and maintenance phase. New versions of the tools may become available, or a tool may become unsupported and require replacement. Tools may be acquired to support new activities, or to support activities that previously took place without them.

The reader should refer to the appropriate guides for the tools that support:

- user requirements definition;
- software requirements definition;
- architectural design;
- detailed design and production;
- transfer;
- software project management;
- software configuration management;
- software verification and validation;
- software quality assurance.

This chapter is concerned with the tools that are normally used for the first time in the life cycle during the operations and maintenance phase. These tools are:

- navigation tools;
- code improvement tools;
- reverse engineering tools.

3.2 NAVIGATION TOOLS

Navigation tools enable software engineers to find quickly and easily the parts of the software that they are interested in. Typical capabilities are:

- identification of where variables are used;
- identification of the modules that use a module;
- display of the call tree;
- display of data structures.

Knowledge of where variables and modules are used is critical to understanding the effect of a change. Display of the call tree and data structures supports understanding of the control and data flow.

In addition, navigation tools for object-oriented software need to be able to:

- distinguish which meaning of an overloaded symbol is implied;
- support the location of inherited attributes and functions.

The maintenance of object-oriented programs is an active research area [Ref 9, 10]. In particular, the behaviour of a polymorphic function can only be known at runtime when argument types are known. This makes it difficult to understand what the code will do by means of static analysis and inspection. Dynamic analysis of the running program may be the only way to understand what it is doing.

3.3 CODE IMPROVEMENT TOOLS

Code improvement tools may:
- reformat source code;
- restructure source code.

Code reformatters, also known as 'pretty printers', read source code and generate output with improved layout and presentation. They can be very useful for converting old code to the style of a new coding standard.

Code restructuring tools read source code and make it more structured, reducing the control flow constructs as far as possible to only sequence, selection and iteration.

3.4 REVERSE ENGINEERING TOOLS

Reverse engineering tools process code to produce another type of software item. They may for example:
- generate source code from object code;
- recover designs from source code.

Decompilers translate object code back to source code. Some debuggers allow software engineers to view the source code alongside the object code. Decompilation capabilities are sometimes useful for diagnosing compiler faults, e.g. erroneous optimisations.

Tools that recover designs from source code examine module dependencies and represent them in terms of a design method such as Yourdon. Tools are available that can generate structure charts from C code for example. These reverse engineering tools may be very useful when documentation of code is non-existent or out of date.

CHAPTER 4
THE PROJECT HISTORY DOCUMENT

4.1 INTRODUCTION

The Project History Document (PHD) summarises the main events and the outcome of the project. The software manager should collect appropriate information, summarise it, and insert it in the PHD phase-by-phase as the project proceeds. Much of the information will already exist in earlier plans and reports. When final acceptance is near, the software manager should update the document taking into account what has happened since the start of the operations and maintenance phase.

4.2 STYLE

The Project History Document should be plain, concise, clear and consistent.

4.3 EVOLUTION

After delivery, the section of the Project History Document on the performance of the software in the OM phase should be updated by the maintenance team at regular intervals (e.g. annually).

4.4 RESPONSIBILITY

The software project manager is responsible for the production of the Project History Document. The software maintenance manager is responsible for the production of subsequent issues.

4.5 MEDIUM

The Project History Document is normally a paper document.

4.6 CONTENT

Software Engineering Standards recommends the following table of contents for the Project History Document.

1 DESCRIPTION OF THE PROJECT
2 MANAGEMENT OF THE PROJECT
    2.1 Contractual approach
    2.2 Project organisation

2.3 Methods and tools[2]
2.4 Planning
3 SOFTWARE PRODUCTION
   3.1 Product size[3]
   3.2 Documentation
   3.3 Effort[4]
   3.4 Computer resources
   3.5 Productivity[5]
4 QUALITY ASSURANCE REVIEW
5 FINANCIAL REVIEW
6 CONCLUSIONS
7 PERFORMANCE OF THE SYSTEM IN OM PHASE

4.6.1 PHD/1 DESCRIPTION OF THE PROJECT

This section should:
- describe the objectives of the project;
- identify the initiator, developer and users;
- identify the primary deliverables;
- state the size of the software and the development effort;
- describe the life cycle approach;
- state the actual dates of all major milestones.

Information that appears in later parts of the document may be summarised in this section.

Critical decisions, for example changes in objectives, should be clearly identified and explained.

4.6.2 PHD/2 MANAGEMENT OF THE PROJECT

4.6.2.1 PHD/2.1 Contractual approach

This section should reference the contract made (if any) between initiator's organisation and the development organisation.

This section should state the type of contract (e.g. fixed price, time and materials).

4.6.2.2 PHD/2.2 Project organisation

This section should describe the:
- internal organisation of the project;
- external interfaces of the project.

The description of the organisation should define for each role:
- major responsibilities;
- number of staff.

---

[2] In *Software Engineering Standards* this section is called "Methods used".
[3] In *Software Engineering Standards* this section is called "Estimated vs. actual amount of code produced"
[4] In *Software Engineering Standards* this section is called "Estimated vs. actual effort"
[5] In *Software Engineering Standards* this section is called "Analysis of productivity factors"

If the organisation and interfaces changed from phase to phase, this section describes the organisation and interfaces in each phase. If the number of staff varied within a phase, the staffing profile should be described.

4.6.2.3 PHD/2.3 Methods and tools

This section should identify the methods used in the project, phase by phase. The methods should be referenced. This section should not describe the rules and procedures of the methods, but critically discuss them from the point of view of the project. Aspects to consider are:
- training requirements.
- applicability.

Any tools used to support the methods should be identified and the quality of the tools discussed, in particular:
- degree of support for the method;
- training requirements;
- reliability;
- ease of integration with other tools;
- whether the benefits of the tools outweighed the costs.

4.6.2.4 PHD/2.4 Planning

This section should summarise the project plan by producing for each phase the:
- initial work breakdown structure (but not the work package descriptions);
- list of work packages added or deleted;
- Gantt chart showing the predicted start and end dates of each activity;
- Gantt chart showing the actual start and end dates of each activity;
- Milestone trend charts showing the movement (if any) of major milestones during the phase.

4.6.3 PHD/3 SOFTWARE PRODUCTION

4.6.3.1 PHD/3.1 Product size

This section should state the number of user requirements and software requirements.

This section should state the number of subsystems, tasks or programs in the architectural design.

This section should state the amount of code, both for the whole system and for each subsystem:
- predicted at the end of the AD phase;
- produced by the end of the TR phase;
- produced by final acceptance.

The actual amount of code produced should be specified in terms of the number of:
- lines of code;
- modules.

This section should make clear the rules used to define a line of code. Comment lines are not usually counted as lines of code. Historically, continuation lines have been counted as separate lines of code, but it may be more meaningful to ignore them and count each complete statement as one line of code. Non-executable statements (e.g. data declarations) are also normally counted as lines of code.

4.6.3.2 PHD/3.2 Documentation

This section should identify each document produced and state for each document the number of pages and words.

These values should be summed to define the total amount of documentation produced.

4.6.3.3 PHD/3.3 Effort

This section should state the estimated and actual effort required for each work package. The unit should be man-hours, man-days or man-months. Significant differences between the estimated and actual effort should be explained.

Values should be summed to give the total amount of effort required for all activities in:

- each of the SR, AD, DD and TR phases;
- the whole development (i.e. sum of the SR, AD, DD and TR phases);
- OM phase.

4.6.3.4 PHD/3.4 Computer resources

This section should state the estimated and actual hardware, operating software and ancillary software required to develop and operate the software. Significant differences between actual and estimated resources should be explained.

4.6.3.5 PHD/3.5 Productivity

This section should state the actual productivity in terms of:

- total number of lines of code produced divided by the total number of man-days in the SR, AD, DD and TR phases;
- total number of lines of code in each subsystem divided by the total number of man-days expended on that subsystem in the DD phase.

The first value gives the global 'productivity' value. The second set of values gives the productivity of each subsystem.

Productivity estimates used should also be stated. Significant differences between the estimated and actual productivity values should be explained.

4.6.4 PHD/4 QUALITY ASSURANCE REVIEW

This section should review the actions taken to achieve quality, particularly reliability, availability, maintainability and safety.

This section should summarise and discuss the effort expended upon activities of:

- software verification and validation;
- software quality assurance.

This section should analyse the quality of all the deliverables by presenting and discussing the number of:

- RIDs per document;
- SPRs and SCRs per month during the DD, TR and OM phases;
- SPRs and SCRs per subsystem per month during the DD, TR and OM phases.

Measurements of Mean Time Between Failures (MTBF) and Mean Time To Repair (MTTR) should be made in the OM phase. SPR, SCR, SMR and operations log data may be useful for the calculation. Measurements should be made at regular intervals (e.g. monthly) and trends monitored.

Average availability may be calculated from the formula MTBF/(MTBF+MTTR). In addition, the durations of all periods when the software was unavailable should be plotted in a histogram to give a picture of the number and frequency of periods of unavailability.

All 'safety' incidents where the software caused a hazard to people or property should be reported. Actions taken to prevent future incidents should be described.

4.6.5 PHD/5 FINANCIAL REVIEW

This section is optional. If included, this section should state the estimate and actual cost of the project. Costs should be divided into labour costs and non-labour costs.

4.6.6 PHD/6 CONCLUSIONS

This section should summarise the lessons learned from the project.

4.6.7 PHD/7 PERFORMANCE OF THE SYSTEM IN THE OM PHASE

This section should summarise in both quantitative and qualitative terms whether the software performance fell below, achieved or exceeded the user requirements, the software requirements and the expectations of the designers.

Performance requirements in the software requirements document may be stated in terms of:

- worst case;
- nominal;
- best case value.

These values, if specified, should be used as benchmarks of performance.

The results of any acceptance tests required for final acceptance should be summarised here.

CHAPTER 5
LIFE CYCLE MANAGEMENT ACTIVITIES

5.1 INTRODUCTION

Software maintenance is a major activity, and needs to be well managed to be effective. *Software Engineering Standards* identifies four software management functions:
- software project management;
- software configuration management;
- software verification and validation;
- software quality assurance.

This chapter discusses the planning of these activities in the operations and maintenance phase.

The plans formulated by the developer at the end of detailed design and production phase should be applied, with updates as necessary, by the development organisation throughout the transfer phase and operations and maintenance phase until final acceptance.

Software Engineering Standards does not mandate the production of any plans after final acceptance. However the maintenance organisation will need to have plans to be effective, and is strongly recommended to:
- produce its own SPMP and SQAP;
- reuse and improve the SCMP and SVVP of the development organisation.

5.2 SOFTWARE PROJECT MANAGEMENT

Until final acceptance, OM phase activities that involve the developer must be carried out according to the plans defined in the SPMP/TR (OM01). After final acceptance, the software maintenance team takes over responsibility for the software. It should produce its own SPMP. Guidelines for producing an SPMP are contained in the *Guide to Software Project Management*.

In the maintenance phase, both plans should define the:
- organisation of the staff responsible for software maintenance;
- work packages;
- resources;
- activity schedule.

5.2.1 Organisation

A maintenance organisation must be designated for every software product in operational use (OM04). A software manager should be appointed for every maintenance organisation. The software manager should define the roles and responsibilities of the maintenance staff in the software project management plan. Individuals should be identified with overall responsibility for:

- each subsystem;
- software configuration management;
- software verification and validation;
- software quality assurance.

Major adaptations of the software for new requirements or environmental changes should be handled by means of the evolutionary life cycle, in which a development project runs in parallel with operations and maintenance. Sometimes an evolutionary approach is decided upon at the start of the project. More commonly the need for such an approach only becomes apparent near the time the software is first released. Whichever way the evolutionary idea arises, software managers should organise their staff accordingly, for example by having separate teams for maintenance and development. Ideally, software engineers should not work on both teams at the same time, although the teams may share the same software manager, software librarian and software quality assurance engineer.

5.2.2 Work packages

Work packages should be defined when software change requests are approved. One work package should produce only one software modification report, but may cover several change requests and problem reports.

5.2.3 Resources

The operations and maintenance phase of software normally consumes more resources than all the other phases added together. Studies have shown that large organisations spend about 50% to 70% of their available effort maintaining existing software [Ref 4, 5]. The high relative cost of maintenance is due to the influence of several factors such as the:

- duration of the operations and maintenance phase being much longer than all the other phases added together;
- occurrence of new requirements that could not have been foreseen when the software was first specified;
- presence of a large number of faults in most delivered software.

Resources must be assigned to the maintenance of product until it is retired (OM07). Software managers must estimate the resources required. The estimates have two components:

- predicted non-labour costs;
- predicted labour costs (i.e. effort).

The cost of the computer equipment and consumables are the major non-labour costs. The cost of travel to user sites and the cost of consumables may have to be considered.

Labour costs can be assessed from:

- the level of effort required from the development organisation to support the software in the transfer phase;

- the number of user requirements outstanding;
- past maintenance projects carried out by the organisation;
- reliability and maintainability data;
- size of the system;
- number of subsystems;
- type of system;
- availability requirements.

Software managers should critically analyse this information. Lehman's laws and a code size method are outlined below to assist the analysis.

6.2.3.1 Lehman's Laws

Lehman and Belady have examined the growth and evolution of several large software systems and formulated five laws to summarise their data [Ref 7]. Three of the laws are directly relevant to estimating software maintenance effort. Simply stated they say:

- the characteristics of a program are fixed from the time when it is first designed and coded (the 'law of large program evolution');
- the rate at which a program develops is approximately constant and (largely) independent of the resources devoted to its development (the 'law of organisational stability');
- the incremental change in each release of a system is approximately constant (the 'law of conservation of familiarity').

The inherent characteristics of a program, introduced when it is first designed and coded, will have a fundamental effect on the amount of maintenance a program needs. Poorly designed software will incur higher maintenance costs. Removing the inherent design defects amounts to rewriting the program from scratch.

The law of diminishing returns applies at a very early stage in software maintenance. No matter how much effort is applied to maintaining software, the need to implement and verify modifications one at a time limits how fast changes can be made. If the mean time to repair the software does not change when the number of maintenance staff is increased, the apparent inefficiency is not the fault of the maintenance staff, but is due to the sequential nature of the work.

Software maintenance projects settle into a cycle of change. Modifications are requested, implemented and released to users at regular intervals. The release rate is constrained by the amount of change users can cope with.

In summary, software managers must be careful not to waste effort by:

- maintaining software that is unmaintainable;
- staffing the maintenance team above a saturation threshold;
- releasing changes too fast for the users to cope with.

6.2.3.2 Code size maintenance cost estimating method

The effort required to produce L lines of code when the productivity is P is L divided by P. For example, the addition or modification of 500 lines of code in a 20000 line of code system that took 1000 man-days to develop would require 500/(20000/1000) = 25 man days. This example assumes that the productivity observed in maintenance is the same as that in development. However productivity in maintenance often falls below that in development because of the need to assess the cause of a problem and perform regression tests.

5.2.4 Activity schedule

The activity schedule should show the dates of the next releases, and the work packages that must be completed for each release. This should be presented in the form of a Gantt chart.

5.3 SOFTWARE CONFIGURATION MANAGEMENT

A good configuration management system is essential for effective software maintenance, not only for the software but also for the tools and ancillary software items. Software configuration management is discussed in the *Guide to Software Configuration Management*.

The maintenance team should define and describe their software configuration management system in a Software Configuration Management Plan (SCMP). The team may reuse the plan and system made by the development team, or produce its own. The SCMP must define the procedures for software modification (OM05). The procedures should be based upon the change process discussed in Section 2.3.1 The SCMP should define, step-by-step, how to modify the software, omitting only the details specific to individual changes.

5.4 SOFTWARE VERIFICATION AND VALIDATION

Software verification and validation consumes a significant proportion of effort during the operations and maintenance phase because of the need to check that changes not only work correctly, but also that they have no adverse side effects. Software verification and validation are discussed in the *Guide to Software Verification and Validation*.

The maintenance team should reuse the Software Verification and Validation Plan (SVVP) produced during the development phases. It should be updated and extended as necessary.

The Software Review Board (SRB) review procedure should have been defined in the SVVP/DD. This procedure may need to be updated or even added to the SVVP either in the TR or OM phase. The SRB should use the technical review procedure described in the *Guide to Software Verification and Validation*, modified as indicated in Section 2.3.1.2.

Walkthroughs and inspections of the design and code are not only useful for training new staff, they are essential for maintaining and improving quality. Even if software inspection procedures were not used during development, consideration should be given to introducing them in the maintenance phase, especially for subsystems that have serious quality problems. All new procedures should be defined in updates to the SVVP.

Every change to the software should be examined from the point of view of:

- what should be done to verify it;
- whether the SVVP defines the verification procedure.

The SVVP will have to be extended to include new test designs, test cases and test procedures for:

- tests of new or modified software components;
- regression tests of the software.

Regression tests may be:

- random selections of existing tests;
- targeted selections of existing tests;
- new tests designed to expose adverse side effects.

Targeted tests and new tests depend upon knowledge of the actual change made. All such regression tests imply a new test design. The first two reuse test cases and test procedures.

Some of the acceptance tests may require a long period of time to complete, and are therefore not required for provisional acceptance. The reports of these tests should be compiled in the operations and maintenance phase. All the tests must be completed before final acceptance (OM02).

5.5 SOFTWARE QUALITY ASSURANCE

Software quality assurance activities must be continued during the operations and maintenance phase. *Software Engineering Standards* specifies ten mandatory practices for OM phase. The *Guide to Software Quality Assurance* contains guidelines on how to check that these practices are carried out. In particular, staff responsible for SQA should:

- be members of the Software Review Board;
- perform functional and physical audits before each release of the software;
- monitor quality, reliability, availability, maintainability and safety.

The SQAP/TR should define the SQA activities that the development team should carry out until final acceptance of the software. The maintenance organisation that takes over after final acceptance should examine that plan, consider the current status of the software and then produce its own plan.

APPENDIX A
GLOSSARY

A.1 LIST OF TERMS

Terms used in this document are consistent with *Software Engineering Standards* [Ref 1] and ANSI/IEEE Std 610.12 [Ref 2]. Additional terms not defined in these standards are listed below.

building
The process of compiling and linking a software system.

development environment
The environment of computer hardware, operating software and external software in which the software system is developed.

end user
A person who utilises the products or services of a system.

installation
The process of copying a software system into the target environment and configuring the target environment to make the software system usable.

operator
A person who controls and monitors the hardware and software of a system.

operational environment
The target environment, external software and users.

target environment
The environment of computer hardware, operating software and external software in which the software system is used.

user
A person who utilises the products or services of a system, or a person who controls and monitors the hardware and software of a system (i.e. an end user, an operator, or both).

A.2 LIST OF ACRONYMS

AD	Architectural Design
ANSI	American National Standards Institute
AT	Acceptance Test
BSSC	Board for Software Standardisation and Control
CASE	Computer Aided Software Engineering
CI	Configuration Item
DD	Detailed Design and production
OM	Operations and Maintenance
PHD	Project History Document
SCM	Software Configuration Management
SCMP	Software Configuration Management Plan
SCR	Software Change Request
SMR	Software Modification Report
SPM	Software Project Management
SPMP	Software Project Management Plan
SPR	Software Problem Report
SQA	Software Quality Assurance
SQAP	Software Quality Assurance Plan
SR	Software Requirements definition
SRD	Software Requirements Document
SRN	Software Release Note
STD	Software Transfer Document
SVV	Software Verification and Validation
SVVP	Software Verification and Validation Plan
TR	Transfer
UR	User Requirements definition
URD	User Requirements Document

APPENDIX B
REFERENCES

1. Software Engineering Standards, C.Mazza, J.Fairclough, B.Melton, D de Pablo, A.Scheffer, R.Stevens, Prentice-Hall, 1994.

2. IEEE Standard Glossary of Software Engineering Terminology, ANSI/IEEE Std 610.12-1990

3. Standard Dictionary of Measures to Produce Reliable Software, ANSI/IEEE Std 982.1-1988

4. Software Engineering, I. Sommerville, Addison Wesley, Fourth Edition, 1992

5. Software Maintenance Management, B.P. Lientz and E.B. Swanson, Addison Wesley, 1980

6. Software Evolution, R.J. Arthur, Wiley, 1988

7. Program Evolution. Processes of Software Change, M.M. Lehman and L. Belady, Academic Press, 1985.

8. Structured Testing: A Software Testing Methodology Using the Cyclomatic Complexity Metric, T.J. McCabe, National Bureau of Standards Special Publications 500-99, 1982.

9. Maintenance support for object-oriented programs, N.Wilde and R. Huitt, IEEE Transactions on Software Engineering, Vol 18 Number 12, IEEE Computer Society, December 1992

10. Support for maintaining object-oriented programs, M. Lejter, S. Meyers and S.P. Reiss, IEEE Transactions on Software Engineering, Vol 18 Number 12, IEEE Computer Society, December 1992.

APPENDIX C
MANDATORY PRACTICES

This appendix is repeated from *Software Engineering Standards* appendix D.7

OM01   Until final acceptance, OM phase activities that involve the developer shall be carried out according to the plans defined in the SPMP/TR.

OM02   All the acceptance tests shall have been successfully completed before the software is finally accepted.

OM03   Even when no contractor is involved, there shall be a final acceptance milestone to arrange the formal hand-over from software development to maintenance.

OM04   A maintenance organisation shall be designated for every software product in operational use.

OM05   Procedures for software modification shall be defined.

OM06   Consistency between code and documentation shall be maintained.

OM07   Resources shall be assigned to a product's maintenance until it is retired.

OM08   The SRB ... shall authorise all modifications to the software.

OM09   The statement of final acceptance shall be produced by the initiator, on behalf of the users, and sent to the developer.

OM10   The PHD shall be delivered to the initiator after final acceptance.

APPENDIX D
INDEX

Guide to
software
project
management

TABLE OF CONTENTS

CHAPTER 1
INTRODUCTION

1.1 PURPOSE

Software Engineering Standards [Ref 1] requires that every software project be planned, organised, staffed, led, monitored and controlled. These activities are called 'Software Project Management' (SPM). Each project must define its Software Project Management activities in a Software Project Management Plan (SPMP).

This guide defines and explains what software project management is, provides guidelines on how to do it, and defines in detail what a Software Project Management Plan should contain.

This guide should be read by software project managers, team leaders, software quality assurance managers, senior managers and initiators of software projects.

1.2 OVERVIEW

Chapter 2 contains a general discussion of the principles of software project management, expanding upon *Software Engineering Standards*. Chapter 3 discusses methods for software project management that can be used to support the activities described in Chapter 2. Chapter 4 discusses tools for software project management. Chapter 5 describes how to write the SPMP. Chapter 6 discusses progress reporting.

All the mandatory practices in *Software Engineering Standards* relevant to software project management are repeated in this document. The identifier of the practice is added in parentheses to mark a repetition. This document contains no new mandatory practices.

CHAPTER 2
SOFTWARE PROJECT MANAGEMENT

2.1 INTRODUCTION

Software project management is 'the process of planning, organising, staffing, monitoring, controlling and leading a software project' [Ref 3]. Every software project must have a manager who leads the development team and is the interface with the initiators, suppliers and senior management. The project manager:
- produces the Software Project Management Plan (SPMP);
- defines the organisational roles and allocates staff to them;
- controls the project by informing staff of their part in the plan;
- leads the project by making the major decisions and by motivating staff to perform well;
- monitors the project by measuring progress;
- reports progress to initiators and senior managers.

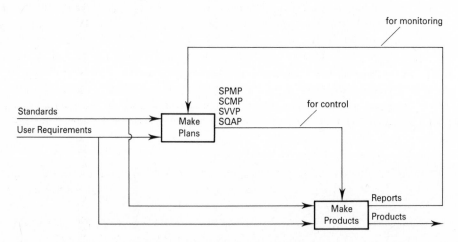

Figure 2.1: Management control loop

Figure 2.1 shows the control and monitoring loop required in every software project. Standards and user requirements are the primary input to both the planning and production processes. Plans are made for project management, configuration management, verification and validation and quality assurance. These plans control production. Reports, such as progress reports, timesheets, work package completion

298

reports, quality assurance reports and test reports provide feedback to the planning process. Plans may be updated to take account of these reports.

The project manager is the driving force in the management control loop. The following sections define the role of the project manager and discuss project management activities.

2.2 THE PROJECT MANAGER'S ROLE AND RESPONSIBILITIES

When they are appointed, project managers should be given terms of reference that define their:
- objectives;
- responsibilities;
- limits of authority.

The objective of every project manager is to deliver the product on time, within budget and with the required quality. Although the precise responsibilities of a project manager will vary from company to company and from project to project, they should always include planning and forecasting. Three additional areas of management responsibility defined by Mintzberg [Ref 16] are:
- interpersonal responsibilities, which include:
  - leading the project team;
  - liaising with initiators, senior management and suppliers;
  - being the 'figurehead', i.e. setting the example to the project team and representing the project on formal occasions.
- informational responsibilities, which include:
  - monitoring the performance of staff and the implementation of the project plan;
  - disseminating information about tasks to the project team;
  - disseminating information about project status to initiators and senior management;
  - acting as the spokesman for the project team.
- decisional responsibilities, which include:
  - allocating resources according to the project plan, and adjusting those allocations when circumstances dictate (i.e. the project manager has responsibility for the budget);
  - negotiating with the initiator about the optimum interpretation of contractual obligations, with the company management for resources, and with project staff about their tasks;
  - handling disturbances to the smooth progress of the project such as equipment failures and personnel problems.

2.3 PROJECT INTERFACES

Project managers must identify the people or groups the project deals with, both within the parent organisation and outside. A project may have interfaces to:
- initiators;
- end users;
- suppliers;
- subcontractors;

- the prime contractor;
- other subsystem developers.

When defining external project interfaces, the project manager should:

- ensure that a single, named point of contact exists both within the project team and each external group;
- channel all communications between the project and external groups through as few people as possible;
- ensure that no person in the project has to liaise with more than seven external groups (the 'rule of seven' principle).

2.4 PROJECT PLANNING

Whatever the size of the project, good planning is essential if it is to succeed. The software project planning process is shown in Figure 2.4. The five major planning activities are:

- define products;
- define activities;
- estimate resources and duration;
- define activity network;
- define schedule and total cost.

This process can be applied to a whole project or to a phase of a project. Each activity may be repeated several times to make a feasible plan. In principle, every activity in Figure 2.4 can be linked to the other activities by 'feedback' loops, in which information gained at a later stage in planning is used to revise earlier planning decisions. These loops have been omitted from the figure for simplicity. Iteration is essential for optimising the plan.

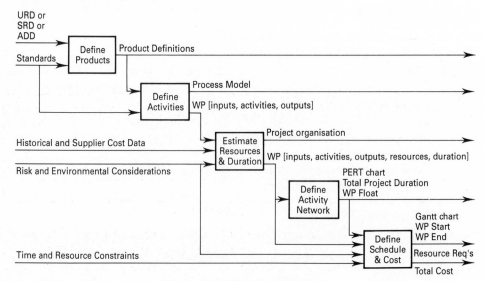

Figure 2.4: Planning process

The inputs to software project planning are:

- User Requirements Document (URD), Software Requirements Document (SRD) or Architectural Design Document (ADD), according to the project phase;
- software standards for products and procedures;
- historical data for estimating resources and duration;
- supplier cost data;
- risks to be considered;
- environmental factors, such as new technology;
- time constraints, such as delivery dates;
- resource constraints, such as the availability of staff.

The primary output of project planning is the Software Project Management Plan. This should contain:

- definitions of the deliverable products;
- a process model defining the life cycle approach and the methods and tools to be used;
- the work breakdown structure, i.e. a hierarchically structured set of work packages defining the work;
- the project organisation, which defines the roles and reporting relationships in the project;
- an activity network defining the dependencies between work packages, the total time for completion of the project, and the float times of each work package;
- a schedule of the project, defining the start and end times of each work package;
- a list of the resources required to implement the project;
- a total cost estimate.

The following subsections describe the five major activities.

2.4.1 Define products

The first activity in project planning is to define the products to be delivered. Table 2.4.1 summarises the software products of each phase as required by *Software Engineering Standards*.

Phase	Input Product	Output Product
SR	URD	SRD
AD	SRD	ADD
DD	ADD	DDD, code, SUM
TR	DDD, code, SUM	STD

Table 2.4.1: Phase input and output products

While standards define the contents of documents, some consideration should be given as to how each section of the document will be prepared. Care should be taken not to overconstrain the analysis and design process in defining the products. Some consideration should also be given to the physical characteristics of the products, such as the medium (e.g. paper or computer file), language (e.g. English, French) or programming language (in the case of code).

2.4.2 Define activities

Once the products are specified, the next step is to define a process model and a set of work packages.

2.4.2.1 Process model

A software process model should define the:
- activities in a software development process;
- the inputs and outputs of each activity;
- roles played in each activity.

The software development process must be based upon the *Software Engineering Standards* life cycle model (SLC03). The key decisions in software process modelling are the:
- selection of the life cycle approach, i.e. the pattern of life cycle phases;
- modifications, if any, to the phase process models (see below);
- selection of methods and tools to support the activities in the phase process models.

2.4.2.1.1 Selection of life cycle approach

Software Engineering Standards defines three life cycle approaches, waterfall, incremental and evolutionary.

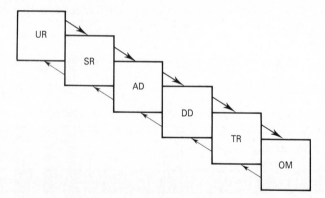

Figure 2.4.2.1.1A: Waterfall approach

The waterfall approach shown in Figure 2.4.2.1.1A executes each phase of the life cycle in sequence. Revisiting earlier phases is permitted to correct errors. The simple waterfall approach is suitable when:
- a set of high quality, stable user requirements exists;
- the length of project is short (i.e. two years or less);
- the users require the complete system all at once.

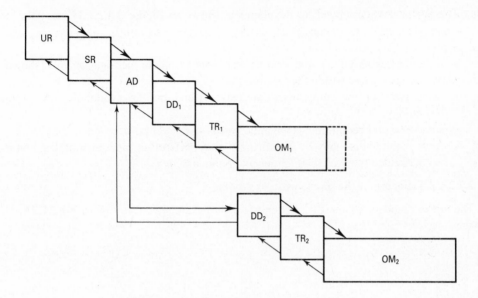

Figure 2.4.2.1.1B: Incremental approach

The incremental approach to development has multiple DD, TR and OM phases as shown in Figure 2.4.2.1.1B. This approach can be useful if:

- delivery of the software has to be according to the priorities set on the user requirements;
- it is necessary to improve the efficiency of integration of the software with other parts of the system (e.g. the telecommanding and telemetry subsystems in a spacecraft control system may be required early for system tests);
- early evidence that products will be acceptable is required.

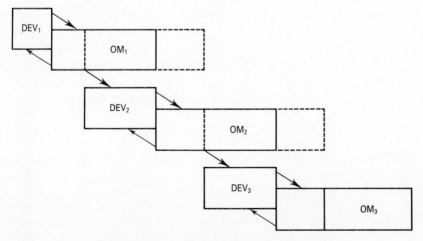

Figure 2.4.2.1.1C: Evolutionary approach

The evolutionary approach to development shown in Figure 2.4.2.1.1C consists of multiple waterfall life cycles with overlap between operations, maintenance and development. This approach may be used if, for example:

- some user experience is required to refine and complete the requirements (shown by the dashed line within the OM boxes);
- some parts of the implementation may depend on the availability of future technology;
- some new user requirements are anticipated but not yet known;
- some requirements may be significantly more difficult to meet than others, and it is not decided to allow them to delay a usable delivery.

2.4.2.1.2 Tailoring of the phase process models

The process models for the SR, AD and DD phases are shown in Figure 2.4.2.1.2A, B and C.

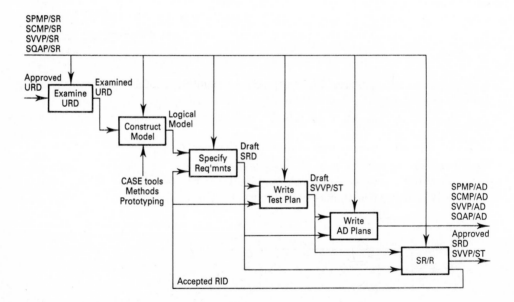

Figure 2.4.2.1.2A: SR phase process model

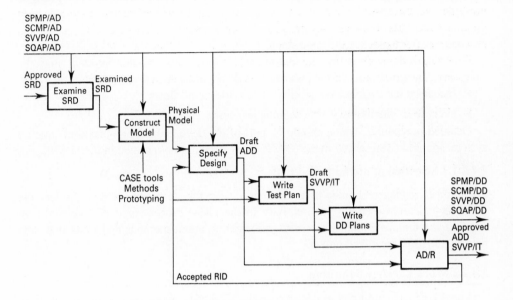

Figure 2.4.2.1.2B: AD phase process model

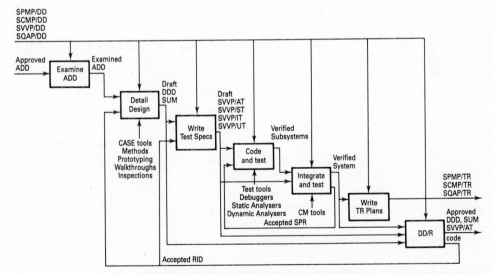

Figure 2.4.2.1.2C: DD phase process model

Project managers should tailor these process models to the needs of their projects. For example the specification of unit tests often has to wait until the code has been produced because there is insufficient information to define the test cases and procedures after the detailed design stage.

Further decomposition of the activities in the phase process models may be necessary. The granularity of the process model should be such that:

- managers have adequate visibility of activities at all times;

- every individual knows what to do at any time.

Detailed procedures, which should be part of the development organisation's quality system, should be referenced in the SPMP. They need not be repeated in the SPMP.

2.4.2.1.3 Selection of methods and tools

The project manager should, in consultation with the development team, select the methods and tools used for each activity in the phase process models. The *Software Engineering Guides* contains extensive information about methods and tools that may be used for software development.

2.4.2.2 Work package definition

The next step in planning is to decompose the work into 'work packages'. Activities in the process model are instantiated as work package tasks. The relationship between activities and tasks may be one-to-one (as in the case of constructing the logical model), or one-to-many (e.g. the code and unit test activity will be performed in many work packages).

Dividing the work into simple practical work packages requires a good understanding of the needs of the project and the logical relationships embedded in the process model. Some criteria for work package design are:

- coherence; tasks within a work package should have the same goal;
- coupling; work package dependencies should be minimised, so that team members can work independently;
- continuity; production work packages should be full-time to maximise efficiency;
- cost; bottom level work packages should require between one man-week and one man-month of effort.

The level of detail in the work breakdown should be driven by the level of accuracy needed for estimating resources and duration in the next stage of planning. This may be too detailed for other purposes, such as progress reporting to senior management. In such cases the higher level work packages are used to describe the work.

The work packages should be hierarchically organised so that related activities, such as software project management, are grouped together. The hierarchy of work packages is called the 'Work Breakdown Structure' (WBS). Table 2.4.2.2 shows an example of a WBS for a medium size project. In this example, each work package has a four digit identifier allowing up to four levels in the WBS.

1000	**Software Project Management**	
1100	UR phase	
	1110	SPMP/SR production
1200	SR phase	
	1210	SPM reports
	1220	SPMP/AD production
1300	AD phase	
	1310	SPM reports
	1320	SPMP/DD production
1400	DD phase	
	1410	SPM reports
	1420	SPMP/TR production
	1430	SPMP/DD updates
1500	TR phase	
	1510	SPM reports
2000	**Software Production**	
2100	UR phase	
	2110	Requirements engineering
2200	SR phase	
	2210	Logical model
	2220	Prototyping
	2230	SRD draft
	2240	SRD final
2300	AD phase	
	2310	Physical model
	2320	Prototyping
	2330	ADD draft
	2340	ADD final
2400	DD phase	
	2410	Unit 1 production
		2411 Unit 1 DDD
		2412 Unit 1 code
		2413 Unit 1 test
	2420	Unit 2 production
		2421 Unit 2 DDD
		2422 Unit 2 code
		2423 Unit 2 test
	2430	Unit 3 production
		2431 Unit 3 DDD
		2432 Unit 3 code
		2433 Unit 3 test
	2440	Unit 4 production
		2441 Unit 4 DDD
		2442 Unit 4 code
		2443 Unit 4 test
	2450	Unit 5 production
		2451 Unit 5 DDD
		2452 Unit 5 code
		2453 Unit 5 test

Table 2.4.2.2: Example Work Breakdown Structure

		2460	Integration and test	
			2461	Integration stage 1
			2462	Integration stage 2
			2463	Integration stage 3
			2464	Integration stage 4
		2470	SUM production	
	2500	TR phase		
		2510	Software installation	
		2520	STD production	
3000	**Software Configuration Management**			
	3100	UR phase		
		3110	SCMP/SR production	
	3200	SR phase		
		3210	Library maintenance	
		3220	Status accounting	
		3230	SCMP/AD production	
	3300	AD phase		
		3310	Library maintenance	
		3320	Status accounting	
		3330	SCMP/DD production	
	3400	DD phase		
		3410	Library maintenance	
		3420	Status accounting	
		3430	SCMP/TR production	
	3500	TR phase		
		3510	Library maintenance	
		3520	Status accounting	
4000	**Software Verification and Validation**			
	4100	UR phase		
		4110	SVVP/SR production	
		4120	SVVP/AT plan production	
		4130	UR review	
	4200	SR phase		
		4210	Walkthroughs	
		4220	Tracing	
		4230	SR review	
		4240	SVVP/ST plan production	
	4300	AD phase		
		4310	Walkthroughs	
		4320	Tracing	
		4330	SR review	
		4340	SVVP/IT plan production	
	4400	DD phase		
		4410	Unit review	
			4411	Unit 1 Review
			4412	Unit 2 Review
			4413	Unit 3 Review
			4414	Unit 4 Review
			4415	Unit 5 Review

Table 2.4.2.2: Example Work Breakdown Structure (continued)

		4420	SVVP/UT production
		4430	SVVP/IT production
		4440	SVVP/ST production
		4450	SVPP/AT production
		4460	System tests
		4470	DD review
	4500	TR phase	
		4510	Acceptance tests
		4520	Provisional Acceptance review
5000	**Software Quality Assurance**		
	5100	UR phase	
		5110	SQAP/SR production
	5200	SR phase	
		5210	SQA reports
		5220	SQAP/AD production
	5300	AD phase	
		5310	SQA reports
		5320	SQAP/DD production
	5400	DD phase	
		5410	SQA reports
		5420	SQAP/TR production
	5500	TR phase	
		5510	SQA reports

Table 2.4.2.2: Example Work Breakdown Structure (continued)

The number of work packages in a project normally increases with project size. Small projects (less than two man years) may have less than ten bottom-level work packages, and large projects (more than twenty man years) more than a hundred. Accordingly, small projects will use one or two levels, medium size projects two to four, and large projects four or five. Medium and large projects may use alphabetic as well as numerical identifiers.

New work packages should be defined for new tasks that are identified during a project. The tasks should not be attached to existing, unrelated, work packages. Some projects find it useful to create an 'unplanned work' package specifically for miscellaneous activities that arise in every project. However such 'unplanned work' packages should never be allocated more than a few per cent of the project resources. New work packages should be defined for tasks that involve significant expenditure.

Work packages are documented in the Work Packages, Schedule and Budget section of the SPMP (see Chapter 5). Work packages may reference standards, guidelines and manuals that define how to carry out the work. An example of a Work Package Description form is given in Appendix D. A form should be completed for every work package. Repetition of information should be minimised.

2.4.3 Estimate resources and duration

The next steps in planning are:
- defining human resources;
- estimating effort;
- estimating non-labour costs;
- estimating duration.

2.4.3.1 Defining human resources

Project managers should analyse the work packages and define the 'human resource requirements'. These define the roles required in the project. Examples of software project roles are:

- project manager;
- team leader;
- programmer;
- test engineer;
- software librarian;
- software quality assurance engineer.

The project manager must also define the relationships between the roles to enable the effective coordination and control of the project. The following rules should be applied when defining organisational structures:

- ensure that each member of the team reports to one and only one person (the 'unity of command principle');
- ensure that each person has no more than seven people reporting directly to him or her (the 'rule of seven' principle).

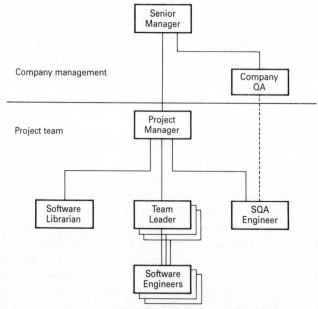

Figure 2.4.3.1.1: Example organigram for a medium-size project

The project team structure should be graphically displayed in an organigram, as shown in Figure 2.4.3.1.1. The 'dotted line' relationship between the project SQA engineer and the Company QA is a violation of the 'unity-of-command' principle that is justified by the need to provide senior management with an alternative, independent view on quality and safety issues.

The senior manager normally defines the activities of the project manager by means of terms of reference (see Section 2.2). The project manager defines the activities of the project team by means of work package descriptions.

2.4.3.2 Estimating effort

The project manager, with the assistance of his team, and, perhaps, external experts, should make a detailed analysis of the work packages and provide an estimate of the effort (e.g. number of man hours, days or months) that will be required.

Where possible these estimates should be compared with historical data. The comparison method can work quite well when good historical data exist. Historical data should be adjusted to take account of factors such as staff experience, project risks, new methods and technology and more efficient work practices.

Formula approaches such as Boehm's Constructive Cost Model (COCOMO) and Function Point Analysis (FPA) should not be used for making estimates at this stage of planning. These methods may be used for verifying the total cost estimate when the plan has been made. These methods are further discussed in Chapter 3.

2.4.3.3 Estimating non-labour costs

Non-labour costs are normally estimated from supplier data. They may include:
- commercial products that form part of the end product;
- commercial products that are used to make the end-product but do not form part of it, e.g. tools;
- materials (i.e. consumables not included in overheads);
- internal facilities (e.g. computer and test facilities);
- external services (e.g. reproduction);
- travel and subsistence;
- packing and shipping;
- insurance.

2.4.3.4 Estimating duration

The duration of the work package may be calculated from effort estimates and historical productivity data or other practical considerations (e.g. the duration of an activity such as a review meeting might be fixed at one day). The duration of each work package is needed for building the activity network and calculating the total project duration in the next stage of planning.

Productivity estimates should describe the average productivity and not the maximum productivity. Studies show that miscellaneous functions can absorb up to about 50% of staff time [Ref 10], reducing the average productivity to much less than the peak. Furthermore, industrial productivity figures (such as the often quoted productivity range of 10 to 20 lines of code per day) are normally averaged over the whole development, and not just the coding stage.

2.4.4 Define activity network

An activity network represents the work packages in the project as a set of nodes with arrows linking them. A sequence of arrows defines a path, or part of a path, through the project. Circular paths are not allowed in an activity network. The primary objective of building an activity network is to design a feasible pattern of activities that takes account of all dependencies. Two important by-products of constructing the activity network are the:

- critical path;
- work package float.

The critical path is the longest path through the network in terms of the total duration of activities. The time to complete the critical path is the time to complete the project.

The float time of a work package is equal to the difference between the earliest and latest work package start (or end) times, and is the amount of time each activity can be moved without affecting the total time to complete the project. Activities on the critical path therefore have zero float time.

In general, activity networks should only include work packages that depend upon other work packages for input, or produce output for other work packages to use.

Activities that are just connected to the start and end nodes should be excluded from the network. This simplifies it without affecting the critical path. Further, the activity network of complex projects should be broken down into subnetworks (e.g. one per phase). Such a modular approach makes the project easier to manage, understand and evaluate.

2.4.5 Define schedule and total cost

The last stage of planning defines the schedule and resource requirements, and finally the total cost.

The activity network constrains the schedule but does not define it. The project manager has to decide the actual schedule by setting the start and end times of work packages so as to:

- comply with time and resource constraints;
- minimise the total cost;
- minimise the fragmentation of resource allocations;
- allow for any risks that might delay the project.

The start and end dates of work packages affected by time constraints (e.g. delivery dates) and resource constraints (e.g. staff and equipment availability) should be set first, as they reduce the number of possibilities to consider. If the total time to complete the project violates the time constraints, project managers should return to the define activities stage, redefine work packages, re-estimate resources and duration, and then modify the activity network.

The minimum total cost of the project is the sum of all the work packages. However labour costs should be calculated from the total amount of time spent by each person on the project. This ensures that the time spent waiting for work packages to start and end is included in the cost estimate. Simply summing the individual costs of each bottom-level work package excludes this overhead. Project managers adjust the schedule to bring the actual cost of the project as close as possible to the minimum.

Activities with high risk factors should be scheduled to start at their earliest possible start times so that the activity float can be used as contingency.

Minimising the fragmentation of a resource allocation is often called 'resource smoothing'. Project managers should adjust the start time of activities using the same resource so that it is used continuously, rather than at discrete intervals. This is because:

- interruptions mean that people have to refamiliarise with the current situation, or relearn procedures that have been forgotten;
- equipment may be charged to the project even when it is not in use.

2.5 LEADING THE PROJECT

Leadership provides direction and guidance to the project team, and is an essential management function. There are numerous studies on leadership in the management literature, and the interested reader should consult them directly.

2.6 TECHNICAL MANAGEMENT OF PROJECTS

Besides the managerial issues, a software project manager must also understand the project technically. He or she is responsible for the major decisions concerning:

- the methods and tools;
- the design and coding standards;
- the logical model;
- the software requirements;
- the physical model;
- the architectural design;
- the detailed design;
- configuration management;
- verification and validation;
- quality assurance.

In medium and large projects the project manager often delegates much of the routine technical management responsibilities to team leaders.

2.7 MANAGEMENT OF PROJECT RISKS

All projects have risks. The point about risk management is not to run away from risks, but to reduce their ability to threaten the success of a project. Project managers should manage risk by:

- continuously looking out for likely threats to the success of the project;
- adjusting the plan to minimise the probability of the threats being realised;
- defining contingency plans for when the threats are realised;
- implementing the contingency plans if necessary.

Risk management never starts from the optimistic premise that 'all will go well'. Instead project managers should always ask themselves 'what is most likely to go wrong?' This is realism, not pessimism.

Project plans should identify the risks to a project and show how the plan takes account of them.

The following sections discuss the common types of risk to software projects, with possible actions that can be taken to counteract them. There are four groups:

- experience factors;
- planning factors;
- technology factors;
- external factors.

2.7.1 Experience factors

Experience factors that can be a source of risk are:

- experience and qualifications of the project manager;
- experience and qualifications of staff;
- maturity of suppliers.

2.7.1.1 Experience and qualifications of the project manager

The project manager is the member of staff whose performance has a critical effect on the outcome of a project. Inexperienced project managers are a significant risk, and organisations making appointments should match the difficulty of the project to the experience of the project manager. Part-time project managers are also a risk, because this reduces the capability of a project to respond to problems quickly.

Project management is a discipline like any other. Untrained project managers are a risk because they may be unaware of what is involved in management. Staff moving into management should receive training for their new role.

Project management should be the responsibility of a single person and not be divided. This ensures unity of command and direction.

2.7.1.2 Experience and qualifications of staff

Staff will be a risk to a project if they have insufficient experience, skills and qualifications for the tasks that they are assigned.

Project managers should avoid such risks by:

- assessing staff before they join the project;
- allocating staff tasks that match their experience, skills and qualifications;
- retaining staff within the project who have the appropriate skills, experience and qualifications to cope with future tasks.

2.7.1.3 Maturity of suppliers

The experience and record of suppliers are key factors in assessing the risks to a project. Indicators of maturity are the:

- successful development of similar systems;
- use of software engineering standards;
- the possession of an ISO 9000 certificate;
- existence of a software process improvement programme.

Experience of developing similar systems is an essential qualification for a project team. Lack of experience results in poor estimates, avoidable errors, and higher costs (because extra work is required to correct the errors).

Standards not only include system development standards such as *Software Engineering Standards*, but also coding standards and administrative standards. Standards may exist within an organisation but ignorance of how best to apply them may prevent their effective use. Project managers should ensure that standards are understood, accepted and applied. Project managers may require additional support from software quality assurance staff to achieve this.

A software process improvement programme is a good sign of maturity. Such a programme should be led by a software process group that is staffed with experienced software engineers. The group should collect data about the current process, analyse it, and decide about improvements to the process.

2.7.2 Planning factors

Planning factors that can be a source of risk are:
- accuracy of estimates;
- short timescales;
- long timescales;
- single-point failures;
- location of staff;
- definition of responsibilities;
- staffing profile evolution.

2.7.2.1 Accuracy of estimates

Accurate estimates of resource requirements are needed to complete a project successfully. Underestimates are especially dangerous if there is no scope for awarding additional resources later. Overestimation can result in waste and can prevent resources from being deployed elsewhere.

Some of the activities which are often poorly estimated for are:
- testing;
- integration, especially of external systems;
- transfer phase;
- reviews, including rework.

Some contingency should always be added to the estimates to cater for errors. The amount of contingency should also be related to the other risks to the project. Estimating the effort required to do something new is particularly difficult.

2.7.2.2 Short timescales

Short timescales increase the amount of parallel working required, resulting in a larger team. Progressive reduction in the timescale increases this proportion to a limit where the project becomes unmanageable [Ref 9]. Project managers should not accept unrealistic timescales.

Project managers should avoid artificially contracting timescales by attempting to deliver software before it is required. They should use the time available to optimise the allocation of resources such as staff.

When faced with accumulating delays and rapidly approaching deadlines, project manager's should remember Brooks' Law: 'adding manpower to a late project makes it later' [Ref 10].

2.7.2.3 Long timescales

Projects with long timescales run the risk of:
- changes in requirements;
- staff turnover;
- being overtaken by technological change.

Long timescales can result from starting too early. Project managers should determine the optimal time to start the project by careful planning.

Long projects should consider using an incremental delivery or evolutionary development life cycle approach. Both approaches aim to deliver some useful functionality within a timescale in which the requirements should be stable. If this cannot be done then the viability of the project should be questioned, as the product may be obsolete or unwanted by the time it appears.

Ambitious objectives, when combined with constraints imposed by annual budgets, often cause projects to have long timescales. As management costs are incurred at a fixed rate, management consumes a larger proportion of the project cost as the timescale lengthens. Furthermore, change, such as technical and economic change, can make the objectives obsolete, resulting in the abandonment of the project before anything is achieved!

2.7.2.4 Single-point failures

A single-point failure occurs in a project when a resource vital to an activity fails and there is no backup. Project managers should look for single-point failures by examining each activity and considering:
- the reliability of the resources;
- whether backup is available.

Project managers should devise contingency plans to reallocate resources when failures occur.

2.7.2.5 Location of staff

Dispersing staff to different locations can result in poor communication. Project managers should co-locate staff in contiguous accommodation wherever possible. This improves communication and allows for more flexible staff allocation.

2.7.2.6 Definition of responsibilities

Poor definition of responsibilities is a major threat to the success of a project. Vital jobs may not be done simply because no-one was assigned to do them. Tasks may be repeated unnecessarily because of ignorance about responsibilities.

Projects should be well organised by defining project roles and allocating tasks to the roles. Responsibilities should be clearly defined in work package descriptions.

2.7.2.7 Staffing profile evolution

Rapid increases in the number of staff can be a problem because new staff need time to familiarise themselves with a project. After the start of the project much of the project knowledge comes from the existing staff. These 'teaching resources' limit the ability of a project to grow quickly.

Rapid decreases in the number of staff can be a problem because the loss of expertise before the project is finished can drastically slow the rate at which problems are solved. When experienced staff leave a project, time should be set aside for them to transfer their knowledge to other staff.

The number of staff on a software project should grow smoothly from a small team in the software requirements definition phase to a peak during coding and unit testing, and fall again to a small team for the transfer phase. Project managers avoid sudden changes in the manpower profile and ensure that the project can absorb the inflow of staff without disruption.

2.7.3 Technological factors

Technological factors that can be a source of risk are:
- technical novelty;
- maturity and suitability of methods;
- maturity and efficiency of tools;
- quality of commercial software.

2.7.3.1 Technical novelty

Technical novelty is an obvious risk. Project managers should assess the technical novelty of every part of the design. Any radically new component can cause problems because the:
- feasibility has not been demonstrated;
- amount of effort required to build it will be difficult to estimate accurately.

Project managers should estimate the costs and benefits of technically novel components. The estimates should include the costs of prototyping the component.

Prototyping should be used to reduce the risk of technical novelty. The cost of prototyping should be significantly less than the cost of developing the rest of the system, so that feasibility is demonstrated before major expenditure is incurred. More accurate cost estimates are an added benefit of prototyping.

2.7.3.2 Maturity and suitability of methods

New methods are often immature, as practical experience with a method is necessary to refine it. Furthermore, new methods normally lack tool support.

Choosing an unsuitable method results in unnecessary work and, possibly, unsuitable software. Analysis and design methods should match the application being built. Verification and validation methods should match the criticality of the software.

Project managers should evaluate the strengths (e.g. high suitability) and the weaknesses (e.g. lack of maturity) of a method before making a choice. Project managers should always check whether the method has been used for similar applications.

2.7.3.3 Maturity and efficiency of tools

Tools can prove to be a hindrance instead of a benefit if:
- staff have not been trained in their use;
- they are unsuitable for the methods selected for the project;
- they are changed during the project;
- they have more overheads than manual techniques.

The aim of using tools is to improve productivity and quality. Project managers should carefully assess the costs and benefits of tools before deciding to use them on a project.

2.7.3.4 Quality of commercial software

The use of proven commercial software with well-known characteristics is normally a low-risk decision. However, including new commercial software, or using commercial software for the first time in a new application area, can be a risk because:
- it may not work as advertised, or as expected;
- it may not have been designed to meet the quality, reliability, maintainability and safety requirements of the project;

New commercial software should be comprehensively evaluated as early as possible in the project so that surprises are avoided later. Besides the technical requirements, other aspects to evaluate when considering the acquisition of commercial software are:
- supplier size, capability and experience;
- availability of support;
- future development plans.

2.7.4 External factors

External factors that can be a source of risk are the:
- quality and stability of user requirements;
- definition and stability of external interfaces;
- quality and availability of external systems.

2.7.4.1 Quality and stability of user requirements

A project is unlikely to succeed without a high quality User Requirements Document. A URD is a well-defined baseline against which to measure success. Project managers should, through the User Requirements Review process, ensure that a coherent set of requirements is available. This may require resources very early in the project to help users define their requirements (e.g. prototyping).

2.7.4.2 Definition and stability of external interfaces

External interfaces can be a risk when their definitions are unstable, poorly defined or non-standard.

Interfaces with external systems should be defined in Interface Control Documents (ICDs). These are needed as early as possible because they constrain the design. Once agreed, changes should be minimised, as a change in an interface implies rework by multiple teams.

Standard interfaces have the advantage of being well-defined and stable. For these reasons a standard interface is always to be preferred, even if the system design has to be modified.

2.7.4.3 Quality and availability of external systems

External systems can be a problem if their quality is poor or if they are not available when required owing to either late delivery or to unreliability.

Project managers should initiate discussions with suppliers of external systems when the project starts. This ensures that suppliers are made aware of project requirements as early as possible. Project managers should allocate adequate resources to the integration of external systems.

The effects of late delivery of the external system can be mitigated by:

- adding the capability of temporarily 'bypassing' the external system;
- development of software to simulate the external system.

The cost of the simulator must be traded-off against the costs incurred by late delivery.

2.8 MEASURING PROJECT PROCESSES AND PRODUCTS

Project managers should as far as possible adopt a quantitative approach to measuring software processes and products. This is essential for effective project control, planning future projects and improving the software development process in the organisation.

The Application of Metrics in Industry (AMI) guide [Ref 17] describes the following measurement steps:

1. assess the project environment and define the primary goals (e.g. financial targets, quality, reliability etc);
2. analyse the primary goals into subgoals that can be quantitatively measured and define a metric (e.g. man-months of effort) for each subgoal;
3. collect the raw metric data and measure the performance relative to the project goals;
4. improve the performance of the project by updating plans to correct deviations from the project goals;
5. improve the performance of the organisation by passing the metric data and measurements to the software process improvement group, who are responsible for the standards and procedures the project uses.

Steps one to four are discussed in the following sections.

2.8.1 Assess environment and define primary goal

The purpose of assessing the environment is to understand the context of the project. An audit aimed at measuring conformance to *Software Engineering Standards* is one means of assessment. Other methods for assessing software development organisations and projects include the Software Engineering Institute's Capability Maturity Model [Ref 4] and the European Software Institute's 'BOOTSTRAP' model, which uses the *Software Engineering Standards* as a definition of basic practices. Whatever the approach taken, the assessment step should define what is needed and what is practical.

The primary software project goal is invariably to deliver the product on time, within budget, with the required quality.

2.8.2 Analyse goals and define metrics

Common subgoals related to the primary goal are:
- do not exceed the planned effort on each activity;
- do not exceed the planned time on each activity;
- ensure that the product is complete;
- ensure that the product is reliable.

A metric is a 'quantitative measure of the degree to which a system, component or process possesses a given attribute' [Ref 2]. Project managers should define one or more metrics related to the subgoals defined for the project. Metric definitions should as far as possible follow organisational standards or industry standards, so that comparisons with other projects are possible [Ref 17].

2.8.2.1 Process metrics

Possible metrics for measuring project development effort are the:
- amount of resources used;
- amount of resources left.

Possible metrics for measuring project development time are the:
- actual duration of activities in days, weeks or months;
- slippage of activities (actual start - planned start).

Possible metrics for measuring project progress are:
- number of work packages completed;
- number of software problems solved.

2.8.2.2 Product metrics

The amount of product produced can be measured in terms of:
- number of lines of source code produced, excluding comments;
- number of modules coded and unit tested;
- number of function points implemented [Ref 11, 15];
- number of pages of documentation written.

Actual values should be compared with target values to measure product completeness.

Possible metrics for measuring product reliability are:
- test coverage;
- cyclomatic complexity of source modules;
- integration complexity of programs;
- number of critical Software Problem Reports;
- number of non-critical Software Problem Reports;

- number of changes to products after first issue or release.

2.8.3 Collect metric data and measure performance

Project managers should ensure that metric data collection is a natural activity within the project. For example the actual effort expended should always be assessed before a Work Package is signed off as completed. Counts of Software Problem Reports should be accumulated in the Configuration Status Accounting process. Cyclomatic complexity can be a routine measurement made before code inspection or unit test design.

2.8.4 Improving performance

Metric data should be made available for project management reporting, planning future projects, and software process improvement studies [Ref 4].

The project manager should use the metric data to improve processes and products. For example:

- comparisons of predicted and actual effort early in a project can quickly identify deficiencies in the initial estimates, and prompt major replanning of the project to improve progress;
- analysis of the trends in software problem occurrence during integration and system testing can show whether further improvement in quality and reliability is necessary before the software is ready for transfer.

2.9 PROJECT REPORTING

Accurate and timely reporting is essential for the control of a project. Project managers report to initiators and senior managers by means of progress reports. Initiators and senior managers should analyse progress reports and arrange regular meetings with the project manager to review the project. The progress report is an essential input to these management reviews.

Project managers should have frequent discussions with team members so that they are always up-to-date with project status. Team members should formally report progress to project managers by means of work package completion reports and timesheets.

2.9.1 Progress reports

Project managers should submit routine (e.g. monthly) progress reports that describe:

- technical status;
- resource status;
- schedule status;
- problems;
- financial status.

Progress reports are discussed in detail in Chapter 6.

2.9.2 Work package completion reports

As each work package is completed, the responsible team member (called the 'work package manager') should notify the project manager by a 'work package completion report'. Project managers accept work package deliverables by issuing 'work package completion certificates'. One way to document this process is to add completion and acceptance fields to the work package description form.

2.9.3 Timesheets

Organisations should have a timesheet system that project managers can use for tracking the time spent by staff on a project. A timesheet describes what each employee has done on a daily or hourly basis during the reporting period. The project manager needs this data to compile progress reports.

A good timesheet system should allow staff to record the work package associated with the expenditure of effort, rather than just the project. This level of granularity in the record keeping eases the collection of data about project development effort, and provides a more precise database for estimating future projects.

CHAPTER 3
SOFTWARE PROJECT MANAGEMENT METHODS

3.1 INTRODUCTION

Various methods and techniques are available for software project management. This chapter discusses some methods for the activities described in Chapter 2. The reader should consult the references for detailed descriptions. Methods are discussed for:
- project planning;
- project risk management;
- project reporting.

3.2 PROJECT PLANNING METHODS

Methods are available for supporting the following project planning activities:
- process modelling;
- estimating resources and duration;
- defining activity networks;
- defining schedules.
    The following sections discuss these methods.

3.2.1 Process modelling methods

The objective of a process modelling method is to construct a model of the software process roles, responsibilities, activities, inputs and outputs. This is often referred to as the 'workflow'.

Process models have been traditionally defined using text or simple diagrams. The Software Lifecycle Model defined in Part 1, Figure 1.2 of *Software Engineering Standards* is an example. Process models have also been defined using notations derived from systems analysis. SADT diagrams can be used for illustrating the flow of products and plans between activities [Ref 6].

Specialised process modelling methods based upon programming languages, predicate logic and Petri Nets are recent developments in software engineering [Ref 7]. These methods allow dynamic modelling of the software process. Dynamic models are required for workflow support.

3.2.2 Estimating methods

Chapter 2 recommends that labour costs of each work package be estimated mainly by expert opinion. The total labour cost is calculated from the total time spent on the project by each team member. The non-labour costs are then added to get the cost to completion of the project. The labour cost estimates should be verified by using another method. This section discusses the alternative methods of:

- historical comparison;
- COCOMO;
- function point analysis;
- activity distribution analysis;
- Delphi methods;
- integration and system test effort estimation;
- documentation effort estimation.

Some of these methods use formulae. Anyone using formula approaches to software cost estimation should take note of the following statement from Albrecht, the originator of Function Point Analysis [Ref 11]:

"It is important to distinguish between two types of work-effort estimates, a primary or 'task analysis' estimate and a 'formula' estimate. The primary work-effort estimate should always be based on an analysis of the tasks , thus providing the project team with an estimate and a work plan... It is recommended that formula estimates be used only to validate and provide perspective on primary estimates".

Boehm gives similar advice, which is all too often ignored by users of his COCOMO method [Ref 9].

3.2.2.1 Historical comparison

The historical comparison method of cost estimation is simply to compare the current project with previous projects. This method can work quite well when:

- the costs of the previous projects have been accurately recorded;
- the previous project has similarities to those of the current project.

If the projects are all identical, then a simple average of the costs can be used. More commonly, minor differences between the projects will lead to a range of actual costs. Estimates can be made by identifying the most similar project, or work package.

Historical comparisons can be very useful for an organisation which develops a series of similar systems, especially when accounts are kept of the effort expended upon each work package. There is no substitute for experience. However, possible disadvantages of the approach are that:

- new methods and tools cannot be accounted for in the estimates;
- inefficient work practices are institutionalised, resulting in waste.

To avoid these problems, it is very important that special features of projects that have influenced the cost are documented, enabling software project managers to adjust their estimates accordingly.

Part of the purpose of the Project History Document (PHD) is to pass on the cost data and the background information needed to understand it.

3.2.2.2 COCOMO

The Constructive Cost Model (COCOMO) is a formula-based method for estimating the total cost of developing software [Ref 9]. The fundamental input to COCOMO is the estimated number of lines of source code. This is its major weakness because:

- the number of lines of code is only accurately predictable at the end of the architectural design phase of a project, and this is too late;
- what constitutes a 'line of code' can vary amongst programming languages and conventions;
- the concept of a line of code does not apply to some modern programming techniques, e.g. visual programming.

COCOMO offers basic, intermediate and detailed methods. The basic method uses simple formulae to derive the total number of man months of effort, and the total elapsed time of the project, from the estimated number of lines of code.

The intermediate method refines the basic effort estimate by multiplying it with an 'effort adjustment factor' derived from fifteen 'effort multipliers'. Wildly inaccurate estimates can result from a poor choice of effort multiplier values. COCOMO supplies objective criteria to help the estimator make a sensible choice. The detailed COCOMO method uses a separate set of effort multipliers for every phase.

When estimating by means of COCOMO, the intermediate method should be used because the detailed method does not appear to perform more accurately than the intermediate method. The basic method provides a level of accuracy that is only adequate for preliminary estimates.

3.2.2.3 Function Point Analysis

Function Point Analysis (FPA) estimates the cost of a project from the estimates of the delivered functionality [Ref 11, 13]. FPA can therefore be applied at the end of the software requirements definition phase to make cost estimates. The method combines quite well with methods such as structured analysis, and has been used for estimating the total effort required to develop an information system.

The FPA approach to cost estimation is based upon counting the numbers of system inputs, outputs and data stores. These counts are weighted, combined and then multiplied by cost drivers, resulting in a 'Function Point' count. The original version of FPA converts the number of function points to lines of code using a language dependent multiplier. The number of lines of code is then fed into COCOMO (see Section 3.2.2.2) to calculate the effort and schedule.

Mark Two Function Point Analysis simplifies the original approach, is more easily applicable to modern systems, and is better calibrated [Ref 15]. Furthermore it does not depend upon the use of language-dependent multipliers to produce an effort estimate. When estimating by means of FPA, the Mark Two version should be used.

3.2.2.4 Activity distribution analysis

Activity distribution analysis uses measurements of the proportion of effort expended on activities in previous projects to:

- derive the effort required for each activity from the total effort;

- verify that the proportion of effort expended upon each activity is realistic;
- verify that the effort required for future activities is in proportion to the effort expended upon completed activities.

Project phases are the top-level activities in a project. The activity distribution technique is called the 'phase per cent method' when it is used to estimate the amount of effort required for project phases.

The activity distribution method requires data about completed projects to be analysed and reduced to derive the relative effort values. As with all methods based upon historical data, the estimates need to be adjusted to take account of factors such as staff experience, project risks, new methods and technology and more efficient work practices. For example the use of modern analysis and design methods and CASE tools requires a higher proportion of effort to be expended in the SR and AD phases.

3.2.2.5 Delphi method

The 'Delphi' method is a useful approach for arriving at software cost estimates [Ref 9]. The assumption of the Delphi method is that experts will independently converge on a good estimate.

The method requires several cost estimation experts and a coordinator to direct the process. The basic steps are:

1. the coordinator presents each expert with a specification and a form upon which to record estimates;
2. the experts fill out forms anonymously, explaining their estimates (they may put questions to the coordinator, but should not discuss the problem with each other);
3. if consensus has not been achieved, the coordinator prepares a summary of all the estimates and distributes them to the experts and the process repeats from step 1.

The summary should just give the results, and not the reasoning behind the results.

A common variation is to hold a review meeting after the first pass to discuss the independent estimates and arrive at a common estimate.

3.2.2.6 Integration and System Test effort estimation

Integration and system test effort depends substantially upon the:
- number and criticality of defects in the software after unit testing;
- number and criticality of defects acceptable upon delivery;
- number and duration of integration and system tests;
- average time to repair a defect.

The effort required for integration and system testing can therefore be estimated from a model of the integration and testing process, assumptions about the number of defects present after unit tests, and an estimate of the mean repair effort per defect [Ref 14].

A typical integration and test process model contains the following cycle:

1. the integration and test team adds components, discovers defects, and reports them to the software modification team;
2. the software modification team repairs the defects;
3. the integration and test team retests the software.

Reference 14 states that twenty to fifty defects per 1000 lines of code typically occur during the life cycle of a software product, and of these, five to fifteen defects per 1000 lines of code remain when integration starts, and one to four defects per 1000 lines of code still exist after system tests.

Repair effort values will vary very widely, but a mean value of half a man-day for a code defect is typical.

3.2.2.7 Documentation effort estimation

Software consists of documentation and code. Documentation is a critical output of software development, not an overhead. When estimating the volume of software that a project should produce, project managers should define not only the amount of code that will be produced, but also the amount of documentation.

Boehm observes that the documentation rates vary between two and four man hours per page [Ref 9]. Boehm also observes that the ratio between code volume and documentation volume ranges from about 10 to about 150 pages of documentation per 1000 lines of code, with a median value of about 50. These figures apply to all the life cycle documents.

The average productivity figure of 20 lines of code per day includes the effort required for documentation. This productivity figure, when combined with the documentation rates given above, implies that software engineers spend half their time on documentation (i.e. the median of 50 pages of documentation per 1000 lines of code implies one page of documentation per 20 lines of code; one page of documentation requires four hours, i.e. half a day, of effort).

3.2.3 Activity network methods

The Program Evaluation and Review Technique (PERT) is the usual method for constructing an activity network [Ref 9]. Most planning tools construct a PERT chart automatically as the planner defines activities and their dependencies.

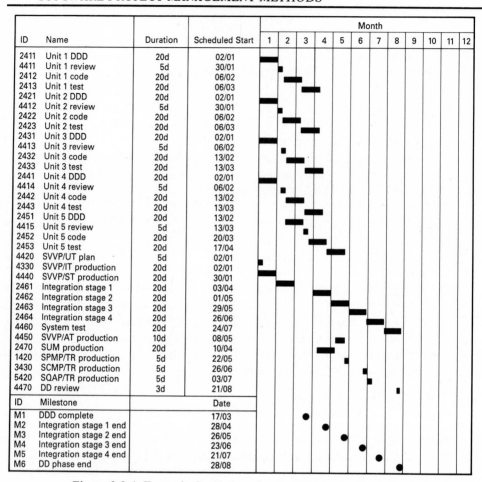

ID	Name	Duration	Scheduled Start
2411	Unit 1 DDD	20d	02/01
4411	Unit 1 review	5d	30/01
2412	Unit 1 code	20d	06/02
2413	Unit 1 test	20d	06/03
2421	Unit 2 DDD	20d	02/01
4412	Unit 2 review	5d	30/01
2422	Unit 2 code	20d	06/02
2423	Unit 2 test	20d	06/03
2431	Unit 3 DDD	20d	02/01
4413	Unit 3 review	5d	06/02
2432	Unit 3 code	20d	13/02
2433	Unit 3 test	20d	13/03
2441	Unit 4 DDD	20d	02/01
4414	Unit 4 review	5d	06/02
2442	Unit 4 code	20d	13/02
2443	Unit 4 test	20d	13/03
2451	Unit 5 DDD	20d	13/02
4415	Unit 5 review	5d	13/03
2452	Unit 5 code	20d	20/03
2453	Unit 5 test	20d	17/04
4420	SVVP/UT plan	5d	02/01
4330	SVVP/IT production	20d	02/01
4440	SVVP/ST production	20d	30/01
2461	Integration stage 1	20d	03/04
2462	Integration stage 2	20d	01/05
2463	Integration stage 3	20d	29/05
2464	Integration stage 4	20d	26/06
4460	System test	20d	24/07
4450	SVVP/AT production	10d	08/05
2470	SUM production	20d	10/04
1420	SPMP/TR production	5d	22/05
3430	SCMP/TR production	5d	26/06
5420	SQAP/TR production	5d	03/07
4470	DD review	3d	21/08

ID	Milestone	Date
M1	DDD complete	17/03
M2	Integration stage 1 end	28/04
M3	Integration stage 2 end	26/05
M4	Integration stage 3 end	23/06
M5	Integration stage 4 end	21/07
M6	DD phase end	28/08

Figure 3.2.4: Example Gantt chart for the DD phase of a project

3.2.4 Scheduling presentation methods

The project schedule defines the start times and duration of each work package and the dates of each milestone. The 'Gantt chart' is the usual method for presenting it. Work packages are marked on a vertical axis and time along the corresponding horizontal axis. Work package activities are shown as horizontal bars (giving rise to synonym of 'bar chart'). Time may be expressed absolutely or relative to the start of the phase.

Figure 3.2.4 shows the schedule for DD phase of the example project described in Chapter 2. Planning tools normally construct the Gantt chart automatically as tasks are defined.

3.3 PROJECT RISK MANAGEMENT METHODS

Two simple and effective methods for risk management are:
- risk table;
- risk matrix.

3.3.1 Risk table

The steps of the risk table method are :

1. list the risks in the project:
2. define the probability of each risk;
3. define the risk reduction action or alternative approach;
4. define the decision date;
5. define the possible impact.

An example is provided in Table 3.3.1.

Risk	Description	Prob.	Action	Decision Date	Impact
1	New user requirements	High	Change to evolutionary development	1/Jun/1997	High
2	Installation of air conditioning	Medium	Relocate staff while work is done	1/April/1998	Medium

Table 3.3.1: Example of a Risk Table

3.3.2 Risk matrix

The steps of the risk matrix method are:

1. list the risks in the project:
2. define the probability of each risk;
3. define the possible impact;
4. plot the risks according to their probability and impact.

An example is provided in Figure 3.3.2, using the data in the risk table in Figure 3.3.1. Risks with high probability and high impact cluster in the top right hand corner of the matrix. These are the risks that should receive the most attention.

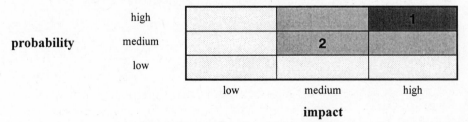

Figure 3.3.2: Example of a Risk Matrix

3.4 PROJECT REPORTING METHODS

Some important methods for progress reporting are:
- progress tables
- progress charts;
- milestone trend charts.

3.4.1 Progress tables and charts

Progress tables and charts are used to report how much has been spent on each work package and how much remains to be spent. For each work package in the WBS an initial estimate of the resources is made. The initial estimates should be in the SPMP. At the end of every reporting period, the following parameters are collected:

1. previous estimate;
2. expenditure for this period;
3. cumulative expenditure up to the end of the reporting period;
4. estimate to completion.

The sum of three and four generates the new estimate, i.e. item one for the following month. The estimate to completion should be re-evaluated each reporting period and not obtained by subtracting the cumulative expenditure from the previous estimate.

Work package expenditure should be summarised in progress tables as shown in Table 3.4.1. Work package identifiers and names are listed in columns one and two. The estimate for the work package in the current SPMP is placed in column three. Subsequent columns contain, for each month, the values of the previous estimate (PrEst), expenditure for the period (ExpP), cumulative expenditure (Cum) and estimate to completion (ToGo). The total in the last column states the current estimated effort for the work package.

Table 3.4.1 shows that the effort required for work packages 2210 and 2220 was underestimated. This underestimate of 10 man days for WP 2210 was detected and corrected in January. The estimate for WP 2220 had to be revised upwards by 5 man days in January and increased again by another 5 man days in February.

WPid	Name	Plan	January		February		March		Total
			PrEst	ToGo	PrEst	ToGo	PrEst	ToGo	
			ExpP	Cum	Exp	Cum	Exp	Cum	
2210	Logical	20	20	10	30	0	30	0	30
	Model		20	20	10	30	0	30	
2220	Prototype	30	30	15	35	5	40	0	40
			20	20	15	35	5	40	
2230	SRD	20	20	20	20	10	20	0	20
	draft		0	0	10	10	10	20	
2240	SRD	5	5	5	5	5	5	0	5
	final		0	0	0	0	5	5	
2200	SR phase	75	75	50	90	20	95	0	95
	total		40	40	35	75	20	95	

Table 3.4.1: Example Progress Table for March

Progress charts plot the estimates against time. They are best used for summarising the trends in the costs of high level work packages. Figure 3.4.1 is an example of a plot showing the trends in the estimates for WP 2200.

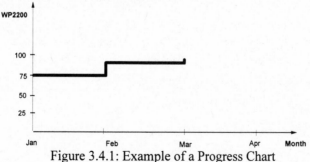

Figure 3.4.1: Example of a Progress Chart

The construction of progress tables and charts every reporting period enables:
- the accuracy of estimates to be measured;
- the degree of completion of each work package to be assessed.

The process of assessing every month what has been accomplished and re-estimating what remains is essential for keeping good control of project resources. Overspend trends are revealed and pinpointed early enough for timely corrective action to be taken.

3.4.2 Milestone trend charts

Milestone trend charts are used to report when milestones have been, or will be, achieved. First, an initial estimate of each milestone date is made. This estimate is put in the schedule section of the SPMP. Then, at the end of every reporting period, the following data are collected:

1. previous estimates of milestone achievement dates;
2. new estimate of milestone achievement dates.

The dates should be plotted in a milestone trend chart to illustrate the changes, if any, of the dates. A sample form is provided in Appendix D.

A milestone trend chart for the example project described in Figure 3.4.1 is shown in Figure 3.4.2. The vertical scale shows that the reporting period is one month. Figure 3.4.2 shows the status after five months. Milestones M1 and M2 have been achieved on schedule. Milestones M3, M4 and M5 have been slipped one month because 'Integration stage 2' took one month longer than expected. Milestone M6, the end of phase, was slipped two months when it was announced that the simulator required for system testing was going to be supplied two months late. Complaints to the supplier resulted in the delivery date being brought forward a month. M6 then moved forward one month.

The example shows how vertical lines indicate that the project is progressing according to schedule. Sloping lines indicate changes. Milestone trend charts are a powerful tool for understanding what is happening in a project. A milestone that slips every reporting period indicates that a serious problem exists.

Milestone trend charts should show milestone dates relative to the current approved plan, not obsolete plans. They should be reinitialised when the SPMP is updated.

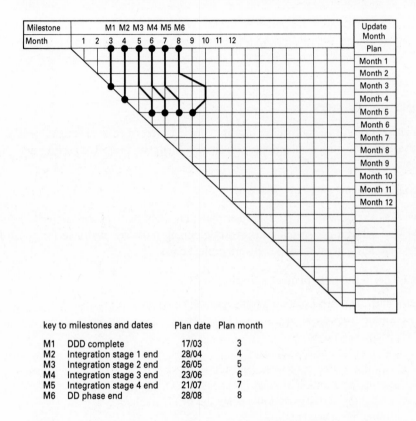

key to milestones and dates		Plan date	Plan month
M1	DDD complete	17/03	3
M2	Integration stage 1 end	28/04	4
M3	Integration stage 2 end	26/05	5
M4	Integration stage 3 end	23/06	6
M5	Integration stage 4 end	21/07	7
M6	DD phase end	28/08	8

Figure 3.4.2: Milestone trend chart for the DD phase of a project

CHAPTER 4
SOFTWARE PROJECT MANAGEMENT TOOLS

4.1 INTRODUCTION

This chapter discusses tool support for the methods described in chapters 2 and 3. Tools are available for project planning, project risk analysis, project reporting and process support.

4.2 PROJECT PLANNING TOOLS

As well as the general purpose project planning tools that support activity definition, PERT and scheduling, specialised project planning tools are available for constructing process models and estimating software project costs.

4.2.1 General purpose project planning tools

General purpose project planning tools normally support:
- defining work packages;
- defining resources;
- defining resource availability;
- allocating resources to work packages;
- defining the duration of work packages;
- constructing activity networks using the PERT method;
- defining the critical path;
- defining the schedule in a Gantt chart.

Managers enter the project activities and define the resources that they require. They then mark the dependencies between the activities. The tool constructs the activity network and Gantt chart. The tools should also include the ability to:
- compute the total amount of resources required;
- provide resource utilisation profiles;
- fix the duration of an activity;
- divide a project into subprojects;
- highlight resource conflicts, or over-utilisation;
- integrate easily with word processors.

Common deficiencies of general purpose project planning tools are:
- fixed rate scheduling, so that work packages have to be split when someone takes a holiday;
- inability to handle fractional allocations of resources (e.g. resource conflicts occur when staff have to share their time between concurrent work packages);

- identifiers that change every time a new work package is inserted;
- too much line crossing in activity networks.

Advanced project planning tools permit variable rate scheduling. The project manager only needs to define:

- the total effort involved in the work package;
- the resources to be allocated to the work package;
- the availability of the allocated resources.

The project planning tool then decides what the resource utilisation profile should be.

4.2.2 Process modelling tools

Process modelling methods are relatively new, and the tools that support them are consequently immature. Process modelling tools should:

- support the definition of procedures;
- contain a library of 'process templates' that can be tailored to each project;
- make the process model available to a process support tool (see Section 4.5).

There are few dedicated software process modelling tools. Analysis tools that support the structured analysis techniques of data flow diagrams and entity relationship diagrams can be effective substitutes.

4.2.3 Estimating Tools

Project costs should be stored in a spreadsheet or database for access during software cost estimating. Project managers estimate by comparing their project with those in the database and extracting the cost data for the most similar project.

Some software cost estimation tools use measurements of software size (e.g. number of lines of code, number of function points) to produce the initial estimate of effort. They then accept estimates of cost drivers (e.g. required reliability, programmer experience) and use them to adjust the initial estimate.

In addition, software cost estimation tools may:

- permit 'what-if' type exploration of costs and timescales;
- produce estimates of the optimum timescale;
- allow input of a range of values instead of a single value, thereby enabling the accuracy to be estimated;
- provide explanations of how estimates were arrived at;
- provide estimates even when some information is absent;
- allow predicted values to be replaced by actual values, thereby allowing progressive refinement of an estimate as the project proceeds;
- permit backtracking to an earlier point in the cost estimation process and subsequent input of new data.

4.3 PROJECT RISK ANALYSIS TOOLS

Risk analysis tools have been applied in other fields, but difficulties in accurately quantifying software risks limits their usefulness.

One approach to risk analysis is to use heuristics or 'rules-of-thumb', derived from experience. Tools are available that have been programmed with the rules related to the common risks to a project. The tools ask a series of questions about the project and then report the most likely risks. Tools of this kind have rarely been used in software development.

4.4 PROJECT REPORTING TOOLS

Project planning tools (see Section 4.2) that are capable of recording the actual resources used, and the dates that events occurred, can be useful for progress reporting. Such tools should use the information to:

- mark up the Gantt chart to indicate schedule progress;
- constrain replanning.

Spreadsheets are useful for constructing progress tables and charts.

4.5 PROCESS SUPPORT TOOLS

Process support tools help guide, control and automate project activities [Ref 8]. They need a formally defined process model in a suitable machine readable format. The absence of complete software process models has limited the application of process support tools.

Process support tools may be integrated into the software engineering environment, coordinating the use of other software tools and guiding and controlling developers through the user interface [Ref 5]. Outside software engineering, process support tools have been used for controlling the work flow in a business process.

Process support tools should provide the following capabilities:

- instantiation of the process model;
- enactment of each process model instance (i.e. the process support tool should contain a 'process engine' that drives activities)
- viewing of the process model instance status.

In addition process support tools should provide:

- interfaces between the process model instance and the actors (i.e. the people playing the project roles);
- interfaces to project planning tools so that coverage of the plan, and the resource expenditure, can be tracked.

CHAPTER 5
THE SOFTWARE PROJECT MANAGEMENT PLAN

5.1 INTRODUCTION

All software project management activities must be documented in the Software Project Management Plan (SPMP) (SPM01). The SPMP is the controlling document for managing a software project.

The SPMP contains four sections dedicated to each development phase. These sections are called:
- Software Project Management Plan for the SR phase (SPMP/SR);
- Software Project Management Plan for the AD phase (SPMP/AD);
- Software Project Management Plan for the DD phase (SPMP/DD);
- Software Project Management Plan for the TR phase (SPMP/TR).

Each section of the SPMP must:
- define the project organisation (SPM01);
- define the managerial process (SPM01);
- outline the technical approach, in particular the methods, tools and techniques (SPM01);
- define the work-breakdown structure (SPM01, SPM10);
- contain estimates of the effort required to complete the project (SPM01, SPM04, SPM06, SPM07, SPM09);
- contain a planning network describing when each work package will be started and finished (SPM01, SPM11);
- allow for the risks to the project (SPM01).

The table of contents for each section of the SPMP is described in Section 5.6. This table of contents is derived from the IEEE Standard for Software Project Management Plans (ANSI/IEEE Std 1058.1-1987).

5.2 STYLE

The SPMP should be plain, concise, clear, consistent and modifiable.

5.3 RESPONSIBILITY

The developer is normally responsible for the production of the SPMP. The software project manager should write the SPMP.

5.4 MEDIUM

It is usually assumed that the SPMP is a paper document. There is no reason why the SPMP should not be distributed electronically to people with the necessary equipment.

5.5 SERVICE INFORMATION

The SR, AD, DD and TR sections of the SPMP are produced at different times in a software project. Each section should be kept separately under configuration control and contain the following service information:

    a - Abstract
    b - Table of Contents
    c - Document Status Sheet
    d - Document Change records made since last issue

5.6 CONTENTS

Software Engineering Standards recommends the following table of contents for each phase section of the SPMP:

1 INTRODUCTION[1]
    1.1 Project overview
    1.2 Project deliverables
    1.3 Evolution of the SPMP
    1.4 Reference materials
    1.5 Definitions and acronyms

2 PROJECT ORGANISATION
    2.1 Process model
    2.2 Organisational structure
    2.3 Organisational boundaries and interfaces
    2.4 Project responsibilities

3 MANAGERIAL PROCESS
    3.1 Management objectives and priorities
    3.2 Assumptions, dependencies and constraints
    3.3 Risk management
    3.4 Monitoring and controlling mechanisms
    3.5 Staffing plan

---

[1] The Software Project Management Plan contents list is based upon extracts from IEEE Std 1058.1-1987, IEEE Standard for Software Project Management Plans, copyright © 1987 by the Institute for Electrical and Electronic Engineers Inc. The IEEE disclaims any responsibility or liability resulting from the placement and use in this publication. Information is reprinted with the permission of the IEEE.

4 TECHNICAL PROCESS
    4.1 Methods, tools and techniques
    4.2 Software documentation
    4.3 Project support functions

5 WORK PACKAGES, SCHEDULE, AND BUDGET
    5.1 Work packages
    5.2 Dependencies
    5.3 Resource requirements
    5.4 Budget and resource allocation
    5.5 Schedule

Material unsuitable for the above contents list should be inserted in additional appendices. If there is no material for a section then the phrase 'Not Applicable' should be inserted and the section numbering preserved.

5.6.1 SPMP/1 Introduction

5.6.1.1 SPMP/1.1 Project overview

This section of the SPMP should provide a summary of the project:
- objectives;
- deliverables;
- life cycle approach;
- major activities;
- milestones;
- resource requirements;
- schedule;
- budget.

This section outlines the plan for whole project and must be provided in the SPMP/SR (SPM01). The overview may be updated in subsequent phases.

5.6.1.2 SPMP/1.2 Project deliverables

This section should list the deliverables of the phase. All *Software Engineering Standards* documents, plans and software releases that will be delivered should be listed. Any other deliverable items such as prototypes, demonstrators and tools should be included.

5.6.1.3 SPMP/1.3 Evolution of the SPMP

This section should summarise the history of the SPMP in this and previous phases of the project.

This section should describe the plan for updating the SPMP in this and subsequent phases of the project.

5.6.1.4 SPMP/1.4 Reference materials

This section should provide a complete list of all the applicable and reference documents, identified by title, author and date. Each document should be marked as applicable or reference. If appropriate, report number, journal name and publishing organisation should be included.

5.6.1.5 SPMP/1.5 Definitions and acronyms

This section should provide the definitions of all terms, acronyms, and abbreviations used in the plan, or refer to other documents where the definitions can be found.

5.6.2 SPMP/2 Project Organisation

5.6.2.1 SPMP/2.1 Process model

This section should define the activities in the phase and their inputs and outputs. The definition should include the major project functions (i.e. activities that span the entire duration of the project, such as project management, configuration management, verification and validation, and quality assurance) and the major production activities needed to achieve the objectives of the phase. The definition of the process model .may be textual or graphic.

5.6.2.2 SPMP/2.2 Organisational structure

This section should describe the internal management structure of the project in the phase. Graphical devices such as organigrams should be used to show the lines of reporting, control and communication.

Roles that often appear in the internal management structure are:
- project manager;
- team leader;
- programmers;
- software librarian;
- software quality assurance engineer.

5.6.2.3 SPMP/2.3 Organisational boundaries and interfaces

This section should describe the relationship between the project and external groups during the phase such as:
- parent organisation;
- client organisation;
- end users;
- subcontractors;
- suppliers;
- independent verification and validation organisation;
- independent quality assurance organisations.

The procedures and responsibilities for the control of each external interface should be summarised. For example:
- name of Interface Control Document (ICD);

- those responsible for the agreement of the ICD;
- those responsible for authorising the ICD.

5.6.2.4 SPMP/2.4 Project responsibilities

This section should define the roles identified in the organisational structure and its boundaries. Each role definition should briefly describe the purpose of the role and list the responsibilities.

5.6.3 SPMP/3 Managerial process

5.6.3.1 SPMP/3.1 Management objectives and priorities

This section should define the management objectives of this project phase and their relative priorities. They should discuss any trade-offs between the objectives.

5.6.3.2 SPMP/3.2 Assumptions, dependencies and constraints

This section should state for the phase the:
- assumptions on which the plan is based;
- external events the project is dependent upon;
- constraints on the project.

Technical issues should only be mentioned if they have an effect on the plan.

Assumptions, dependencies and constraints are often difficult to distinguish. The best approach is not to categorise them but to list them. For example:
- limitations on the budget;
- schedule constraints (e.g. launch dates);
- constraints on the location of staff (e.g. they must work at developer's premises);
- commercial hardware or software that will be used by the system;
- availability of simulators and other test devices;
- availability of external systems with which the system must interface.

5.6.3.3 SPMP/3.3 Risk management

This section of the plan should identify and assess the risks to the project, and describe the actions that will be taken in this phase to manage them. A risk table (see Section 3.3.1) may be used.

5.6.3.4 SPMP/3.4 Monitoring and controlling mechanisms

This section of the plan should define the monitoring and controlling mechanisms for managing the work. Possible monitoring and controlling mechanisms are:
- work package descriptions;
- work package completion reports;
- progress reports;
- reviews;
- audits.

This section should define or reference the formats for all documents and forms used for monitoring and controlling the project.

This section should specify the:
- frequency of progress meeting with initiators and management;
- frequency of submission of progress reports;
- modifications (if any) to the progress report template provided in Chapter 6;
- general policy regarding reviews and audits (the details will be in the SVVP).

5.6.3.5 SPMP/3.5 Staffing plan

This section of the plan should specify the names, roles and grades of staff that will be involved in the phase. The utilisation of the staff should be given for each reporting period. A staff profile giving the total number of staff on the project each month may also be given.

5.6.4 SPMP/4 Technical Process

5.6.4.1 SPMP/4.1 Methods, tools and techniques

This section should specify the methods, tools and techniques to be used to produce the phase deliverables.

5.6.4.2 SPMP/4.2 Software documentation

This section should define or reference the documentation plan for the phase. For each document to be produced, the documentation plan should specify:
- document name;
- review requirements;
- approval requirements.

Some documents will be deliverable items. Others will be internal documents, such as technical notes, or plans, such as the SCMP. All documents should be listed.

The documentation plan may contain or reference a 'style' guide that describes the format and layout of documents.

5.6.4.3 SPMP/4.3 Project support functions

This section should contain an overview of the plans for the project support functions of:
- software configuration management;
- software verification and validation;
- software quality assurance.

This section should reference the SCMP, SVVP and SQAP.

5.6.5 SPMP/5 Work Packages, Schedule, and Budget

5.6.5.1 SPMP/5.1 Work packages

This section should describe the breakdown of the phase activities into work packages.

This section may begin with a Work Breakdown Structure (WBS) diagram to describe the hierarchical relationships between the work packages. Each box should show the title and identifier of the work package. Alternatively, the work breakdown may be described by listing the work package titles and identifiers as shown in Section 2.4.2.2.

The full Work Package Descriptions may be contained in this section or put in an appendix. Each Work Package description should define the:

- work package title;
- work package reference number;
- responsible organisation;
- major constituent activity;
- work package manager;
- start event;
- end event;
- inputs;
- activities;
- outputs.

Work packages should be defined for all activities, including project functions such as project management, configuration management, verification and validation and quality assurance.

5.6.5.2 SPMP/5.2 Dependencies

This section should define the ordering relations between the work packages. This may be done by using a planning network technique, such as the Program Evaluation and Review Technique (PERT), to order the execution of work packages according to their dependencies (see Section 3.5). Dependency analysis should define the critical path to completion of the project and derive the 'float' for activities off the critical path.

5.6.5.3 SPMP/5.3 Resource requirements

This section should describe, for each work package:

- the total resource requirements;
- the resource requirements as a function of time.

Labour resources should be evaluated in man-hours, man-days or man-months. Other resources should be identified (e.g. equipment).

5.6.5.4 SPMP/5.4 Budget and resource allocation

The project budget allocation should be specified by showing how the available financial resources will be deployed on the project. This is normally done by providing a table listing the amount of money budgeted for each major work package. The manner in which this section is completed depends upon the contractual relationship.

5.6.5.5 SPMP/5.5 Schedule

This section should define when each work package starts and ends. This is normally done by drawing a Gantt chart (see Section 3.6).

This section should describe the milestones in the project, providing for each milestone:

- an identifier;
- a description (e.g. a list of deliverables);
- the planned date of achievement;
- the actual date of achievement (for plan updates).

Milestones should be marked on or alongside the Gantt chart.

5.7 EVOLUTION

Project planning is a continuous process. Project managers should review their plan when:

- making progress reports;
- new risks are identified;
- problems occur.

It is good practice to draft sections of the plan as soon as the necessary information is available, and not wait to begin planning until just before the start of the phase that the SPMP section applies to. Some parts of the SPMP/DD need to be drafted at the start of the project to arrive at a total cost estimate, for example.

The evolution of the plan is closely connected with progress reporting (see Chapter 6). Reports are produced and reviewed. Reports may propose changes to the plan. Alternatively, changes to the plan may be defined during the progress meeting.

5.7.1 UR phase

By the end of the UR review, the SR phase section of the SPMP must be produced (SPMP/SR) (SPM02). The SPMP/SR describes, in detail, the project activities to be carried out in the SR phase.

As part of its introduction, the SPMP/SR must outline a plan for the whole project (SPM03), and provide a rough estimate of the total cost. The project manager will need to draft the work breakdown, schedule and budget section of the SPMP/AD, SPMP/DD and SPMP/TR at the start of the project to provide the overview and estimate the total cost of the project.

A precise estimate of the effort involved in the SR phase must be included in the SPMP/SR (SPM04). Specific factors affecting estimates for the work required in the SR phase are the:

- number of user requirements;
- level of user requirements;
- stability of user requirements;
- level of definition of external interfaces;
- quality of the URD.

An estimate based simply on the number of user requirements might be very misleading - a large number of detailed low-level user requirements might be more useful, and save more time in the SR phase, than a few high-level user requirements. A poor quality URD with few requirements might imply that a lot of requirements analysis is required in the SR phase.

5.7.2 SR phase

During the SR phase, the AD phase section of the SPMP must be produced (SPMP/AD) (SPM05). The SPMP/AD describes, in detail, the project activities to be carried out in the AD phase.

As part of its introduction, the SPMP/AD must include an outline plan for the rest of the project, and provide an estimate of the total cost of the whole project accurate to at least 30% (SPM06). The project manager will need to draft the work breakdown, schedule and budget section of the SPMP/DD and SPMP/TR at the end of the SR phase to provide the overview and estimate the total cost of the project.

A precise estimate of the effort involved in the AD phase must be included in the SPMP/AD (SPM07). Specific factors that affect estimates for the work required in the AD phase are the:

- number of software requirements;
- level of detail of software requirements;
- stability of software requirements;
- level of definition of external interfaces;
- quality of the SRD.

If an evolutionary development life cycle approach is to be used, then this should be stated in the SPMP/AD.

5.7.3 AD phase

During the AD phase, the DD phase section of the SPMP must be produced (SPMP/DD) (SPM08). The SPMP/DD describes, in detail, the project activities to be carried out in the DD phase.

An estimate of the total project cost must be included in the SPMP/DD (SPM09). An accuracy of 10% should be aimed at.

The SPMP/DD must contain a WBS that is directly related to the decomposition of the software into components (SPM10).

The SPMP/DD must contain a planning network (i.e. activity network) showing the relationships between the coding, integration and testing activities (SPM11).

5.7.4 DD phase

As the detailed design work proceeds to lower levels, the WBS and job schedule need to be refined to reflect this. To achieve the necessary level of visibility, software production work packages in the SPMP/DD must not last longer than one man-month (SPM12).

During the DD phase, the TR phase section of the SPMP must be produced (SPMP/TR) (SPM13). The SPMP/TR describes, in detail, project activities until final acceptance, in the OM phase.

CHAPTER 6
THE SOFTWARE PROJECT PROGRESS REPORT

6.1 INTRODUCTION

Accurate and timely reporting is essential for the control of a project. Software project managers should produce progress reports at regular intervals or when events occur that meet agreed criteria. The progress report is an essential tool for controlling a project because:

- preparing the progress report forces re-evaluation of the resources required to complete the project;
- the progress report provides initiators and senior management with visibility of the status of the project.

Progress reports describe the project status in relation to the applicable Software Project Management Plan. They should cover technical status, resource status, schedule status, problems and financial status (which may be provided separately).

Progress reports should be distributed to senior management and the initiator. The progress report sent to senior management should contain the information described in Section 6.6. Although the progress report sent to the initiator should have the same structure, the level of detail provided may not be the same because of the contractual situation. For example in a fixed price contract, it is acceptable to omit detailed information about resource status and financial status.

6.2 STYLE

The progress report should be plain, concise, clear, complete and consistent. Brevity, honesty and relevance are the watchwords of the good progress report.

6.3 RESPONSIBILITY

The software project manager is normally responsible for the production of the progress report.

6.4 MEDIUM

It is usually assumed that the progress report is a paper document. There is no reason why it should not be distributed electronically to people with the necessary equipment.

6.5 SERVICE INFORMATION

Progress reports should contain the following service information:
a - Abstract
b - Table of Contents

6.6 CONTENTS

The following table of contents is recommended for the progress report:

1 INTRODUCTION
  1.1 Purpose
  1.2 Summary
  1.3 References
  1.4 Definitions and acronyms

2 TECHNICAL STATUS
  2.1 Work package technical status
  2.2 Configuration status
  2.3 Forecast for next reporting period

3 RESOURCE STATUS
  3.1 Staff utilisation
  3.2 Work package resource status
  3.3 Resource summary

4 SCHEDULE STATUS
  4.1 Milestone trends
  4.2 Schedule summary

5 PROBLEMS

6 FINANCIAL STATUS REPORT
  6.1 Costs for the reporting period
  6.2 Cost to completion
  6.3 Limit of liability
  6.4 Payments

6.6.1 Progress Report/1 Introduction

6.6.1.1 Progress Report/1.1 Purpose

This section should describe the purpose of the report. This section should include:
- the name of the project;
- a reference to the applicable SPMP;
- a reference to the applicable contract (if any);
- a statement of the reporting period.

6.6.1.2 Progress Report/1.2 Summary

This section should summarise the main activities and achievements during the reporting period.

Any change in the total cost to completion should be stated in this section. Changes to work package resource estimates should be summarised.

6.6.1.3 Progress Report/1.3 References

This section should list any documents referenced in the report or applicable to it (e.g. this guide, the SPMP etc).

6.6.1.4 Progress Report/1.4 Definitions and acronyms

This section should list any special terms, acronyms or abbreviations used in the report and explain their meaning.

6.6.2 Progress Report/2 Technical status

6.6.2.1 Progress Report/2.1 Work package technical status

This section should list the work packages completed during the reporting period. There should be some indication of whether each work package was completed successfully or not.

This section should list the work packages continued or started during the reporting period. The outstanding tasks for each work package should be identified.

6.6.2.2 Progress Report/2.2 Configuration status

This section should summarise the changes to the configuration status in the reporting period, e.g:
- RID statistics;
- issues and revisions of documents;
- SCR, SPR and SMR statistics;
- releases of software.

6.6.2.3 Progress Report/2.3 Forecast for next reporting period

This section should forecast what technical progress is expected on each work package in the next reporting period.

Any events that are expected to take place in the reporting period should be described (e.g. milestones, deliveries).

6.6.3 Progress Report/3 Resource status

6.6.3.1 Progress Report/3.1 Staff utilisation

This section should comprise:
- a table of hours booked by each member of the team;

- the hours staff have booked for a number of past reporting periods (e.g. from the beginning of the current phase, or beginning of the year, or beginning of the project, as appropriate);
- a forecast for the man-hours staff will book for future reporting periods (e.g. up to the end of the current phase, or the end of the project, or other milestone).

6.6.3.2 Progress Report/3.2 Work package resource status

This section should contain a work package progress table (see Section 3.7.1) summarising for each work package:
- previous estimate of the effort required for completion;
- effort expended in this period;
- cumulative effort expenditure up to the end of the reporting period;
- estimate of remaining effort required for completion.

6.6.3.3 Progress Report/3.3 Resource status summary

This section should present the aggregated effort expenditure for the reporting period for:
- the project;
- subsystems (for medium and large-size projects).

6.6.4 Progress Report/4 Schedule status

6.6.4.1 Progress Report/4.1 Milestone trend charts

This section should provide an updated milestone trend chart (see Section 3.4.2) for all the milestones described in the SPMP section to which this progress report applies. All changes to milestone dates made in this reporting period should be explained and justified.

6.6.4.2 Progress Report/4.2 Schedule summary

This section should provide an updated bar chart (i.e. Gantt chart) marked to show work packages completed and milestones achieved. Progress on partially completed work packages may also be shown.

6.6.5 Progress Report/5 Problems

This section should identify any problems which are affecting or could affect progress. These may include technical problems with the software under development, environmental problems (e.g. computers, communications, and accommodation) and resource problems (e.g. staffing problems). This list is not exhaustive.

6.6.6 Progress Report/6 Financial status report

The Financial Status Report (sometimes called the Cost Report) provides the total amounts, in currency units, to be billed during the reporting period. The Financial Status Report may be provided separately.

6.6.6.1 Progress Report/6.1 Costs for the reporting period

This section should provide a table listing the hours worked, rates and costs (hours worked multiplied by rate) for each team member. Total labour costs should be stated.

Non-labour costs should be listed and a total stated.

6.6.6.2 Progress Report/6.2 Cost to completion

This section should state the accumulated cost so far and the planned cost to completion of the project and project phase.

A progress chart plotting the cost to completion values reported since the start of the project or project phase may be provided (see Section 3.4.1).

6.6.6.3 Progress Report/6.3 Limit of liability

This section states:
- the Limit Of Liability (LOL);
- how much has been spent;
- how much there is to go.

6.6.6.4 Progress Report/6.4 Payments

This section should state what payments are due for the reporting period (e.g. contractual stage payments on achievement of a given milestone).

APPENDIX A
GLOSSARY

Terms used in this document are consistent with *Software Engineering Standards* [Ref 1] and ANSI/IEEE Std 610.12-1990 [Ref 2].

A.1 LIST OF ACRONYMS

AD	Architectural Design
AD/R	Architectural Design Review
ADD	Architectural Design Document
AMI	Applications of Metrics in Industry
ANSI	American National Standards Institute
AT	Acceptance Test
BSSC	Board for Software Standardisation and Control
CASE	Computer Aided Software Engineering
COCOMO	Constructive Cost Model
DCR	Document Change Record
DD	Detailed Design and production
DD/R	Detailed Design and production Review
DDD	Detailed Design and production Document
ESA	European Space Agency
FPA	Function Point Analysis
ICD	Interface Control Document
IEEE	Institute of Electrical and Electronics Engineers
IT	Integration Test
LOL	Limit Of Liability
PERT	Program Evaluation and Review Technique
PSS	Procedures, Specifications and Standards
QA	Quality Assurance
RID	Review Item Discrepancy
SCMP	Software Configuration Management Plan
SCR	Software Change Request
SMR	Software Modification Report
SPR	Software Problem Report
SR	Software Requirements
SR/R	Software Requirements Review
SRD	Software Requirements Document
ST	System Test

SUT	Software Under Test
SVV	Software Verification and Validation
SVVP	Software Verification and Validation Plan
UR	User Requirements
UR/R	User Requirements Review
URD	User Requirements Document
UT	Unit Test

APPENDIX B
REFERENCES

1. Software Engineering Standards, C.Mazza, J.Fairclough, B.Melton, D. dePablo, A.Scheffer, R.Stevens, Prentice-Hall 1994.
2. IEEE Standard Glossary of Software Engineering Terminology, ANSI/IEEE Std 610.12-1990.
3. IEEE Standard for Software Project Management Plans, ANSI/IEEE Std 1058.1-1987.
4. Managing the Software Process, Watts S. Humphrey, SEI Series in Software Engineering, Addison-Wesley, August 1990.
5. Reference Model for Frameworks of Software Engineering Environments, European Computer Manufacturer's Association, TR/55, 1991.
6. Evolution of the ESA Software Engineering Standards, J.Fairclough and C.Mazza, in Proceedings of the IEEE Fourth Software Engineering Standards Application Workshop, 1991.
7. Software Process Themes and Issues, M. Dowson, in Proceedings of 2nd International Conference on the Software Process, IEEE Computer Society Press, 1993.
8. Tool Support for Software Process Definition and Enactment, C. Fernström, Proceedings of the ESA/ESTEC workshop on European Space Software Development Environment, ESA, 1992.
9. Software Engineering Economics, B.Boehm, Prentice-Hall, 1981
10. The Mythical Man-Month, F. Brooks, Addison-Wesley, 1975
11. Software Function, source lines of code and development effort prediction - a software science validation, A. Albrecht and J. Gaffney Jr, IEEE Transactions on Software Engineering, SE-9, (6), 1983.
12. SOCRAT, Software Cost Resources Assessment Tool, ESA Study Contract Report, J.Fairclough, R. Blake, I. Alexander, 1992.
13. Function Point Analysis: Difficulties and Improvements, IEEE Transactions on Software Engineering, Vol 14, 1, 1988.
14. Managing Computer Projects, R. Gibson, Prentice-Hall, 1992.
15. Software Sizing and Estimating, C.R. Symons, Wiley, 1991.
16. The Nature of Managerial Work, H. Mintzberg, Prentice-Hall, 1980.
17. Applications of Metrics in Industry Handbook, a quantitative approach to software management, Centre for Systems and Software Engineering, South Bank University, London, 1992.

APPENDIX C
MANDATORY PRACTICES

This appendix is repeated from *Software Engineering Standards*, appendix D.8.

SPM01   All software project management activities shall be documented in the Software Project Management Plan (SPMP).

SPM02   By the end of the UR review, the SR phase section of the SPMP shall be produced (SPMP/SR).

SPM03   The SPMP/SR shall outline a plan for the whole project.

SPM04   A precise estimate of the effort involved in the SR phase shall be included in the SPMP/SR.

SPM05   During the SR phase, the AD phase section of the SPMP shall be produced (SPMP/AD).

SPM06   An estimate of the total project cost shall be included in the SPMP/AD.

SPM07   A precise estimate of the effort involved in the AD phase shall be included in the SPMP/AD.

SPM08   During the AD phase, the DD phase section of the SPMP shall be produced (SPMP/DD).

SPM09   An estimate of the total project cost shall be included in the SPMP/DD.

SPM10   The SPMP/DD shall contain a WBS that is directly related to the decomposition of the software into components.

SPM11   The SPMP/DD shall contain a planning network showing relationships of coding, integration and testing activities.

SPM12   No software production work packages in the SPMP/DD shall last longer than 1 man-month.

SPM13   During the DD phase, the TR phase section of the SPMP shall be produced (SPMP/TR).

APPENDIX D
PROJECT MANAGEMENT FORMS

D.1   WORK PACKAGE DESCRIPTION

PROJECT:	PHASE:	W.P. REF:
W.P. TITLE: CONTRACTOR: MAJOR CONSTITUENT: START EVENT: PLANNED DATE: END EVENT: PLANNED DATE: W.P. MANAGER		SHEET 1 OF 1 ISSUE REF: ISSUE DATE:
Inputs Activities Outputs		

D.2 MILESTONE TREND CHART

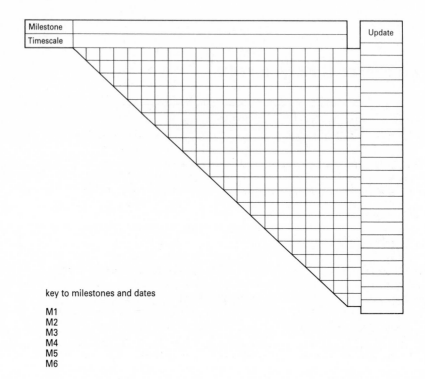

key to milestones and dates

M1
M2
M3
M4
M5
M6

APPENDIX E
INDEX

Guide to software configuration management

TABLE OF CONTENTS

CHAPTER 1
INTRODUCTION

1.1 PURPOSE

Software Engineering Standards [Ref 1] requires that documentation and code be controlled throughout the software life cycle. This activity is called 'Software Configuration Management' (SCM). Each project must define its Software Configuration Management activities in a Software Configuration Management Plan (SCMP).

This guide defines and explains what software configuration management is, provides guidelines on how to do it, and defines in detail what a Software Configuration Management Plan should contain.

This guide should be read by everyone concerned with developing, installing and changing software, i.e. software project managers, software librarians and software engineers. Some sections describing procedures for handling software problems and changing documents will be of interest to users.

1.2 OVERVIEW

Chapter 2 discusses the principles of software configuration management, expanding upon *Software Engineering Standards*. Chapter 3 discusses tools for software configuration management. Chapter 4 describes how to write the SCMP.

All the mandatory practices in *Software Engineering Standards* relevant to software configuration management are repeated in this document. The identifier of the practice is added in parentheses to mark a repetition. This document contains no new mandatory practices.

CHAPTER 2
SOFTWARE CONFIGURATION MANAGEMENT

2.1 INTRODUCTION

The purpose of software configuration management is to plan, organise, control and coordinate the identification, storage and change of software through development, integration and transfer (SCM02). Every project must establish a software configuration management system. All software items, for example documentation, source code, executable code, files, tools, test software and data, must be subjected to SCM (SCM01). Software configuration management must ensure that:
- software components can be identified;
- software is built from a consistent set of components;
- software components are available and accessible;
- software components never get lost (e.g. after media failure or operator error);
- every change to the software is approved and documented;
- changes do not get lost (e.g. through simultaneous updates);
- it is always possible to go back to a previous version;
- a history of changes is kept, so that is always possible to discover who did what and when.

Project management is responsible for organising software configuration management activities, defining software configuration management roles (e.g. software librarian), and allocating staff to those roles. In the TR and OM phases, responsibility for software configuration management lies with the Software Review Board (SRB).

Each group has its own characteristic requirements for software configuration management [Ref 5]. Project management requires accurate identification of all items, and their status, to control and monitor progress. Development personnel need to share items safely and efficiently. Quality assurance personnel need to be able to trace the derivation of each item and establish the completeness and correctness of each configuration. The configuration management system provides visibility of the product to everyone.

In large developments, spread across multiple hardware platforms, configuration management procedures may differ in physical details. However, a common set of configuration management procedures must be used (SCM03).

No matter how large the project may be, software configuration management has a critical effect on quality. Good software configuration management is essential for efficient development and maintenance, and for ensuring that the integrity of the software is never compromised. Bad software configuration management can paralyse a project. Sensible change requests may fail to be approved because of fears that they cannot be implemented correctly and will degrade the system.

This chapter summarises the principles of software configuration management described in *Software Engineering Standards* and then discusses the application of these principles first to documents and then to code.

2.2 PRINCIPLES OF SOFTWARE CONFIGURATION MANAGEMENT

The subject matter of all software configuration management activities is the 'configuration item' (CI). A CI is an aggregation of hardware, software or both that is designated as a unit for configuration management, and treated as a single entity in the configuration management process [Ref 2]. A CI can be an aggregation of other CIs, organised in a hierarchy. Any member of this hierarchy can exist in several versions, each being a separate CI. For code, the CI hierarchy will normally be based on the design hierarchy, but may be modified for more efficient configuration management. Figure 2.2.A shows an example CI hierarchy.

Examples of configuration items are:

- software component, such as a version of a source module, object module, executable program or data file;
- support software item, such as a version of a compiler or a linker;
- baseline, such as a software system under development;
- release, such as a software system in operational use;
- document, such as an ADD.

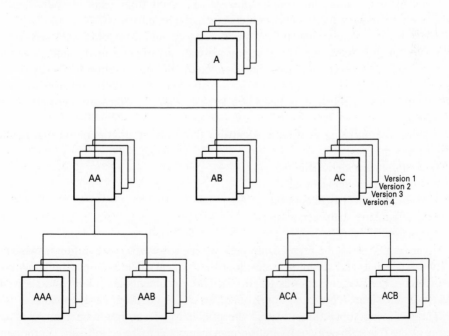

Figure 2.2.A: Example Configuration Item hierarchy

Software configuration management is formally defined in ANSI/IEEE Std 610.12-1990 [Ref 2] as the discipline of applying technical and administrative direction and administration to:

- identify and document the functional and physical characteristics of a configuration item;
- control changes to those characteristics;
- record and report change processing and implementation status;
- verify compliance with specified requirements.

All configuration items, from modules to entire software releases, must be defined as early as possible and systematically labelled when they are created. Software development can only proceed smoothly if the development team are able to work on correct and consistent configuration items. Responsibilities for the creation and modification of configuration items must be allocated to individuals and respected by others. Although this allocation is defined in the Work Breakdown Structure (WBS) of the Software Project Management Plan (SPMP), the Software Configuration Management Plan (SCMP) defines the procedures that coordinate the efforts of the developers.

Software develops from baseline to baseline until it can be released. Changes to baselines must be controlled throughout the life cycle by documenting the:

- problems, so that they can be understood;
- changes that are proposed to solve the problem;
- modifications that result.

Problems that initiate the change process can result from bugs in code, faults in design, errors in the requirements or omissions in the requirements.

The change process must be monitored. Accurate records and reports of configuration item status are needed to provide visibility of controlled change.

Verification of the completeness and correctness of configuration items (by reviews and audits) is classified by *Software Engineering Standards* as a software verification and validation activity, and is discussed in the *Guide to Software Verification and Validation*.

Software Engineering Standards identifies five primary configuration management activities:

- configuration identification;
- configuration item storage;
- configuration change control;
- configuration status accounting;
- release.

Figure 2.2.B shows the relationship between the software configuration management activities (shaded) and component development, system integration and build activities (unshaded). The diagram applies to all CIs, both documents and code, and shows the change control loop, a primary feature of software configuration management.

The following subsections discuss the principles of configuration management in terms of the five software configuration management activities. Software configuration management terms are collected in Appendix A for reference.

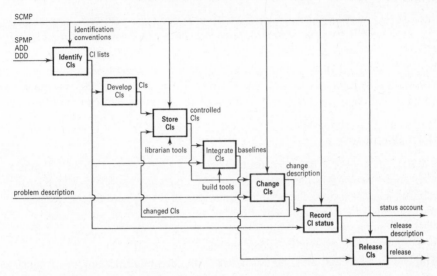

Figure 2.2B: Software Configuration Management Activities

2.2.1 Configuration identification

The first step in configuration management is to define the CIs and the conventions for their identification.

The inputs to the configuration identification activity are the SPMP (which lists the project documents), the ADD and the DDD (which list the software components). These inputs are used to define the hierarchy of CIs. The output is a configuration item list, defining what will be built using the naming conventions described in the SCMP. The configuration item list physically defines the components to be developed and the baselines to be integrated. For example an SPMP will say that an SRD will be written, but the configuration item list will define its file specification.

Configuration identification conventions should state how to:

- name a CI;
- decide who is the control authority of a CI;
- describe the history of a CI.

2.2.1.1 What to identify as configuration items

At the top level, the whole system is a CI. The system CI is composed of lower level CIs, which are derived from the design and planning documentation. Several factors may be relevant in deciding what to identify as the lowest level CI, such as the:

- software design defined in the ADD and DDD (the lowest level of the software design sets the lowest possible level of configuration management);
- capabilities of the software development tools (e.g. the units that the compiler or linkers input and output);
- bottom-level work packages defined in the SPMP.

Configurations must be practical from the physical point of view (i.e. each CI is easy to create and modify) and practical from the logical point of view (i.e. the purpose of each CI is easy to understand). A configuration should have sufficient 'granularity' (i.e. the lowest level CIs are small enough), to ensure that precise control is possible.

CIs should be easy to manage as discrete physical entities (e.g. files), and so the choice of what to make CIs can depend very much upon the tools available. A basic configuration management toolset (see Chapter 3) might rely on the file management facilities of the operating system. It is no accident therefore that CIs are often discrete files.

2.2.1.1.1 Baselines

A 'baseline' is a CI that has been formally reviewed and agreed upon (i.e. approved), and declared a basis for further development. Although any approved CI in a system can be referred to as a baseline, the term is normally used for the complete system.

Software development proceeds from baseline to baseline, accumulating new or revised CIs in the process. Early baselines contain only documents specifying the software to be built; later baselines contain the code as well.

The CIs in a baseline must be consistent with each other. Examples of consistency are:

- code CIs are compatible with the design document CIs;
- design document CIs are compatible with the requirements document CIs;
- user manual CIs describe the operation of the code CIs.

Baselines should be established when sharing software between developers becomes necessary. As soon as more than one person is using a piece of software, development of that software must be controlled.

Key baselines are tied to the major milestones in the life cycle (i.e. UR/R, SR/R, AD/R, DD/R, provisional acceptance and final acceptance). Baselines are also tied to milestones during integration. Unit-tested software components are assembled and integration-tested to form the initial baseline. New baselines are generated as other software components are integrated. The baselines provide a development and test environment for the new software components undergoing development and integration.

2.2.1.1.2 Variants

The term 'variant' is often used to identify CIs that, although offering almost identical functionality, differ in aspects such as:

- hardware environment;
- communications protocol;
- user language (e.g. English, French).

Variants may also be made to help diagnose software problems. The usefulness of such variants is often temporary, and they should be withdrawn when the problem has been solved.

The need to develop and maintain several variants can greatly complicate configuration management, so the number of variants should be minimised. One way to do this is to include conditional code in modules, so that one module can handle every variation. However modules can become very much more complicated, and developers need to trade-off code complexity with configuration complexity.

2.2.1.2 How to identify configuration items

Each configuration item must possess an identifier (SCM06). The identifier contains the name, type and version attributes of the configuration item (SCM07, SCM08, SCM09). The configuration management system should automatically ensure that all identifiers are unique.

Good names help developers quickly locate parts they need to work on, and ease traceability. Documents should have standard names (note that *Software Engineering Standards* predefines the names of documents) and code items should be named after the software components they contain.

The type field of a CI identifier should identify the processing the CI is intended for. There are three main types of CI:

- source CIs;
- derived CIs;
- tools to generate derived CIs from source CIs.

Source CIs (e.g. documents, source code) are created by software engineers. Corrections and modifications to CIs should always be done at source level.

Derived CIs (e.g. object files, executable files) are generated by processing source CIs with tools (e.g. compilers and linkers). The type field of a CI identifier should allow easy distinction between source CIs, derived CIs, and the tools used to make derived CIs.

Version numbers allow changes to CIs to be distinguished. Whenever a CI is changed, the version number changes. In most configuration management systems the version number is an integer.

Some configuration management systems distinguish between 'versions' and 'revisions'. Revision numbers track minor changes that do not change the functionality, such as bug fixes. When this approach is used, the version number actually consists of two numbers. The first marks major changes and the second, the revision number, marks minor changes. For example a software release might be referred to as 'Version 5.4'. For documents, the first number is called the 'issue' number. A version of a document might be referred to as 'Issue 2 Revision 1', for example.

The configuration identification method must accommodate new CIs, without requiring the modification of the identifiers of any existing CIs (SCM11). This is the 'extensibility' requirement. A method that sets a limit on the number of CIs does not meet the extensibility requirement, for example. When the limit has been reached, existing CIs have to be merged or deleted to make room for new CIs.

2.2.1.3 Configuration item control authority

Every CI should have a unique control authority that decides what changes will be made to a CI. The control authority may be an individual or a group of people. Three levels of control authority are normally distinguished in a software project:

- software author;
- software project manager;
- review board.

Large projects may have more levels. As a CI passes through the stages of verification (formal review meeting in the case of documents, unit, integration, system and acceptance tests in the case of code), so the control authority changes to match the higher verification status of the CI.

2.2.1.3.1 Software author

Software authors create low-level CIs, such as documents and code. Document writers are usually the control authority for draft documents. Programmers are normally the control authority for code until unit testing is complete.

2.2.1.3.2 Software project manager

Software project managers are responsible for the assembly of high-level CIs (i.e. baselines and releases) from the low-level CIs provided by software authors. Software project managers are the control authorities for all these CIs. Low-level CIs are maintained in software libraries (see Section 2.2.2.1). On most projects the software project manager is supported by a software librarian.

2.2.1.3.3 Review board

The review board approves baselines and changes to them. During development phases, formal review of baselines is done by the UR/R, SR/R, AD/R and DD/R boards. During the TR and OM phases, baselines are controlled by the Software Review Board (SRB).

The review board is the control authority for all baselines that have been approved or are under review. The review board may decide that a baseline should be changed, and authorises the development or maintenance team to implement the change. Control authority rights are not returned. Those responsible for implementing changes must resist the temptation to make any changes that have not been authorised. New problems found should be reported in the normal way (see Sections 2.3.3 and 2.4.3).

Review boards should be composed of members with sufficient authority and expertise to resolve any problems with the software. The nature of the review board depends upon the project. On a small project it might just consist of two people, such as the project manager and a user representative. On a large project the membership might include the project manager, the technical manager, the software librarian, the team leaders, user representatives and quality assurance personnel. Review board procedures are discussed in the *Guide to Software Verification and Validation*.

2.2.1.4 Configuration item history

The development history of each CI must be recorded from the moment it is first submitted for review or integration. For documents, this history is stored in Document Change Records (DCRs) and Document Status Sheets (DSS). For source code, the development history is stored in the module header (SCM18). Change records in module headers should reference the Software Change Request (SCR) that actioned them. For derived code, the development history is stored in the librarian's database. The development history should include records of the tests that have been performed. The Software Modification Report (SMR) should summarise the changes to CIs that have been revised in response to an SCR.

Development histories may be stored as tables of 'derivation records'. Each derivation record records one event in the life of the CI (e.g. source code change, compilation, testing etc.).

2.2.2 Configuration item storage

All CIs must be stored securely so that they never get lost. Software projects can accumulate thousands of low-level CIs, and just as books are stored in libraries, it is necessary to store low-level CIs in software libraries. The software libraries are themselves CIs.

Software CIs reside on hardware media (e.g. paper, magnetic disk). Storage media must be maintained securely and safely so that software is never lost or its integrity compromised.

2.2.2.1 Software libraries

A software library is a controlled collection of configuration items (e.g. source module, object module and document). Low-level CIs are developed and stored in libraries (e.g. source and object libraries), and then extracted to build high-level CIs (e.g. executable images).

As a minimum, every project must use the following software libraries to store CIs:

- development (or dynamic) libraries (SCM23);
- master (or controlled) libraries (SCM24);
- archive (or static) libraries (SCM25).

Development libraries store CIs that are being written or unit tested. Master libraries store CIs in the current baselines. Archive libraries store CIs in releases or retired baselines. CIs in archive libraries must not be modified (SCM26).

Development libraries are created and maintained by the software authors in their own work space. Master and archive libraries are created and maintained by the software librarian, who is responsible for:

- establishing new master libraries;
- updating master libraries;
- backup of master libraries to archive libraries;
- control of access to master libraries and archive libraries.

To make Figure 2.2B simple, the only storage activity shown is that of the software librarian storing new and changed CIs in master libraries. CIs are also stored in development libraries during development and change activities. CIs are stored in archive libraries when the software is released or routinely saved. In Figure 2.2B the outputs of the storage activity are the controlled CIs which are input to the integration process, or to the software change process.

Software libraries are fundamental to a software configuration management system. Whatever the library, the software configuration management system should permit CIs in libraries to be read, inserted, replaced and deleted.

Access to software libraries should be controlled so that it is impossible:

- to access CIs without the correct authorisation;
- for two people to simultaneously update the same CI.

Tables 2.2.2.1A and B show the software library access rights that should be granted to development staff and software librarians. Read access allows a CI to be examined or copied. The insert access right allows a new CI to be added to a software library. The delete access right allows a CI to be removed from a library. The replace right allows a CI to be removed from a library and another version inserted.

library \ access right	read	insert	replace	delete
development libraries	y	y	y	y
master libraries	y	n	n	n
archive libraries	y	n	n	n

Table 2.2.2.1A: Development staff access rights

library \ access right	read	insert	replace	delete
development libraries	y	y	y	y
master libraries	y	n	n	n
archive libraries	y	n	n	n

Table 2.2.2.1B: Software librarian access rights

Table 2.2.2.1A does not mean that a development library should be accessible to all developers. On the contrary, apart from the software librarian, only the person directly responsible for developing or maintaining the CIs in a development library should have access to them. For sharing software, master libraries should be used, not development libraries.

Simultaneous update occurs when two or more developers take a copy of a CI and make changes to it. When a developer returns a modified CI to the master library, modifications made by developers who have returned their CI earlier are lost. A charge-in/charge-out or 'locking' mechanism is required to prevent simultaneous update.

2.2.2.2 Media control

All CIs should be stored on controlled media (e.g. tapes, disks). Media should be labelled, both visibly (e.g. sticky label) and electronically (e.g. tape header). The label should have a standard format, and must contain the:
- project name (SCM19);
- configuration item identifier (name, type, version) (SCM20);
- date of storage (SCM21);
- content description (SCM22).

Procedures for the regular backup of development libraries must be established (SCM28). Up-to-date security copies of master and archive libraries must always be available (SCM27). An aim of good media control is to be able to recover from media loss quickly.

2.2.3 Configuration change control

Changes are normal in the evolution of a system. Proper change control is the essence of good configuration management.

Software configuration control evaluates proposed changes to configuration items and coordinates the implementation of approved changes. The change control process (see Figure 2.2B) analyses problem descriptions (such as RIDs and SPRs), decides which (if any) controlled CIs are to be changed, retrieves them from the master library for change, and returns changed CIs to the master library for storage. The process also outputs descriptions of the changes.

The change process is a miniature software development itself. Problems must be identified, analysed and a solution designed and implemented. Each stage in the process must be documented. *Software Engineering Standards* describes procedures for changing documents and code that are part of a baseline. These procedures are discussed in detail in Section 2.3.3 and 2.4.3.

Changes must be verified before the next changes are implemented. If changes are done in a group, each change must be separately verifiable. For documents, this just means that the Document Change Record (DCR) at the beginning of a document should describe each change precisely, or that a revised document is issued with change bars. For code, groups of changes must be carefully analysed to eliminate any confusion about the source of a fault during regression testing. If time permits, changes are best done one at a time, testing each change before implementing the next. This 'one-at-a-time' principle applies at all levels: code modification and unit testing; integration and integration testing, and system testing.

If an evolutionary or incremental delivery life cycle approach is used, changes may be propagated backwards to releases in use, as well as forwards to releases under development. Consider two releases of software, 1 and 2. Release 1 is in operational use and release 2 is undergoing development. As release 2 is developed, release 1 may evolve through several baselines (e.g. release 1.0, 1.1, 1.2 etc.) as problems discovered in operation are fixed.

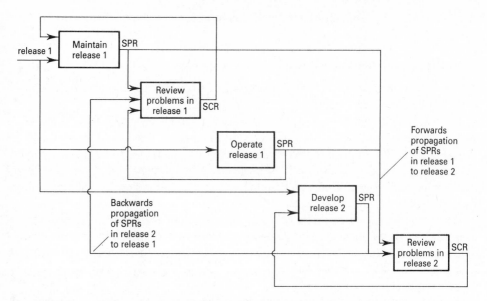

Figure 2.2.3: Software problem report propagation

Reports of problems found in release 1 must be fed forwards to the developers of release 2. Reports of problems in release 2 must also be fed backward to the maintainers of release 1, so that they can decide if the problems need to be fixed in release 1. Figure 2.2.3 shows how this can be done. The maintainers of release 1 should consider whether the problems pose a hazard to the users of release 1, and update it if they do.

2.2.4 Configuration status accounting

Software configuration status accounting is 'the recording and reporting of information needed to manage a configuration effectively, including a listing of the approved configuration identification, the status of proposed changes to the configuration, and the implementation status of the proposed changes' [Ref 2]. The status of all configuration items must be recorded (SCM31). Configuration status accounting continues throughout the life cycle.

In Figure 2.2.B, the Record CI Status process examines the configuration item lists output by the Identify CIs process, and the change descriptions output by the Change CIs process, to produce the status accounts.

The software librarian is normally responsible for maintaining the configuration status accounts, and for checking that the 'as-built' configuration status complies with the 'as-designed' status defined in the SCMP.

Configuration status accounts are composed of:

- records that describe the contents, dates and version/issue of each baseline (SCM32 and SCM35);
- records that describe the status of problem reports and their solutions (SCM33 and SCM34).

Configuration status accounts can be presented as tables of these two types of records.

Table 2.2.4 is an example of a table of baseline records. Each column of the table lists CIs in a baseline. The table shows the issue and revision number of each document, and the version number of the code in seven baselines. Six of the baselines are associated with the six major milestones of the software project. An extra interim baseline is created during integration. Table 2.2.4 assumes that revisions to each document are required between each baseline to show how the version numbers change. This is an extreme case.

Each management document (i.e. SPMP, SCMP, SVVP, SQAP) is reissued at each major milestone. This corresponds to the inclusion of new sections describing the plans for the next phase.

Baseline	1	2	3	4	5	6	7
CI\Milestone	URD approval	SRD approval	ADD approval	Interim Baseline	DDD approval	Prov' Accept'	Final Accept'
SPMP	1.0	2.0	3.0	4.0	4.0	4.1	4.2
SCMP	1.0	2.0	3.0	4.0	4.0	4.0	4.0
SVVP	1.0	2.0	3.0	4.0	4.1	4.2	4.3
SQAP	1.0	2.0	3.0	4.0	4.0	4.0	4.0
URD issue	1.0	1.1	1.2	1.3	1.4	1.5	1.6
SRD issue		1.0	1.1	1.2	1.3	1.4	1.5
ADD issue			1.0	1.1	1.2	1.3	1.4
DDD issue				1.0	1.1	1.2	1.3
SUM issue				1.0	1.1	1.2	1.3
Program A				1.0	1.1	1.2	1.3
Program B				1.0	1.1	1.2	1.3
Compiler				5.2	5.2	5.2	5.2
Linker				3.1	3.1	3.1	3.1
Oper. Sys				6.1	6.1	6.1	6.1
Program C					1.0	1.1	1.2
STD issue						1.0	1.0
SRD issue							1.0

Table 2.2.4: Example of baseline records

Records should be kept of the progress of Software Problem Reports (SPR) and Review Item Discrepancies (RID). A record should be created for each RID and SPR when it is received.

Each record should contain fields for noting:
- whether the SPR or RID has been approved;
- the corresponding SCR, SMR or RID.

The records do not actually describe the changes - this is what the CI history does (see Section 2.2.1.4).

Configuration status accounts are important instruments of project control, and should be made available to all project members for up-to-date information on baseline status. When a program works one day and not the next, the first question is 'what has changed?'. The configuration status accounts should answer such questions quickly and accurately. It should be possible to reproduce the original baseline, verify correct operation, and individually reintroduce the changes until the problem recurs [Ref 6].

Values of quality metrics (e.g. reliability) might be derived by means of data in the configuration status accounts, and these metrics might be used to decide the acceptability of the software. Sometimes quite simple pieces of information can be highly significant. A module that requires frequent 'bug fixes' may have more serious structural problems, and redesign may be necessary.

Sections 2.3.4 and 2.4.4 discuss the details of the configuration status accounting of documents and code.

2.2.5 Release

When a CI is distributed outside the project it is said to be 'released'. In Figure 2.2B, inputs to the release process are the baselines that have been successfully system tested, and the status accounts (for deciding the readiness for release). Outputs of the release process are the release itself and its 'release description'.

The Software Transfer Document (STD) describes the first release. The configuration item list in the first release must be included in the STD (SCM12). A Software Release Note (SRN) describes subsequent releases of the software (SCM14). A list of changed configuration items must be included in each SRN (SCM13).

2.3 DOCUMENTATION CONFIGURATION MANAGEMENT

Software Engineering Standards requires several documents to be produced in the software life cycle. The documents may specify the product (e.g. Software Requirements Document, Architectural Design Document) or some part of the process (e.g. Software Verification and Validation Plan, Software Configuration Management Plan). Whatever the document, it must be subject to configuration management procedures (SCM01).

The following subsections discuss the configuration management functions from the point of view of documentation.

2.3.1 Document configuration identification

A document CI may be:
- an entire document;
- a part of a document (e.g. a diagram).

The general principle established in *Software Engineering Standards* is that any configuration identification method must accommodate new CIs without modifying any existing CIs (SCM11). This principle applies to documents and parts of documents just as much as to code.

For documentation, the CI identifier must include:
- a number or name related to the purpose of the CI (SCM07);
- an indication of the type of processing for which the CI is intended (SCM08);
- an issue number and a revision number (SCM10).

As an example, the identifier of Issue 1, Revision 3 of the Software Requirements Document for a project called XXXX, produced with a word processor that attaches the filetype DOC, might be:

XXXX/SRD/DOC/Issue 1/Revision 3

The DOC field relates to SCM08, the Issue and Revision fields contain the version information required by SCM10, and the remaining fields name the item, as required by SCM07.

The title page(s) of a document should include:

- project name (SCM19);
- configuration item identifier (name, type, version) (SCM20);
- date (SCM21);
- content description (SCM22) (i.e. abstract and table of contents).

2.3.2 Document configuration item storage

Software Engineering Standards requires that all CIs be stored in software libraries. Paper versions of documents should be systematically filed in the project library. Electronic documents should be managed with the aid of software configuration management tools and should be stored in electronic libraries.

2.3.3 Document configuration change control

The procedure for controlling changes to a document is shown in Figure 2.3.3. This diagram shows the decomposition of the 'Change CIs' process in Figure 2.3.3.B. The process is used when a document that is part of a major baseline is modified, and is a mandatory requirement of *Software Engineering Standards* (SCM29).

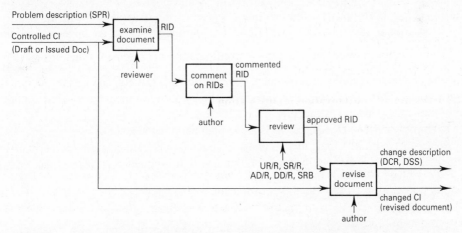

Figure 2.3.3: Document configuration change control activities

Examination is the first step in the document release process. Copies of the documents are circulated to everyone concerned (who should be identified in the Software Verification and Validation Plan). In the DD, TR and OM phases, SPRs may be input to the examination stage, to guide reviewers looking for errors in the URD, SRD, ADD, DDD and SUM.

Reviewers describe the defects that they find in the document on Review Item Discrepancy (RID) forms. RIDs permit reviewers to describe the:

- CI identifier of the document;
- problem location (in terms of a lower level CI identifier, if appropriate);
- problem;
- possible solution recommended by the reviewer.

RIDs are returned to the document authors for comment. Authors need to study problems identified in RIDs prior to the review meeting and mark their response on the RIDs, recording their views on the problems and the recommended solutions. Their responses may include preliminary assessments of the resources required to make the recommended changes, and the risks involved.

The commented RIDs and draft document are then input to the formal review meeting. Procedures for formal review meetings are discussed in the *Guide to Software Verification and Validation*. The review meeting may be a UR/R, SR/R, AD/R, DD/R or SRB meeting, depending upon the phase of the project.

The review meeting should discuss the RIDs and decide whether to:

- close the review item because the update has been completed;
- update (i.e. change) the document on the basis of the review item comments;
- reject the review item;
- define actions needed before a decision to close, update or reject can be made.

Each meeting should consider the level of authority required to approve each update. Agreements with other organisations may be necessary before decisions on some RIDs can be made.

The review meeting ends with a decision on whether to approve the document. A document may be approved although some changes have been agreed. Until the document has been updated, the baseline consists of the examined document and the RIDs describing the updates. Such RIDs are normally put in an appendix to the document.

A new version of the document incorporating the updates is then prepared. All updates should be recorded in Document Change Records (DCRs) and on the Document Status Sheet (DSS). Because the updates have the authority of the review board, authors must implement update instructions in the RIDs exactly.

Examples of RIDs, DCRs and DSSs are contained in Appendix D.

Sometimes a project finds that so many changes to a document are required that the RID method of recording problems is too clumsy. In this situation reviewers may prefer to:

- mark up a copy of the document;
- describe the problems in a note.

Review by these methods is acceptable only when the first issue of a document is being prepared, because there is no baseline for comparison until the first issue appears. After the first issue, the RID/DCR/DSS method must be used, because it allows the accurate tracking of changes to baselines, which the other methods do not.

2.3.4 Document configuration status accounting

Configuration status accounting keeps track of the contents of baselines. The configuration status accounts should describe the issue and revision number of each document in every baseline (see Section 2.2.4).

The configuration status accounts must record the status of every RID outstanding against every document in the baseline (SCM33). Table 2.3.4 describes the configuration status accounts of the RIDs in baseline 3 in Table 2.2.4.

RID Number	CI	Date submitted	Date reviewed	Status	DCR Number	CI with DCR
1	URD 1.1	1/6/92	1/7/92	closed	1	URD 1.2
2	URD 1.1	5/6/92	1/7/92	rejected	-	-
3	URD 1.1	6/6/92	1/7/92	action		
4	SRD 1.0	7/6/92	2/7/92	update		

Table 2.3.4: Records of the status RIDs in baseline 3

It is also important to track the RIDs outstanding against documents. Configuration status accounts need to be organised in a variety of ways (e.g. CI identifier order) and a DBMS is useful for managing them.

2.3.5 Document release

A document is released when it is formally 'issued'. The Document Status Sheet (DSS) is updated to mark this event, and any DCRs (remaining from previous revisions) are omitted. There should be no outstanding RIDs when a document is issued.

A formal issue must carry the approval of the responsible review body. Only formally issued documents can be made applicable. Approvals should be marked on the title page.

2.4 CODE CONFIGURATION MANAGEMENT

Source code, object code, executable code, data files, tools, test software and data must be subjected to configuration management procedures (SCM01). Procedures for the configuration management of code need to be defined before any code is written. This may be as early as the UR phase if prototypes are needed. DD phase code configuration management procedures need to be defined at the end of the AD phase in the SCMP/AD. These procedures may differ very much from those used in previous phases.

2.4.1 Code configuration identification

A code CI may be:
- a data file;
- an executable program;
- an object module;
- a source module.

The CI name must represent its function or specific purpose (SCM07). Since the name used for a software component in the ADD or DDD must also summarise the function of the component, the software component name should be used in the configuration identifier. The name of a source module that calculates an average might be called 'CALC_MEAN', for example. This configuration identification method allows easy traceability between the design and the CIs that implement it.

The CI type must summarise the processing for which the item is intended. If CALC_MEAN is a FORTRAN source file, its type would be written as 'FOR'. The configuration identifier of the first version of the file is then 'CALC_MEAN.FOR.1'.

The identifier of a CI must distinguish it from other items with different:

- requirements, especially functionality and interfaces (e.g. CALC_ARITHMETIC_MEAN and CALC_GEOMETRIC_MEAN) (SCM04);
- implementation (e.g. CALC_MEAN coded in FORTRAN and CALC_MEAN coded in C) (SCM05).

Source modules must have a header that includes:

- configuration item identifier (name, type, version) (SCM15);
- author (SCM16);
- creation date (SCM17);
- change history (version/date/author/description) (SCM18).

Projects should define a standard module header in the DDD. The format of the header must follow the rules of the selected programming language. Configuration management tools and documentation tools may be built to handle header information.

Code configuration identification conventions need to be established before any design work is done. They should be strictly observed throughout the design, coding, integration and testing.

2.4.2 Code configuration item storage

Librarians are perhaps the most widely used software development tools after editors, compilers and linkers. Librarian tools are used to:

- store source and object modules;
- keep records of library transactions;
- cross-reference source and object modules.

Once a source code module has been created and successfully compiled, source and object code are inserted into the development libraries. These libraries are owned by the programmer.

Programmers must observe configuration management procedures during coding and unit testing. The CI identifiers for the modules stored in their development libraries should be the same as the identifiers for the corresponding modules in master libraries. This makes CI status easy to track. Programmers should not, for example, write a module called CM.FOR and then rename it CALC_MEAN.FOR when it is submitted for promotion to the master library.

Code should be portable. Absolute file references should not be hardwired in source modules. Information relating names in software to names in the environment should be stored in tables that can be easily accessed.

2.4.3 Code configuration change control

The procedure for controlling changes to released code is shown in Figure 2.4.3. This diagram is a decomposition of the 'Change CIs' process in Figure 2.2B. The process is used when code that is part of a baseline is modified, and is a mandatory requirement of *Software Engineering Standards* (SCM30).

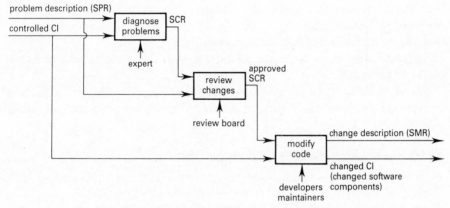

Figure 2.4.3: Code configuration change control activities

Problems may be identified during integration, system testing, acceptance testing or operations by users, development staff and quality assurance personnel. Software Problem Reports (SPRs) contain:

- CI title or name;
- CI version or release number;
- priority of the problem with respect to other problems;
- a description of the problem;
- operating environment;
- recommended solution (if possible).

The SPR is then assigned to an expert for diagnosis. Some debugging of code is often required, and the expert will need to have access to all the software in the baseline. The expert must prepare a Software Change Request (SCR) if modifications to the software are required. The SCR describes the:

- CI title or name;
- CI version or release number;
- priority of the problem with respect to other problems;
- changes required;
- responsible staff;
- estimated start date, end date and manpower effort.

The review board (i.e. the DD/R, SRB or a delegated individual) then reviews each SPR and associated SCRs and decides whether to:

- close the SPR because the update has been completed;
- update (i.e. change) the software on the basis of the
- recommendations in the associated SCR;
- reject the SPR;

- define an action that needs to be taken before a decision to close, update or reject can be made.

Approved SCRs are passed to the developers or maintainers for implementation, who produce a Software Modification Report (SMR) for each SCR. An SMR must describe the:

- CI title or name;
- CI version or release number;
- changes implemented;
- actual start date, end date and manpower effort.

Attachments may accompany the SPR, SCR and SMR to detail the problem, the change and the modification.

The code to be changed is taken from the master library used to build the baseline that exhibited the problem. Regression testing is necessary when changes are made (SCM39).

2.4.4 Code configuration status accounting

Configuration status accounting keeps track of the contents of baselines, allowing software evolution to be followed, and old baselines to be reconstructed.

Records of the status of each CI should be kept. These should describe whether the CI has passed project milestones, such as unit testing and integration testing. The table of these records provides a snapshot of baseline status, and provides management with visibility of product development.

The configuration status accounts must record the status of every SPR, SCR and SMR related to every CI in the baseline (SCM34). Table 2.4.4 shows how such records might be kept.

CI Name Version	SPR	Date submitted	Review Date	SPR Decision	Related SCR	Related SMR	Completion Date
LOADER v1.1	2	5/8/92	1/9/92	update	2	2	1/10/92
LOADER v1.1	3	7/8/92	1/9/92	update	3	2	1/10/92
EDITOR v1.2	4	9/8/92	1/9/92	rejected	-	-	-
MERGER v1.0	1	1/8/92	1/9/92	update	1	1	3/10/92

Table 2.4.4: Configuration status accounts example

2.4.5 Code release

The first release of the code must be documented in the STD. Subsequent releases must be accompanied by a Software Release Note (SRN). STDs and SRNs provide an overview of a release. They include a configuration item list that catalogues the CIs in the release. They must summarise any faults that have been repaired and the new requirements that have been incorporated (SCM36). One way to do this is to list the SPRs that have been dealt with.

For each release, documentation and code must be consistent (SCM37). Furthermore, old releases must be retained, for reference (SCM38). Where possible, the previous release should be kept online during a change-over period, to allow comparisons, and as a fallback. The number of releases in operational use should be minimised.

Releases should be self-identifying (e.g. label, display or printed output) so that users know what the software is. Some form of software protection may be desirable to avoid unauthorised use of a release.

Modified software must be retested before release (SCM29). Tests should be selected from the SVVP to demonstrate its operational capability.

CHAPTER 3
SOFTWARE CONFIGURATION MANAGEMENT TOOLS

3.1 INTRODUCTION

Software configuration management is often described as simple in concept but complex in detail. Tools that support software configuration management are widely available and their use is strongly recommended.

This chapter does not describe particular tools. Instead, this chapter discusses software configuration management tools in terms of their capabilities. No single tool can be expected to provide all of them, and developers need to define their own software configuration management tool requirements and assemble a 'toolset' that meets them.

ANSI/IEEE Std 1042-1987, IEEE Guide to Software Configuration Management, recognises four types of toolset:

- basic;
- advanced;
- online;
- integrated.

This classification is used to organise software configuration management tools. Each toolset includes the capabilities of preceding toolsets.

3.2 BASIC TOOLSET REQUIREMENTS

Basic toolsets use standard operating system utilities such as the editor and librarian system, perhaps supplemented by a database management system. They rely heavily on personal discipline. The capability requirements for a basic toolset are listed below.

1. A basic toolset should permit the structured definition, identification and storage of configuration items.

2. The file systems of operating systems allows storage of CIs in files. A file system should object if the user tries to create a file with the same name as an existing file, i.e. it should ensure that names are unique.

3. A basic toolset should permit the structured storage of configuration items.

4. The file systems of operating systems should allow the creation of directory trees for storing files.

5. A basic toolset should provide a librarian system that supports:
   - insertion of modules;
   - extraction of modules;
   - replacement of modules by updated modules;

- deletion of modules;
- production of cross-reference listings to show which modules refer to which;
- storage of the transaction history;
- all the above features for both source (i.e. text) and object (i.e. binary) files.

4. A basic toolset should provide facilities for building executable software from designated sources.
   This implies the capability to create a command file of build instructions with a text editor.

5. A basic toolset should provide security features so that access to CIs can be restricted to authorised personnel.
   This means that the operating system should allow the owner of a file to control access to it.

6. A basic toolset should provide facilities for comparing source modules so that changes can be identified.
   Most operating systems provide a tool for differencing ASCII files.

7. A basic toolset should include tools for the systematic backup of CIs. Specifically:
   - automatic electronic labelling of media;
   - complete system backup;
   - incremental backup;
   - restore;
   - production of backup logs.
   Most operating systems have commands for backing-up and restoring files.

3.3 ADVANCED TOOLSET REQUIREMENTS

Advanced toolsets supplement the basic toolset with standalone tools such as source code control systems and module management systems. The extra capability requirements for an advanced toolset are listed below.

1. An advanced toolset should provide a locking system with the library to ensure that only one person can work on a module at a time.
   Most operating system librarians do not provide this feature; it is a characteristic of dedicated software configuration management librarian tools.

2. An advanced toolset should minimise the storage space needed.
   One way to do this is store the latest version and the changes, usually called 'deltas', required to generate earlier versions.

3. An advanced librarian tool should allow long names to be used in identifiers.
   Some operating systems force the use of shorter names than the compiler or programming language standard allows, and this can make it impossible to make the configuration identifiers contain the names used in design.

4. An advanced toolset should permit rollback, so that software configuration management operations can be undone.
   A simple but highly desirable type of backtracking operation is the 'undelete'. Some tools can reverse deletion operations.

5. An advanced toolset should provide facilities for rebuilding executable software from up-to-date versions of designated sources.
   This capability requires the build tool to examine the dependencies between the modules in the build and recompile those modules that have been changed since the last build.

6. An advanced toolset should record the version of each module that was used to build a product baseline, so that product baselines can always be reproduced.

7. An advanced toolset should provide facilities for the handling of configuration status accounts, specifically:
   - insertion of new RID, SPR, SCR and SMR status records;
   - modification of RID, SPR, SCR and SMR status records;
   - deletion of RID, SPR, SCR and SMR status records;
   - search of RID, SPR, SCR and SMR records on any field;
   - differencing of configuration status accounts, so that changes can be identified;
   - report generation.

3.4 ONLINE TOOLSET REQUIREMENTS

Online toolsets supplement the capabilities of advanced toolsets by providing facilities for interactive entry of change control information. The extra capability requirements for an online toolset are listed below.

1. An online toolset should provide facilities for the direct entry of RID, SPR, SCR and SMR information into the database;

2. An online toolset should provide an authentication system that permits online approval of changes.

3.5 INTEGRATED TOOLSET REQUIREMENTS

Integrated toolsets supplement the capabilities of online toolsets by extending the change control system to documentation. Integrated Toolsets form part of so-called 'Integrated Project Support Environments' (IPSEs), 'Project Support Environments' (PSEs) and 'Software Development Environments' (SDEs). The extra capabilities of an integrated toolset are listed below.

1. An integrated toolset should recognise all the dependencies between CIs, so that consistency can be controlled.
   This capability requires a super-library called a 'repository'. The Online Toolset has to be integrated with the CASE tools used for design. This facility permits the system to be automatically rebuilt from a design change, not just a code change.

2. An integrated toolset should have standard interfaces to other tools (e.g. project management tools).
   Standards for interfacing software tools have been proposed, such as the Portable Common Tools Environment (PCTE) [Ref 7] and the Common APSE Interface Set (CAIS) [Ref 8].

CHAPTER 4
THE SOFTWARE CONFIGURATION MANAGEMENT PLAN

4.1 INTRODUCTION

All software configuration management activities shall be documented in the Software Configuration Management Plan (SCM40). A new section of the SCMP must be produced for each development phase (SCM42, SCM44, SCM46, SCM48). Each SCMP section must document all software configuration management activities (SCM40), specifically the:

- organisation of configuration management;
- procedures for configuration identification;
- procedures for change control;
- procedures for configuration status accounting;
- tools, techniques and methods for software configuration management;
- procedures for supplier control;
- procedures for the collection and retention of records.

The size and content of the SCMP should reflect the complexity of the project. ANSI/IEEE Std 1042-1987, IEEE Guide to Software Configuration Management contains examples of plans for:

- a complex, critical computer system;
- a small software development project;
- maintaining programs developed by other activities or organisations;
- developing and maintaining embedded software.

Configuration management procedures must be in place before software production (code and documentation) starts (SCM41). Software configuration management procedures should be easy to follow and efficient. Wherever possible, procedures should be reusable in later phases. Instability in software configuration management procedures can impede progress in a software project.

4.2 STYLE

The SCMP should be plain and concise. The document should be clear, consistent and modifiable.

The author of the SCMP should assume familiarity with the purpose of the software, and not repeat information that is explained in other documents.

4.3 RESPONSIBILITY

The developer is responsible for the production of the SCMP.

4.4 MEDIUM

It is usually assumed that the SCMP is a paper document. There is no reason why the SCMP should not be distributed electronically to participants with the necessary equipment.

4.5 CONTENT

The SCMP is divided into four sections, one for each development phase. These sections are called:
- Software Configuration Management Plan for the SR phase (SCMP/SR);
- Software Configuration Management Plan for the AD phase (SCMP/AD);
- Software Configuration Management Plan for the DD phase (SCMP/DD);
- Software Configuration Management Plan for the TR phase (SCMP/TR).

Software Engineering Standards recommends the following table of contents for each section of the SCMP, which as been derived from the IEEE Standard for Software Configuration Management Plans (ANSI/IEEE Std 828-1990).

Service Information:
a - Abstract
b - Table of Contents
c - Document Status Sheet
d - Document Change records made since last issue

1 INTRODUCTION[1]
    1.1 Purpose
    1.2 Scope
    1.3 Glossary
    1.4 References
2 MANAGEMENT
3 CONFIGURATION IDENTIFICATION
4 CONFIGURATION CONTROL
    4.1 Code (and document) control
    4.2 Media control
    4.3 Change control
5 CONFIGURATION STATUS ACCOUNTING
6 TOOLS TECHNIQUES AND METHODS FOR SCM
7 SUPPLIER CONTROL
8 RECORDS COLLECTION AND RETENTION

---

[1] The Software Configuration Management Plan contents list is based upon extracts from IEEE Std 828-1990, IEEE Standard for Software Configuration Management Plans, copyright © 1990 by the Institute for Electrical and Electronic Engineers Inc. The IEEE disclaims any responsibility or liability resulting from the placement and use in this publication. Information is reprinted with the permission of the IEEE.

Material unsuitable for the above contents list should be inserted in additional appendices. If there is no material for a section then the phrase 'Not Applicable' should be inserted and the section numbering preserved.

4.5.1 SCMP/1 INTRODUCTION

The following subsections should provide an introduction to the plan.

4.5.1.1 SCMP/1.1 Purpose

This section should:
(1) briefly define the purpose of the particular SCMP;
(2) specify the intended readership of the SCMP.

4.5.1.2 SCMP/1.2 Scope

This section should identify the:
(1) configuration items to be managed;
(2) configuration management activities in this plan;
(3) organisations the plan applies to;
(4) phase of the life cycle the plan applies to.

4.5.1.3 SCMP/1.3 Glossary

This section should define all terms, acronyms, and abbreviations used in the plan, or refer to other documents where the definitions can be found.

4.5.1.4 SCMP/1.4 References

This section should provide a complete list of all the applicable and reference documents, identified by title, author and date. Each document should be marked as applicable or reference. If appropriate, report number, journal name and publishing organisation should be included.

4.5.2 SCMP/2 MANAGEMENT

This section should describe the organisation of configuration management, and the associated responsibilities. It should define the roles to be carried out. ANSI/IEEE Std 828-1990, 'Standard for Software Configuration Management Plans' [Ref 3] recommends that the following structure be used for this section.

4.5.2.1 SCMP/2.1 Organisation

This section should:
- identify the organisational roles that influence the software configuration management function (e.g. project managers, programmers, quality assurance personnel and review boards);
- describe the relationships between the organisational roles;
- describe the interface with the user organisation.

Relationships between the organisational roles may be shown by means of an organigram. This section may reference the SPMP.

4.5.2.2 SCMP/2.2 SCM responsibilities

This section should identify the:
- software configuration management functions each organisational role is responsible for (e.g. identification, storage, change control, status accounting);
- responsibilities of each organisational role in the review, audit and approval process;
- responsibilities of the users in the review, audit and approval process.

4.5.2.3 SCMP/2.3 Interface management

This section should define the procedures for the management of external hardware and software interfaces. In particular it should identify the:
- external organisations responsible for the systems or subsystems with which the software interfaces;
- points of contact in the external organisations for jointly managing the interface;
- groups responsible for the management of each interface.

4.5.2.4 SCMP/2.4 SCMP implementation

This section should establish the key events in the implementation of the SCMP, for example the:
- readiness of the configuration management system for use;
- establishment of the Software Review Board;
- establishment of baselines;
- release of products.

The scheduling of the software configuration management resources should be shown (e.g. availability of software librarian, software configuration management tools and SRB). This section may cross-reference the SPMP.

4.5.2.5 SCMP/2.5 Applicable policies, directives and procedures

This section should:
- identify all applicable software configuration management policies, directives or procedures to be implemented as part of this plan (corporate software configuration management documents may be referenced here, with notes describing the parts of the documents that apply);
- describe any software configuration management polices, directives or procedures specific to this project, for example:
  - project-specific interpretations of corporate software configuration management documents;
  - level of authority required for each level of control;
  - level of review, testing or assurance required for promotion.

4.5.3 SCMP/3 CONFIGURATION IDENTIFICATION

This section should describe the conventions for identifying the software items and then define the baselines used to control their evolution.

4.5.3.1 SCMP/3.1 Conventions

This section should:
- define project CI naming conventions;
- define or reference CI labelling conventions.

4.5.3.2 SCMP/3.2 Baselines

For each baseline, this section should give the:
- identifier of the baseline;
- contents, i.e. the:
    - software itself (e.g. URD, SRD, ADD, DDD, modules, executables, SUM, SVVP);
    - tools for making derived items in the baseline (e.g. compiler, linker and build procedures);
    - test software (e.g. data, harnesses and stubs);
    - RIDs, SPRs etc that relate to the baseline;
- ICDs, if any, which define the interfaces of the software;
- review and approval events, and the acceptance criteria, associated with establishing each baseline;
- participation required of developers and users in establishing baselines.

Because the SCMP is a plan, the precise contents of each baseline may not be known when it is written (e.g. names of modules before the detailed design is started). When this occurs, procedures for getting a report of the contents of the baseline should be defined (e.g. a directory list). An example of a report may be supplied in this section.

If appropriate, the description of each baseline should:
- distinguish software being developed from software being reused or purchased;
- define the hardware environment needed for each configuration;
- trace CIs to deliverable items listed in the SPMP, and, for code, to the software components described in the ADD and DDD.

4.5.4 SCMP/4 CONFIGURATION CONTROL

In ANSI/IEEE Std 610.12-1990 [Ref 2], configuration control covers only configuration item change control. In *Software Engineering Standards*, the definition of configuration control is expanded to include configuration item storage. Sections 4.1, 'Code Control' and 4.2, 'Media Control' therefore describe the procedures for configuration item storage. Section 4.3 of the plan describes the procedures for configuration item change control.

4.5.4.1 SCMP/4.1 Code (and document) control

This section should describe the software library handling procedures. *Software Engineering Standards* calls for three types of library:

- development (or dynamic);
- master (or controlled);
- archive (or static).

Ideally the same set of procedures should be used for each type of library.

While Section 6 of the SCMP, 'Tools, Techniques and Methods', gives background information, this section should describe, in a stepwise manner, how these are applied.

4.5.4.2 SCMP/4.2 Media control

This section should describe the procedure for handling the hardware on which the software resides, such as:

- magnetic disk;
- magnetic tape;
- Read-Only Memory (ROM);
- Erasable Programmable Read-Only Memory (EPROM);
- optical disk.

Whatever media is used, this section should describe the procedures for:

- labelling media (which should be based on *Software Engineering Standards*, Part 2, Section 3.2.1);
- storing the media (e.g. fire-proof safes, redundant off-site locations);
- recycling the media (e.g. always use new magnetic tapes when archiving).

4.5.4.3 SCMP/4.3 Change control

This section should define the procedures for processing changes to baselines described in Section 3.2 of the plan.

4.5.4.3.1 SCMP/4.3.1 Levels of authority

This section should define the level of authority required to authorise changes to a baseline (e.g. software librarian, project manager).

4.5.4.3.2 SCMP/4.3.2 Change procedures

This section should define the procedures for processing change proposals to software.

The documentation change process (i.e. URD, SRD, ADD, DDD, SUM) should be based on the procedures defined in *Software Engineering Standards*, Part 2, Section 3.2.3.2.1, 'Documentation Change Procedures'. These procedures use the RID, DCR and DSS forms.

The code change process should be based on the procedures *Software Engineering Standards*, Part 2, Section 3.2.3.2.2, 'Software Problem Reporting procedures'. These procedures use the SPR, SCR and SMR forms.

4.5.4.3.3 SCMP/4.3.3 Review board

This section should define the:

- membership of the review board (e.g. DD/R, SRB);
- levels of authority required for different types of change.

The second point implies that the review board may delegate some of their responsibilities for change.

4.5.4.3.4 SCMP/4.3.4 Interface control

This section should define the procedures for controlling the interfaces. In particular it should define the:

- change control process for ICDs;
- status accounting process for ICDs.

4.5.4.3.5 SCMP/4.3.5 Support software change procedures

This section should define the change control procedures for support software items. Support software items are not produced by the developer, but may be components of the delivered system, or may be tools used to make it. Examples are:

- commercial software;
- reused software;
- compilers;
- linkers.

4.5.5 SCMP/5 CONFIGURATION STATUS ACCOUNTING

This section should:

- define how configuration item status information is to be collected, stored, processed and reported;
- identify the periodic reports to be provided about the status of the CIs, and their distribution;
- state what dynamic inquiry capabilities, if any, are to be provided;
- describe how to implement any special status accounting requirements specified by users.

In summary, this section defines how the project will keep an audit trail of changes.

4.5.6 SCMP/6 TOOLS, TECHNIQUES AND METHODS FOR SCM

This section should describe the tools, techniques and methods to support:

- configuration identification (e.g. controlled allocation of identifiers);
- configuration item storage (e.g. source code control systems);
- configuration change control (e.g. online problem reporting systems);
- configuration status accounting (e.g. tools to generate accounts).

4.5.7 SCMP/7 SUPPLIER CONTROL

This section should describe the requirements for software configuration management to be placed on external organisations such as:

- subcontractors;
- suppliers of commercial software (i.e. vendors).

This section should reference the review and audit procedures in the SVVP for evaluating the acceptability of supplied software.

This section may reference contractual requirements.

4.5.8 SCMP/8 RECORDS COLLECTION AND RETENTION

This section should:
- identify the software configuration management records to be retained (e.g. CIDLs, RIDs, DCRs, DSSs, SPRs, SCRs, SMRs, configuration status accounts);
- state the methods to be used for retention (e.g. fire-proof safe, on paper, magnetic tape);
- state the retention period (e.g. retain all records for all baselines or only the last three baselines).

4.6 EVOLUTION

4.6.1 UR phase

By the end of the UR review, the SR phase section of the SCMP must be produced (SCMP/SR) (SCM42). The SCMP/SR must cover the configuration management procedures for all documentation, CASE tool outputs or prototype code produced in the SR phase (SCM43).

Since the SCMP/SR is the first section to be produced, Section 3.2 of the SCMP should identify the libraries in which the URD, SRD, SCMP and SVVP will be stored. Section 3.3 of the SCMP should describe the UR/R and SR/R board.

4.6.2 SR phase

During the SR phase, the AD phase section of the SCMP must be produced (SCMP/AD) (SCM44). The SCMP/AD must cover the configuration management procedures for documentation, CASE tool outputs or prototype code produced in the AD phase (SCM45). Unless there is a good reason to change (e.g. different CASE tool used), SR phase procedures should be reused.

Section 3.2 should identify the libraries in which the ADD will be stored. Section 3.3 should describe the AD/R board.

4.6.3 AD phase

During the AD phase, the DD phase section of the SCMP must be produced (SCMP/DD) (SCM46). The SCMP/DD must cover the configuration management procedures for documentation, deliverable code, CASE tool outputs or prototype code produced in the DD phase (SCM47). Unless there is a good reason to change, AD phase procedures should be reused.

Section 3.2 should identify the libraries in which the DDD, SUM, and code will be stored. Section 3.3 should describe the DD/R board.

4.6.4 DD phase

During the DD phase, the TR phase section of the SCMP must be produced (SCMP/TR) (SCM48). The SCMP/TR must cover the procedures for the configuration management of the deliverables in the operational environment (SCM49).

APPENDIX A
GLOSSARY

A.1 LIST OF TERMS

Terms used in this document are consistent with *Software Engineering Standards* [Ref 1] and ANSI/IEEE Std 610.12 [Ref 2]. This section defines the software configuration management terms used in this guide.

archive library
A software library used for storing CIs in releases or retired baselines.

backup
A copy of a software item for use in the event of the loss of the original.

baseline
A configuration item that has been formally reviewed and agreed upon, that thereafter serves as a basis for further development, and that can be changed only through formal change control procedures.

change control
An element of configuration management, consisting of the evaluation, coordination, approval or disapproval, and implementation of changes to configuration items after formal establishment of their configuration identification [Ref 2].

charge-in
The process of inserting or replacing a configuration item in a master library.

charge-out
The process of obtaining a copy of a configuration item from a master library and preventing charge-out operations on the item until it is charged back in.

configuration identification
An element of configuration management, consisting of selecting the configuration items for a system and recording their functional and physical characteristics in technical documentation [Ref 2].

configuration item
A aggregation of hardware, software, or both, that is designated for configuration management and treated as a single entity in the configuration management process [Ref 2].

configuration item identifier

A data structure that describes the name, type and version number of a configuration item.

configuration item list

A catalogue of configuration items in a baseline or release.

configuration item storage

The process of storing configuration items in software libraries and on hardware media.

configuration status accounting

An element of configuration management, consisting of the recording and reporting of information needed to manage a configuration effectively [Ref 2].

control authority

The individual or group who decides upon the changes to a configuration item; a configuration item cannot be changed without the control authority's consent.

controlled configuration item

A configuration item that has been accepted by the project for integration into a baseline. Controlled configuration items are stored in master libraries. Controlled configuration items are subject to formal change control.

derivation record

A record of one event in the life of the configuration item (e.g. source code change, compilation, testing etc).

development history

A set of time-ordered derivation records; there is a development history for each configuration item.

development library

A software library that is used for storing software components that are being coded (or modified) and unit tested.

document change record

A description of one or more changes to a document.

document status sheet

An issue-by-issue description of the history of a document.

formal

Used to describe activities that have explicit and definite rules of procedure (e.g. formal review) or reasoning (e.g. formal method and formal proof).

issue

A version of a document that has undergone major changes since the previous version.

level of authority

The position in the project hierarchy that is responsible for deciding upon a change.

master library

A software library that is used for storing controlled configuration items.

media control
The process of labelling and storing the hardware items on which the software is stored.

release
A baseline made available for use.

review board
The authority responsible for evaluating proposed ... changes, and ensuring implementation of the approved changes; same as configuration control board in Reference 2.

review item discrepancy
A description of a problem with a document and its recommended solution.

revision
A version of a document with minor changes from the previous version.

simultaneous update
The phenomenon of two updates being made by different people on different copies of the same configuration item; one of the updates is always lost.

software change request
A description of the changes required to documentation and code, the responsible staff, schedule and effort.

software configuration management
A discipline of applying technical and administrative direction and surveillance to identify and document the functional and physical characteristics of a configuration item, control changes to those characteristics, record and report change processing and implementation status, and verify compliance with specified requirements [Ref 2].

software librarian
A person responsible for establishing, controlling, and maintaining a software library.

software library
A controlled collection of software and related documentation designed to aid in software development, use, or maintenance [Ref 2].

software modification report
A report that describes the implementation of a software change request.

software problem report
A report that describes a problem with the software, the urgency of the problem, the environment in which it occurs, and the recommended solution.

software release note
A document that describes the changes and configuration items in a software release

software review board
The name for the review board in the OM phase.

variant
A configuration item that meets special requirements.

A.2 LIST OF ACRONYMS

AD	Architectural Design
AD/R	Architectural Design Review
ADD	Architectural Design Document
ANSI	American National Standards Institute
APSE	Ada Programming Support Environment
AT	Acceptance Test
BSSC	Board for Software Standardisation and Control
CASE	Computer Aided Software Engineering
DBMS	Data Base Management System
DCR	Document Change Record
DD	Detailed Design and production
DD/R	Detailed Design and production Review
DDD	Detailed Design and production Document
DSS	Document Status Sheet
EPROM	Erasable Programmable Read-Only Memory
ESA	European Space Agency
ICD	Interface Control Document
IEEE	Institute of Electrical and Electronics Engineers
ISO	International Standards Organisation
IT	Integration Test
PA	Product Assurance
PCTE	Portable Common Tools Environment
PSS	Procedures, Specifications and Standards
QA	Quality Assurance
RID	Review Item Discrepancy
ROM	Read-Only Memory
SCM	Software Configuration Management
SCMP	Software Configuration Management Plan
SCR	Software Change Request
SMR	Software Modification Report
SPM	Software Project Management
SPMP	Software Project Management Plan
SPR	Software Problem Report
SQA	Software Quality Assurance
SQAP	Software Quality Assurance Plan
SR	Software Requirements
SR/R	Software Requirements Review
SRD	Software Requirements Document
SRN	Software Release Note
ST	System Test
STD	Software Transfer Document
SUM	Software User Manual
SVVP	Software Verification and Validation Plan

UR	User Requirements
UR/R	User Requirements Review
URD	User Requirements Document
UT	Unit Test

APPENDIX B
REFERENCES

1. Software Engineering Standards, C.Mazza, J.Fairclough, B.Melton, D.dePablo, A.Scheffer, R.Stevens, Prentice-Hall 1994.
2. IEEE Standard Glossary of Software Engineering Terminology, ANSI/IEEE Std 610.12-1990.
3. IEEE Standard for Software Configuration Management Plans, ANSI/IEEE Std 828-1990.
4. IEEE Guide to Software Configuration Management, ANSI/IEEE Std 1042-1987.
5. The STARTs Guide - a guide to methods and software tools for the construction of large real-time systems, NCC Publications, 1987.
6. Managing the Software Process, Watts S. Humphrey, SEI Series in Software Engineering, Addison-Wesley, August 1990.
7. Portable Common Tool Environment (PCTE) Abstract Specification, Standard ECMA-149, European Computer Manufacturers Association, December 1990.
8. Requirements for Ada Programming Support Environments, STONEMAN, U.S Department of Defense, February 1980.

APPENDIX C
MANDATORY PRACTICES

This appendix is repeated from *Software Engineering Standards*, appendix D.9.

SCM01   All software items, for example documentation, source code, object or relocatable code, executable code, files, tools, test software and data, shall be subjected to configuration management procedures.

SCM02   The configuration management procedures shall establish methods for identifying, storing and changing software items through development, integration and transfer.

SCM03   A common set of configuration management procedures shall be used.

Every configuration item shall have an identifier that distinguishes it from other items with different:

SCM04   • requirements, especially functionality and interfaces;

SCM05   • implementation.

SCM06   Each component defined in the design process shall be designated as a CI and include an identifier.

SCM07   The identifier shall include a number or a name related to the purpose of the CI.

SCM08   The identifier shall include an indication of the type of processing the CI is intended for (e.g. filetype information).

SCM09   The identifier of a CI shall include a version number.

SCM10   The identifier of documents shall include an issue number and a revision number.

SCM11   The configuration identification method shall be capable of accommodating new CIs, without requiring the modification of the identifiers of any existing CIs.

SCM12   In the TR phase, a list of configuration items in the first release shall be included in the STD.

SCM13   In the OM phase, a list of changed configuration items shall be included in each Software Release Note (SRN).

SCM14   An SRN shall accompany each release made in the OM phase.

As part of the configuration identification method, a software module shall have a standard header that includes:

SCM15 • configuration item identifier (name, type, version);

SCM16 • original author;

SCM17 • creation date;

SCM18 • change history (version/date/author/description).

All documentation and storage media shall be clearly labelled in a standard format, with at least the following data:

SCM19 • project name;

SCM20 • configuration item identifier (name, type, version);

SCM21 • date;

SCM22 • content description.

To ensure security and control of the software, at a minimum, the following software libraries shall be implemented for storing all the deliverable components (e.g. documentation, source and executable code, test files, command procedures):

SCM23 • Development (or Dynamic) library;

SCM24 • Master (or Controlled) library;

SCM25 • Static (or Archive) library.

SCM26 • Static libraries shall not be modified.

SCM27 Up-to-date security copies of master and static libraries shall always be available.

SCM28 Procedures for the regular backup of development libraries shall be established.

SCM29 The change procedure described (in Part 2, Section 3.2.3.2.1) shall be observed when changes are needed to a delivered document.

SCM30 Software problems and change proposals shall be handled by the procedure described (in Part 2, Section 3.2.3.2.2).

SCM31 The status of all configuration items shall be recorded.

To perform software status accounting, each software project shall record:

SCM32 • the date and version/issue of each baseline;

SCM33 • the date and status of each RID and DCR;

SCM34 • the date and status of each SPR, SCR and SMR;

SCM35 • a summary description of each Configuration Item.

SCM36   As a minimum, the SRN shall record the faults that have been repaired and the new requirements that have been incorporated.

SCM37   For each release, documentation and code shall be consistent.

SCM38   Old releases shall be retained, for reference.

SCM39   Modified software shall be retested before release.

SCM40   All software configuration management activities shall be documented in the Software Configuration Management Plan (SCMP).

SCM41   Configuration management procedures shall be in place before the production of software (code and documentation) starts.

SCM42   By the end of the UR review, the SR phase section of the SCMP shall be produced (SCMP/SR).

SCM43   The SCMP/SR shall cover the configuration management procedures for documentation, and any CASE tool outputs or prototype code, to be produced in the SR phase.

SCM44   During the SR phase, the AD phase section of the SCMP shall be produced (SCMP/AD).

SCM45   The SCMP/AD shall cover the configuration management procedures for documentation, and CASE tool outputs or prototype code, to be produced in the AD phase.

SCM46   During the AD phase, the DD phase section of the SCMP shall be produced (SCMP/DD).

SCM47   The SCMP/DD shall cover the configuration management procedures for documentation, deliverable code, and any CASE tool outputs or prototype code, to be produced in the DD phase.

SCM48   During the DD phase, the TR phase section of the SCMP shall be produced (SCMP/TR).

SCM49   The SCMP/TR shall cover the procedures for the configuration management of the deliverables in the operational environment.

APPENDIX D
FORM TEMPLATES

Template forms are provided for:

DCR   Document Change Record
DSS   Document Status Sheet
RID   Review Item Discrepancy
SCR   Software Change Request
SMR   Software Modification Report
SPR   Software Problem Report
SRN   Software Release Note

DOCUMENT CHANGE RECORD	DCR NO	
	DATE	
	ORIGINATOR	
	APPROVED BY	

1. DOCUMENT TITLE:

2. DOCUMENT REFERENCE NUMBER:

3. DOCUMENT ISSUE/REVISION NUMBER:

4. PAGE	5. PARAGRAPH	6. REASON FOR CHANGE

DOCUMENT STATUS SHEET			
1. DOCUMENT TITLE:			
2. DOCUMENT REFERENCE NUMBER:			
3. ISSUE	4. REVISION	5. DATE	6. REASON FOR CHANGE

REVIEW ITEM DISCREPANCY	RID NO	
	DATE	
	ORIGINATOR	

1. DOCUMENT TITLE:

2. DOCUMENT REFERENCE NUMBER:

3. DOCUMENT ISSUE/REVISION NUMBER:

4. PROBLEM LOCATION:

5. PROBLEM DESCRIPTION:

6. RECOMMENDED SOLUTION;

7. AUTHOR'S RESPONSE:

8. REVIEW DECISION: CLOSE/UPDATE/ACTION/REJECT (underline choice)

SOFTWARE PROBLEM REPORT	SPR NO	
	DATE	
	ORIGINATOR	

1. SOFTWARE ITEM TITLE:

2. SOFTWARE ITEM VERSION/RELEASE NUMBER:

3. PRIORITY: CRITICAL/URGENT/ROUTINE (underline choice)

4. PROBLEM DESCRIPTION:

5. DESCRIPTION OF ENVIRONMENT:

6. RECOMMENDED SOLUTION;

7. REVIEW DECISION: CLOSE/UPDATE/ACTION/REJECT (underline choice)

8. ATTACHMENTS:

SOFTWARE RELEASE NOTE	SRN NO	
	DATE	
	ORIGINATOR	

1. SOFTWARE ITEM TITLE:

2. SOFTWARE ITEM VERSION/RELEASE NUMBER:

3. CHANGES IN THIS RELEASE:

4. CONFIGURATION ITEMS INCLUDED IN THIS RELEASE:

5. INSTALLATION INSTRUCTIONS:

APPENDIX E
INDEX

Guide to software verification and validation

TABLE OF CONTENTS

CHAPTER 1
INTRODUCTION

1.1 PURPOSE

Software Engineering Standards [Ref 1] requires that software be verified during every phase of its development life cycle and validated when it is transferred. These activities are called 'Software Verification and Validation' (SVV). Each project must define its Software Verification and Validation activities in a Software Verification and Validation Plan (SVVP).

This guide defines and explains what software verification and validation is, provides guidelines on how to do it, and defines in detail what a Software Verification and Validation Plan should contain.

This guide should be read by everyone concerned with developing software, such as software project managers, software engineers and software quality assurance staff. Sections on acceptance testing and formal reviews should be of interest to users.

1.2 OVERVIEW

Chapter 2 contains a general discussion of the principles of software verification and validation, expanding upon the ideas in *Software Engineering Standards*. Chapter 3 discusses methods for software verification and validation that can be used to supplement the basic methods described in Chapter 2. Chapter 4 discusses tools for software verification and validation. Chapter 5 describes how to write the SVVP.

All the mandatory practices in *Software Engineering Standards* concerning software verification and validation are repeated in this document. The identifier of the practice is added in parentheses to mark a repetition. This document contains no new mandatory practices.

1.3 IEEE STANDARDS USED FOR THIS GUIDE

Six standards of the Institute of Electrical and Electronics Engineers (IEEE) have been used to ensure that this guide complies as far as possible with internationally accepted standards for verification and validation terminology and documentation. The IEEE standards are listed in Table 1.3 below.

Reference	Title
610.12-1990	Standard Glossary of Software Engineering Terminology
829-1983	Standard for Software Test Documentation
1008-1987	Standard for Software Unit Testing
1012-1986	Standard for Software Verification and Validation Plans
1028-1988	Standard for Software Reviews and Audits

Table 1.3: IEEE Standards used for this guide.

IEEE Standard 829-1983 was used to define the table of contents for the SVVP sections that document the unit, integration, system and acceptance testing activities (i.e. SVVP/UT, SVVP/IT, SVVP/ST, SVVP/AT).

IEEE Standard 1008-1987 provides a detailed specification of the unit testing process. Readers who require further information on the unit testing should consult this standard.

IEEE Standard 1012-1986 was used to define the table of contents for the SVVP sections that document the non-testing verification and validation activities (i.e. SVVP/SR, SVVP/AD, SVVP/DD).

IEEE Standard 1028-1988 was used to define the technical review, walkthrough, inspection and audit processes.

Because of the need to integrate the requirements of six standards into a single approach to software verification and validation, users of this guide should not claim complete compliance with any one of the IEEE standards.

CHAPTER 2
SOFTWARE VERIFICATION AND VALIDATION

2.1 INTRODUCTION

Software verification and validation activities check the software against its specifications. Every project must verify and validate the software it produces. This is done by:

- checking that each software item meets specified requirements;
- checking each software item before it is used as an input to another activity;
- ensuring that checks on each software item are done, as far as possible, by someone other than the author;
- ensuring that the amount of verification and validation effort is adequate to show each software item is suitable for operational use.

Project management is responsible for organising software verification and validation activities, the definition of software verification and validation roles (e.g. review team leaders), and the allocation of staff to those roles.

Whatever the size of project, software verification and validation greatly affects software quality. People are not infallible, and software that has not been verified has little chance of working. Typically, 20 to 50 errors per 1000 lines of code are found during development, and 1.5 to 4 per 1000 lines of code remain even after system testing [Ref 17]. Each of these errors could lead to an operational failure or non-compliance with a requirement. The objective of software verification and validation is to reduce software errors to an acceptable level. The effort needed can range from 30% to 90% of the total project resources, depending upon the criticality and complexity of the software [Ref 9].

This chapter summarises the principles of software verification and validation described in *Software Engineering Standards* and then discusses the application of these principles first to documents and then to code.

2.2 PRINCIPLES OF SOFTWARE VERIFICATION AND VALIDATION

Verification can mean the:

- act of reviewing, inspecting, testing, checking, auditing, or otherwise establishing and documenting whether items, processes, services or documents conform to specified requirements [Ref 1];
- process of evaluating a system or component to determine whether the products of a given development phase satisfy the conditions imposed at the start of the phase [Ref 1]

- formal proof of program correctness [Ref 1].

The first definition of verification in the list above is the most general and includes the other two. In *Software Engineering Standards*, the first definition applies.

Validation is, according to its ANSI/IEEE definition, 'the process of evaluating a system or component during or at the end of the development process to determine whether it satisfies specified requirements'. Validation is, therefore, 'end-to-end' verification.

Verification activities include:

- technical reviews, walkthroughs and software inspections;
- checking that software requirements are traceable to user requirements;
- checking that design components are traceable to software requirements;
- unit testing;
- integration testing;
- system testing;
- acceptance testing;
- audit.

Verification activities may include carrying out formal proofs.

The activities to be conducted in a project are described in the Software Verification and Validation Plan (SVVP).

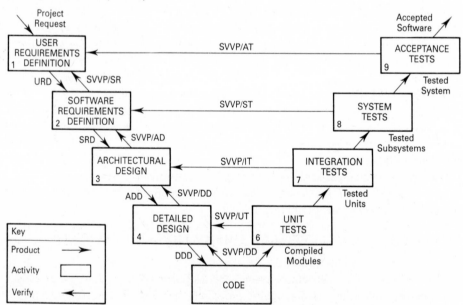

Figure 2.2: Life cycle verification approach

Figure 2.2 shows the life cycle verification approach. Software development starts in the top left-hand corner, progresses down the left-hand 'specification' side to the bottom of the 'V' and then onwards up the right-hand 'production' side. The V-formation emphasises the need to verify each output specification against its input specification, and the need to verify the software at each stage of production against its corresponding specification.

In particular the:

- SRD must be verified with respect to the URD by means of the SVVP/SR;
- ADD must be verified with respect to the SRD by means of the SVVP/AD;
- DDD must be verified with respect to the ADD by means of the SVVP/DD;
- code must be verified with respect to the DDD by means of the SVVP/DD;
- unit tests verify that the software subsystems and components work correctly in isolation, and as specified in the detailed design, by means of the SVVP/UT;
- integration tests verify that the major software components work correctly with the rest of the system, and as specified in the architectural design, by means of the SVVP/IT;
- system tests verify that the software system meets the software requirements, by means of the SVVP/ST;
- acceptance tests verify that the software system meets the user requirements, by means of the SVVP/AT.

These verification activities demonstrate compliance to specifications. This may be done by showing that the product:

- performs as specified;
- contains no defects that prevent it performing as specified.

Demonstration that a product meets its specification is a mechanical activity that is driven by the specification. This part of verification is efficient for demonstrating conformance to functional requirements (e.g. to validate that the system has a function it is only necessary to exercise the function). In contrast, demonstration that a product contains no defects that prevent it from meeting its specification requires expert knowledge of what the system must do, and the technology the system uses. This expertise is needed if the non-functional requirements (e.g. those for reliability) are to be met. Skill and ingenuity are needed to show up defects.

In summary, software verification and validation should show that the product conforms to all the requirements. Users will have more confidence in a product that has been through a rigorous verification programme than one subjected to minimal examination and testing before release.

2.3 REVIEWS

A review is 'a process or meeting during which a work product, or set of work products, is presented to project personnel, managers, users, customers, or other interested parties for comment or approval' [Ref 3].

Reviews may be formal or informal. Formal reviews have explicit and definite rules of procedure. Informal reviews have no predefined procedures. Although informal reviews can be very useful for educating project members and solving problems, this section is only concerned with reviews that have set procedures, i.e. formal reviews.

Three kinds of formal review are normally used for software verification:

- technical review;
- walkthrough;
- audits.

These reviews are all 'formal reviews' in the sense that all have specific objectives and procedures. They seek to identify defects and discrepancies of the software against specifications, plans and standards.

Software inspections are a more rigorous alternative to walkthroughs, and are strongly recommended for software with stringent reliability, security and safety requirements. Methods for software inspections are described in Section 3.2.

The software problem reporting procedure and document change procedure defined in Part 2, Section 3.2.3.2 of *Software Engineering Standards*, and in more detail in *Guide to Software Configuration Management*, calls for a formal review process for all changes to code and documentation. Any of the first two kinds of formal review procedure can be applied for change control. The SRB, for example, may choose to hold a technical review or walkthrough as necessary.

2.3.1 Technical reviews

Technical reviews evaluate specific software elements to verify progress against the plan. The technical review process should be used for the UR/R, SR/R, AD/R, DD/R and any critical design reviews.

The UR/R, SR/R, AD/R and DD/R are formal reviews held at the end of a phase to evaluate the products of the phase, and to decide whether the next phase may be started (UR08, SR09, AD16 and DD11).

Critical design reviews are held in the DD phase to review the detailed design of a major component to certify its readiness for implementation (DD10).

The following sections describe the technical review process. This process is based upon the ANSI/IEEE Std 1028-1988, 'IEEE Standard for Software Reviews and Audits' [Ref 7], and best practice.

2.3.1.1 Objectives

The objective of a technical review is to evaluate a specific set of review items (e.g. document, source module) and provide management with evidence that:
- they conform to specifications made in previous phases;
- they have been produced according to the project standards and procedures;
- any changes have been properly implemented, and affect only those systems identified by the change specification (described in a RID, DCR or SCR).

2.3.1.2 Organisation

The technical review process is carried out by a review team, which is made up of:
- a leader;
- a secretary;
- members.

In large and/or critical projects, the review team may be split into a review board and a technical panel. The technical panel is usually responsible for processing RIDs and the technical assessment of review items, producing as output a technical panel report. The review board oversees the review procedures and then independently assesses the status of the review items based upon the technical panel report.

The review team members should have skills to cover all aspects of the review items. Depending upon the phase, the review team may be drawn from:

- users;
- software project managers;
- software engineers;
- software librarians;
- software quality assurance staff;
- independent software verification and validation staff;
- independent experts not involved in the software development.

Some continuity of representation should be provided to ensure consistency.

The leader's responsibilities include:

- nominating the review team;
- organising the review and informing all participants of its date, place and agenda;
- distribution of the review items to all participants before the meeting;
- organising as necessary the work of the review team;
- chairing the review meetings;
- issuing the technical review report.

The secretary will assist the leader as necessary and will be responsible for documenting the findings, decisions and recommendations of the review team.

Team members examine the review items and attend review meetings. If the review items are large, complex, or require a range of specialist skills for effective review, the leader may share the review items among members.

2.3.1.3 Input

Input to the technical review process includes as appropriate:

- a review meeting agenda;
- a statement of objectives;
- the review items;
- specifications for the review items;
- plans, standards and guidelines that apply to the review items;
- RID, SPR and SCR forms concerning the review items;
- marked up copies of the review items;
- reports of software quality assurance staff.

2.3.1.4 Activities

The technical review process consists of the following activities:

- preparation;
- review meeting.

The review process may start when the leader considers the review items to be stable and complete. Obvious signs of instability are the presence of TBDs or of changes recommended at an earlier review meeting not yet implemented.

Adequate time should be allowed for the review process. This depends on the size of project. A typical schedule for a large project (20 man years or more) is shown in Table 2.3.1.4.

Event	Time
Review items distributed	R - 20 days
RIDs categorised and distributed	R - 10 days
Review Meeting	R
Issue of Report	R + 20 days

Table 2.3.1.4: Review Schedule for a large project

Members may have to combine their review activities with other commitments, and the review schedule should reflect this.

2.3.1.4.1 Preparation

The leader creates the agenda and distributes it, with the statements of objectives, review items, specifications, plans, standards and guidelines (as appropriate) to the review team.

Members then examine the review items. Each problem is recorded by completing boxes one to six of the RID form. A RID should record only one problem, or group of related problems. Members then pass their RIDs to the secretary, who numbers each RID uniquely and forwards them to the author for comment. Authors add their responses in box seven and then return the RIDs to the secretary.

The leader then categorises each RID as major, minor, or editorial. Major RIDs relate to a problem that would affect capabilities, performance, quality, schedule and cost. Minor RIDs request clarification on specific points and point out inconsistencies. Editorial RIDs point out defects in format, spelling and grammar. Several hundred RIDs can be generated in a large project review, and classification is essential if the RIDs are to be dealt with efficiently. Failure to categorise the RIDs can result in long meetings that concentrate on minor problems at the expense of major ones.

Finally the secretary sorts the RIDs in order of the position of the discrepancy in the review item. The RIDs are now ready for input to the review meeting.

Preparation for a Software Review Board follows a similar pattern, with RIDs being replaced by SPRs and SCRs.

2.3.1.4.2 Review meeting

A typical review meeting agenda consists of:
1. Introduction;
2. Presentation of the review items;
3. Classification of RIDs;
4. Review of the major RIDs;
5. Review of the other RIDs;
6. Conclusion.

The introduction includes agreeing the agenda, approving the report of any previous meetings and reviewing the status of outstanding actions.

After the preliminaries, authors present an overview of the review items. If this is not the first meeting, emphasis should be given to any changes made since the items were last discussed.

The leader then summarises the classification of the RIDs. Members may request that RIDs be reclassified (e.g. the severity of a RID may be changed from minor to major). RIDs that originate during the meeting should be held over for decision at a later meeting, to allow time for authors to respond.

Major RIDs are then discussed, followed by the minor and editorial RIDs. The outcome of the discussion of any defects should be noted by the secretary in the review decision box of the RID form. This may be one of CLOSE, UPDATE, ACTION or REJECT. The reason for each decision should be recorded. Closure should be associated with the successful completion of an update. The nature of an update should be agreed. Actions should be properly formulated, the person responsible identified, and the completion date specified. Rejection is equivalent to closing a RID with no action or update.

The conclusions of a review meeting should be agreed during the meeting. Typical conclusions are:
- authorisation to proceed to the next phase, subject to updates and actions being completed;
- authorisation to proceed with a restricted part of the system;
- a decision to perform additional work.

One or more of the above may be applicable.

If the review meeting cannot reach a consensus on RID dispositions and conclusions, possible actions are:
- recording a minority opinion in the review report;
- for one or more members to find a solution outside the meeting;
- referring the problem to the next level of management.

2.3.1.5 Output

The output from the review is a technical review report that should contain the following:
- abstract of the report;
- a list of the members;
- an identification of the review items;
- tables of RIDs, SPRs and SCRs organised according to category, with dispositions marked;
- a list of actions, with persons responsible identified and expected dates for completion defined;
- conclusions.

This output can take the form of the minutes of the meeting, or be a self-standing report. If there are several meetings, the collections of minutes can form the report, or the minutes can be appended to a report summarising the findings. The report should be detailed enough for management to judge what happened. If there have been difficulties in reaching consensus during the review, it is advisable that the output be signed off by members.

2.3.2 Walkthroughs

Walkthroughs should be used for the early evaluation of documents, models, designs and code in the SR, AD and DD phases. The following sections describe the walkthrough process, and are based upon the ANSI/IEEE Std 1028-1988, 'IEEE Standard for Software Reviews and Audits' [Ref 7].

2.3.2.1 Objectives

The objective of a walkthrough is to evaluate a specific software element (e.g. document, source module). A walkthrough should attempt to identify defects and consider possible solutions. In contrast with other forms of review, secondary objectives are to educate, and to resolve stylistic problems.

2.3.2.2 Organisation

The walkthrough process is carried out by a walkthrough team, which is made up of:
- a leader;
- a secretary;
- the author (or authors);
- members.

The leader, helped by the secretary, is responsible for management tasks associated with the walkthrough. The specific responsibilities of the leader include:
- nominating the walkthrough team;
- organising the walkthrough and informing all participants of the date, place and agenda of walkthrough meetings;
- distribution of the review items to all participants before walkthrough meetings;
- organising as necessary the work of the walkthrough team;
- chairing the walkthrough meeting;
- issuing the walkthrough report.

The author is responsible for the production of the review items, and for presenting them at the walkthrough meeting.

Members examine review items, report errors and recommend solutions.

2.3.2.3 Input

Input to the walkthrough consists of:
- a statement of objectives in the form of an agenda;
- the review items;
- standards that apply to the review items;
- specifications that apply to the review items.

2.3.2.4 Activities

The walkthrough process consists of the following activities:
- preparation;
- review meeting.

2.3.2.4.1 Preparation

The moderator or author distributes the review items when the author decides that they are ready for walkthrough. Members should examine the review items prior to the meeting. Concerns should be noted on RID forms so that they can be raised at the appropriate point in the walkthrough meeting.

2.3.2.4.2 Review meeting

The review meeting begins with a discussion of the agenda and the report of the previous meeting. The author then provides an overview of the review items.

A general discussion follows, during which issues of the structure, function and scope of the review items should be raised.

The author then steps through the review items, such as documents and source modules (in contrast technical reviews step through RIDs, not the items themselves). Members raise issues about specific points as they are reached in the walkthrough.

As the walkthrough proceeds, errors, suggested changes and improvements are noted on RID forms by the secretary.

2.3.2.5 Output

The output from the walkthrough is a walkthrough report that should contain the following:

- a list of the members;
- an identification of the review items;
- a list of changes and defects noted during the walkthrough;
- completed RID forms;
- a list of actions, with persons responsible identified and expected dates for completion defined;
- recommendations made by the walkthrough team on how to remedy defects and dispose of unresolved issues (e.g. further walkthrough meetings).

This output can take the form of the minutes of the meeting, or be a self-standing report.

2.3.3 Audits

Audits are independent reviews that assess compliance with software requirements, specifications, baselines, standards, procedures, instructions, codes and contractual and licensing requirements. To ensure their objectivity, audits should be carried out by people independent of the development team. The audited organisation should make resources (e.g. development team members, office space) available to support the audit.

A 'physical audit' checks that all items identified as part of the configuration are present in the product baseline. A 'functional audit' checks that unit, integration and system tests have been carried out and records their success or failure. Other types of audits may examine any part of the software development process, and take their name from the part of the process being examined, e.g. a 'code audit' checks code against coding standards.

Audits may be routine or non-routine. Examples of routine audits are the functional and physical audits that must be performed before the release of the software (SVV03). Non-routine audits may be initiated by the organisation receiving the software, or management and quality assurance personnel in the organisation producing the software.

The following sections describe the audit process, and are based upon the ANSI/IEEE Std 1028-1988, 'IEEE Standard for Software Reviews and Audits' [Ref 7].

2.3.3.1 Objectives

The objective of an audit is to verify that software products and processes comply with standards, guidelines, specifications and procedures.

2.3.3.2 Organisation

The audit process is carried out by an audit team, which is made up of:
- a leader;
- members.

The leader is responsible for administrative tasks associated with the audit. The specific responsibilities of the leader include:
- nominating the audit team;
- organising the audit and informing all participants of the schedule of activities;
- issuing the audit report.

Members interview the development team, examine review items, report errors and recommend solutions.

2.3.3.3 Input

The following items should be input to an audit:
- terms of reference defining the purpose and scope of the audit;
- criteria for deciding the correctness of products and processes such as contracts, plans, specifications, procedures, guidelines and standards;
- software products;
- software process records;
- management plans defining the organisation of the project being audited.

2.3.3.4 Activities

The team formed to carry out the audit should produce a plan that defines the:
- products or processes to be examined;
- schedule of audit activities;
- sampling criteria, if a statistical approach is being used;
- criteria for judging correctness (e.g. the SCM procedures might be audited against the SCMP);
- checklists defining aspects to be audited;
- audit staffing plan;
- date, time and place of the audit kick-off meeting.

The audit team should prepare for the audit by familiarising themselves with the organisation being audited, its products and its processes. All the team must understand the audit criteria and know how to apply them. Training may be necessary.

The audit team then examines the software products and processes, interviewing project team members as necessary. This is the primary activity in any audit. Project team members should co-operate fully with the auditors. Auditors should fully investigate all problems, document them, and make recommendations about how to rectify them. If the system is very large, the audit team may have to employ a sampling approach.

When their investigations are complete, the audit team should issue a draft report for comment by the audited organisation, so that any misunderstandings can be eliminated. After receiving the audited organisation's comments, the audit team should produce a final report. A follow-up audit may be required to check that actions are implemented.

2.3.3.5 Output

The output from an audit is an audit report that:
- identifies the organisation being audited, the audit team, and the date and place of the audit;
- defines the products and processes being audited;
- defines the scope of the audit, particularly the audit criteria for products and processes being audited;
- states conclusions;
- makes recommendations;
- lists actions.

2.4 TRACING

Tracing is 'the act of establishing a relationship between two or more products of the development process; for example, to establish the relationship between a given requirement and the design element that implements that requirement' [Ref 3]. There are two kinds of traceability:
- forward traceability;
- backward traceability.

Forward traceability requires that each input to a phase must be traceable to an output of that phase (SVV01). Forward traceability shows completeness, and is normally done by constructing traceability matrices. These are normally implemented by tabulating the correspondence between input and output (see the example in *Guide to the Software Requirements Definition Phase*). Missing entries in the matrix display incompleteness quite vividly. Forward traceability can also show duplication. Inputs that trace to more than one output may be a sign of duplication.

Backward traceability requires that each output of a phase must be traceable to an input to that phase (SVV02). Outputs that cannot be traced to inputs are superfluous, unless it is acknowledged that the inputs themselves were incomplete. Backward tracing is normally done by including with each item a statement of why it exists (e.g. source of a software requirement, requirements for a software component).

During the software life cycle it is necessary to trace:

- user requirements to software requirements and vice-versa;
- software requirements to component descriptions and vice versa;
- integration tests to architectural units and vice-versa;
- unit tests to the modules of the detailed design;
- system tests to software requirements and vice-versa;
- acceptance tests to user requirements and vice-versa.

To support traceability, all components and requirements are identified. The SVVP should define how tracing is to be done. References to components and requirements should include identifiers. The SCMP defines the identification conventions for documents and software components. The SVVP should define additional identification conventions to be used within documents (e.g. requirements) and software components.

2.5 FORMAL PROOF

Formal proof attempts to demonstrate logically that software is correct. Whereas a test empirically demonstrates that specific inputs result in specific outputs, formal proofs logically demonstrate that all inputs meeting defined preconditions will result in defined postconditions being met.

Where practical, formal proof of the correctness of software may be attempted. Formal proof techniques are often difficult to justify because of the additional effort required above the necessary verification techniques of reviewing, tracing and testing.

The difficulty of expressing software requirements and designs in the mathematical form necessary for formal proof has prevented the wide application of the technique. Some areas where formal methods have been successful are for the specification and verification of:

- protocols;
- secure systems.

Good protocols and very secure systems depend upon having precise, logical specifications with no loopholes.

Ideally, if formal techniques can prove that software is correct, separate verification (e.g. testing) should not be necessary. However, human errors in proofs are still possible, and ways should be sought to avoid them, for example by ensuring that all proofs are checked independently.

Sections 3.3 and 3.4 discuss Formal Methods and formal Program Verification Techniques.

2.6 TESTING

A test is 'an activity in which a system or component is executed under specified conditions, the results are observed or recorded, and an evaluation is made of some aspect of the system or component' [Ref 3]. Compared with other verification techniques, testing is the most direct because it executes the software, and is therefore always to be preferred. When parts of a specification cannot be verified by a test, another verification technique (e.g. inspection) should be substituted in the test plan. For example a test of a portability requirement might be to run the software in the alternative environment. If this not possible, the substitute approach might be to inspect the code for statements that are not portable.

Testing skills are just as important as the ability to program, design and analyse. Good testers find problems quickly. Myers defines testing as 'the process of executing a program with the intent of finding errors' [Ref 11]. While this definition is too narrow for *Software Engineering Standards*, it expresses the sceptical, critical attitude required for effective testing.

The testability of software should be evaluated as it is designed, not when coding is complete. Designs should be iterated until they are testable. Complexity is the enemy of testability. When faced with a complex design, developers should ask themselves:

- can the software be simplified without compromising its capabilities?
- are the resources available to test software of this complexity?

Users, managers and developers all need to be assured that the software does what it is supposed to do. An important objective of testing is to show that software meets its specification. The 'V diagram' in Figure 2.2 shows that unit tests compare code with its detailed design, integration tests compare major components with the architectural design, system tests compare the software with the software requirements, and acceptance tests compare the software with the user requirements. All these tests aim to 'verify' the software, i.e. show that it truly conforms to specifications.

In *Software Engineering Standards* test plans are made as soon as the corresponding specifications exist. These plans outline the approach to testing and are essential for estimating the resources required to complete the project. Tests are specified in more detail in the DD phase. Test designs, test cases and test procedures are defined and included in the SVVP. Tests are then executed and results recorded.

Figure 2.6 shows the testing activities common to unit, integration, system and acceptance tests. Input at the top left of the figure are the Software Under Test (SUT), the test plans in the SVVP, and the URD, SRD, ADD and DDD that define the baselines for testing against. This sequence of activities is executed for unit testing, integration testing, system testing and acceptance testing in turn.

The following paragraphs address each activity depicted in Figure 2.6. Section 4.5 discusses the tools needed to support the activities.

1. The 'specify tests' activity takes the test plan in the SVVP, and the product specification in one of the URD, SRD, ADD or DDD and produces a test design for each requirement or component. Each design will imply a family of test cases. The Software Under Test (SUT) is required for the specification of unit tests.

2. The 'make test software' activity takes the test case specifications and produces the test code (stubs, drivers, simulators, harnesses), input data files and test procedures needed to run the tests.

3. The 'link SUT' activity takes the test code and links it with the SUT, and (optionally) existing tested code, producing the executable SUT.

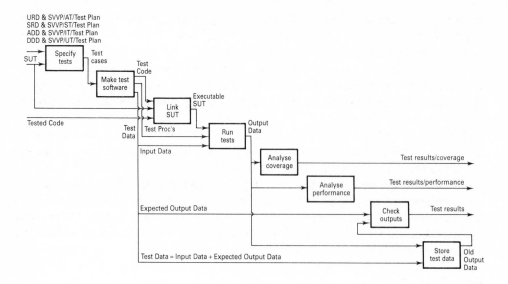

Figure 2.6: Testing activities

4. The 'run tests' activity executes the tests according to the test procedures, by means of the input data. The output data produced may include coverage information, performance information, or data produced by the normal functioning of the SUT.

5. The 'analyse coverage' activity checks that the tests have in fact executed those parts of the SUT that they were intended to test.

6. The 'analyse performance' activity studies the resource consumption of the SUT (e.g. CPU time, disk space, memory).

7. The 'check outputs' activity compares the outputs with the expected output data or the outputs of previous tests, and decides whether the tests have passed or failed.

8. The 'store test data' activity stores test data for reruns of tests. Test output data needs to be retained as evidence that the tests have been performed.

The following sections discuss the specific approaches to unit testing, integration testing, system testing and acceptance testing. For each type of testing sections are provided on:

- test planning;
- test design;
- test case specification;
- test procedure definition;
- test reporting.

2.6.1 Unit tests

A 'unit' of software is composed of one or more modules. In *Software Engineering Standards*, 'unit testing' refers to the process of testing modules against the detailed design. The inputs to unit testing are the successfully compiled modules from the coding process. These are assembled during unit testing to make the largest units, i.e. the components of architectural design. The successfully tested architectural design components are the outputs of unit testing.

An incremental assembly sequence is normally best. When the sequence is top-down, the unit grows during unit testing from a kernel module to the major component required in the architectural design. When the sequence is bottom-up, units are assembled from smaller units. Normally a combination of the two approaches is used, with the objective of minimising the amount of test software, measured both in terms of the number of test modules and the number of lines of test code. This enables the test software to be easily verified by inspection.

Studies of traditional developments show that approximately 65% of bugs can be caught in unit testing, and that half these bugs will be caught by 'white-box' tests [Ref 9]. These results show that unit testing is the most effective type of testing for removing bugs. This is because less software is involved when the test is performed, and so bugs are easier to isolate.

2.6.1.1 Unit test planning

The first step in unit testing is to construct a unit test plan and document it in the SVVP (SVV18). This plan is defined in the DD phase and should describe the scope, approach, resources and schedule of the intended unit tests. The scope of unit testing is to verify the design and implementation of all components from the lowest level defined in the detailed design up to and including the lowest level in the architectural design. The approach should outline the types of tests, and the amounts of testing, required.

The amount of unit testing required is dictated by the need to execute every statement in a module at least once (DD06). The simplest measure of the amount of testing required is therefore just the number of lines of code.

Execution of every statement in the software is normally not sufficient, and coverage of every branch in the logic may be required. The amount of unit testing then depends principally on the complexity of the software. The 'Structured Testing' method (see Section 3.6) uses the cyclomatic complexity metric to evaluate the testability of module designs. The number of test cases necessary to ensure that every branch in the module logic is covered during testing is equivalent to the cyclomatic complexity of the module. The Structured Testing method is strongly recommended when full branch coverage is a requirement.

2.6.1.2 Unit test design

The next step in unit testing is unit test design (SVV19). Unit test designs should specify the details of the test approach for each software component defined in the DDD, and identify the associated test cases and test procedures. The description of the test approach should state the assembly sequence for constructing the architectural design units, and the types of tests necessary for individual modules (e.g. white-box, black-box).

The three rules of incremental assembly are:
- assemble the architectural design units incrementally, module-by-module if possible, because problems that arise in a unit test are most likely to be related to the module that has just been added;
- introduce producer modules before consumer modules, because the former can provide control and data flows required by the latter.
- ensure that each step is reversible, so that rollback to a previous stage in the assembly is always possible.

A simple example of unit test design is shown in Figure 2.6.1.2A. The unit U1 is a major component of the architectural design. U1 is composed of modules M1, M2 and M3. Module M1 calls M2 and then M3, as shown by the structure chart. Two possible assembly sequences are shown. The sequence starting with M1 is 'top-down' and the sequence starting with M2 is 'bottom-up'. Figure 2.6.1.2B shows that data flows from M2 to M3 under the control of M1.

Each sequence in Figure 2.6.1.2A requires two test modules. The top-down sequence requires the two stub modules S2 and S3 to simulate M2 and M3. The bottom-up sequence requires the drivers D2 and D3 to simulate M1, because each driver simulates a different interface. If M1, M2 and M3 were tested individually before assembly, four drivers and stubs would be required. The incremental approach only requires two.

The rules of incremental assembly argue for top-down assembly instead of bottom-up because the top-down sequence introduces the:
- modules one-by-one;
- producer modules before consumer modules (i.e. M1 before M2 before M3).

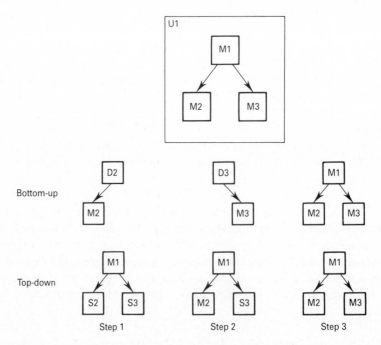

Figure 2.6.1.2A: Example of unit test design

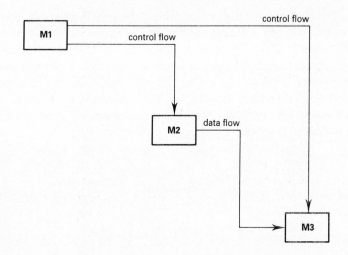

Figure 2.6.1.2B: Data flow dependencies between the modules of U1

2.6.1.2.1 White-box unit tests

The objective of white-box testing is to check the internal logic of the software. White-box tests are sometimes known as 'path tests', 'structure tests' or 'logic tests'. A more appropriate title for this kind of test is 'glass-box test', as the engineer can see almost everything that the code is doing.

White-box unit tests are designed by examining the internal logic of each module and defining the input data sets that force the execution of different paths through the logic. Each input data set is a test case.

Traditionally, programmers used to insert diagnostic code to follow the internal processing (e.g. statements that print out the values of program variables during execution). Debugging tools that allow programmers to observe the execution of a program step-by-step in a screen display make the insertion of diagnostic code unnecessary, unless manual control of execution is not appropriate, such as when real-time code is tested.

When debugging tools are used for white-box testing, prior preparation of test cases and procedures is still necessary. Test cases and procedures should not be invented during debugging. The Structured Testing method (see Section 3.6) is the best known method for white-box unit testing. The cyclomatic complexity value gives the number of paths that must be executed, and the 'baseline method' is used to define the paths. Lastly, input values are selected that will cause each path to be executed. This is called 'sensitising the path'.

A limitation of white-box testing is its inability to show missing logic. Black-box tests remedy this deficiency.

2.6.1.2.2 Black-box unit tests

The objective of black-box tests is to verify the functionality of the software. The tester treats the module as 'black-box' whose internals cannot be seen. Black-box tests are sometimes called 'function tests'.

Black-box unit tests are designed by examining the specification of each module and defining input data sets that will result in different behaviour (e.g. outputs). Each input data set is a test case.

Black-box tests should be designed to exercise the software for its whole range of inputs. Most software items will have many possible input data sets and using them all is impractical. Test designers should partition the range of possible inputs into 'equivalence classes'. For any given error, input data sets in the same equivalence class will produce the same error [Ref 11].

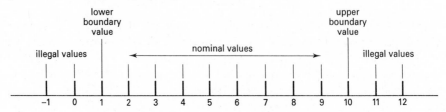

Figure 2.6.1.2.2: Equivalence partitioning example

Consider a module that accepts integers in the range 1 to 10 as input, for example. The input data can be partitioned into five equivalence classes as shown in Figure 2.6.1.2.2. The five equivalence classes are the illegal values below the lower boundary, such as 0, the lower boundary value 1, the nominal values 2 to 9, the upper boundary value 10, and the illegal values above the upper boundary, such as 11.

Output values can be used to generate additional equivalence classes. In the example above, if the output of the routine generated the result TRUE for input numbers less than or equal to 5 and FALSE for numbers greater than 5, the nominal value equivalence class should be split into two subclasses:

- nominal values giving a TRUE result, such as 3;
- boundary nominal value, i.e. 5;
- nominal values giving a FALSE result, such as 7.

Equivalence classes may be defined by considering all possible data types. For example the module above accepts integers only. Test cases could be devised using real, logical and character data.

Having defined the equivalence classes, the next step is to select suitable input values from each equivalence class. Input values close to the boundary values are normally selected because they are usually more effective in causing test failures (e.g. 11 might be expected to be more likely to produce a test failure than 99).

Although equivalence partitioning combined with boundary-value selection is a useful technique for generating efficient input data sets, it will not expose bugs linked to combinations of input data values. Techniques such as decision tables [Ref 9] and cause-effect graphs [Ref 11] can be very useful for defining tests that will expose such bugs.

	1	2	3	4
open_pressed	TRUE	TRUE	FALSE	FALSE
close_pressed	TRUE	FALSE	TRUE	FALSE
action	?	OPEN	CLOSE	?

Table 2.6.1.2.2: Decision table example

Table 2.6.1.2.2 shows the decision table for a module that has Boolean inputs that indicate whether the OPEN or CLOSE buttons of an elevator door have been pressed. When open_pressed is true and close_pressed is false, the action is OPEN. When close_pressed is true and open_pressed is false, the action is CLOSE. Table 2.6.1.2.2 shows that the outcomes for when open_pressed and close_pressed are both true and both false are undefined. Additional test cases setting open_pressed and close_pressed both true and then both false are likely to expose problems.

A useful technique for designing tests for real-time systems is the state-transition table. These tables define what messages can be processed in each state. For example, sending the message 'open doors' to an elevator in the state 'moving' should be rejected. Just as with decision tables, undefined outcomes shown by blank table entries make good candidates for testing.

Decision tables, cause-effect graphs and state-transition diagrams are just three of the many analysis techniques that can be employed for test design. After tests have been devised by means of these techniques, test designers should examine them to see whether additional tests are needed, their judgement being based upon their experience of similar systems or their involvement in the development of the system. This technique, called 'error guessing' [Ref 11], should be risk-driven, focusing on the parts of the design that are novel or difficult to verify by other means, or where quality problems have occurred before.

Test tools that allow the automatic creation of drivers, stubs and test data sets help make black-box testing easier (see Chapter 4). Such tools can define equivalence classes based upon boundary values in the input, but the identification of more complex test cases requires knowledge of the how the software should work.

2.6.1.2.3 Performance tests

The DDD may have placed resource constraints on the performance of a module. For example a module may have to execute within a specified elapsed time, or use less than a specified amount of CPU time, or consume less than a specified amount of memory. Compliance with these constraints should be tested as directly as possible, for example by means of:

- performance analysis tools;
- diagnostic code;
- system monitoring tools.

2.6.1.3 Unit test case definition

Each unit test design will use one or more unit test cases, which must also be documented in the SVVP (SVV20). Test cases should specify the inputs, predicted results and execution conditions for a test case.

2.6.1.4 Unit test procedure definition

The unit test procedures must be described in the SVVP (SVV21). These should provide a step-by-step description of how to carry out each test case. One test procedure may execute one or more test cases. The procedures may use executable 'scripts' that control the operation of test tools. With the incremental approach, the input data required to test a module may be created by executing an already tested module (e.g. M2 is used to create data for M1 and M3 in the example above). The test procedure should define the steps needed to create such data.

2.6.1.5 Unit test reporting

Unit test results may be reported in a variety of ways. Some common means of recording results are:
- unit test result forms, recording the date and outcome of the test cases executed by the procedure;
- execution logfile.

2.6.2 Integration tests

A software system is composed of one or more subsystems, which are composed of one or more units (which are composed of one or more modules). In *Software Engineering Standards*, 'integration testing' refers to the process of testing units against the architectural design. During integration testing, the architectural design units are integrated to make the system.

The 'function-by-function' integration method described in Section 3.3.2.1 of the *Guide to the Detailed Design and Production Phase* should be used to integrate the software. As with the approach described for unit testing, this method minimises the amount of test software required. The steps are to:
1. select the functions to be integrated;
2. identify the components that carry out the functions;
3. order the components by the number of dependencies (i.e. fewest dependencies first);
4. create a driver to simulate the input of the component later in the order when a component depends on another later in the order;
5. introduce the components with fewest dependencies first.

Though the errors found in integration testing should be much fewer than those found in unit testing, they are more time-consuming to diagnose and fix. Studies of testing [Ref 12] have shown architectural errors can be as much as thirty times as costly to repair as detailed design errors.

2.6.2.1 Integration test planning

The first step in integration testing is to construct an integration test plan and document it in the SVVP (SVV17). This plan is defined in the AD phase and should describe the scope, approach, resources and schedule of the intended integration tests.

The scope of integration testing is to verify the design and implementation of all components from the lowest level defined in the architectural design up to the system level. The approach should outline the types of tests, and the amounts of testing, required.

The amount of integration testing required is dictated by the need to:
- check that all data exchanged across an interface agree with the data structure specifications in the ADD (DD07);
- confirm that all the control flows in the ADD have been implemented (DD08).

The amount of control flow testing required depends on the complexity of the software. The Structured Integration Testing method (see Section 3.7) uses the integration complexity metric to evaluate the testability of architectural designs. The integration complexity value is the number of integration tests required to obtain full coverage of the control flow. The Structured Integration Testing method is strongly recommended for estimating the amount of integration testing.

2.6.2.2 Integration test design

The next step in integration testing is integration test design (SVV19). This and subsequent steps are performed in the DD phase, although integration test design may be attempted in the AD phase. Integration test designs should specify the details of the test approach for each software component defined in the ADD, and identify the associated test cases and test procedures.

The description of the test approach should state the:
- integration sequence for constructing the system;
- types of tests necessary for individual components (e.g. white-box, black-box).

With the function-by-function method, the system grows during integration testing from the kernel units that depend upon few other units, but are depended upon by many other units. The early availability of these kernel units eases subsequent testing.

For incremental delivery, the delivery plan will normally specify what functions are required in each delivery. Even so, the number of dependencies can be used to decide the order of integration of components in each delivery.

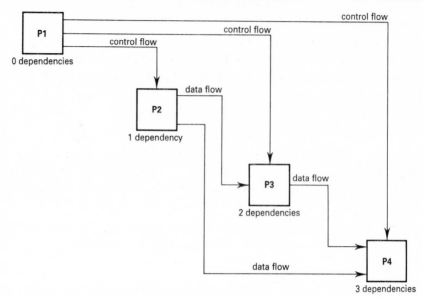

Figure 2.6.2A: Incremental integration sequences

Figure 2.6.2A shows a system composed of four programs P1, P2, P3 and P4. P1 is the 'program manager', providing the user interface and controlling the other programs. Program P2 supplies data to P3, and both P2 and P3 supply data to P4. User inputs are ignored. P1 has zero dependencies, P2 has one, P3 has two and P4 has three. The integration sequence is therefore P1, P2, P3 and then P4.

2.6.2.2.1 White-box integration tests

White-box integration tests should be defined to verify the data and control flow across interfaces between the major components defined in the ADD (DD07 and DD08). For file interfaces, test programs that print the contents of the files provide the visibility required. With real-time systems, facilities for trapping messages and copying them to a log file can be employed. Debuggers that set break points at interfaces can also be useful. When control or data flow traverses an interface where a break point is set, control is passed to the debugger, enabling inspection and logging of the flow.

The Structured Integration Testing method (see Section 3.7) is the best known method for white-box integration testing. The integration complexity value gives the number of control flow paths that must be executed, and the 'design integration testing method' is used to define the control flow paths. The function-by-function integration method (see Section 2.6.2) can be used to define the order of testing the required control flow paths.

The addition of new components to a system often introduces new execution paths through it. Integration test design should identify paths suitable for testing and define test cases to check them. This type of path testing is sometimes called 'thread testing'. All new control flows should be tested.

2.6.2.2.2 Black-box integration tests

Black-box integration tests should be used to fully exercise the functions of each component specified in the ADD. Black-box tests may also be used to verify that data exchanged across an interface agree with the data structure specifications in the ADD (DD07).

2.6.2.2.3   Performance tests

The ADD may have placed resource constraints on the performance of a unit. For example a program may have to respond to user input within a specified elapsed time, or process a defined number of records within a specified CPU time, or occupy less than a specified amount of disk space or memory. Compliance with these constraints should be tested as directly as possible, for example by means of:
- performance analysis tools;
- diagnostic code;
- system monitoring tools.

2.6.2.3 Integration test case definition

Each integration test design will use one or more integration test cases, which must also be documented in the SVVP (SVV20). Test cases should specify the inputs, predicted results and execution conditions for a test case.

2.6.2.4 Integration test procedure definition

The integration test procedures must be described in the SVVP (SVV21). These should provide a step-by-step description of how to carry out each test case. One test procedure may execute one or more test cases. The procedures may use executable 'scripts' that control the operation of test tools.

2.6.2.5 Integration test reporting

Integration test results may be reported in a variety of ways. Some common means of recording results are:
- integration test result forms, recording the date and outcome of the test cases executed by the procedure;
- execution logfile.

2.6.3 System tests

In *Software Engineering Standards*, 'system testing' refers to the process of testing the system against the software requirements. The input to system testing is the successfully integrated system.

Wherever possible, system tests should be specified and performed by an independent testing team. This increases the objectivity of the tests and reduces the likelihood of defects escaping the software verification and validation net.

2.6.3.1 System test planning

The first step in system testing is to construct a system test plan and document it in the SVVP (SVV14). This plan is defined in the SR phase and should describe the scope, approach, resources and schedule of the intended system tests. The scope of system testing is to verify compliance with the system objectives, as stated in the SRD (DD09). System testing must continue until readiness for transfer can be demonstrated.

The amount of testing required is dictated by the need to cover all the software requirements in the SRD. A test should be defined for every essential software requirement, and for every desirable requirement that has been implemented.

2.6.3.2 System test design

The next step in system testing is system test design (SVV19). This and subsequent steps are performed in the DD phase, although system test design may be attempted in the SR and AD phases. System test designs should specify the details of the test approach for each software requirement specified in the SRD, and identify the associated test cases and test procedures. The description of the test approach should state the types of tests necessary (e.g. function test, stress test etc).

Knowledge of the internal workings of the software should not be required for system testing, and so white-box tests should be avoided. Black-box and other types of test should be used wherever possible. When a test of a requirement is not possible, an alternative method of verification should be used (e.g. inspection).

System testing tools can often be used for problem investigation during the TR and OM phases. Effort invested in producing efficient easy-to-use diagnostic tools at this stage of development is often worthwhile.

If an incremental delivery or evolutionary development approach is being used, system tests of each release of the system should include regression tests of software requirements verified in earlier releases.

The SRD will contain several types of requirements, each of which needs a distinct test approach. The following subsections discuss possible approaches.

2.6.3.2.1 Function tests

System test design should begin by designing black-box tests to verify each functional requirement. Working from the functional requirements in the SRD, techniques such as decision tables, state-transition tables and error guessing are used to design function tests.

2.6.3.2.2 Performance tests

Performance requirements should contain quantitative statements about system performance. They may be specified by stating the:
- worst case that is acceptable;
- nominal value, to be used for design;
- best case value, to show where growth potential is needed.

System test cases should be designed to verify:
- that all worst case performance targets have been met;
- that nominal performance targets are usually achieved;
- whether any best-case performance targets have been met.

In addition, stress tests (see Section 2.6.3.2.13) should be designed to measure the absolute limits of performance.

2.6.3.2.3 Interface tests

System tests should be designed to verify conformance to external interface requirements. Interface Control Documents (ICDs) form the baseline for testing external interfaces. Simulators and other test tools will be necessary if the software cannot be tested in the operational environment.

Tools (not debuggers) should be provided to:
- convert data flows into a form readable by human operators;
- edit the contents of data stores.

2.6.3.2.4 Operations tests

Operations tests include all tests of the user interface, man machine interface, or human computer interaction requirements. They also cover the logistical and organisational requirements. These are essential before the software is delivered to the users.

Operations tests should be designed to show up deficiencies in usability such as:
- instructions that are difficult to follow;
- screens that are difficult to read;
- commonly-used operations with too many steps;
- meaningless error messages.

The operational requirements may have defined the time required to learn and operate the software. Such requirements can be made the basis of straightforward tests. For example a test of usability might be to measure the time an operator with average skill takes to learn how to restart the system.

Other kinds of tests may be run throughout the system-testing period, for example:
- do all warning messages have a red background?
- is there help on this command?

If there is a help system, every topic should be systematically inspected for accuracy and appropriateness.

Response times should normally be specified in the performance requirements (as opposed to operational requirements). Even so, system tests should verify that the response time is short enough to make the system usable.

2.6.3.2.5 Resource tests

Requirements for the usage of resources such as CPU time, storage space and memory may have been set in the SRD. The best way to test for compliance to these requirements is to allocate these resources and no more, so that a failure occurs if a resource is exhausted. If this is not suitable (e.g. it is usually not possible to specify the maximum size of a particular file), alternative approaches are to:
- use a system monitoring tool to collect statistics on resource consumption;

- check directories for file space used.

2.6.3.2.6 Security tests

Security tests should check that the system is protected against threats to confidentiality, integrity and availability.

Tests should be designed to verify that basic security mechanisms specified in the SRD have been provided, for example:
- password protection;
- resource locking.

Deliberate attempts to break the security mechanisms are an effective way of detecting security errors. Possible tests are attempts to:
- access the files of another user;
- break into the system authorisation files;
- access a resource when it is locked;
- stop processes being run by other users.

Security problems can often arise when users are granted system privileges unnecessarily. The Software User Manual should clearly state the privileges required to run the software.

Experience of past security problems should be used to check new systems. Security loopholes often recur.

2.6.3.2.7 Portability tests

Portability requirements may require the software to be run in a variety of environments. Attempts should be made to verify portability by running a representative selection of system tests in all the required environments. If this is not possible, indirect techniques may be attempted. For example if a program is supposed to run on two different platforms, a programming language standard (e.g. ANSI C) might be specified and a static analyser tool used to check conformance to the standard. Successfully executing the program on one platform and passing the static analysis checks might be adequate proof that the software will run on the other platform.

2.6.3.2.8 Reliability tests

Reliability requirements should define the Mean Time Between Failure (MTBF) of the software. Separate MTBF values may have been specified for different parts of the software.

Reliability can be estimated from the software problems reported during system testing. Tests designed to measure the performance limits should be excluded from the counts, and test case failures should be categorised (e.g. critical, non-critical). The mean time between failures can then be estimated by dividing the system testing time by the number of critical failures.

2.6.3.2.9 Maintainability tests

Maintainability requirements should define the Mean Time To Repair (MTTR) of the software. Separate MTTR values may have been specified for different parts of the software.

Maintainability should be estimated by averaging the difference between the dates of Software Problem Reports (SPRs) reporting critical failures that occur during system testing, and the corresponding Software Modification Reports (SMRs) reporting the completion of the repairs.

Maintainability requirements may have included restrictions on the size and complexity of modules, or even the use of the programming language. These should be tested by means of a static analysis tool. If a static analysis tool is not available, samples of the code should be manually inspected.

2.6.3.2.10 Safety tests

Safety requirements may specify that the software must avoid injury to people, or damage to property, when it fails. Compliance to safety requirements can be tested by:
- deliberately causing problems under controlled conditions and observing the system behaviour (e.g. disconnecting the power during system operations);
- observing system behaviour when faults occur during tests.

Simulators may have to be built to perform safety tests.

Safety analysis classifies events and states according to how much of a hazard they cause to people or property. Hazards may be catastrophic (i.e. life-threatening), critical, marginal or negligible. Safety requirements may identify functions whose failure may cause a catastrophic or critical hazard. Safety tests may require exhaustive testing of these functions to establish their reliability.

2.6.3.2.11 Miscellaneous tests

An SRD may contain other requirements for:
- documentation (particularly the SUM);
- verification;
- acceptance testing;
- quality, other than reliability, maintainability and safety.

It is usually not possible to test for compliance to these requirements, and they are normally verified by inspection.

2.6.3.2.12 Regression tests

Regression testing is 'selective retesting of a system or component, to verify that modifications have not caused unintended effects, and that the system or component still complies with its specified requirements' [Ref 3].

Regression tests should be performed before every release of the software in the OM phase. If an incremental delivery or evolutionary development approach is being used, regression tests should be performed to verify that the capabilities of earlier releases are unchanged.

Traditionally, regression testing often requires much effort, increasing the cost of change and reducing its speed. Test tools that automate regression testing are now widely available and can greatly increase the speed and accuracy of regression testing (see Chapter 4). Careful selection of test cases also reduces the cost of regression testing, and increases its effectiveness.

2.6.3.2.13 Stress tests

Stress tests 'evaluate a system or software component at or beyond the limits of its specified requirements' [Ref 3]. The most common kind of stress test is to measure the maximum load the SUT can sustain for a time, for example the:

- maximum number of activities that can be supported simultaneously;
- maximum quantity of data that can be processed in a given time.

Another kind of stress test, sometimes called a 'volume test' [Ref 11], exercises the SUT with an abnormally large quantity of input data. For example a compiler might be fed a source file with very many lines of code, or a database management system with a file containing very many records. Time is not of the essence in a volume test.

Most software has capacity limits. Testers should examine the software documentation for statements about the amount of input the software can accept, and design tests to check that the stated capacity is provided. In addition, testers should look for inputs that have no constraint on capacity, and design tests to check whether undocumented constraints do exist.

2.6.3.3 System test case definition

The system test cases must be described in the SVVP (SVV20). These should specify the inputs, predicted results and execution conditions for a test case.

2.6.3.4 System test procedure definition

The system test procedures must be described in the SVVP (SVV21). These should provide a step-by-step description of how to carry out each test case. One test procedure may execute one or more test cases. The procedures may use executable 'scripts' that control the operation of test tools.

2.6.3.5 System test reporting

System test results may be reported in a variety of ways. Some common means of recording results are:

- system test result forms recording the date and outcome of the test cases executed by the procedure;
- execution logfile.

System test results should reference any Software Problem Reports raised during the test.

2.6.4 Acceptance tests

In *Software Engineering Standards*, 'acceptance testing' refers to the process of testing the system against the user requirements. The input to acceptance testing is the software that has been successfully tested at system level.

Acceptance tests should always be done by the user or their representatives. If this is not possible, they should witness the acceptance tests and sign off the results.

2.6.4.1 Acceptance test planning

The first step in acceptance testing is to construct an acceptance test plan and document it in the SVVP (SVV11). This plan is defined in the UR phase and should describe the scope, approach, resources and schedule of the intended acceptance tests. The scope of acceptance testing is to validate that the software is compliant with the user requirements, as stated in the URD. Acceptance tests are performed in the TR phase, although some acceptance tests of quality, reliability, maintainability and safety may continue into the OM phase until final acceptance is possible.

The amount of testing required is dictated by the need to cover all the user requirements in the URD. A test should be defined for every essential user requirement, and for every desirable requirement that has been implemented

2.6.4.2 Acceptance test design

The next step in acceptance testing is acceptance test design (SVV19). This and subsequent steps are performed in the DD phase, although acceptance test design may be attempted in the UR, SR and AD phases. Acceptance test designs should specify the details of the test approach for a user requirement, or combination of user requirements, and identify the associated test cases and test procedures. The description of the test approach should state the necessary types of tests.

Acceptance testing should require no knowledge of the internal workings of the software, so white-box tests cannot be used.

If an incremental delivery or evolutionary development approach is being used, acceptance tests should only address the user requirements of the new release. Regression tests should have been performed in system testing.

Dry-runs of acceptance tests should be performed before transfer of the software. Besides exposing any faults that have been overlooked, dry-runs allow the acceptance test procedures to be checked for accuracy and ease of understanding.

The specific requirements in the URD should be divided into capability requirements and constraint requirements. The following subsections describe approaches to testing each type of user requirement.

2.6.4.2.1 Capability tests

Capability requirements describe what the user can do with the software. Tests should be designed that exercise each capability. System test cases that verify functional, performance and operational requirements may be reused to validate capability requirements.

2.6.4.2.2 Constraint tests

Constraint requirements place restrictions on how the software can be built and operated. They may predefine external interfaces or specify attributes such as adaptability, availability, portability and security. System test cases that verify compliance with requirements for interfaces, resources, security, portability, reliability, maintainability and safety may be reused to validate constraint requirements.

2.6.4.3 Acceptance test case specification

The acceptance test cases must be described in the SVVP (SVV20). These should specify the inputs, predicted results and execution conditions for a test case.

2.6.4.4 Acceptance test procedure specification

The acceptance test procedures must be described in the SVVP (SVV21). These should provide a step-by-step description of how to carry out each test case. The effort required of users to validate the software should be minimised by means of test tools.

2.6.4.5 Acceptance test reporting

Acceptance test results may be reported in a variety of ways. Some common means of recording results are:

- acceptance test result forms recording the date and outcome of the test cases executed by the procedure;
- execution logfile.

Acceptance test results should reference any Software Problem Reports raised during the test.

CHAPTER 3
SOFTWARE VERIFICATION AND VALIDATION METHODS

3.1 INTRODUCTION

This chapter discusses methods for software verification and validation that may be used to enhance the basic approach described in Chapter 2. The structure of this chapter follows that of the previous chapter, as shown in Table 3.1. Supplementary methods are described for reviews, formal proof and testing.

Activity	Supplementary method
review	software inspection
tracing	none
formal proof	formal methods program verification techniques
testing	structured testing structured integration testing

Table 3.1: Structure of Chapter 3

3.2 SOFTWARE INSPECTIONS

Software inspections can be used for the detection of defects in detailed designs before coding, and in code before testing. They may also be used to verify test designs, test cases and test procedures. More generally, inspections can be used for verifying the products of any development process that is defined in terms of:

- operations (e.g. 'code module');
- exit criteria (e.g. 'module successfully compiles').

Software inspections are efficient. Projects can detect over 50% of the total number of defects introduced in development by doing them [Ref 18, 19].

Software inspections are economical because they result in significant reductions in both the number of defects and the cost of their removal. Detection of a defect as close as possible to the time of its introduction results in:

- an increase in the developers' awareness of the reason for the defect's occurrence, so that the likelihood that a similar defect will recur again is reduced;
- reduced effort in locating the defect, since no effort is required to diagnose which component, out of many possible components, contains the defect.

Software inspections are formal processes. They differ from walkthroughs (see Section 2.3.2) by:

- repeating the process until an acceptable defect rate (e.g. number of errors per thousand lines of code) has been achieved;
- analysing the results of the process and feeding them back to improve the production process, and forward to give early measurements of software quality;
- avoiding discussion of solutions;
- including rework and follow-up activities.

The following subsections summarise the software inspection process. The discussion is based closely on the description given by Fagan [Ref 18 and 19] and ANSI/IEEE Std 1028-1988, 'IEEE Standard for Software Reviews and Audits' [Ref 7].

3.2.1 Objectives

The objective of a software inspection is to detect defects in documents or code.

3.2.2 Organisation

There are five roles in a software inspection:

- moderator;
- secretary;
- reader;
- inspector;
- author.

The moderator leads the inspection and chairs the inspection meeting. The person should have implementation skills, but not necessarily be knowledgeable about the item under inspection. He or she must be impartial and objective. For this reason moderators are often drawn from staff outside the project. Ideally they should receive some training in inspection procedures.

The secretary is responsible for recording the minutes of inspection meetings, particularly the details about each defect found.

The reader guides the inspection team through the review items during the inspection meetings.

Inspectors identify and describe defects in the review items under inspection. They should be selected to represent a variety of viewpoints (e.g. designer, coder and tester).

The author is the person who has produced the items under inspection. The author is present to answer questions about the items under inspection, and is responsible for all rework.

A person may have one or more of the roles above. In the interests of objectivity, no person may share the author role with another role.

3.2.3 Input

The inputs to an inspection are the:
- review items;
- specifications of the review items;
- inspection checklist;
- standards and guidelines that apply to the review items;
- inspection reporting forms;
- defect list from a previous inspection.

3.2.4 Activities

A software inspection consists of the following activities:
- overview;
- preparation;
- review meeting;
- rework;
- follow-up.

The overview is a presentation of the items being inspected. Inspectors then prepare themselves for the review meeting by familiarising themselves with the review items. They then examine the review items, identify defects, and decide whether they should be corrected or not, at the review meeting. Rework activities consist of the repair of faults. Follow-up activities check that all decisions made by the review meeting are carried out.

Before the overview, the moderator should:
- check that the review items are ready for inspection;
- arrange a date, time and place for the overview and review meetings;
- distribute the inputs if no overview meeting is scheduled.

Organisations should collect their own inspection statistics and use them for deciding the number and duration of inspections. The following figures may be used as the starting point for inspections of code [Ref 18]:
- preparation: 125 non-comment lines of source code per hour;
- review meeting: 90 non-comment lines of source code per hour.

These figures should be doubled for inspections of pseudo code or program design language.

Review meetings should not last more than two hours. The efficiency of defect detection falls significantly when meetings last longer than this.

3.2.4.1 Overview

The purpose of the overview is to introduce the review items to the inspection team. The moderator describes the area being addressed and then the specific area that has been designed in detail.

For a reinspection, the moderator should flag areas that have been subject to rework since the previous inspection.

The moderator then distributes the inputs to participants.

3.2.4.2 Preparation

Moderators, readers and inspectors then familiarise themselves with the inputs. They might prepare for a code inspection by reading:

- design specifications for the code under inspection;
- coding standards;
- checklists of common coding errors derived from previous inspections;
- code to be inspected.

Any defects in the review items should be noted on RID forms and declared at the appropriate point in the examination. Preparation should be done individually and not in a meeting.

3.2.4.3 Review meeting

The moderator checks that all the members have performed the preparatory activities (see Section 3.2.4.2). The amount of time spent by each member should be reported and noted.

The reader then leads the meeting through the review items. For documents, the reader may summarise the contents of some sections and cover others line-by-line, as appropriate. For code, the reader covers every piece of logic, traversing every branch at least once. Data declarations should be summarised. Inspectors use the checklist to find common errors.

Defects discovered during the reading should be immediately noted by the secretary. The defect list should cover the:

- severity (e.g. major, minor);
- technical area (e.g. logic error, logic omission, comment error);
- location;
- description.

Any solutions identified should be noted. The inspection team should avoid searching for solutions and concentrate on finding defects.

At the end of the meeting, the inspection team takes one of the following decisions:

- accept the item when the rework (if any) is completed;
- make the moderator responsible for accepting the item when the rework is completed;
- reinspect the whole item (usually necessary if more than 5% of the material requires rework).

The secretary should produce the minutes immediately after the review meeting, so that rework can start without delay.

3.2.4.4 Rework

After examination, software authors correct the defects described in the defect list.

3.2.4.5 Follow-up

After rework, follow-up activities verify that all the defects have been properly corrected and that no secondary defects have been introduced. The moderator is responsible for follow-up.

Other follow-up activities are the:

- updating of the checklist as the frequency of different types of errors change;
- analysis of defect statistics, perhaps resulting in the redirection of SVV effort.

3.2.5 Output

The outputs of an inspection are the:

- defect list;
- defect statistics;
- inspection report.

The inspection report should give the:

- names of the participants;
- duration of the meeting;
- amount of material inspected;
- amount of preparation time spent;
- review decision on acceptance;
- estimates of rework effort and schedule.

3.3 FORMAL METHODS

Formal Methods, such as LOTOS, Z and VDM, possess an agreed notation, with well-defined semantics, and a calculus, which allow proofs to be constructed. The first property is shared with other methods for software specification, but the second sets them apart.

Formal Methods may be used in the software requirements definition phase for the construction of specifications. They are discussed in the *Guide to the Software Requirements Definition Phase*.

3.4 PROGRAM VERIFICATION TECHNIQUES

Program verification techniques may be used in the detailed design and production phase to show that a program is consistent with its specification. These techniques require that the:

- semantics of the programming language are formally defined;
- program be formally specified in a notation that is consistent with the mathematical verification techniques used.

If these conditions are not met, formal program verification cannot be attempted [Ref 13].

A common approach to formal program verification is to derive, by stepwise refinement of the formal specification, 'assertions' (e.g. preconditions or postconditions) that must be true at each stage in the processing. Formal proof of the program is achieved by demonstrating that program statements separating assertions transform each assertion into its successor. In addition, it is necessary to show that the program will always terminate (i.e. one or more of the postconditions will always be met).

Formal program verification is usually not possible because the programming language has not been formally defined. Even so, a more pragmatic approach to formal proof is to show that the:

- program code is logically consistent with the program specification;
- program will always terminate.

Assertions are placed in the code as comments. Verification is achieved by arguing that the code complies with the requirements present in the assertions.

3.5 CLEANROOM METHOD

The cleanroom method [Ref 20] replaces unit testing and integration testing with software inspections and program verification techniques. System testing is carried out by an independent testing team.

 The cleanroom method is not fully compliant with *Software Engineering Standards* because:

- full statement coverage is not achieved (DD06);
- unit and integration testing are omitted (DD07, DD08).

3.6 STRUCTURED TESTING

Structured Testing is a method for verifying software based upon the mathematical properties of control graphs [Ref 10]. The method:

- improves testability by limiting complexity during detailed design;
- guides the definition of test cases during unit testing.

Software with high complexity is hard to test. The Structured Testing method uses the cyclomatic complexity metric for measuring complexity, and recommends that module designs be simplified until they are within the complexity limits.

Structured Testing provides a technique, called the 'baseline method', for defining test cases. The objective is to cover every branch of the program logic during unit testing. The minimum number of test cases is the cyclomatic complexity value measured in the first step of the method.

The discussion of Structured Testing given below is a summary of that given in Reference 10. The reader is encouraged to consult the reference for a full discussion.

3.6.1 Testability

The testability of software should be evaluated during the detailed design phase by measuring its complexity.

The relationships between the parts of an entity determine its complexity. The parts of a software module are the statements in it. These are related to each other by sequence, selection (i.e. branches or conditions) and iteration (i.e. loops). As loops can be simulated by branching on a condition, McCabe defined a metric that gives a complexity of 1 for a simple sequence of statements with no branches. Only one test is required to execute every statement in the sequence. Each branch added to a module increases the complexity by one, and requires an extra test to cover it.

A control graph represents the control flow in a module. Control graphs are simplified flowcharts. Blocks of statements with sequential logic are represented as 'nodes' in the graph. Branches between blocks of statements (called 'edges') are represented as arrows connecting the nodes. McCabe defines the cyclomatic complexity 'v' of a control graph as:

$$v = e - n + 2$$

where:
- e is the number of edges;
- n is the number of nodes.

Figure 3.6.1A, B and C show several examples of control graphs.

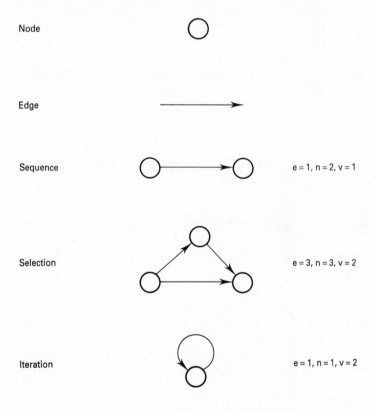

Figure 3.6.1A: Basic control graphs

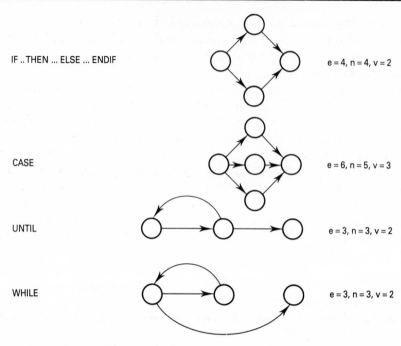

Figure 3.6.1B: Control graphs for structured programming elements

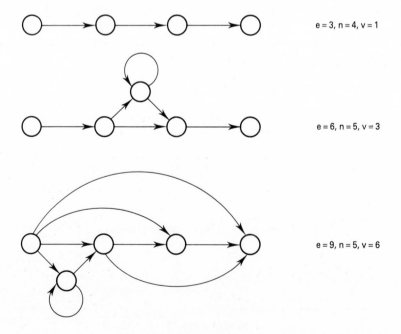

Figure 3.6.1C: Example control graphs

Alternative ways to measure cyclomatic complexity are to count the:
- number of separate regions in the control graph (i.e. areas separated by edges);
- number of decisions (i.e. the second and subsequent branches emanating from a node) and add one.

Myers [Ref 11] has pointed out that decision statements with multiple predicates must be separated into simple predicates before cyclomatic complexity is measured. The decision IF (A .AND. B .AND. C) THEN ... is really three separate decisions, not one.

The Structured Testing Method recommends that the cyclomatic complexity of a module be limited to 10. Studies have shown that errors concentrate in modules with complexities greater than this value. During detailed design, the limit of 7 should be applied because complexity always increases during coding. Modules that exceed these limits should be redesigned. Case statements are the only exception permitted.

The total cyclomatic complexity of a program can be obtained by summing the cyclomatic complexities of the constituent modules. The full cyclomatic complexity formula given by McCabe is:

$$v = e - n + 2p$$

where p is the number of modules. Each module has a separate control graph. Figure 3.6.1D shows how the total cyclomatic complexity can be evaluated by:
- counting all edges (18), nodes (14) and modules (3) and applying the complexity formula, $18 - 14 + 2*3 = 10$;
- adding the complexity of the components, $1 + 3 + 6 = 10$.

Combining the modules in Figure 3.6.1D into one module gives a module with complexity of eight. Although the total complexity is reduced, this is higher than the complexity of any of the separate modules. In general, decomposing a module into smaller modules increases the total complexity but reduces the maximum module complexity. A useful rule for design decomposition is to continue decomposition until the complexity of each of the modules is 10 or less.

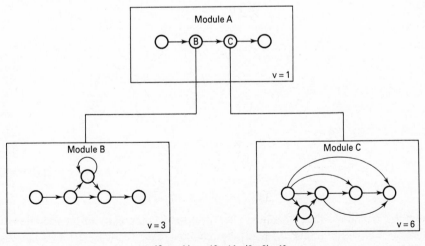

$e = 18, n = 14, v = 18 - 14 + (2 \times 3) = 10$

Figure 3.6.1D: Evaluating total cyclomatic complexity

3.6.2 Branch testing

Each branch added to a control graph adds a new path, and in this lies the importance of McCabe's complexity metric for the software tester: the cyclomatic complexity metric, denoted as 'v' by McCabe, measures the minimum number of paths through the software required to ensure that:

- every statement in a program is executed at least once (DD06);
- each decision outcome is executed at least once.

These two criteria imply full 'branch testing' of the software. Every clause of every statement is executed. In simple statement testing, every clause of every statement may not be executed. For example, branch testing of IF (A .EQ. B) X = X/Y requires that test cases be provided for both 'A equal to B' and 'A not equal to B'. For statement testing, only one test case needs to be provided. *Software Engineering Standards* places statement coverage as the minimum requirement. Branch testing should be the verification requirement in most projects.

3.6.3 Baseline method

The baseline method is used in structured testing to decide what paths should be used to traverse every branch. The test designer should examine the main function of the module and define the 'baseline path' that directly achieves it. Special cases and errors are ignored.

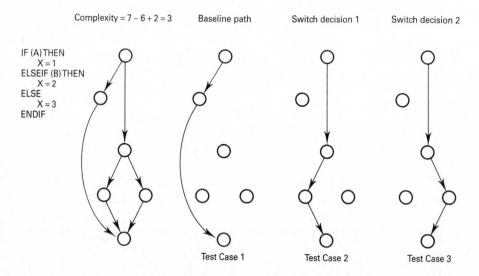

Figure 3.6.3: Baseline Method example.

Figure 3.6.3 shows the principles. The cyclomatic complexity of the module is three, so three test cases are required for full branch coverage. Test case 1 traces the baseline path. The baseline method proceeds by taking each decision in turn and switching it, as shown in test cases 2 and 3. Each switch is reset before switching the next, resulting in the checking of each deviation from the baseline. The baseline method does not require the testing of all possible paths. See the example of untested path of Figure 3.6.3. Tests for paths that are not tested by the baseline method may have to be added to the test design (e.g paths for testing safety-critical functions).

3.7 STRUCTURED INTEGRATION TESTING

Structured Integration Testing [Ref 12] is a method based upon the Structured Testing Method that:
- improves testability by limiting complexity during software architectural design;
- guides the definition of test cases during integration testing.

The method can be applied at all levels of design above the module level. Therefore it may also be applied in unit testing when units assembled from modules are tested.

The discussion of Structured Integration Testing given below is a summary of that given in Reference 12. The reader is encouraged to consult the references for a full discussion.

3.7.1 Testability

Structured Integration Testing defines three metrics for measuring testability:
- module design complexity;
- design complexity;
- integration complexity.

Module design complexity, denoted as 'iv' by McCabe, measures the individual effect of a module upon the program design [Ref 12]. The module design complexity is evaluated by drawing the control graph of the module and then marking the nodes that contain calls to external modules. The control graph is then 'reduced' according to the rules listed below and shown in Figure 3.7.1A:
1. marked nodes cannot be removed;
2. unmarked nodes that contain no decisions are removed;
3. edges that return control to the start of a loop that only contains unmarked nodes are removed;
4. edges that branch from the start of a case statement to the end are removed if none of the other cases contain marked nodes.

As in all control graphs, edges that 'duplicate' other edges are removed. The module design complexity is the cyclomatic complexity of the reduced graph.

In summary, module design complexity ignores paths covered in module testing that do not result in calls to external modules. The remaining paths are needed to test module interfaces.

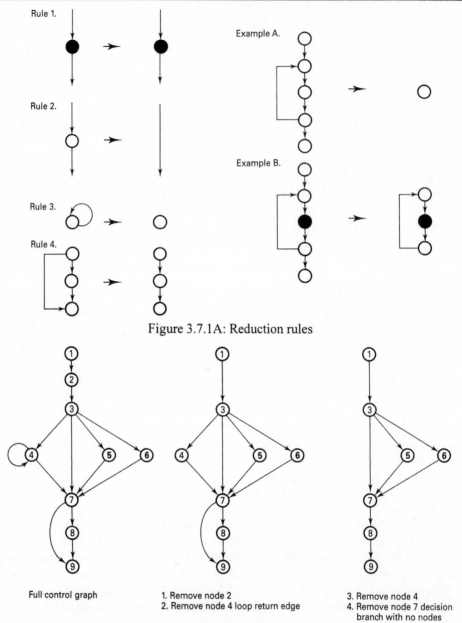

Figure 3.7.1A: Reduction rules

Full control graph

1. Remove node 2
2. Remove node 4 loop return edge

3. Remove node 4
4. Remove node 7 decision branch with no nodes

Figure 3.7.1B: Calculating module design complexity - part 1

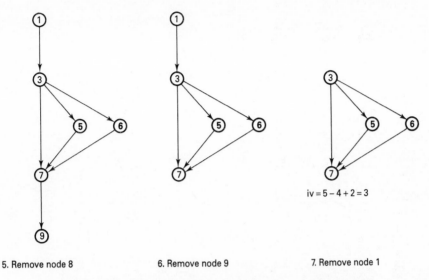

5. Remove node 8   6. Remove node 9   7. Remove node 1

Figure 3.7.1C: Calculating module design complexity - part 2

Figures 3.7.1B and C show an example of the application of these rules. The shaded nodes 5 and 6 call lower level modules. The unshaded nodes do not. In the first reduction step, rule 2 is applied to remove node 2. Rule 3 is then applied to remove the edge returning control in the loop around node 4. Rule 2 is applied to remove node 4. Rule 4 is then applied to remove the edge branching from node 7 to node 9. Rule 2 is then applied to remove nodes 8, 9 and 1. The module design complexity is the cyclomatic complexity (see Section 3.6.1) of the reduced control graph, 3.

The design complexity, denoted as 'S_0' by McCabe, of an assembly of modules is evaluated by summing the module design complexities of each module in the assembly.

The integration complexity, denoted as 'S_1' by McCabe, of an assembly of modules, counts the number of paths through the control flow. The integration complexity of an assembly of 'N' modules is given by the formula:

$$S_1 = S_0 - N + 1$$

The integration complexity of N modules each containing no branches is therefore 1.

The testability of a design is measured by evaluating its integration complexity. Formally the integration complexity depends on measuring the module design complexity of each module. During architectural design, the full control graph of each constituent module will not usually be available. However sufficient information should be available to define the module design complexity without knowing all the module logic.

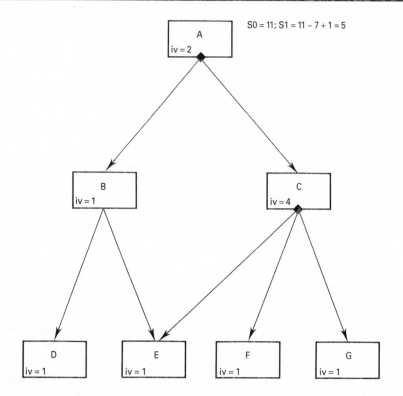

Figure 3.7.1D: Estimating integration complexity from a structure chart

Figure 3.7.1D shows a structure chart illustrating how S_1 can be evaluated just from knowing the conditions that govern the invocation of each component, i.e. the control flow. Boxes in the chart correspond to design components, and arrows mark transfer of the control flow. A diamond indicates that the transfer is conditional. The control flow is defined to be:

- component A calls either component B or component C;
- component B sequentially calls component D and then component E;
- component C calls either component E or component F or component G or none of them.

The integration complexity of the design in shown Figure 3.7.1D is therefore 5.

3.7.2 Control flow testing

Just as cyclomatic complexity measures the number of test cases required to cover every branch of a module, integration complexity measures the number of tests required to cover all the control flow paths. Structured integration testing can therefore be used for verifying that all the control flows defined in the ADD have been implemented (DD08).

3.7.3 Design integration testing method

The design integration testing method is used in structured integration testing to enable the test designer to decide what control flow paths should be tested. The test designer should:

- evaluate the integration complexity, S_1 for the N modules in the design (see Section 3.7.1);
- construct a blank matrix of dimension S_1 rows by N columns, called the 'integration path test matrix';
- mark each column, the module of which is conditionally called, with a 'p' (for predicate), followed by a sequence number for the predicate;
- fill in the matrix with 1's or 0's to show whether the module is called in each test case.

The example design shown in Figure 3.7.1D has an integration complexity of 5. The five integration test cases to verify the control flow are shown in Table 3.7.3.

		P1	P2		P3	P4	P5	
Case	A	B	C	D	E	F	G	Control flow path
1	1	1	0	1	1	0	0	A calls B; B calls D and E
2	1	0	1	0	0	0	0	A calls C and then returns
3	1	0	1	0	1	0	0	A calls C and then C calls E
4	1	0	1	0	0	1	0	A calls C and then C calls F
5	1	0	1	0	0	0	1	A ca⌐ ⌐ and then C calls G

Table 3.7.3: Example Integration Path Test Matrix

In Table 3.7.3, P1 and P2 are two predicates (contained within module A) that decide whether B or C are called. Similarly, P3, P4 and P5 are three predicates (contained within module C) that decide whether E, F or G are called.

CHAPTER 4
SOFTWARE VERIFICATION AND VALIDATION TOOLS

4.1 INTRODUCTION

A software tool is a 'computer program used in the development, testing, analysis, or maintenance of a program or its documentation' [Ref 3]. Software tools, more commonly called 'Computer Aided Software Engineering' (CASE) tools enhance the software verification and validation process by:

- reducing the effort needed for mechanical tasks, therefore increasing the amount of software verification and validation work that can be done;
- improving the accuracy of software verification and validation (for example, measuring test coverage is not only very time consuming, it is also very difficult to do accurately without tools).

Both these benefits result in improved software quality and productivity.

Software Engineering Standards defines the primary software verification and validation activities as:

- reviewing;
- tracing;
- formal proof;
- testing;
- auditing.

The following sections discuss tools for supporting each activity. This chapter does not describe specific products, but contains guidelines for their selection.

4.2 TOOLS FOR REVIEWING

4.2.1 General administrative tools

General administrative tools may be used for supporting reviewing, as appropriate. Examples are:

- word processors that allow commenting on documents;
- word processors that can show changes made to documents;
- electronic mail systems that support the distribution of review items;
- notes systems that enable communal commenting on a review item;
- conferencing systems that allow remote participation in reviews.

4.2.2 Static analysers

Static analysis is the process of evaluating a system or component based on its form, structure, content or documentation [Ref 3]. Reviews, especially software inspections, may include activities such as:

- control flow analysis to find errors such as unreachable code, endless loops, violations of recursion conventions, and loops with multiple entry and exit points;
- data-use analysis to find errors such as data used before initialisation, variables declared but not used, and redundant writes;
- range-bound analysis to find errors such as array indices outside the boundaries of the array;
- interface analysis to find errors such as mismatches in argument lists between called modules and calling modules;
- information flow analysis to check the dependency relations between input and output;
- verification of conformance to language standards (e.g. ANSI C);
- verification of conformance to project coding standards, such as departures from naming conventions;
- code volume analysis, such as counts of the numbers of modules and the number of lines of code in each module;
- complexity analysis, such as measurements of cyclomatic complexity and integration complexity.

Tools that support one or more of these static analysis activities are available and their use is strongly recommended.

Compilers often perform some control flow and data-use analysis. Some compile/link systems, such as those for Ada and Modula-2, automatically do interface analysis to enforce the strong type checking demanded by the language standards. Compilers for many languages, such as FORTRAN and C, do not do any interface analysis. Static analysis tools are especially necessary when compilers do not check control flow, data flow, range bounds and interfaces. The use of a static analyser should be an essential step in C program development, for example.

Static analysers for measuring complexity and constructing call graphs are essential when the Structured Testing method is used for unit testing (see Section 4.5.1). Producing call graphs at higher levels (i.e. module tree and program tree) is also of use in the review and testing of the detailed design and architectural design.

4.2.3 Configuration management tools

Reviewing is an essential part of the change control process and therefore some configuration management tools also support review processes. The preparation and tracking of RIDs and SPRs can be supported by database management systems for example. See the *Guide to Software Configuration Management*.

4.2.4 Reverse engineering tools

Although reverse engineering tools are more commonly used during maintenance to enable code to be understood, they can be used during development to permit verification that 'as-built' conforms to 'as-designed'. For example the as-built structure chart of a program can be generated from the code by means of a reverse engineering tool, and then compared with the as-designed structure chart in the ADD or DDD.

4.3 TOOLS FOR TRACING

The basic tracing method is to:
- uniquely identify the items to be tracked;
- record relationships between items.

Software Engineering Standards states that cross-reference matrices must be used to record relationships between:
- user requirements and software requirements;
- software requirements and architectural design components;
- software requirements and detailed design components.

In addition, test designs should be traced to software components and requirements. Tracing tools should:
- ensure that identifiers obey the naming conventions of the project;
- ensure that identifiers are unique;
- allow attributes to be attached to the identified items such as the need, priority, or stability of a requirement, or the status of a software component (e.g. coded, unit tested, integration tested, system tested, acceptance tested);
- record all instances where an identified part of a document references an identified part of another document (e.g. when software requirement SR100 references user requirement UR49, the tool should record the relationship SR100-UR49);
- accept input in a variety of formats;
- store the traceability records (e.g. a table can be used to store a traceability matrix);
- allow easy querying of the traceability records;
- allow the extraction of information associated with a specific traceability record (e.g. the user requirement related to a software requirement);
- generate traceability reports (e.g. cross-reference matrices);
- inform users of the entities that may be affected when a related entity is updated or deleted;
- be integrated with the project repository so that the relationship database is automatically updated after a change to a document or a software component;
- provide access to the change history of a review item so that the consistency of changes can be monitored.

In summary, tracing tools should allow easy and efficient navigation through the software.

Most word processors have indexing and cross-referencing capabilities. These can also support traceability; for example, traceability from software requirements to user requirements can be done by creating index entries for the user requirement identifiers in the SRD. The disadvantage of this approach is that there is no system-wide database of relationships. Consequently dedicated tracing tools, normally based upon commercial database management systems, are used to build relationship databases. Customised frontends are required to make tracing tool capabilities easily accessible. The database may form part of, or be integrated with, the software development environment's repository. Tracing tools should accept review items (with embedded identifiers) and generate the traceability records from that input.

Traceability tool functionality is also provided by 'requirements engineering' tools, which directly support the requirements creation and maintenance process. Requirements engineering tools contain all the specific requirements information in addition to the information about the relationships between the requirements and the other parts of the software.

4.4 TOOLS FOR FORMAL PROOF

Formal Methods (e.g. Z and VDM) are discussed in the *Guide to the Software Requirements Definition Phase*. This guide also discusses the criteria for the selection of CASE tools for software requirements definition. These criteria should be used for the selection of tools to support Formal Methods.

Completely automated program verification is not possible without a formally defined programming language. However subsets of some languages (e.g. Pascal, Ada) can be formally defined. Preprocessors are available that automatically check that the code is consistent with assertion statements placed in it. These tools can be very effective in verifying small well-structured programs.

Semantics is the relationship of symbols and groups of symbols to their meaning in a given language [Ref 3]. In software engineering, semantic analysis is the symbolic execution of a program by means of algebraic symbols instead of test input data. Semantic analysers use a source code interpreter to substitute algebraic symbols into the program variables and present the results as algebraic formulae [Ref 14]. Like program verifiers, semantic analysers may be useful for the verification of small well-structured programs.

4.5 TOOLS FOR TESTING

Testing involves many activities, most of which benefit from tool support. Figure 4.5 shows what test tools can be used to support the testing activities defined in Section 2.6.

The following paragraphs step through each activity depicted in Figure 4.5, discussing the tools indicated by the arrows into the bottom of the activity boxes.

1. The 'specify tests' activity may use the Structured Testing Method and Structured Integration Testing methods (see Sections 3.6 and 3.7). Static analysers should be used to measure the cyclomatic complexity and integration complexity metrics. This activity may also use the equivalence partitioning method for defining unit test cases. Test case generators should support this method.

2. The 'make test software' activity should be supported with a test harness tool. At the unit level, test harness tools that link to the SUT act as drivers for software modules, providing all the user interface functions required for the control of unit tests. At the integration and system levels, test harness tools external to the SUT (e.g. simulators) may be required. Test procedures should be encoded in scripts that can be read by the test harness tool.

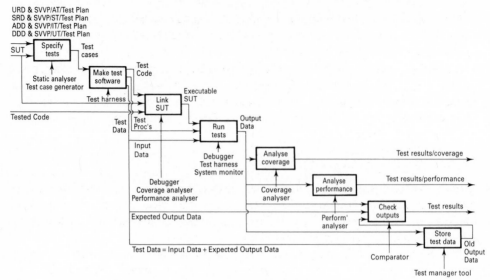

Figure 4.5: Testing Tools

3. The 'link SUT' activity links the test code, SUT, and existing tested code, producing the executable SUT. Debuggers, coverage analysers and performance analysers may also be built into the executable SUT. Coverage analysers and performance analysers (collectively known as 'dynamic analysers') require 'instrumentation' of the code so that post-test analysis data can be collected.

4. The 'run tests' activity executes the tests according to the test procedures, using the input data. Test harnesses permit control of the test. These should have a capture and playback capability if the SUT has an interactive user interface. White-box test runs may be conducted under the control of a debugger. This permits monitoring of each step of execution, and immediate detection of defects that cause test failures. System monitoring tools can be used to study program resource usage during tests.

5. The 'analyse coverage' activity checks that the tests have executed the parts of the SUT they were intended to. Coverage analysers show the paths that have been executed, helping testers keep track of coverage.

6. The 'analyser performance' activity should be supported with a performance analyser (also called a 'profiler'). These examine the performance data collected during the test run and produce reports of resource usage at component level and statement level.

7. The 'check outputs' activity should be supported with a comparator. This tool can automatically compare the test output data with the outputs of previous tests or the expected output data.

8. The 'store test data' activity should be supported by test manager tools that store the test scripts, test input and output data for future use.

Tool support for testing is weakest in the area of test design and test case generation. Tool support is strongest in the area of running tests, analysing the results and managing test software. Human involvement is required to specify the tests, but tools should do most of the tedious, repetitive work involved in running them. Automated support for regression testing is especially good. In an evolving system this is where it is most needed. The bulk of software costs usually accrue during the operations and maintenance phase of a project. Often this is due to the amount of regression testing required to verify that changes have not introduced faults in the system.

The following subsections discuss the capabilities of test tools in more detail.

4.5.1 Static analysers

Static analysers that measure complexity are needed to support the Structured Testing method and for checking adherence to coding standards. These tools may also support review activities (see Section 4.2.2). The measure of complexity defines the minimum number of test cases required for full branch coverage. Static analysers should also produce module control graphs to support path definition.

The output of a static analyser should be readable by the test harness tool so that checks on values measured during static analysis can be included in test scripts (e.g. check that the complexity of a module has not exceeded some threshold, such as 10). This capability eases regression testing.

4.5.2 Test case generators

A test case generator (or automated test generator) is 'a software tool that accepts as input source code, test criteria, specifications, or data structure definitions; uses these inputs to generate test input data; and, sometimes, determines the expected results' [Ref 3].

The test case generation methods of equivalence partitioning and boundary value analysis can be supported by test case generators. These methods are used in unit testing. Automated test case generation at integration, system and acceptance test level is not usually possible.

Expected output data need to be in a form usable by comparators.

4.5.3 Test harnesses

A test harness (or test driver) is a 'software module used to invoke a module under test and, often, provide test inputs, control and monitor execution, and report test results' [Ref 3]. Test harness tools should:

- provide a language for programming test procedures (i.e. a script language);
- generate stubs for software components called by the SUT;
- not require any modifications to the SUT;
- provide a means of interactive control (for debugging);
- provide a batch mode (for regression testing);
- enable stubs to be informed about the test cases in use, so that they will read the appropriate test input data;
- execute all test cases required of a unit, subsystem or system;
- handle exceptions, so that testing can continue after test failures;
- record the results of all test cases in a log file;

- check all returns from the SUT;
- record in the test results log whether the test was passed or failed;
- be usable in development and target environments.

A test harness is written as a driver for the SUT. The harness is written in a scripting language that provides module, sequence, selection and iteration constructs. Scripting languages are normally based upon a standard programming language. The ability to call one script module from another, just as in a conventional programming language, is very important as test cases may only differ in their input data. The scripting language should include directives to set up, execute, stop and check the results of each test case. Software components that implement these directives are provided as part of the test harness tool. Test harnesses may be compiled and linked with the SUT, or exist externally as a control program.

Test harness tools can generate input at one or more of the following levels [Ref 16]:
- application software level, either as input files or call arguments;
- operating system level, for example as X-server messages;
- hardware level, as keyboard or mouse input.

Test harness tools should capture output at the level at which they input it. It should be possible to generate multiple input and output data streams. This is required in stress tests (e.g. multiple users logging on simultaneously) and security tests (e.g. resource locking).

A synchronisation mechanism is required to co-ordinate the test harness and the software under test. During unit testing this is rarely a problem, as the driver and the SUT form a single program. Synchronisation may be difficult to achieve during integration and system testing, when the test harness and SUT are separate programs. Synchronisation techniques include:
- recording and using the delays of the human operators;
- waiting for a specific output (i.e. a handshake technique);
- using an algorithm to decide the wait time;
- monitoring keyboard lock indicators.

The first technique is not very robust. The other techniques are preferable.

For interactive testing, the most efficient way to define the test script is to capture the manually generated input and store it for later playback. For graphical user interfaces this may be the only practical method.

Graphical user interfaces have window managers to control the use of screen resources by multiple applications. This can cause problems to test harness tools because the meaning of a mouse click depends upon what is beneath the cursor. The window manager decides this, not the test harness. This type of problem can mean that test scripts need to be frequently modified to cope with changes in layout. Comparators that can filter out irrelevant changes in screen layout (see Section 4.5.7) reduce the problems of testing software with a graphical user interface.

4.5.4 Debuggers

Debuggers are used in white-box testing for controlling the execution of the SUT. Capabilities required for testing include the ability to:

- display and interact with the tester using the symbols employed in the source code;
- step through code instruction-by-instruction;
- set watch points on variables;
- set break points;
- maintain screen displays of the source code during test execution;
- log the session for inclusion in the test results.

Session logs can act as test procedure files for subsequent tests and also as coverage reports, since they describe what happened.

4.5.5 Coverage analysers

Coverage analysis is the process of:
- instrumenting the code so that information is collected on the parts of it that are executed when it is run;
- analysing the data collected to see what parts of the SUT have been executed.

Instrumentation of the code should not affect its logic. Any effects on performance should be easy to allow for. Simple coverage analysers will just provide information about statement coverage, such as indications of the program statements executed in one run. More advanced coverage analysers can:

- sum coverage data to make reports of total coverage achieved in a series of runs;
- display control graphs, so that branch coverage and path coverage can be monitored;
- output test coverage information so that coverage can be checked by the test harness, therefore aiding regression testing;
- operate in development and target environments.

4.5.6 Performance analysers

Performance analysis is the process of:
- instrumenting the code so that information is collected about resources used when it is run;
- analysing the data collected to evaluate resource utilisation;
- optimising performance.

Instrumentation of the code should not affect the measured performance. Performance analysers should provide information on a variety of metrics such as:
- CPU usage by each line of code;
- CPU usage by each module;
- memory usage;
- input/output volume.

Coverage analysers are often integrated with performance analysers to make 'dynamic analysers'.

4.5.7 Comparators

A comparator is a 'software tool used to compare two computer programs, files, or sets of data to identify commonalities and differences' [Ref 3]. Differencing tools are types of comparators. In testing, comparators are needed to compare actual test output data with expected test output data.

Expected test output data may have originated from:
- test case generators;
- previous runs.

Comparators should report about differences between actual and expected output data. It should be possible to specify tolerances on differences (floating point operations can produce slightly different results each time they are done). The output of comparators should be usable by test harness tools, so that differences can be used to flag a test failure. This makes regression testing more efficient.

Screen comparators [Ref 16] are useful for testing interactive software. These may operate at the character or bitmap level. The ability to select parts of the data, and attributes of the data, for comparison is a key requirement of a screen comparator. Powerful screen comparison capabilities are important when testing software with a graphical user interface.

Some comparators may be run during tests. When a difference is detected the test procedure is suspended. Other comparators run off-line, checking for differences after the test run.

4.5.8 Test management tools

All the software associated with testing: test specifications, SUT, drivers, stubs, scripts, tools, input data, expected output data and output data must be placed under configuration management (SCM01). The configuration management system is responsible for identifying, storing, controlling and accounting for all configuration items.

Test data management tools provide configuration management functions for the test data and scripts. Specifically designed for supporting testing, they should:
- enable tests to be set up and run with the minimum of steps;
- automatically manage the storage of outputs and results;
- provide test report generation facilities;
- provide quality and reliability statistics;
- provide support for capture and playback of input and output data during interactive testing.

Test managers are essential for efficient regression testing.

CHAPTER 5
THE SOFTWARE VERIFICATION AND VALIDATION PLAN

5.1 INTRODUCTION

All software verification and validation activities must be documented in the Software Verification and Validation Plan (SVVP) (SVV04). The SVVP is divided into seven sections that contain the verification plans for the SR, AD and DD phases and the unit, integration, system and acceptance test specifications. Figure 5.1A summarises when and where each software verification and validation activity is documented in the SVVP.

PHASE / SVVP SECTION	USER REQUIREMENTS DEFINITION	SOFTWARE REQUIREMENTS DEFINITION	ARCHITECTURAL DESIGN	DETAILED DESIGN AND PRODUCTION	TRANSFER
SVVP/SR	SR Phase Plan				
SVVP/AD		AD Phase Plan			
SVVP/DD			DD Phase Plan		
SVVP/AT	AT Plan			AT Designs AT Cases AT Procedures	AT Reports
SVVP/ST		ST Plan		ST Designs ST Cases ST Procedures ST Reports	
SVVP/IT			IT Plan	IT Designs IT Cases IT Procedures IT Reports	
SVVP/UT				UT Plan UT Designs UT Cases UT Procedures UT Reports	

Figure 5.1A: Life cycle production of SVV documentation

Each row of Figure 5.1A corresponds to a section of the SVVP and each column entry corresponds to a subsection. For example, the entry 'ST Plan' in the SVVP/ST row means that the System Test Plan is drawn up in the SR phase and placed in the SVVP section 'System Tests', subsection 'Test Plan'.

The SVVP must ensure that the verification activities:
- are appropriate for the degree of criticality of the software (SVV05);
- meet the verification and acceptance testing requirements (stated in the SRD) (SVV06);
- verify that the product will meet the quality, reliability, maintainability and safety requirements (stated in the SRD) (SVV07);
- are sufficient to assure the quality of the product (SVV08).

The table of contents for the verification sections is derived from the IEEE Standard for Verification and Validation Plans (ANSI/IEEE Std 1012-1986). For the test sections it is derived from the IEEE Standard for Software Test Documentation (ANSI/IEEE Std 829-1983).

The relationship between test specifications, test plans, test designs, test cases, test procedures and test results may sometimes be a simple hierarchy but usually it will not be. Figure 5.1B shows the relationships between the sections and subsections of the SVVP. Sections are shown in boxes. Relationships between sections are shown by lines labelled with the verb in the relationship (e.g. 'contains'). The one-to-one relationships are shown by a plain line and one-to-many relationships are shown by the crow's feet.

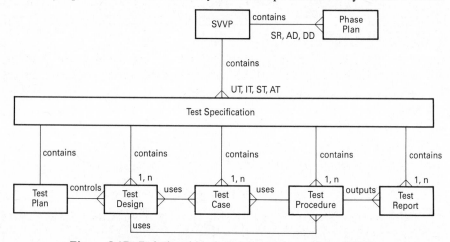

Figure 5.1B: Relationships between sections of the SVVP

Figure 5.1B illustrates that a test plan controls the test design process, defining the software items to be tested. Test designs define the features of each software item to be tested, and specify the test cases and test procedures that will be used to test the features. Test cases may be used by many test designs and many test procedures. Each execution of a test procedure produces a new set of test results.

Software verification and validation procedures should be easy to follow, efficient and wherever possible, reusable in later phases. Poor test definition and record keeping can significantly reduce the maintainability of the software.

The key criterion for deciding the level of documentation of testing is repeatability. Tests should be sufficiently documented to allow repetition by different people, yet still yield the same results for the same software. The level of test documentation depends very much upon the software tools used to support testing. Good testing tools should relieve the developer from much of the effort of documenting tests.

5.2 STYLE

The SVVP should be plain and concise. The document should be clear, consistent and modifiable.

Authors should assume familiarity with the purpose of the software, and not repeat information that is explained in other documents.

5.3 RESPONSIBILITY

The developer is normally responsible for the production of the SVVP. The user may take responsibility for producing the Acceptance Test Specification (SVVP/AT), especially when the software is to be embedded in a larger system.

5.4 MEDIUM

It is usually assumed that the SVVP is a paper document. The SVVP could be distributed electronically to participants with the necessary equipment.

5.5 SERVICE INFORMATION

The SR, AD, DD, UT, IT, ST and AT sections of the SVVP are produced at different times in a software project. Each section should be kept separately under configuration control and contain the following service information:

    a - Abstract
    b - Table of Contents
    c - Document Status Sheet
    d - Document Change records made since last issue

5.6 CONTENT OF SVVP/SR, SVVP/AD & SVVP/DD SECTIONS

These sections define the review, proof and tracing activities in the SR, AD and DD phases of the lifecycle. While the SPMP may summarise these activities, the SVVP should provide the detailed information. For example the SPMP may schedule an AD/R, but this section of the SVVP defines the activities for the whole AD phase review process.

These sections of the SVVP should avoid repeating material from the standards and guidelines and instead define how the procedures will be applied.

Software Engineering Standards recommends the following table of contents for the SVVP/SR, SVVP/AD and SVVP/DD sections:

1 PURPOSE[1]
2 REFERENCE DOCUMENTS
3 DEFINITIONS
4 VERIFICATION OVERVIEW
    4.1 Organisation
    4.2 Master schedule
    4.3 Resources summary
    4.4 Responsibilities
    4.5 Tools, techniques and methods
5 VERIFICATION ADMINISTRATIVE PROCEDURES
    5.1 Anomaly reporting and resolution
    5.2 Task iteration policy
    5.3 Deviation policy
    5.4 Control procedures
    5.5 Standards, practices and conventions
6 VERIFICATION ACTIVITIES
    6.1 Tracing[2]
    6.2 Formal proofs
    6.3 Reviews
7 SOFTWARE VERIFICATION REPORTING

Additional material should be inserted in additional appendices. If there is no material for a section then the phrase 'Not Applicable' should be inserted and the section numbering preserved.

5.6.1 SVVP/SR/1 PURPOSE

This section should:

- briefly define the purpose of this part of the SVVP, stating the part of the lifecycle to which it applies;
- identify the software project for which the SVVP is written;
- identify the products to be verified, and the specifications that they are to be verified against;
- outline the goals of verification and validation;
- specify the intended readers of this part of the SVVP.

---

[1] The Software Verification and Validation Plan phase section contents list is based upon extracts from IEEE Std 1012-1986, IEEE Standard for Software Verification and Validation Plans, copyright © 1986 by the Institute for Electrical and Electronic Engineers Inc. The IEEE disclaims any responsibility or liability resulting from the placement and use in this publication. Information is reprinted with the permission of the IEEE.

[2] Note that in *Software Engineering Standards* this section is called 'traceability matrix template'

5.6.2 SVVP/SR/2 REFERENCE DOCUMENTS

This section should provide a complete list of all the applicable and reference documents, such as the *Software Engineering Standards* and *Software Engineering Guides*. Each document should be identified by title, author and date. Each document should be marked as applicable or reference. If appropriate, report number, journal name and publishing organisation should be included.

5.6.3 SVVP/SR/3 DEFINITIONS

This section should provide the definitions of all terms, acronyms, and abbreviations used in the plan, or refer to other documents where the definitions can be found.

5.6.4 SVVP/SR/4 VERIFICATION OVERVIEW

This section should describe the organisation, schedule, resources, responsibilities, tools, techniques and methods necessary to perform reviews, proofs and tracing.

5.6.4.1 SVVP/SR/4.1 Organisation

This section should describe the organisation of the review, proofs and tracing activities for the phase. Topics that should be included are:

- roles;
- reporting channels;
- levels of authority for resolving problems;
- relationships to the other activities such as project management, development, configuration management and quality assurance.

The description should identify the people associated with the roles. Elsewhere the plan should only refer to roles.

5.6.4.2 SVVP/SR/4.2 Master schedule

This section should define the schedule for the review, proofs and tracing activities in the phase.

Reviews of large systems should be broken down by subsystem. In the DD phase, critical design reviews of subsystems should be held when the subsystem is ready, not when all subsystems have been designed.

5.6.4.2 SVVP/SR/4.3 Resources summary

This section should summarise the resources needed to perform reviews, proofs and tracing such as staff, computer facilities, and software tools.

5.6.4.4 SVVP/SR/4.4 Responsibilities

This section should define the specific responsibilities associated with the roles described in section 4.1.

5.6.4.5 SVVP/SR/4.5 Tools, techniques and methods

This section should identify the software tools, techniques and methods used for reviews, proofs and tracing in the phase. Training plans for the tools, techniques and methods may be included.

5.6.5 SVVP/SR/5 VERIFICATION ADMINISTRATIVE PROCEDURES

5.6.5.1 SVVP/SR/5.1 Anomaly reporting and resolution

The Review Item Discrepancy (RID) form is normally used for reporting and resolving anomalies found in documents and code submitted for formal review. The procedure for handling this form is normally described in Section 4.3.2 of the SCMP, which should be referenced here and not repeated. This section should define the criteria for activating the anomaly reporting and resolution process.

5.6.5.2 SVVP/SR/5.2 Task iteration policy

This section should define the criteria for deciding whether a task should be repeated when a change has been made. The criteria may include assessments of the scope of a change, the criticality of the function(s) affected, and any quality effects.

5.6.5.3 SVVP/SR/5.3 Deviation policy

This section should describe the procedures for deviating from the plan, and define the levels of authorisation required for the approval of deviations. The information required for deviations should include task identification, deviation rationale and the effect on software quality.

5.6.5.4 SVVP/SR/5.4 Control procedures

This section should identify the configuration management procedures of the products of review, proofs and tracing. Adequate assurance that they are secure from accidental or deliberate alteration is required.

5.6.5.4 SVVP/SR/5.5 Standards, practices and conventions

This section should identify the standards, practices and conventions that govern review, proof and tracing tasks, including internal organisational standards, practices and policies (e.g. practices for safety-critical software).

5.6.6 SVVP/SR/6 VERIFICATION ACTIVITIES

This section should describe the procedures for review, proof and tracing activities.

5.6.6.1 SVVP/SR/6.1 Tracing

This section should describe the procedures for tracing each part of the input products to the output products, and vice-versa.

5.6.6.2 SVVP/SR/6.2 Formal proofs

This section should define or reference the methods and procedures used (if any) for proving theorems about the behaviour of the software.

5.6.6.3 SVVP/SR/6.3 Reviews

This section should define or reference the methods and procedures used for technical reviews, walkthroughs, software inspections and audits.

This section should list the reviews, walkthroughs and audits that will take place during the phase and identify the roles of the people participating in them.

This section should not repeat material found in the standards and guides, but should specify project-specific modifications and additions.

5.6.7 SVVP/SR/7 SOFTWARE VERIFICATION REPORTING

This section should describe how the results of implementing the plan will be documented. Types of reports might include:
- summary report for the phase;
- technical review report;
- walkthrough report;
- audit report.

RIDs should be attached to the appropriate verification report.

5.7 CONTENT OF SVVP/UT, SVVP/IT, SVVP/ST & SVVP/AT SECTIONS

The SVVP contains four sections dedicated to each test development phase. These sections are called:
- Unit Test Specification (SVVP/UT);
- Integration Test Specification (SVVP/IT);
- System Test Specification (SVVP/ST);
- Acceptance Test Specification (SVVP/AT).

Software Engineering Standards recommends the following table of contents for each test section of the SVVP.

1 TEST PLAN[3]

   1.1   Introduction
   1.2   Test items
   1.3   Features to be tested
   1.4   Features not to be tested
   1.5   Approach
   1.6   Item pass/fail criteria
   1.7   Suspension criteria and resumption requirements
   1.8   Test deliverables

---

[3] The Software Verification and Validation Plan test section contents list is based upon extracts from IEEE Std 829-1983, IEEE Standard for Software Test Documentation, copyright © 1983 by the Institute for Electrical and Electronic Engineers Inc. The IEEE disclaims any responsibility or liability resulting from the placement and use in this publication. Information is reprinted with the permission of the IEEE.

1.9   Testing tasks
1.10 Environmental needs
1.11 Responsibilities
1.12 Staffing and training needs
1.13 Schedule
1.14 Risks and contingencies
1.15 Approvals

2 TEST DESIGNS (FOR EACH TEST DESIGN...)

2.n.1 Test design identifier
2.n.2 Features to be tested
2.n.3 Approach refinements
2.n.4 Test case identification
2.n.5 Feature pass/fail criteria

3 TEST CASE SPECIFICATIONS (FOR EACH TEST CASE...)

3.n.1 Test case identifier
3.n.2 Test items
3.n.3 Input specifications
3.n.4 Output specifications
3.n.5 Environmental needs
3.n.6 Special procedural requirements
3.n.7 Intercase dependencies

4 TEST PROCEDURES (FOR EACH TEST CASE...)

4.n.1 Test procedure identifier
4.n.2 Purpose
4.n.3 Special requirements
4.n.4 Procedure steps

5 TEST REPORTS (FOR EACH EXECUTION OF A TEST PROCEDURE ...)

5.n.1 Test report identifier
5.n.2 Description
5.n.3 Activity and event entries

5.7.1 SVVP/AT/1 TEST PLAN

5.7.1.1 SVVP/AT/1.1 Introduction

This section should summarise the software items and software features to be tested. A justification of the need for testing may be included.

5.7.1.2 SVVP/AT/1.2 Test items

This section should identify the test items. References to other software documents should be supplied to provide information about what the test items are supposed to do, how they work, and how they are operated.

Test items should be grouped according to release number when delivery is incremental.

5.7.1.3 SVVP/AT/1.3 Features to be tested

This section should identify all the features and combinations of features that are to be tested. This may be done by referencing sections of requirements or design documents.
References should be precise yet economical, e.g:
- 'the acceptance tests will cover all requirements in the User Requirements Document except those identified in Section 1.4';
- 'the unit tests will cover all modules specified in the Detailed Design Document except those modules listed in Section 1.4'.

Features should be grouped according to release number when delivery is incremental.

5.7.1.4 SVVP/AT/1.4 Features not to be tested

This section should identify all the features and significant combinations of features that are not to be tested, and why.

5.7.1.5 SVVP/AT/1.5 Approach

This section should specify the major activities, methods (e.g. structured testing) and tools that are to be used to test the designated groups of features.
Activities should be described in sufficient detail to allow identification of the major testing tasks and estimation of the resources and time needed for the tests. The coverage required should be specified.

5.7.1.6 SVVP/AT/1.6 Item pass/fail criteria

This section should specify the criteria to be used to decide whether each test item has passed or failed testing.

5.7.1.7 SVVP/AT/1.7 Suspension criteria and resumption requirements

This section should specify the criteria used to suspend all, or a part of, the testing activities on the test items associated with the plan.
This section should specify the testing activities that must be repeated when testing is resumed.

5.7.1.8 SVVP/AT/1.8 Test deliverables

This section should identify the items that must be delivered before testing begins, which should include:
- test plan;
- test designs;
- test cases;
- test procedures;
- test input data;

- test tools.

This section should identify the items that must be delivered when testing is finished, which should include:

- test reports;
- test output data;
- problem reports.

5.7.1.9 SVVP/AT/1.9 Testing tasks

This section should identify the set of tasks necessary to prepare for and perform testing. This section should identify all inter-task dependencies and any special skills required.

Testing tasks should be grouped according to release number when delivery is incremental.

5.7.1.10 SVVP/AT/1.10 Environmental needs

This section should specify both the necessary and desired properties of the test environment, including:

- physical characteristics of the facilities including hardware;
- communications software;
- system software;
- mode of use (i.e. standalone, networked);
- security;
- test tools.

Environmental needs should be grouped according to release number when delivery is incremental.

5.7.1.11 SVVP/AT/1.11 Responsibilities

This section should identify the groups responsible for managing, designing, preparing, executing, witnessing, and checking tests.

Groups may include developers, operations staff, user representatives, technical support staff, data administration staff, independent verification and validation personnel and quality assurance staff.

5.7.1.12 SVVP/AT/1.12 Staffing and training needs

This section should specify staffing needs according to skill. Identify training options for providing necessary skills.

5.7.1.13 SVVP/AT/1.13 Schedule

This section should include test milestones identified in the software project schedule and all item delivery events, for example:

- programmer delivers unit for integration testing;
- developers deliver system for independent verification.

This section should specify:

- any additional test milestones and state the time required for each testing task;
- the schedule for each testing task and test milestone;

- the period of use for all test resources (e.g. facilities, tools, staff).

5.7.1.14 SVVP/AT/1.14 Risks and contingencies

This section should identify the high-risk assumptions of the test plan. It should specify contingency plans for each.

5.7.1.15 SVVP/AT/1.15 Approvals

This section should specify the names and titles of all persons who must approve this plan. Alternatively, approvals may be shown on the title page of the plan.

5.7.2 SVVP/AT/2 TEST DESIGNS

5.7.2.1 SVVP/AT/2.n.1 Test Design identifier

The title of this section should specify the test design uniquely. The content of this section should briefly describe the test design.

5.7.2.2 SVVP/AT/2.n.2 Features to be tested

This section should identify the test items and describe the features, and combinations of features, that are to be tested.

For each feature or feature combination, a reference to its associated requirements in the item requirement specification (URD, SRD) or design description (ADD, DDD) should be included.

5.7.2.3 SVVP/AT/2.n.3 Approach refinements

This section should describe the results of the application of the methods described in the approach section of the test plan. Specifically it may define the:

- module assembly sequence (for unit testing);
- paths through the module logic (for unit testing);
- component integration sequence (for integration testing);
- paths through the control flow (for integration testing);
- types of test (e.g. white-box, black-box, performance, stress etc).

The description should provide the rationale for test-case selection and the packaging of test cases into procedures. The method for analysing test results should be identified (e.g. compare with expected output, compare with old results, proof of consistency etc).

The tools required to support testing should be identified.

5.7.2.4 SVVP/AT/2.n.4 Test case identification

This section should list the test cases associated with the design and give a brief description of each.

5.7.2.5 SVVP/AT/2.n.5 Feature pass/fail criteria

This section should specify the criteria to be used to decide whether the feature or feature combination has passed or failed.

5.7.3. SVVP/AT/3 TEST CASE SPECIFICATION

5.7.3.1 SVVP/AT/3.n.1 Test Case identifier

The title of this section should specify the test case uniquely. The content of this section should briefly describe the test case.

5.7.3.2 SVVP/AT/3.n.2 Test items

This section should identify the test items. References to other software documents should be supplied to help understand the purpose of the test items, how they work and how they are operated.

5.7.3.3 SVVP/AT/3.n.3 Input specifications

This section should specify the inputs required to execute the test case. File names, parameter values and user responses are possible types of input specification. This section should not duplicate information held elsewhere (e.g. in test data files).

5.7.3.4 SVVP/AT/3.n.4 Output specifications

This section should specify the outputs expected from executing the test case relevant to deciding upon pass or failure. File names and system messages are possible types of output specification. This section should not duplicate information held elsewhere (e.g. in log files).

5.7.3.5 SVVP/AT/3.n.5 Environmental needs

5.7.3.5.1 SVVP/AT/3.n.5.1 Hardware

This section should specify the characteristics and configurations of the hardware required to execute this test case.

5.7.3.5.2 SVVP/AT/3.n.5.2 Software

This section should specify the system and application software required to execute this test case.

5.7.3.5.3 SVVP/AT/3.n.5.3 Other

This section should specify any other requirements such as special equipment or specially trained personnel.

5.7.3.6 SVVP/AT/3.n.6 Special procedural requirements

This section should describe any special constraints on the test procedures that execute this test case.

5.7.3.7 SVVP/AT/3.n.7 Intercase dependencies

This section should list the identifiers of test cases that must be executed before this test case. The nature of the dependencies should be summarised.

5.7.4 SVVP/AT/4 TEST PROCEDURES

5.7.4.1 SVVP/AT/4.n.1 Test Procedure identifier

The title of this section should specify the test procedure uniquely. This section should reference the related test design.

5.7.4.2 SVVP/AT/4.n.2 Purpose

This section should describe the purpose of this procedure. A reference for each test case the test procedure uses should be given.

5.7.4.3 SVVP/AT/4.n.3 Special requirements

This section should identify any special requirements for the execution of this procedure.

5.7.4.4 SVVP/AT/4.n.4 Procedure steps

This section should include the steps described in the subsections below as applicable.

5.7.4.4.1 SVVP/AT/4.n.4.1 Log

This section should describe any special methods or formats for logging the results of test execution, the incidents observed, and any other events pertinent to the test.

5.7.4.4.2 SVVP/AT/4.n.4.2 Set up

This section should describe the sequence of actions necessary to prepare for execution of the procedure.

5.7.4.4.3 SVVP/AT/4.n.4.3 Start

This section should describe the actions necessary to begin execution of the procedure.

5.7.4.4.4 SVVP/AT/4.n.4.4 Proceed

This section should describe the actions necessary during the execution of the procedure.

5.7.4.4.5 SVVP/AT/4.n.4.5 Measure

This section should describe how the test measurements will be made.

5.7.4.4.6 SVVP/AT/4.n.4.6 Shut down

This section should describe the actions necessary to suspend testing when interruption is forced by unscheduled events.

5.7.4.4.7 SVVP/AT/4.n.4.7 Restart

This section should identify any procedural restart points and describe the actions necessary to restart the procedure at each of these points.

5.7.4.4.8 SVVP/AT/4.n.4.8 Stop

This section should describe the actions necessary to bring execution to an orderly halt.

5.7.4.4.9 SVVP/AT/4.n.4.9 Wrap up

This section should describe the actions necessary to terminate testing.

5.7.4.4.10 SVVP/AT/4.n.4.10 Contingencies

This section should describe the actions necessary to deal with anomalous events that may occur during execution.

5.7.5 SVVP/AT/5 TEST REPORTS

5.7.5.1 SVVP/AT/5.n.1 Test Report identifier

The title of this section should specify the test report uniquely.

5.7.5.2 SVVP/AT/5.n.2 Description

This section should identify the items being tested including their version numbers. The attributes of the environment in which testing was conducted should be identified.

5.7.5.3 SVVP/AT/5.n.3 Activity and event entries

This section should define the start and end time of each activity or event. The author should be identified.

One or more of the descriptions in the following subsections should be included.

5.7.5.3.1 SVVP/AT/5.n.3.1 Execution description

This section should identify the test procedure being executed and supply a reference to its specification.

The people who witnessed each event should be identified.

5.7.5.3.2 SVVP/AT/5.n.3.2 Procedure results

For each execution, this section should record the visually observable results (e.g. error messages generated, aborts and requests for operator action). The location of any output, and the result of the test, should be recorded.

5.7.5.3.3 SVVP/AT/5.n.3.3 Environmental information

This section should record any environmental conditions specific for this entry, particularly deviations from the normal.

5.8 EVOLUTION

5.8.1 UR phase

By the end of the UR review, the SR phase section of the SVVP must be produced (SVVP/SR) (SVV09). The SVVP/SR must define how to trace user requirements to software requirements so that each software requirement can be justified (SVV10). It should describe how the SRD is to be evaluated by defining the review procedures. The SVVP/SR may include specifications of the tests to be done with prototypes.

The initiator(s) of the user requirements should lay down the principles upon which the acceptance tests should be based. The developer must construct an acceptance test plan in the UR phase and document it in the SVVP (SVV11). This plan should define the scope, approach, resources and schedule of acceptance testing activities.

5.8.2 SR phase

During the SR phase, the AD phase section of the SVVP must be produced (SVVP/AD) (SVV12). The SVVP/AD must define how to trace software requirements to components, so that each software component can be justified (SVV13). It should describe how the ADD is to be evaluated by defining the review procedures. The SVVP/AD may include specifications of the tests to be done with prototypes.

During the SR Phase, the developer analyses the user requirements and may insert 'acceptance testing requirements' in the SRD. These requirements constrain the design of the acceptance tests. This must be recognised in the statement of the purpose and scope of the acceptance tests.

The planning of the system tests should proceed in parallel with the definition of the software requirements. The developer may identify 'verification requirements' for the software. These are additional constraints on the unit, integration and system testing activities. These requirements are also stated in the SRD.

The developer must construct a system test plan in the SR phase and document it in the SVVP (SVV14). This plan should define the scope, approach, resources and schedule of system testing activities.

5.8.3 AD phase

During the AD phase, the DD phase section of the SVVP must be produced (SVVP/DD) (SVV15). The SVVP/AD must describe how the DDD and code are to be evaluated by defining the review and traceability procedures (SVV16).

The developer must construct an integration test plan in the AD phase and document it in the SVVP (SVV17). This plan should describe the scope, approach, resources and schedule of intended integration tests. Note that the items to be integrated are the software components described in the ADD.

5.8.4 DD phase

In the DD phase, the SVVP sections on testing are developed as the detailed design and implementation information become available.

The developer must construct a unit test plan in the DD phase and document it in the SVVP (SVV18). This plan should describe the scope, approach, resources and schedule of the intended unit tests.

The test items are the software components described in the DDD.

The unit, integration, system and acceptance test designs must be described in the SVVP (SVV19). These should specify the details of the test approach for a software feature, or combination of software features, and identify the associated test cases and test procedures.

The unit integration, system and acceptance test cases must be described in the SVVP (SVV20). These should specify the inputs, predicted results and execution conditions for a test case.

The unit, integration, system and acceptance test procedures must be described in the SVVP (SVV21). These should provide a step-by-step description of how to carry out each test case.

The unit, integration, system and acceptance test reports must be contained in the SVVP (SVV22).

APPENDIX A
GLOSSARY

A.1 LIST OF TERMS

Definitions of SVV terms are taken from IEEE Standard Glossary of Software Engineering Terminology ANSI/IEEE Std 610.12-1990 [Ref 3]. If no suitable definition is found in the glossary, the definition is taken from a referenced text or the Concise Oxford Dictionary.

acceptance testing
Formal testing conducted to determine whether or not a system satisfies its acceptance criteria (i.e. the user requirements) to enable the customer (i.e. initiator) to determine whether or not to accept the system [Ref 3].

assertion
A logical expression specifying a program state that must exist or a set of conditions that program variables must satisfy at a particular point during program execution [Ref 3].

audit
An independent examination of a work product or set of work products to assess compliance with specifications, baselines, standards, contractual agreements or other criteria [Ref 3].

back-to-back test
Back-to-back tests execute two or more variants of a program with the same inputs. The outputs are compared, and any discrepancies are analysed to check whether or not they indicate a fault [Ref 3].

comparator
A software tool that compares two computer programs, files, or sets of data to identify commonalities and differences [Ref 3].

component
One of the parts that make up a system [Ref 3]. A component may be a module, a unit or a subsystem. This definition is similar to that used in Reference 1 and more general than the one in Reference 2.

critical design review
A review conducted to verify that the detailed design of one or more configuration items satisfies specified requirements [Ref 3]. Critical design reviews must be held in the DD

phase to review the detailed design of a major component to certify its readiness for implementation (DD10).

decision table
A table used to show sets of conditions and the actions resulting from them [Ref 3].

defect
An instance in which a requirement is not satisfied [Ref 19].

driver
A software module that invokes and, perhaps, controls and monitors the execution of one or more other software modules [Ref 3].

dynamic analysis
The process of evaluating a computer program based upon its behaviour during execution [Ref 3].

formal
Used to describe activities that have explicit and definite rules of procedure (e.g. formal review) or reasoning (e.g. formal method and formal proof).

formal review
A review that has explicit and definite rules of procedure such as a technical review, walkthrough or software inspection [Ref 1].

inspection
A static analysis technique that relies on visual examination of development products to detect errors, violations of development standards, and other problems [Ref 3]. Same as 'software inspection'.

integration
The process of combining software elements, hardware elements or both into an overall system [Ref 3].

integration testing
Testing in which software components, hardware components, or both are combined and tested to evaluate the interaction between them [Ref 3]. In *Software Engineering Standards*, the lowest level software elements tested during integration are the lowest level components of the architectural design.

module
A program unit that is discrete and identifiable with respect to compiling, combining with other units, and loading; for example the input or output from a compiler or linker; also a logically separable part of a program [Ref 3].

regression test
Selective retesting of a system or component to verify that modifications have not caused unintended effects and that the system or component still complies with its specified requirements [Ref 3].

review
A process or meeting during which a work product, or set of work products, is presented to project personnel, managers, users, customers, or other interested parties for comment or approval [Ref 3].

semantics
The relationships of symbols and groups of symbols to their meanings in a given language [Ref 3].

semantic analyser
A software tool that substitutes algebraic symbols into the program variables and present the results as algebraic formulae [Ref 14].

static analysis
The process of evaluating a system or component based on its form, structure, content or documentation [Ref 3].

stress test
A test that evaluates a system or software component at or beyond the limits of its specified requirements [Ref 3].

system
A collection of components organised to accomplish a specific function or set of functions [Ref 3]. A system is composed of one or more subsystems.

subsystem
A secondary or subordinate system within a larger system [Ref 3]. A subsystem is composed of one or more units.

system testing
Testing conducted on a complete, integrated system to evaluate the system's compliance with its specified requirements [Ref 3].

test
An activity in which a system or component is executed under specified conditions, the results are observed or recorded, and an evaluation is made of some aspect of the system or component [Ref 3].

test case
A set of test inputs, execution conditions, and expected results developed for a particular objective, such as to exercise a particular program path or to verify compliance with a specified requirement [Ref 3].

test design
Documentation specifying the details of the test approach for a software feature or combination of software features and identifying associated tests [Ref 3].

test case generator
A software tool that accepts as input source code, test criteria, specifications, or data structure definitions; uses these inputs to generate test input data, and, sometimes, determines the expected results [Ref 3].

test coverage

The degree to which a given test or set of tests addresses all specified requirements for a given system or component [Ref 3]; the proportion of branches in the logic that have been traversed during testing.

test harness

A software module used to invoke a module under test and, often, provide test inputs, control and monitor execution, and report test results [Ref 3].

test plan

A document prescribing the scope, approach resources, and schedule of intended test activities [Ref 3].

test procedure

Detailed instructions for the setup, operation, and evaluation of the results for a given test [Ref 3].

test report

A document that describes the conduct and results of the testing carried out for a system or component [Ref 3].

testability

The degree to which a system or component facilitates the establishment of test criteria and the performance of tests to determine whether those criteria have been met [Ref 3].

tool

A computer program used in the development, testing, analysis, or maintenance of a program or its documentation [Ref 3].

tracing

The act of establishing a relationship between two or more products of the development process; for example, to establish the relationship between a given requirement and the design element that implements that requirement [Ref 3].

unit

A separately testable element specified in the design of a computer software component [Ref 3]. A unit is composed of one or more modules.

validation

The process of evaluating a system or component during or at the end of the development process to determine whether it satisfies specified requirements [Ref 3].

verification

The act of reviewing, inspecting, testing, checking, auditing, or otherwise establishing and documenting whether items, processes, services or documents conform to specified requirements [Ref 2].

walkthrough

A static analysis technique in which a designer or programmer leads members of the development team and other interested parties through a segment of documentation or code, and the participants ask questions and make comments about possible errors, violation of development standards, and other problems [Ref 3].

A.2   LIST OF ACRONYMS

AD	Architectural Design
AD/R	Architectural Design Review
ADD	Architectural Design Document
ANSI	American National Standards Institute
AT	Acceptance Test
BSSC	Board for Software Standardisation and Control
CASE	Computer Aided Software Engineering
DCR	Document Change Record
DD	Detailed Design and production
DD/R	Detailed Design and production Review
DDD	Detailed Design and production Document
ESA	European Space Agency
ICD	Interface Control Document
IEEE	Institute of Electrical and Electronics Engineers
IT	Integration Test
PSS	Procedures, Specifications and Standards
QA	Quality Assurance
RID	Review Item Discrepancy
SCMP	Software Configuration Management Plan
SCR	Software Change Request
SMR	Software Modification Report
SPR	Software Problem Report
SR	Software Requirements
SR/R	Software Requirements Review
SRD	Software Requirements Document
ST	System Test
SUT	Software Under Test
SVV	Software Verification and Validation
SVVP	Software Verification and Validation Plan
UR	User Requirements
UR/R	User Requirements Review
URD	User Requirements Document
UT	Unit Test

APPENDIX B
REFERENCES

1. Software Engineering Standards, C.Mazza, J.Fairclough, B.Melton, D.dePablo, A.Scheffer and R.Stevens, Prentice-Hall 1994.
2. ANSI/ASQC A3-1978, Quality Systems Terminology
3. IEEE Standard Glossary of Software Engineering Terminology, ANSI/IEEE Std 610.12-1990.
4. IEEE Standard for Software Test Documentation, ANSI/IEEE Std 829-1983.
5. IEEE Standard for Software Unit Testing, ANSI/IEEE Std 1008-1987.
6. IEEE Standard for Software Verification and Validation Plans, ANSI/IEEE Std 1012-1986.
7. IEEE Standard for Software Reviews and Audits, ANSI/IEEE Std 1028-1988.
8. Managing the Software Process, Watts S. Humphrey, SEI Series in Software Engineering, Addison-Wesley, August 1990.
9. Software Testing Techniques, B.Beizer, Van Nostrand Reinhold, 1983.
10. Structured Testing: A Software Testing Methodology Using the Cyclomatic Complexity Metric, T.J.McCabe, National Bureau of Standards Special Publication 500-99, 1982.
11. The Art of Software Testing, G.J.Myers, Wiley-Interscience, 1979.
12. Design Complexity Measurement and Testing, T.J.McCabe and C.W.Butler, Communications of the ACM, Vol 32, No 12, December 1989.
13. Software Engineering, I.Sommerville, Addison-Wesley, 1992.
14. The STARTs Guide - a guide to methods and software tools for the construction of large real-time systems, NCC Publications, 1987.
15. Engineering software under statistical quality control, R.H.Cobb and H.D.Mills, IEEE Software, 7 (6), 1990.
16. Dynamic Testing Tools, a Detailed Product Evaluation, S.Norman, Ovum, 1992.
17. Managing Computer Projects, R.Gibson, Prentice-Hall, 1992.
18. Design and Code Inspections to Reduce Errors in Program Development, M.E.Fagan, IBM Systems Journal, No 3, 1976
19. Advances in Software Inspections, M.E.Fagan, IEEE Transactions on Software Engineering, Vol. SE-12, No. 7, July 1986.
20. The Cleanroom Approach to Quality Software Development, Dyer, Wiley, 1992.

APPENDIX C
MANDATORY PRACTICES

This appendix is repeated from *Software Engineering Standards*, appendix D.10.

SVV01   Forward traceability requires that each input to a phase shall be traceable to an output of that phase.

SVV02   Backward traceability requires that each output of a phase shall be traceable to an input to that phase.

SVV03   Functional and physical audits shall be performed before the release of the software.

SVV04   All software verification and validation activities shall be documented in the Software Verification and Validation Plan (SVVP).

The SVVP shall ensure that the verification activities:

SVV05   • are appropriate for the degree of criticality of the software;

SVV06   • meet the verification and acceptance testing requirements (stated in the SRD);

SVV07   • verify that the product will meet the quality, reliability, maintainability and safety requirements (stated in the SRD);

SVV08   • are sufficient to assure the quality of the product.

SVV09   By the end of the UR review, the SR phase section of the SVVP shall be produced (SVVP/SR).

SVV10   The SVVP/SR shall define how to trace user requirements to software requirements, so that each software requirement can be justified.

SVV11   The developer shall construct an acceptance test plan in the UR phase and document it in the SVVP.

SVV12   During the SR phase, the AD phase section of the SVVP shall be produced (SVVP/AD).

SVV13   The SVVP/AD shall define how to trace software requirements to components, so that each software component can be justified.

SVV14   The developer shall construct a system test plan in the SR phase and document it in the SVVP.

SVV15   During the AD phase, the DD phase section of the SVVP shall be produced (SVVP/DD).

SVV16   The SVVP/AD shall describe how the DDD and code are to be evaluated by defining the review and traceability procedures.

SVV17   The developer shall construct an integration test plan in the AD phase and document it in the SVVP.

SVV18   The developer shall construct a unit test plan in the DD phase and document it in the SVVP.

SVV19   The unit, integration, system and acceptance test designs shall be described in the SVVP.

SVV20   The unit integration, system and acceptance test cases shall be described in the SVVP.

SVV21   The unit, integration, system and acceptance test procedures shall be described in the SVVP.

SVV22   The unit, integration, system and acceptance test reports shall be described in the SVVP.

APPENDIX D
INDEX

Guide to software quality assurance

TABLE OF CONTENTS

CHAPTER 1
INTRODUCTION

1.1 PURPOSE

Software Engineering Standards [Ref 1] requires that all software projects assure that products and procedures conform to standards and plans. This is called 'Software Quality Assurance' (SQA). Projects must define their software quality assurance activities in a Software Quality Assurance Plan (SQAP).

This guide defines and explains what software quality assurance is, provides guidelines on how to do it, and defines in detail what a Software Quality Assurance Plan should contain.

Everyone who is concerned with software quality should read this guide, i.e. software project managers, software engineers and software quality assurance personnel.

1.2 OVERVIEW

Chapter 2 contains a general discussion of the principles of Software Quality Assurance, expanding upon *Software Engineering Standards*. Chapter 3 describes how to write the SQAP, in particular how to fill out the document template.

All the mandatory practices in *Software Engineering Standards* that apply to software quality assurance are repeated in this document. The identifier of the practice in parentheses marks a repetition. Practices that apply to other chapters of *Software Engineering Standards* are referenced in the same way. This document contains no new mandatory practices.

CHAPTER 2
SOFTWARE QUALITY ASSURANCE

2.1 INTRODUCTION

Software Engineering Standards defines Software Quality Assurance (SQA) as a 'planned and systematic pattern of all actions necessary to provide adequate confidence that the item or product conforms to established technical requirements'. SQA does this by checking that:

- plans are defined according to standards;
- procedures are performed according to plans;
- products are implemented according to standards.

A procedure defines how an activity will be conducted. Procedures are defined in plans, such as a Software Configuration Management Plan. A product is a deliverable to a customer. Software products are code, user manuals and technical documents, such as an Architectural Design Document. Examples of product standards are design and coding standards, and the standard document templates in *Software Engineering Standards*.

SQA is not the only checking activity in a project. Whereas SQA checks procedures against plans and output products against standards, Software Verification and Validation (SVV) checks output products against input products. Figure 2.1A illustrates the difference.

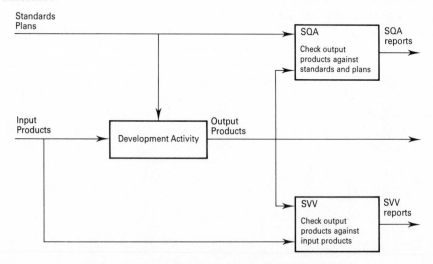

Figure 2.1A: Differences between SQA and SVV

Complete checking is never possible, and the amount required depends upon the type of project. All projects must do some checks. Projects developing safety-critical software should be checked more rigorously.

SQA must plan what checks to do early in the project. The most important selection criterion for software quality assurance planning is risk. Common risk areas in software development are novelty, complexity, staff capability, staff experience, manual procedures and organisational maturity.

SQA staff should concentrate on those items that have a strong influence on product quality. They should check as early as possible that the:

- project is properly organised, with an appropriate life cycle;
- development team members have defined tasks and responsibilities;
- documentation plans are implemented;
- documentation contains what it should contain;
- documentation and coding standards are followed;
- standards, practices and conventions are adhered to;
- metric data is collected and used to improve products and processes;
- reviews and audits take place and are properly conducted;
- tests are specified and rigorously carried out;
- problems are recorded and tracked;
- projects use appropriate tools, techniques and methods;
- software is stored in controlled libraries;
- software is stored safely and securely;
- software from external suppliers meets applicable standards;
- proper records are kept of all activities;
- staff are properly trained;
- risks to the project are minimised.

Project management is responsible for the organisation of SQA activities, the definition of SQA roles and the allocation of staff to those roles.

Within a project, different groups have their own characteristic requirements for SQA. Project management needs to know that the software is built according to the plans and procedures it has defined. Development personnel need to know that their work is of good quality and meets the standards. Users should get visibility of SQA activities, so that they will be assured that the product will be fit for its purpose.

The effective management of a project depends upon the control loop shown in Figure 2.1B.

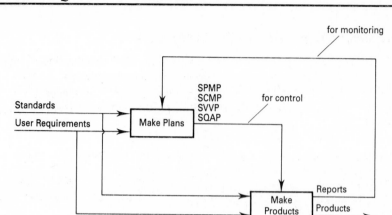

Figure 2.1B: Management control loop

SQA staff make a critical contribution to both control and monitoring activities in the management of a project by:

- writing the SQAP;
- reviewing the SPMP, SCMP and SVVP;
- advising project management on how to apply the standards to planning;
- advising development staff on how to apply the standards to production tasks;
- reporting to the development organisation's management about the implementation of plans and adherence to standards.

The project manager supervises the work of the development staff, and normally carries out the SQA role in small projects (two man years or less). In large projects (twenty man-years or more), specialist personnel should be dedicated to the SQA role because of the amount of work required. It is normal for the SQA staff to report to both the project manager and the corporate SQA manager.

On some projects, SQA functions may be performed in parallel by a separate team, independent of the development organisation, which reports directly to the user or customer. Such teams should have their own SQAP.

In a multi-contractor project, the SQA staff of the prime contractor oversee the activities of the subcontractors by participating in reviews and conducting audits.

The rest of this chapter discusses the software quality assurance activities required in each life cycle phase. As verifying conformance to *Software Engineering Standards* is the primary SQA task, each section discusses all the mandatory practices for the phase from the SQA point of view. Each practice is marked in parentheses and indexed for ease of reference. Management practices that are of special importance in the phase are also included. Each section is therefore an annotated SQA checklist for a life cycle phase. The guidelines should be used to prepare the SQAP for each phase.

In each phase, SQA staff should prepare a report of their activities in time for the formal review (SR/R, AD/R, DD/R). The report should cover all the activities described in the SQAP and should contain recommendations about the readiness to proceed. SQA may also prepare interim reports during the phase to bring concerns to the attention of management.

2.2 USER REQUIREMENTS DEFINITION PHASE

Software quality assurance staff should be involved in a software development project at the earliest opportunity. They should check the user requirements and plans for conformance to standards. These documents have a strong influence on the whole development, and it is extremely cost-effective for any problems in them to be identified and corrected as early as possible.

2.2.1 Checking technical activities

The user requirements document is the users' input to the project. The users are responsible for it (UR01), and SQA should not permit a software development project to start until it has been produced (UR10, UR11).

SQA staff should check the URD for conformance to standards by reading the whole document. They should look for a general description of the software (UR12). This must contain a step-by-step account of what the user wants the software to do (UR14). The URD must also contain specific requirements with identifiers, need attributes, priority attributes and references to sources (UR02, UR03, UR04 UR05). The URD should contain all the known user requirements (UR13). To confirm completeness, SQA should look for evidence of requirements capture activities such as surveys and interviews.

SQA should check that users have stated in the URD all the constraints they want to impose on the software, such as portability, availability and usability (UR15). The URD must also describe all the external interfaces, or reference them in Interface Control Documents (UR16). External interfaces constrain the design.

The user requirements must be verifiable (UR06). The acceptance test plan defines the scope and approach towards validation, and SQA staff should check that the plan will allow the user requirements to be validated. This plan is documented in the Software Verification and Validation Plan, Acceptance Test section (SVVP/AT).

An important responsibility of SQA staff is to check that the user has described the consequences of losses of availability or breaches of security (UR07). This is needed if the developers are to fully appreciate the criticality of each function.

At the end of the phase the URD is reviewed at the formal user requirements review (UR08). SQA staff should take part in the review, and check that the proper procedures are observed. The review may decide that some requirements should not be made applicable. Such requirements must be clearly flagged in the URD (UR09). They should not be deleted, as they indicate to developers where future growth potential may be needed.

2.2.2 Checking the management plans

Four plans must be produced by the developers by the end of the user requirements review to define how the development will be managed in the SR phase. These are the:
- Software Project Management Plan (SPMP/SR) (SPM02);
- Software Configuration Management Plan (SCMP/SR) (SCM42);
- Software Verification and Validation Plan (SVVP/SR) (SVV09);
- Software Quality Assurance Plan (SQAP/SR) (SQA03).

SQA staff must produce the SQAP/SR. They also need to review the other plans to check that they conform to standards. The SQAP/SR also outlines SQA activities for the whole of the project.

The same structure is used for each plan in every phase of the project. The importance of different parts of the structure varies with the phase. The rest of this section picks out the parts of each plan that are important for the SQA activities in the SR phase.

2.2.2.1 Software project management plan

Every project must produce a software project management plan (SPM01). The plan should declare the objectives of the project. These may take the form of statements of deliverables and delivery dates, or of statements of required functionality, performance and quality. The objectives should be prioritised. SQA staff should examine the statement of objectives and check that all plans are consistent with them.

The plan should describe all the SR phase activities and contain a precise estimate of the SR phase cost (SPM04). The plan should outline activities in the remaining phases (SPM03) and estimate the total cost of the project.

The plan should define the life cycle approach to be used in the project, such as waterfall, incremental delivery or evolutionary. The choice of life cycle approach is crucial to the success of the project. SQA should check that the life cycle approach is appropriate and has been correctly tailored to the project.

A 'process model', based upon the selected life cycle approach should be described in the plan. The process model defines all the major activities. For each activity it should define:

- entry criteria;
- inputs;
- tasks;
- outputs;
- exit criteria.

SQA staff should check the model for consistency. Common problems are documents with no destination, impossible entry criteria and the absence of exit criteria (e.g. successful review).

SQA should check that the plan is sufficient to minimise the risks on the project. For example prototyping is an important risk reduction activity, especially when the project is developing novel software.

SQA should check that the project management plan is realistic. The plan should explicitly declare the:

- assumptions made in planning (e.g. feasibility);
- dependencies upon external events (e.g. supplier delivery);
- constraints on the plan (e.g. availability of staff).

All plans make assumptions, have dependencies, and are subject to constraints. SQA should check that the assumptions, dependencies and constraints have been addressed in the risk analysis.

Quantitative measures (metrics) are important for evaluating project performance [Ref 5]. SQA should check that any metrics proposed in plans are appropriate.

2.2.2.2 Software configuration management plan

SQA need to check that the development of the software is properly controlled. Each project defines the control procedures in the SCMP, before the production starts (SCM41). SQA should verify that they are properly defined and carried out. Examples of poor software configuration management planning are:

- no SCMP;
- an incomplete SCMP;
- no-one with overall responsibility for SCM;
- no identification conventions;
- no change control procedures;
- inefficient change control procedures;
- no approval procedures;
- no storage procedures;
- no mechanisms for tracking changes.

Documents are the primary output of the SR phase. The software configuration management plan for the phase must describe the documentation configuration management procedures. These should be flexible enough to be usable throughout the project. Key aspects that must be addressed are:

- document identification;
- document storage;
- document change control;
- document status accounting.

All relevant project documentation must be uniquely identified (SCM06). Document identifiers should include the company name, the project name, the document type, the document number and/or name, and the document version number (SCM07, SCM08, SCM09, SCM10). The identification scheme must be extensible (SCM11). Every page of the document should be marked with the identifier. SQA staff should check that all project documents have been included in the configuration identification scheme. One way to do this is to examine the process model and decide what kind of documents are input to and output from each activity in the model.

Multiple versions of documents will be generated during a project. A copy of the current issue of every project document must be stored in the master library. Another copy must be archived. SQA staff check that master and archive libraries are complete by performing physical audits.

Software Engineering Standards defines the Review Item Discrepancy (RID) procedure for document change control (SCM29). This procedure must be used for reporting problems in documents that undergo formal review. SQA should confirm that all problems discovered during formal review are reported on RID forms and processed by the review.

Document status accounting includes the management of the RID status information (one of CLOSE/UPDATE/ACTION/REJECT). Hundreds of RIDs can be generated on small projects. Large projects, with many reviewers, can produce thousands. Tool support for analysing and reporting RID status is therefore usually needed. SQA staff should ensure that the RID status accounting system is efficient, accurate and gives good visibility of status.

The software configuration management plan should address the identification, storage, control and status accounting of CASE tool outputs, such as files containing design information (SCM43). Plans for the configuration management of prototype software should also be made. Key project decisions may turn upon the results of prototyping, and SQA staff should ensure that the prototypes can be trusted. Poor configuration management of prototypes can cause spurious results.

2.2.2.3 Software verification and validation plan

By the end of the UR phase, the software verification and validation plan needs to include:

- a plan for verifying the outputs of the SR phase;
- an acceptance test plan (SVV11).

Verification techniques used in the SR phase include reviewing, formal proof and tracing. Plans for reviews should include intermediate and formal reviews. Intermediate reviews are used to verify products, and later to clear up problems before formal review. The primary formal review is the Software Requirements Review (SR/R).

SQA should examine the software verification and validation plan and check that the review procedures are well-defined, the right people are involved, and that enough reviews are held. Documents that have not been reviewed are just as likely to contain problems as code that has not been tested.

SQA staff should examine the software verification and validation plan and check that the verification approach is sufficiently rigorous to assure the correctness of the software requirements document. Formal methods for specification and verification of software are often necessary when safety and security issues are involved.

The software verification and validation plan needs to define how user requirements will be traced to software requirements. SQA staff often have to check the traceability matrix later in the project, and it is important that traceability procedures are easy to use.

The acceptance test plan must be produced as soon as the URD is available (SVV11). Although the level of detail required depends upon the project, all plans should define the approach to validating the user requirements. SQA staff should check that the plan is sufficiently detailed to allow estimation of the effort required for acceptance testing. Overlooking the need for expensive items of test equipment, such as a simulator, is all too common.

2.3 SOFTWARE REQUIREMENTS DEFINITION PHASE

Software quality assurance staff's primary responsibility in the SR phase is to check that the planned activities are carried out (SR01).

2.3.1 Checking technical activities

All projects should adopt a recognised method for software requirements analysis that is appropriate for the project, and then apply it consistently. The best sign of recognition of a method is publication in a book or journal. All methods should produce a 'logical model' that expresses the logic of the system without using implementation terminology, such as 'record', 'file' or 'event flag', to describe how the software will work (SR02, SR15, SR16, SR17).

Modelling is an essential technical activity in the SR phase and SQA should check that modelling is being done. SQA should check at the beginning of the phase that:

- an analysis method will be used;
- staff have used the analysis method before, or will receive training;
- the analysis method can be supported with CASE tools.

SQA should check that methods, tools and techniques are being properly applied. An important reason for using a tool is that it enforces the correct use of the method. Even though using a tool can slow the creative stages, it pays off in the long run by minimising the amount of work that needs to be redone because rules were broken. CASE tools are not mandatory, but they are strongly recommended.

Techniques such as:

- Failure Modes, Effects and Criticality Analysis (FMECA);
- Common Mode Failure Analysis (CMFA);
- Fault Tree Analysis (FTA);
- Hazard Analysis;

may be employed by developers to verify that software will meet requirements for reliability, maintainability and safety [Ref 8]. The role of SQA is to check that appropriate analysis methods have been properly applied. SQA may introduce requirements for quality, reliability, maintainability and safety based upon the results of the analysis.

The software requirements should specify metrics for measuring quality, reliability (e.g. MTBF), and maintainability (e.g. MTTR). Additional quality-related metrics may be defined by the project. Values of complexity metrics may be defined in the quality requirements to limit design complexity for example.

The Software Requirements Document (SRD) is the primary product of the SR phase (SR10). SQA should read the whole document and check that it has the structure and contents required by the standards (SR18). The general description section should contain the logical model, and SQA should check that it conforms to the rules of the method. If no CASE tool has been used, SQA should check the consistency of the model. An unbalanced data flow can give rise to an interface problem at a later stage, for example. During the intermediate review process, SQA should help analysts make the model understandable to non-experts.

Each requirement in the specific requirements section needs to have an identifier, for traceability (SR04), a flag marking it as essential or desirable (SR05), a flag marking priority (SR06), and references to the URD (SR07). The requirements should be structured according to the logical model.

The SRD needs to be complete, consistent and cover all the requirements in the URD (SR11, SR12, and SR14). SQA should verify completeness by checking the traceability matrix in the SRD (SR13).

The software requirements must be verifiable (SR08). Developers check verifiability by examining each specific requirement and deciding whether it can be verified by testing. If a requirement cannot be tested, other methods, such as inspection or formal proof, must be found. The system test plan defines the scope and approach towards verification of the SRD. This plan is documented in the Software Verification and Validation Plan, System Test section (SVVP/ST). SQA should check that the SVVP/ST defines, in outline, how the software requirements will be verified.

At the end of the phase the SRD is reviewed at the formal software requirements review (SR09). SQA staff should take part in the review, and check that the proper procedures are observed.

2.3.2 Checking the management plans

During the SR phase, four plans must be produced by the developers to define how the development will be managed in the AD phase. These are the:

- Software Project Management Plan (SPMP/AD) (SPM05);
- Software Configuration Management Plan (SCMP/AD) (SCM44);
- Software Verification and Validation Plan (SVVP/AD) (SVV12);
- Software Quality Assurance Plan (SQAP/AD) (SQA06).

SQA staff must produce the SQAP/AD. They also need to review the other plans to check that they conform to standards. The rest of this section picks out the parts of each plan that are important for the AD phase.

2.3.2.1 Software project management plan

In most respects, the SPMP/AD will resemble the SPMP/SR. SQA staff should check that the plan analyses the risks to the project and devotes adequate resources to them. Experimental prototyping may be required for the demonstration of feasibility, for example.

The plan should describe all the AD phase activities and contain a precise estimate of the AD phase cost (SPM07). The most important new component of the plan is the refined cost estimate for the whole project (SPM06). Using the logical model, managers should be able to produce a cost estimate accurate to 30%. SQA staff should check that the cost estimate has been obtained methodically and includes all the necessary development activities. Possible methods include using historical cost data from similar projects, and Albrecht's function point analysis method [Ref 6].

Projects with few technical risks should require little or no experimental prototyping. Accurate cost estimates should therefore be possible. SQA staff should check that there is no discrepancy between the amount of prototyping planned and accuracy of cost estimates.

2.3.2.2 Software configuration management plan

Software configuration management procedures in the AD phase are normally similar to the those used in the SR phase. New procedures might be necessary for the CASE tools used for design, however.

2.3.2.3 Software verification and validation plan

The software verification and validation plan needs to be extended during the SR phase to include:

- a plan for verifying the outputs of the AD phase;

- a system test plan (SVV14).

Verification techniques used in the AD phase are similar to the SR phase. Intermediate reviews are used to agree the design layer by layer, and to clear up problems in the ADD before formal review. The primary formal review is the Architectural Design Review (AD/R).

The system test plan must be produced as soon as the SRD is available (SVV14). Although the level of detail required depends upon the project, all plans should define the approach to verifying the software requirements. Implementation of the verification requirements in the SRD should be considered in the plan.

2.4 ARCHITECTURAL DESIGN PHASE

Software quality assurance staff's primary responsibility in the AD phase is to check that the planned activities are carried out (AD01).

2.4.1 Checking technical activities

A recognised method for software design shall be adopted and applied consistently in the AD phase (AD02). This method must support the construction of 'physical model' that defines how the software works (AD03). The method used to decompose the software into its components must permit a top-down approach (AD04).

Just as in the SR phase, SQA should check at the beginning of the phase that:
- an appropriate design method will be used;
- the developers have used the design method before, or will receive training;
- the design method can be supported with CASE tools;
- the lowest level of the architectural design has been agreed.

The architectural design should be reviewed layer-by-layer as it is developed. SQA should attend these intermediate reviews to help, for example:
- prevent the design becoming too complex to test;
- check that feasibility of each major component has been proven;
- ensure that the design will be reliable, maintainable and safe.

SQA should check that design quality has been optimised using the guidelines in the *Guide to the Software Architectural Design Phase*.

The primary output of the AD phase is the Architectural Design Document (ADD) (AD19). Although several designs may have been considered in the AD phase, only one design should be presented (AD05). Records of the investigation of alternatives should have been retained for inclusion in the Project History Document.

SQA should check that the ADD defines the functions, inputs and outputs of all the major components of the software (AD06, AD07, AD08, AD17). The ADD must also contain definitions of the data structures that interface components (AD09, AD10, AD11, AD12, AD13, AD18), or reference them in Interface Control Documents (ICDs). The ADD must define the control flow between the components (AD14).

The ADD must define the computer resources needed (AD15). Trade-offs should have been performed during the AD phase to define them. Prototyping may have been required. SQA staff should look for evidence that the resource estimates have been obtained methodically.

The ADD gives everyone on the project visibility of the system as a whole. SQA staff have a special responsibility to ensure that the designers make the document easy to understand. They should review the whole ADD and familiarise themselves with the design. This will improve their effectiveness during the DD phase.

The ADD needs to be complete (AD20) and should include a cross-reference matrix tracing software requirements to components (AD21). SQA should check this table, and that the ADD contains the standard contents (AD24), to confirm completeness. SQA staff should confirm that the ADD has been checked for inconsistencies (AD22), such as mismatched interfaces. The checks need to be very thorough when CASE tools have not been used. The ADD needs to be detailed enough for subgroups of developers to be able to work independently in the DD phase (AD23). The functions of major components and their interfaces need to be well defined for this to be possible.

At the end of the phase the ADD is reviewed at the formal architectural design review (AD16). SQA staff should take part in the review, and check that the proper procedures are observed.

2.4.2 Checking the management plans

During the AD phase, four plans must be produced by the developers to define how the development will be managed in the DD phase. These are the:
- Software Project Management Plan (SPMP/DD)(SPM08);
- Software Configuration Management Plan (SCMP/DD)(SCM46);
- Software Verification and Validation Plan (SVVP/DD) (SVV15);
- Software Quality Assurance Plan (SQAP/DD) (SQA08).

SQA staff must produce the SQAP/DD. They also need to review the other plans to check that they conform to standards. The rest of this section picks out the parts of each plan that are important for the DD phase.

2.4.2.1 Software project management plan

The software project management plan for the DD phase is larger and more complex than SR and AD phase plans because:
- most of the development effort is expended in the DD phase;
- software production work packages must not consume more than one man-month of effort (SPM12);
- parallel working is usually required.

The work-breakdown structure is based upon the component breakdown (SPM10). The level of detail required should result in a cost estimate that is accurate to 10% (SPM09).

SQA should check that the plan contains a network showing the relation of coding, integration and testing activities (SPM11). This network should have been optimised to make the best use of resources such as staff and computing equipment. SQA should check that the plan:
- defines a critical path showing the time required for completion of the phase;
- includes essential activities such as reviews;
- makes realistic estimates of the effort required for each activity (e.g. it is usual to spend at least half the time in the DD phase in testing);

- schedules SQA activities such as audits.

Projects should define criteria, ideally based upon software metrics, to help decide such issues as the readiness of:

- a software component for integration;
- the software for system testing;
- the software for delivery.

SQA should check that the management plan describes the criteria for making these decisions.

2.4.2.2 Software configuration management plan

The primary output of the DD phase is the code, and the software configuration management plan needs to be extended to cover:

- code identification;
- code storage;
- code change control;
- code status accounting.

An efficient configuration management system is vital to the success of the DD phase, and this system must be described in detail in the SCMP/DD (SCM02).

SQA staff should review the SCMP/DD to confirm that all software items, documentation, source code, object code, executable code, data files and test software, are covered by the plan (SCM01). The parts of the SCMP related to document handling can be carried over from earlier phases.

All code must be uniquely identified (SCM06). Identifiers must include the module name, type and version number (SCM07, SCM08, SCM09, SCM10, and SCM11). SQA staff should check that the names of configuration items reflect their purpose.

The SCMP should define the standard header for all source code modules (SCM15, SCM16, SCM17 SCM18). Documentation and storage media should be clearly labelled (SCM19, SCM20, SCM21 SCM22). Clear labelling is a sign of a well-run project. Poor labelling is readily apparent in a physical audit. SQA conduct physical audits to verify that the tangible software items such as disks, tapes and files are present and in their correct location.

The core of the software configuration management plan is the software library system (SCM23, SCM24, SCM25). The library procedures should be vetted by SQA to check that access to libraries is controlled (SCM26). SQA should check that software cannot be lost through simultaneous update.

The SCMP must contain a backup plan (SCM27, SCM28). All versions of software should be retained. SQA should check backup logs and stores in physical audits.

Good change control procedures are essential. SQA should examine these procedures and estimate the total time needed to process a change through the configuration management system. This time should be small compared with the time required to do the necessary technical work. If the change process is too time-consuming then there is a high probability of it breaking down at periods of stress, such as when a delivery is approaching. When this happens, configuration management problems will add to technical problems, increasing the pressure on developers. SQA staff should check that the configuration management system can handle the expected volume of change, and if necessary help make it more efficient. Special fast-track procedures may be required for urgent changes, for example.

Configuration status accounting is needed for the effective control of a project. It also gives customers and users visibility of problem tracking and corrective action. SQA should examine the configuration status accounting procedures and confirm that the evolution of baselines is tracked (SCM32, SCM33) and records are kept of the status of RIDs, SPRs, SCRs and SMRs (SCM34). SQA may define software quality metrics that use data in the configuration status accounts. Tools for monitoring quality attributes (e.g. fault rate, repair time) may use the accounts data.

SQA should monitor the execution of the procedures, described in the SCMP, and examine trends in problem occurrence. To make meaningful comparisons, SQA should check that problems are classified. A possible classification is:

- user error;
- user documentation error;
- coding error;
- design error;
- requirements specification error.

Problems may also be categorised by subsystem, or even software component. For each problem category, projects should record:

- number of problems reported;
- number of problems open;
- number of problems closed
- problem reporting rate;
- problem close-out time.

SQA should use these statistics to evaluate product quality and readiness for transfer.

2.4.2.3 Software verification and validation plan

The software verification and validation plan needs to be extended during the AD phase to include:

- a plan for verifying the outputs of the DD phase;
- an integration test plan (SVV17).

The techniques used to verify the detailed design are similar to those used in the AD phase. As before, intermediate reviews are used to agree the design layer by layer. The last review is the code inspection. This is done after modules have been successfully compiled but before unit testing. Peer review of code before unit testing has been shown to be very cost-effective. SQA staff should ensure that this vital step is not missed. Inspection metrics should include:

- lines of code per module;
- cyclomatic complexity per module;
- number of errors per module.

SQA should check that the values of these metrics are within the limits defined in the design and coding standards.

The primary formal review is the Detailed Design Review (DD/R). This is held at the end of the phase to decide whether the software is ready for transfer.

The integration test plan should be produced as soon as the ADD is available. The plan should define the integration approach, and should aim to put the major infrastructure functions in place as early as possible. Thereafter the integration plan should maximise the use of integrated software and minimise the use of test software that substitutes for components that are integrated later.

2.5 DETAILED DESIGN AND PRODUCTION PHASE

Software quality assurance staff's primary responsibility in the DD phase is to check that the planned activities are carried out (DD01).

2.5.1 Checking technical activities

2.5.1.1 Detailed design

Software Engineering Standards calls for the detailed design and production of software to be based upon the principles of top-down decomposition and structured programming (DD02, DD03). Technical staff should describe how they will implement these design practices in part 1 of the DDD. SQA should examine the DDD and check that the practices are implemented when they review the software.

SQA should check that the software is documented as it is produced (DD04). Documentation is often deferred when staff are under pressure, and this is always a mistake. SQA can ensure that documentation and production are concurrent by reviewing software as soon as it is produced. If SQA delay their review, developers may defer writing documentation until just before SQA are ready.

The detailed design should be reviewed layer-by-layer. These reviews should include technical managers and the designers concerned. When the design of a major component is finished, a critical design review of the relevant DDD sections must be held to decide upon its readiness for coding (DD10). SQA should attend some of these review meetings, especially when they relate to the implementation of quality, reliability, maintainability and safety requirements. SQA should also check that part 2 of the DDD is a logical extension of the structure defined in the ADD, and that there is a section for every software component (DD14).

2.5.1.2 Coding

SQA should inspect the code. This activity may be part of an inspection process used by development staff, or may be a standalone quality assurance activity. They should verify that the coding standards have been observed. The quality of code should be evaluated with the aid of standard metrics such as module length, complexity and comment rate. Static analysis tools should be used to support metric data collection and evaluation.

2.5.1.3 Reuse

The 'reuse' of software from project to project is increasingly common. SQA should check that the reused software was developed according to acceptable standards.

Software may be reliable in one operational environment but not in another. SQA should treat with extreme caution claims that the quality of reusable software is proven through successful operational use. SQA should check that the development and maintenance standards and records of the software make it fit for reuse.

Reused software is frequently purchased off-the-shelf. Such software is usually called 'commercial software'. SQA should check that the quality certification of the commercial software supplier meets the standards of the project.

2.5.1.4 Testing

Software that has not been tested is very unlikely to work. SQA have a vital role to play in reassuring management and the users that testing has been done properly. To do this, SQA should check that testing activities:

- are appropriate for the degree of criticality of the software (SVV05);
- comply with verification and acceptance testing requirements (stated in the SRD) (SVV06);
- are properly documented in the SVVP (SVV17, SVV18, SVV19, SVV20, SVV21, SVV22).

SQA carry out these checks by reviewing test specifications, observing tests being carried out, participating in selected tests, and reviewing the results. As part of this reviewing activity, SQA may request additions or modification to the test specifications.

Normally SQA will not be able to observe all the tests. The SQAP should identify the tests they intend to observe or participate in.

SQA should monitor the progress of the project through the results of tests. SQA should define a metrics programme that includes measures such as:

- number of failures;
- number of failures for each test;
- number of failures per test cycle.

Progress can be measured by a declining number of failures per test cycle (i.e. edit, compile, link, test).

The unit test plan should be written early in the DD phase (SVV18) and SQA should review it. They should check that its level of detail is consistent with the software quality, reliability and safety requirements. The first unit tests should be white-box tests because they give assurance that the software is performing its job in the way it was intended. When full coverage has been achieved (see below), black-box tests should be applied to verify functionality. Black-box tests should also be used to check for the occurrence of likely errors (e.g. invalid input data).

SQA should check that the unit test plan defines the coverage requirements. *Software Engineering Standards's* basic requirement is for full statement coverage (DD06). This is a minimum requirement. For most projects, full branch coverage should be achieved during unit testing [Ref 7]. This is because coverage verification requires the tester to trace the path of execution. Debuggers, dynamic testing tools and test harnesses are usually needed to do this, and are most conveniently applied during unit testing. SQA should examine the coverage records. Dynamic testing tools should be used to produce them.

The software verification and validation plan is expanded in the DD phase to include:

- unit, integration and system test designs (SVV19);
- unit, integration and system test cases (SVV20);

- unit, integration and system test procedures (SVV21).

Each test design may have several test cases. A test procedure should be defined for each test case. SQA should review all these extensions to the SVVP test sections.

An important SQA check is to confirm that enough test cases have been specified. When full branch coverage has been specified, SQA should check that the:

- number of test cases for each module is greater than or equal to the cyclomatic complexity of the module [Ref 7];
- paths traversed in the test cases actually result in every branch being traversed.

In applying these rules, a module is assumed to contain a single software component such as a FORTRAN subroutine or a PASCAL procedure. Path coverage should be done for a representative set of test cases. Complete checking is most efficiently done during the testing process with a dynamic testing tool.

There should be an integration test design for every interface (DD07). The test cases should vary the input data so that nominal and limit situations are explored. Integration tests should also exercise the control flows defined in the ADD (DD08).

The system tests must verify compliance with system objectives (DD09). There should be a system test design for each software requirement. System test cases should check for likely ways in which the system may fail to comply with the software requirement.

Test procedures should be written so that they can be executed by someone other than the software author. SQA should review the test procedures and confirm that they are self-explanatory.

The outcome of testing activities must be recorded (SVV22). Reviewing test results is an important SQA responsibility. SQA should check that the causes of test failures are diagnosed and corrective action taken. The problem reporting and corrective action mechanism should be invoked whenever a fault is detected in an item of software whose control authority is not the software author. Normally this means that SPRs are used to record problems discovered during integration testing and system testing. However SPRs also need to be used to record problems when unit tests are done by an independent SVV team.

SQA staff should ensure that failed tests are repeated after repairs have been made. SPRs cannot be closed until the tests that originated them have been passed.

Whereas the integration test plan defines the sequence for building the system from the major components, the software configuration management plan defines the procedures to be used when components are promoted to the master libraries for integration testing (DD05). SQA should check that control authority rights are formally transferred when each component is promoted. The usual means of formal notification is signing-off unit test results. SQA should also check that software authors cannot modify components that are stored in master libraries.

2.5.1.5 Formal review

Every project must hold a DD/R before delivering software to check readiness for transfer (DD11). SQA should participate in the review process and make recommendations based upon:

- test results;

- audit results;
- analysis of outstanding problems.

SQA should conduct a physical audit of the software by checking the configuration item list before transfer. The list should contain every deliverable software item specified in the project plan. The DDD, code and SUM must be included, as these are mandatory outputs of the phase (DD12, DD13 and DD17).

SQA should conduct a functional audit of the software by checking the software requirements versus software components traceability matrix in the DDD (DD16). This checks that the DDD is complete, and accounts for all software requirements (DD15). A second activity is to check that the SVVP/ST contains tests for every software requirement, and that these tests have been run. Functional audit activities should start as early as possible, as soon as the inputs, such as the DDD and test specifications, are available.

SQA's most important role at the DD/R is to analyse the trends in problem occurrence and repair, and advise management about readiness. SQA should categorise failures into major and minor. Major problems put provisional acceptance at risk. Using the records of SPRs in the configuration status accounts, SQA should estimate for each failure category:

- Mean Time Between Failures (MTBF);
- Mean Time To Repair (MTTR);
- number of outstanding problems;
- time required to repair the outstanding problems.

Using this data, management should be able to decide when the software will be ready for transfer. SQA should not approve the transfer of software with major problems outstanding.

2.5.2 Checking the management plans

During the DD phase, three plans must be produced by the developers to define how the development will be managed in the TR phase. These are the:

- Software Project Management Plan (SPMP/TR) (SPM13);
- Software Configuration Management Plan (SCMP/TR) (SCM48);
- Software Quality Assurance Plan (SQAP/TR) (SQA10).

In addition, the Software Verification and Validation Plan must be extended to define the acceptance tests in detail.

SQA staff must produce the SQAP/TR. They also need to review the other plans to check that they conform to standards. The rest of this section picks out the parts of each plan that are important for the TR phase.

2.5.2.1 Software project management plan

Customer confidence in software is greatly increased when the transfer phase is trouble-free. This is most likely when the installation and acceptance testing activities are carefully planned.

The transfer phase plan can be simple for a standalone product developed in the same environment as that used for operations. The software is installed and acceptance tests are run. SQA should check that both these activities have been rehearsed in the DD phase. These rehearsals should allow accurate estimation of TR phase effort.

When the software is to be embedded in a larger system or operated in a different environment, the transfer of software can be much more complicated. The acceptance tests check that the software integrates correctly with the target environment. Problems will always occur when software meets its target environment for the first time. Changes will be necessary and the software project management plan should allow for them.

SQA should check the SPMP/TR plan for realistic estimates for the testing and repair work. They should also check that key development staff will be retained during the phase so that new problems can be diagnosed and corrected quickly. The SPMP/TR should say who is to be involved during the phase. Users, development staff and SQA should attend acceptance tests.

2.5.2.2 Software configuration management plan

The SCMP/TR must define the software configuration management procedures for deliverables in the operational environment (SCM49). SQA should check that the SCMP/TR:

- identifies the deliverable items;
- defines procedures for the storage and backup of deliverables;
- defines the change control procedures;
- defines the problem reporting procedures.

Users may have to apply the procedures defined in the SCMP/TR. This section of the SCMP should be simple and easy to follow, and integrate well with the SUM and STD. SQA should confirm this.

The change control section of the SCMP/TR should include a definition of the terms of reference and procedures of the Software Review Board (SRB). SQA staff should be members of the SRB.

2.5.2.3 Software verification and validation plan

The SVVP is expanded in the DD phase to include test designs, test cases, test procedures and test results for unit tests, integration tests and systems tests, as discussed in Section 2.5.1.4. This section deals with the additions to the SVVP necessary for the TR phase.

During the DD phase, the Acceptance Test section of the Software Verification and Validation Plan (SVVP/AT) is extended to contain:

- acceptance test designs (SVV19);
- acceptance test cases (SVV20);
- acceptance test procedures (SVV21).

SQA should confirm that there is a test design for each user requirement. A test design versus user requirement cross-reference matrix may be inserted in the SVVP/AT to demonstrate compliance.

Test cases should be flagged for use in provisional or final acceptance (TR05). Some properties, such as reliability, may only be demonstrable after a period of operations.

Every project should rehearse the acceptance tests before the DD/R to confirm readiness for transfer. SQA should ensure that the rehearsals (often called 'dry runs') are done.

2.6 TRANSFER PHASE

Software quality assurance staff's primary responsibility in the TR phase is to check that the planned activities are carried out (TR03).

The first TR phase activity is to build the software. This should be done using the components directly modifiable by the maintenance team (TR04). The build procedures must have been defined in the Software Transfer Document (STD). After building, the software is installed using the procedures also defined in the STD. SQA should monitor the installation and build process.

The acceptance tests necessary for provisional acceptance are then run (TR05). SQA should check that the users are present to witness the acceptance tests, and that each test is signed off by developers and users (TR01).

A Software Review Board (SRB) meeting is held after the acceptance tests to review the software's performance and decide whether the software can be provisionally accepted (TR02). For the purposes of acceptance, the 'software' is the outputs of the SR, AD, DD and TR phases. Together with the URD, these outputs constitute the software system (TR07). SQA should attend this meeting. Three outcomes are possible:

- rejection of the software;
- unconditional provisional acceptance of the software;
- conditional provisional acceptance of the software.

The third outcome is the most common. Acceptance is made conditional upon the completion of actions defined by the SRB meeting. These 'close-out' actions usually include the completion of modifications found to be necessary during the acceptance tests.

SQA should check that the statement of provisional acceptance (TR06) is signed by the:

- initiator;
- project manager;
- project SQA manager.

The STD is a mandatory output of the TR phase and SQA should inspect it (TR08). The first STD inspection should be done at the beginning of the phase, before delivery. At this stage the STD contains sections listing the deliverables (i.e. configuration item list), installation procedures and build procedures. The second inspection should be done at the end of the TR phase when the sections describing the acceptance test results, software problem reports, software change requests and software modification results are added (TR10). The last step in the TR phase is the formal hand-over of the STD (TR09).

2.7 OPERATIONS AND MAINTENANCE PHASE

Good software can be ruined by poor maintenance. SQA should monitor software quality throughout the OM phase to check that it is not degraded. SQA should check that the:

- software configuration is properly managed (OM05);
- documentation and code are kept up-to-date (OM06);
- MTBF increases;
- MTTR decreases.

MTBF and MTTR should be regularly estimated from the data in the configuration status accounts.

The SRB authorises all modifications to the software (OM08). SQA should participate in SRB meetings and advise it on issues related to quality, reliability, maintainability and safety.

Development plans should cover the period up to final acceptance (OM01). All projects must have a final acceptance milestone (OM03). Before it arrives, SQA should check that:

- all acceptance tests have been successfully completed (OM02);
- the Project History Document is ready for delivery (OM10).
- SQA should check that the statement of final acceptance (OM09) is signed by the:
  - initiator;
  - project manager;
  - project SQA manager.

After final acceptance, an organisation must be defined to take over maintenance (OM04). SQA should check that the maintenance organisation is properly resourced (OM07). Estimates of the resource requirements should be based upon:

- MTBF;
- MTTR;
- size of the system;
- number of subsystems;
- type of system;
- usage pattern.

CHAPTER 3
THE SOFTWARE QUALITY ASSURANCE PLAN

3.1 INTRODUCTION

Plans for software quality assurance activities must be documented in the Software Quality Assurance Plan (SQAP) (SQA02). The first issue of the SQAP must be prepared by the end of the UR review. This issue must outline the SQA activities for the whole project and define in detail SR phase SQA activities (SQA04 SQA05). Sections of the SQAP must be produced for the AD, DD and TR phases (SQA06, SQA08, SQA10), to cover in detail all the SQA activities that will take place in those phases (SQA07, SQA09 SQA11).

The table of contents for each section is derived from the IEEE Standard for Software Quality Assurance Plans (ANSI/IEEE Std 730-1989) [Ref 3], which adds the proviso that the table of contents 'should not be construed to prohibit additional content in the SQAP'. The size and content of the SQAP should reflect the complexity of the project. Additional guidelines on the completion of an SQAP can be found in IEEE Guide for Software Quality Assurance Plans (ANSI/IEEE Std 983-1989) [Ref 4].

3.2 STYLE

The SQAP should be plain and concise. The document should be clear, consistent and modifiable.

The author of the SQAP should assume familiarity with the purpose of the software, and not repeat information that is explained in other documents.

3.3 RESPONSIBILITY

A SQAP must be produced by each contractor developing software (SQA01). Review of the SQAPs produced by each contractor is part of the supplier control activity.

The SQAP should be produced by the SQA staff. It should be reviewed by those to whom the SQA personnel report.

3.4 MEDIUM

It is usually assumed that the SQAP is a paper document. There is no reason why the SQAP should not be distributed electronically to participants with the necessary equipment.

3.5 CONTENT

The SQAP is divided into four sections, one for each development phase. These sections are called:

- Software Quality Assurance Plan for the SR phase (SQAP/SR);
- Software Quality Assurance Plan for the AD phase (SQAP/AD);
- Software Quality Assurance Plan for the DD phase (SQAP/DD);
- Software Quality Assurance Plan for the TR phase (SQAP/TR).

Software Engineering Standards recommends the following table of contents for each section of the SQAP:

Service Information:

a - Abstract

b - Table of Contents

c - Document Status Sheet

d - Document Change records made since last issue

1 PURPOSE[1]

2 REFERENCE DOCUMENTS

3 MANAGEMENT

4 DOCUMENTATION

5 STANDARDS, PRACTICES, CONVENTIONS AND METRICS

      5.1 Documentation standards

      5.2 Design standards

      5.3 Coding standards

      5.4 Commentary standards

      5.5 Testing standards and practices

      5.6 Selected software quality assurance metrics

      5.7 Statement of how compliance is to be monitored

6 REVIEW AND AUDITS

7 TEST

8 PROBLEM REPORTING AND CORRECTIVE ACTION

9 TOOLS, TECHNIQUES AND METHODS

10 CODE CONTROL

11 MEDIA CONTROL

12 SUPPLIER CONTROL

13 RECORDS COLLECTION, MAINTENANCE AND RETENTION

14 TRAINING

15 RISK MANAGEMENT

16 OUTLINE OF THE REST OF THE PROJECT

APPENDIX A GLOSSARY

---

[1] The Software Quality Assurance Plan phase contents list is based upon extracts from IEEE Std 730-1989, IEEE Standard for Software Quality Assurance Plans, copyright © 1989 by the Institute for Electrical and Electronic Engineers Inc. The IEEE disclaims any responsibility or liability resulting from the placement and use in this publication. Information is reprinted with the permission of the IEEE.

Material unsuitable for the above contents list should be inserted in additional appendices. If there is no material for a section then the phrase 'Not Applicable' should be inserted and the section numbering preserved.

Sections 3 to 15 of the SQAP should describe how the technical activities and management plans will be checked. Table 3.5 traces each section of SQAP to the complementary documents or document sections that describe what is to be checked. The SQAP should identify (i.e. reference) the material in each of the other documents, but not repeat it. Sections 3 to 15 of the SQAP should also describe how SQA activities will be reported.

SQAP section	Document/Document section
Management	SPMP
	SCMP/Management
	SVVP/SR-AD-DD-TR/Reporting
Documentation	SPMP/Software documentation
Standards, practices and conventions	SPMP/Methods, tools and techniques
	SVVP/SR-AD-DD-TR/Administrative procedures
	DDD/Project standards, conventions and procedures
Reviews and audits	SVVP/SR-AD-DD-TR/Activities
Test	SVVP/AT-ST-IT-UT
Problem reporting and corrective action	SCMP/Change control
	SVVP/SR-AD-DD-TR/Administrative procedures
Tools, techniques and methods	SPMP/Methods, tools and techniques
	SCMP/Tools, techniques and methods
	SVVP/SR-AD-DD-TR/Overview
	ADD/Design method
Code control	SCMP/Code control
Media control	SCMP/Media control
Records collection, maintenance and retention	SCMP/Configuration status accounting
	SCMP/Records collection and retention
Supplier control	SCMP/Supplier control
Training	SPMP
Risk management	SPMP/Risk Management

Table 3.5 Software quality assurance plan sections traced to other project documents

3.5.1 SQAP/1 Purpose

This section should briefly:
- describe the purpose of the SQAP;
- specify the intended readership of the SQAP;
- list the software products to be developed;
- describe the intended use of the software;
- identify the phase of the life cycle to which the plan applies.

3.5.2 SQAP/2 Reference Documents

This section should provide a complete list of all the applicable and reference documents, identified by title, author and date. Each document should be marked as applicable or reference. If appropriate, report number, journal name and publishing organisation should be included.

3.5.3 SQAP/3 Management

This section should describe the organisation of quality assurance, and the associated responsibilities. The SQAP should define the roles to be carried out, but not allocate people to roles, or define the effort and schedule. ANSI/IEEE Std 730-1989, 'Standard for Software Quality Assurance Plans' [Ref 3] recommends that the following structure be used for this section.

3.5.3.1 SQAP/3.1 Organisation

This section should:
- identify the organisational roles that control and monitor software quality (e.g. project manager, team leaders, software engineers, software librarian, software verification and validation team leader, software quality assurance engineer);
- describe the relationships between the organisational roles;
- describe the interface with the user organisation.

Relationships between the organisational roles may be shown by means of an organigram. This section may reference the SPMP, SCMP and SVVP.

This section should describe how the implementation of the organisational plan will be verified.

3.5.3.2 SQAP/3.2 Tasks

This section should define the SQA tasks (selected from SQAP sections 3.4 to 3.13) that are to be carried out in the phase of the life cycle to which this SQAP applies. This section should define the sequencing of the selected tasks. Additional tasks may be included.

3.5.3.3 SQAP/3.3 Responsibilities

This section should identify the SQA tasks for which each organisational role is responsible. A cross-reference matrix may be used to show that each SQA task has been allocated.

3.5.4 SQAP/4 Documentation

This section should identify the documents to be produced in the phase. The SPMP normally contains (or references) a documentation plan listing all the documents to be produced in the phase.

This section should state how the documents will be checked for conformance to *Software Engineering Standards* and the project documentation plan.

3.5.5 SQAP/5 Standards, practices, conventions and metrics

The following subsections should identify the standards, practices, conventions and metrics used to specify software quality, and explain how SQA will check that the required quality will be achieved.

3.5.5.1 SQAP/5.1 Documentation standards

This section should identify the standards, practices, and conventions that will be used to produce the documents of the phase. Documentation standards are normally defined in the documentation plan (see section 4 of the SQAP).

3.5.5.2 SQAP/5.2 Design standards

This section should identify the standards, practices and conventions that will be used in the phase to design the software. Design standards are normally defined or referenced in the ADD and DDD.

3.5.5.3 SQAP/5.3 Coding standards

This section should identify the standards, practices, and conventions that will be used in the phase to write code. Coding standards are normally defined or referenced in the DDD.

3.5.5.4 SQAP/5.4 Commentary standards

This section should identify the standards, practices and conventions that will be used in the phase to comment code. Commentary standards are normally included in the coding standards.

3.5.5.5 SQAP/5.5 Testing standards and practices

This section should identify the standards, practices and conventions that will be used in the phase to test the software. Testing standards are normally defined in the SRD and SVVP.

3.5.5.6 SQAP/5.6 Selected software quality assurance metrics

This section should identify the metrics that will be used in the phase to measure the quality of the software. Metrics are normally defined in the project standards and plans.

3.5.5.7 SQAP/5.7 Statement of how compliance is to be monitored

This section should describe how SQA will monitor compliance to the standards, practices, conventions and metrics.

3.5.6 SQAP/6 Review and audits

This section should identify the technical reviews, inspections, walkthroughs and audits that will be held during the phase, and the purpose of each. It should describe how adherence to the review and audit procedures (defined in the SVVP) will be monitored, and the role of SQA personnel in the review and audit process.

3.5.7 SQAP/7 Test

This section should describe how the testing activities described in the SVVP will be monitored and how compliance with verification and acceptance-testing requirements in the SRD will be checked.

3.5.8 SQAP/8 Problem reporting and corrective action

This section should identify (by referencing the SCMP) the problem reporting and corrective action procedures (e.g. RID and SPR handling procedures).

This section should describe how adherence to the problem reporting procedures described in the SCMP will be monitored.

This section may describe the metrics that will be applied to problem reporting process to estimate the software quality.

3.5.9 SQAP/9 Tools, techniques and methods

This section should identify the tools, techniques and methods used to develop the software.

This section should describe how the use of the tools, techniques and methods will be monitored.

Additional tools, techniques and methods for supporting SQA tasks may be described here (or in the section on the task).

3.5.10 SQAP/10 Code (and document) control

This section should identify the procedures used to maintain, store, secure and document software. These procedures should be defined in the SCMP.

This section should describe how adherence to the procedures will be monitored.

3.5.11 SQAP/11 Media control

This section should identify the procedures used to maintain, store, secure and document controlled versions of the physical media on which the identified software resides. These procedures should be defined in the SCMP.

This section should describe how adherence to the procedures will be monitored.

3.5.12 SQAP/12 Supplier control

A supplier is any external organisation that develops or provides software to the project (e.g. subcontractor developing software for the project, or a company providing off-the-shelf commercial software).

This section should identify the standards that will be applied by suppliers.

This section should describe how adherence of the suppliers to the applicable standards will be monitored.

This section should identify the procedures that will be applied to goods supplied, such as commercial software and hardware.

This section should describe how adherence to the incoming inspections (i.e. goods-in procedures) will be monitored.

3.5.13 SQAP/13 Records collection, maintenance and retention

This section should identify the procedures kept by the project for recording activities such as meetings, reviews, walkthroughs, audits and correspondence. It should describe where the records are kept, and for how long.

This section should describe how adherence to the record-keeping procedures will be monitored.

3.5.14 SQAP/14 Training

This section should identify any training programmes defined for the project staff and explain how SQA will check that they have been implemented.

3.5.15 SQAP/15 Risk Management

This section should identify the risk management procedures used in the project (which should be described in the SPMP).

This section should describe how adherence to the risk management procedures will be monitored.

3.5.16 SQAP/16 Outline of the rest of the project

This section should be included in the SQAP/SR to provide an overview of SQA activities in the AD, DD and TR phases.

3.5.17 SQAP/APPENDIX A Glossary

This section should provide the definitions of all terms, acronyms, and abbreviations used in the plan, or refer to other documents where the definitions can be found.

3.6 EVOLUTION

3.6.1 UR phase

By the end of the UR review, the SR phase section of the SQAP must be produced (SQAP/SR) (SQA03). The SQAP/SR must describe, in detail, the quality assurance activities to be carried out in the SR phase (SQA04). The SQAP/SR must outline the quality assurance plan for the rest of the project (SQA05).

3.6.2 SR phase

During the SR phase, the AD phase section of the SQAP must be produced (SQAP/AD) (SQA06). The SQAP/AD must cover in detail all the quality assurance activities to be carried out in the AD phase (SQA07).

In the SR phase, the SRD should be analysed to extract any constraints that relate to software quality assurance (e.g. standards and documentation requirements).

3.6.3 AD phase

During the AD phase, the DD phase section of the SQAP must be produced (SQAP/DD) (SQA08). The SQAP/DD must cover in detail all the quality assurance activities to be carried out in the DD phase (SQA09).

3.6.4 DD phase

During the DD phase, the TR phase section of the SQAP must be produced (SQAP/TR) (SQA10). The SQAP/TR must cover in detail all the quality assurance activities to be carried out from the start of the TR phase until final acceptance in the OM phase (SQA11).

APPENDIX A
GLOSSARY

A.1 LIST OF ACRONYMS

AD	Architectural Design
AD/R	Architectural Design Review
ADD	Architectural Design Document
ANSI	American National Standards Institute
AT	Acceptance Test
BSSC	Board for Software Standardisation and Control
CASE	Computer-Aided Software Engineering
CMFA	Common Mode Failure Analysis
DCR	Document Change Record
DD	Detailed Design and production
DD/R	Detailed Design and production Review
DDD	Detailed Design and production Document
DSS	Document Status Sheet
ESA	European Space Agency
FMECA	Failure Modes, Effects and Criticality Analysis
FTA	Fault Tree Analysis
IEEE	Institute of Electrical and Electronics Engineers
IT	Integration Test
MTBF	Mean Time Between Failures
MTTR	Mean Time To Repair
PA	Product Assurance
PSS	Procedures, Specifications and Standards
QA	Quality Assurance
RID	Review Item Discrepancy
SCM	Software Configuration Management
SCMP	Software Configuration Management Plan
SCR	Software Change Request
SMR	Software Modification Report
SPM	Software Project Management
SPMP	Software Project Management Plan
SPR	Software Problem Report
SQA	Software Quality Assurance
SQAP	Software Quality Assurance Plan

SR	Software Requirements
SR/R	Software Requirements Review
SRD	Software Requirements Document
ST	System Test
STD	Software Transfer Document
SVVP	Software Verification and Validation Plan
UR	User Requirements
UR/R	User Requirements Review
URD	User Requirements Document
UT	Unit Tests

APPENDIX B
REFERENCES

1. Software Engineering Standards, C.Mazza, J.Fairclough, B.Melton, D.dePablo, A.Scheffer, R.Stevens, Prentice-Hall 1994.
2. IEEE Standard Glossary of Software Engineering Terminology, ANSI/IEEE Std 610.12-1990.
3. IEEE Standard for Software Quality Assurance Plans, ANSI/IEEE Std 730-1989.
4. IEEE Guide for Software Quality Assurance Planning, ANSI/IEEE Std 983-1986.
5. Application of Metrics in Industry Handbook, AMI Project, Centre for Systems and Software Engineering, South Bank University, London, UK, 1992.
6. Software function, source lines of code, and development effort prediction: a software science validation, A.J.Albrecht and J.E.Gaffney, IEEE Transactions on Software Engineering, vol SE-9, No 6, November 1983.
7. Structured Testing; A Software testing Methodology Using the Cyclomatic Complexity Metric, T.J. McCabe, NBS Special Publication 500-99, 1992.
8. Software Engineering, Design, Reliability and Management, M.L.Shooman, McGraw-Hill, 1983.

APPENDIX C
MANDATORY PRACTICES

This appendix is repeated from *Software Engineering Standards*, appendix D.12

SQA01   An SQAP shall be produced by each contractor developing software.

SQA02   All software quality assurance activities shall be documented in the Software Quality Assurance Plan (SQAP).

SQA03   By the end of the UR review, the SR phase section of the SQAP shall be produced (SQAP/SR).

SQA04   The SQAP/SR shall describe, in detail, the quality assurance activities to be carried out in the SR phase.

SQA05   The SQAP/SR shall outline the quality assurance plan for the rest of the project.

SQA06   During the SR phase, the AD phase section of the SQAP shall be produced (SQAP/AD).

SQA07   The SQAP/AD shall cover in detail all the quality assurance activities to be carried out in the AD phase.

SQA08   During the AD phase, the DD phase section of the SQAP shall be produced (SQAP/DD).

SQA09   The SQAP/DD shall cover in detail all the quality assurance activities to be carried out in the DD phase.

SQA10   During the DD phase, the TR phase section of the SQAP shall be produced (SQAP/TR).

SQA11   The SQAP/TR shall cover in detail all the quality assurance activities to be carried out from the start the TR phase until final acceptance in the OM phase.

APPENDIX D
INDEX